Integrating Doctrine and Diversity

Integrating Doctrine and Diversity

Inclusion and Equity in the
Law School Classroom

Edited by

Nicole P. Dyszlewski

HEAD OF REFERENCE, INSTRUCTION, AND ENGAGEMENT
ROGERS WILLIAMS UNIVERSITY LAW LIBRARY

Raquel J. Gabriel

PROFESSOR OF LAW & DIRECTOR OF THE LAW LIBRARY
CITY UNIVERSITY OF NEW YORK (CUNY) SCHOOL OF LAW

Suzanne Harrington-Steppen

ASSOCIATE DIRECTOR OF PRO BONO PROGRAMS
ROGERS WILLIAMS UNIVERSITY SCHOOL OF LAW

Anna Russell

LIBRARIAN
NINTH CIRCUIT COURT OF APPEALS LIBRARY

Genevieve B. Tung

ASSOCIATE DIRECTOR FOR EDUCATIONAL PROGRAMS
BIDDLE LAW LIBRARY, UNIVERSITY OF PENNSYLVANIA CAREY LAW SCHOOL

CAROLINA ACADEMIC PRESS
Durham, North Carolina

Library of Congress Cataloging-in-Publication Data

Names: Dyszlewski, Nicole.
Title: Integrating doctrine and diversity : inclusion and equity in the law
  school classroom / by Nicole P. Dyszlewski, Raquel J. Gabriel, Suzanne
  Harrington-Steppen, Anna Russell, Genevieve B. Tung.
Description: Durham, North Carolina : Carolina Academic Press, LLC, [2021]
Identifiers: LCCN 2020058004 (print) | LCCN 2020058005 (ebook) | ISBN
  9781531017019 (paperback) | ISBN 9781531017026 (ebook)
Subjects: LCSH: Law—Study and teaching—United States. | Law
  schools—Curricula—United States.
Classification: LCC KF273 .I58 2021 (print) | LCC KF273 (ebook) | DDC
  340.071/173—dc23
LC record available at https://lccn.loc.gov/2020058004
LC ebook record available at https://lccn.loc.gov/2020058005

Carolina Academic Press
700 Kent Street
Durham, North Carolina 27701
Telephone (919) 489-7486
Fax (919) 493-5668
www.cap-press.com

Contents

Foreword

When Professor Nicole P. Dyszlewski asked me to write the foreword for her book, *Integrating Doctrine and Diversity: Inclusion and Equity in the Law School Classroom*, I immediately replied with an enthusiastic yes. Just weeks before, Boston University School of Law (BU Law), the school where I serve as Dean, had hosted a conference entitled "Racial Bias, Disparities, and Oppression in the 1L Curriculum: A Critical Approach to the Canonical First Year Law Subjects." During that symposium, distinguished faculty from BU Law and law schools across the country, plus 1L, 2L, and 3L students from BU Law, offered their insights about how the longstanding insistence upon presenting legal doctrine as neutral and objective and the enduring practice of ignoring hierarchy and subordination in the 1L curriculum had consistently worked to deprive students of color, LGBTQ+ students, and other students from marginalized groups of equitable access to the education offered within their institutions. Additionally, they highlighted how the same traditions and practices worked to produce law school graduates who are completely unaware of how to be critical consumers of the law and who were largely ill-equipped to represent a diverse clientele, work with and manage a diverse group of lawyers, and serve as leaders in their increasingly diverse and interdependent communities, cities, states, and nation. The lessons that faculty and students conveyed at that conference made it clear that law faculty everywhere desperately needed to learn and absorb the practical advice that *Integrating Doctrine and Diversity* promises to offer and, indeed, offers instructors about fully integrating and incorporating diversity, equity, and inclusion into all parts of their law school courses and the law school curriculum.

Tragedies from the spring and summer of 2020, such as the killings of Breonna Taylor, George Floyd, and Rayshard Brooks, reinforced the long overdue need for law schools and law faculty to transform their thinking and their operations to expose the many ways in which the law excludes and oppresses as much as it protects and includes; the numerous means by which the law maintains structures that reify disadvantage rather than tears them down; and the consistent manner in which law schools pressure students, both implicitly and explicitly, to conform to a model that was not designed with so many of them in mind.

The faculty who have provided contributions to *Integrating Doctrine and Diversity* have brilliantly uncovered these flaws, and many more, within the law, law teaching, law schools, and the legal profession. In so doing, they have pushed us all to embrace and adopt an antisubordination approach to legal education and practice, an approach that is needed to ensure that law students and lawyers are fully equipped to use the powerful tool of law to ensure justice, rather than thwart it, whether knowingly or unknowingly.

As I read *Integrating Doctrine and Diversity*, I found myself continuously reliving my own law school experience and wishing I had attended a law school where the book's contributors had all formed a magical, dream faculty that is committed to engaging inclusive pedagogies; helping to break the silences for students lost in the new world of law, as Professor Kali Murray has so beautifully done for her own students; working toward equitable outcomes, as Professor Genevieve Blake Tung has shown us how to do through her work; uncovering biases in assigned cases and individuals' minds, as Professor Jeremiah Ho revealed an urgency for; and integrating the reflection that is necessary for an antiracist approach to professional identity development, as Professors Eduardo Capulong, Andrew King-Ries, and Monte Mills have shown us is critical. It was this type of instruction and learning that I desperately craved as a law student, as a law student who often sensed and felt that my voice and my experiences had been cast to the margins, even as the assigned cases and materials I was reading demanded otherwise, insisting to me (and others) that they offered objective, all-inclusive understandings and perspectives of the law. As a law student, I neither had the words nor the legal expertise to specify or highlight the gaps in history, context, narratology, and logic that were in my assigned reading materials; nor could I articulate, understand, or explain these very realities of mine as an outsider within a discipline and profession that had not yet figured out ways of fully including me and my experiences. *Integrating Doctrine and Diversity* offers students today those very tools. It provides them with the language, and, to some extent, the expertise that can extend the possibilities that law schools and the legal profession will provide space for them, their differing realities, and the important insights they will bring to law and society.

Just as *Integrating Doctrine and Diversity* caused me to relive my own law student experiences, it also pushed me to think more deeply about my current students' experiences and to reflect, quite sadly at times, on how much their experiences were still mirroring my own twenty-five years later. As a Dean, it is difficult to both recognize and watch how little has changed in our discipline's approach to education and our profession's approach to practice, diversity, inclusion, and equity, even as my allies and I have worked our entire careers to create change in both. However, *Integrating Doctrine and Diversity* has provided me not only with additional tools to employ in this fight, but also the hope that I need to believe that my dreams of a magical faculty—a faculty that is fully committed to integrating doctrine, diversity, equity, inclusion, and transformation in the law—can exist and flourish not just in my imagination but in all law schools across the country. As Professor Dyszlewski tells us in her introduction to *Integrating Doctrine and Diversity*, "this book is a way forward if [we] choose it, but [we] must choose it." May all of us as faculty choose to find our way forward as teachers, mentors, scholars, and examples of what our profession can become with the right choices.

Dean Angela Onwuachi-Willig,
Boston University School of Law

Introduction

Nicole P. Dyszlewski[*]

This book is not going to try to convince you that diversity, equity, and inclusion in law and legal academia is critical or important or vital or necessary or long overdue. Other authors have covered this ground with care and conviction.[1] For example, in *Diversity Matters: Race, Gender, and Ethnicity in Legal Education*, Nancy Dowd and colleagues plainly state, "for law school to be relevant to women and people of color, the subject matter, examples, and stories of the law cannot revolve solely around white men."[2] This book is also not going to argue that it is especially important that

---

[*] Head of Reference, Instruction, & Engagement, Roger Williams University School of Law. I would like to profusely thank my co-editors for joining on this adventure. We are a sisterhood and the introduction is a product of all of us, with my name and mistakes, only. I would also like to thank my support network of family and friends and amazing library and law school colleagues (many of whom you will meet in these chapters). Finally, I would like to thank my students, especially Zach Lyons, Michael Thomas, Linda Tappa, Jonathan Pierre, Kendra Hosein, Sebastien Voigt, Brianna Jordan, and Caitlyn Forrester-Johnson. You have taught me so much about how to be a better teacher and a better librarian by witnessing your journey through classrooms and courtrooms. I am so grateful.

1. *See* Henry F. Fradella, *Integrating the Study of Sexuality into the Core Law School Curriculum: Suggestions for Substantive Criminal Law Courses*, 57 J. Legal Educ. 60 (2007).

> For far too long, gays, lesbians, bisexuals, and transgendered ("GLBT") people were invisible in America's law school classrooms, and the curriculum studied was silent on matters of sexuality and the law. Not only did such invisibility and silence deny GLBT people the "privilege of community," but it allowed generations of lawyers to be educated without regard to the social and legal concerns of this sizable minority population in much the same way women have historically experienced exclusion or alienation from legal discourse. This invisibility of GLBT students, faculty, and issues in the law school curriculum perpetuated heterosexism and individualized homophobia.

Id. at 60–61. *See also* Lolita Buckner Inniss, *"Other Spaces" in Legal Pedagogy*, 28 Harv. J. Racial & Ethnic Just. 67, 88 (2012) ("To take racial inclusion and the norms of CRT seriously, law schools must work to incorporate such norms throughout the curriculum in order to eliminate racial barriers to understanding."); Alexi Nunn Freeman & Lindsey Webb, *Positive Disruption: Addressing Race in A Time of Social Change Through A Team-Taught, Reflection-Based, Outward-Looking Law School Seminar*, 21 U. Pa. J.L. & Soc. Change 121 (2018).

2. Nancy E. Dowd, Kenneth B. Nunn & Jane E. Pendergast, *Diversity Matters: Race, Gender, and Ethnicity in Legal Education*, 15 U. Fla. J.L. & Pub. Pol'y 11, 41 (2003).

> Curricula and subject matter within particular course areas deserve our examination. Learning for all students must be contextualized. That is, students learn best about subjects that are interesting, familiar, and relevant to their life experiences. For law school to be relevant to women and people of color, the subject matter, examples, and stories of the law cannot

issues of diversity and inclusion are critical or important or vital or necessary or long overdue to be integrated fully in the first year curriculum. These points have been argued for many years and this is not the goal of this work.[3] Instead of being a scholarly work on the value or business case for diversity, this book is something different. This text assumes you already agree that diversity and inclusion are profoundly important to the first year curriculum in American law schools and you are looking for resources on how to improve your skills or knowledge in these areas. This text also takes an expansive view of what "diversity" means in legal education and the facets of identity to which it can refer. Throughout this introduction I will use the term "diversity." I choose this term to include a variety of issues that may touch diversity but are also distinct, such as equity, equality, inclusion, racial injustice, gender discrimination, and other forms of social inequality. I also intend diversity to be defined broadly to include race, ethnicity, religion, spirituality, national origin, citizenship, age, domicile, gender identity, ability, gender expression, sexual orientation, status, culture, difference, and the many places where those descriptors intersect. As editors, we have certain freedom to define the boundaries of the work we have created instead of allowing the boundaries of the topic to define the work for us. In this case, we are making a choice to answer the question *how* and not *why*.

The work on this book, and the writing of this introduction, began long before the summer of 2020 and the murders of Ahmaud Arbery, Breonna Taylor, George Floyd (and countless others murdered whose deaths have come before 2020 and continue beyond it). The events of 2020 have set off a much-needed change in these discussions within law and beyond it. Because of this new climate some readers may be more aware of the need for sustained curricular change and may be approaching this work for the first time, perhaps with quiet skepticism. We welcome you to this book despite how uncomfortable this might be. We do not intend the matter-of-factness on the importance of these topics to turn you away. Rather, we are adamant that this book is a way forward if you choose it, but *you* must choose it.

This book sites itself at the intersection of pedagogy and critical reflections on social diversity and the law, two fields of great importance to legal academia. Both, however, can be daunting and overwhelming in their importance and rhetoric. I can recall sitting down to read a book on teaching and feeling unease set in when the au-

---

revolve solely around white men. Nor should the law predominantly address the legal concerns of the wealthy, to the exclusion of the interests of middle-class Americans or the poor. If legal education is to be meaningful, then it must include what Professor Martha Fineman calls "uncomfortable conversations": challenges to both traditional analysis but also the critiques of traditional analysis; talking about difficult issues and assumptions regarding class, race, ethnicity, and gender; not privileging any perspective by immunizing it from critical consideration and ensuring that all voices in the room are heard and respected.
Id. (referencing Martha Albertson Fineman, *Contract and Care*, 76 CHI.-KENT L. REV. 1403 (2001)).
    3. *See* Kim Forde-Mazrui, *Learning Law Through the Lens of Race*, 21 J.L. & POL. 1, 3 n.9 (2005); Cruz Reynoso & Cory Amron, *Diversity in Legal Education: A Broader View, A Deeper Commitment*, 52 J. LEGAL EDUC. 491 (2002).

thor used the phrase "pedagogical praxis." I can also remember picking up a book on race and gender and feeling daunted by my unfamiliarity with terms like "kyriarchies." Informed by my own experiences feeling anxious about the heft and depth of the two topics we find ourselves addressing, this text is our attempt at being reader-focused, practical, and hands-on.

We created this to be a resource by law professors for law professors. The authors come from a variety of institutions across the country and have diverse backgrounds, diverse perspectives, and diverse methodologies. We approached and selected authors to maximize diversity of identity, style, institutional affiliation, and experience. We have tried to create a space for law teachers to talk about teaching diversity based on their own experiences in the classroom and their own pedagogic styles. We have sought to create something which is not just a pep talk but also not heavy-handed. Our focus is, and has always been, on presenting tools and relevant examples to law professors in a way that is easily navigable.

Is this book necessary? Isn't diversity already being taught in the first year curriculum?

Yes and it might be. It also might not be.

Are issues related to diversity inextricably woven into the standard American first year law school curriculum? Of course.[4] Issues of racial injustice, gender discrimination, and other forms of social inequality fill the pages of every casebook and are implicated in every narrative we tell about American law, even if they are typically unacknowledged. However, *how* professors choose to confront these issues varies.[5] Explicitly and intentionally confronting diversity, inclusion, and equity is exhausting, time-consuming, and nuanced work. Student reactions to these topics can also be caustic, defensive, and unpredictable. Some students may be triggered by certain words, phrases, or concepts, and may find the topics uncover and expose past traumas. Consequently, some professors have learned to reduce this friction by minimizing in-class discussions of fraught topics in favor of discussions which may be more productive when measured against some other, purportedly more "objective" metric, like bar exam preparation or covering a preferred casebook.

When I've talked about this with law professors, there are several themes. Most acknowledge the importance of diversity and inclusion in the curriculum. It is not as if there are many faculty standing up to decry diversity and inclusion in the law and legal academia. Instead, professors speak about already having too much ground to cover in too few class sessions and not knowing exactly

---

4. Nunn, Freeman & Webb, *supra* note 2, at 124 ("Whether or not law professors explicitly discuss race in their classes, law students are absorbing lessons about race and the law. Academic silence regarding race does not mean that race is invisible or absent; rather, many argue, the void left by this silence contains the presumption that the law is for and about white people or is somehow racially 'neutral.'").

5. Not talking about these issues is also a choice.

how to weave diversity into their courses. These teachers want tools to learn how to facilitate difficult conversations, set the stage for these discussions, and encourage conversations within the scope of the doctrine.

When I began to engage on this topic and heard some of these concerns, I was skeptical. Was expressing a need for tools on how to integrate diversity, equity, and inclusion more seamlessly into the curriculum a pretext for not wanting to change the status quo? Was not having training or a collection of resources on integrating diversity into the curriculum an excuse for feeling uncomfortable with the discussions, and thus protecting and perpetuating whiteness and maleness? As Wendy Leo Moore states, "whether white people are not comfortable engaging issues of race because they are fearful or because they do not see race as relevant to their lives or the law, the result is racialized practices that reify white space."[6] The conclusion that I came to is that there is a need for resources on this topic to be available to law professors in an easy to access way and this book is one way to address some of the faculty concerns.

How is this book organized?

This book is envisioned as a Choose Your Own Adventure, of sorts.

Chapter 1 is a must-read for all. It provides the foundational grounding for anyone engaged in law school curricular development, including faculty, staff, and administrators. Readers will take away from the chapter how, on a macro level, diversity, equity, and inclusion can be integrated across the first year curriculum. Chapter 1 sets the stage for the chapters which follow. This book is organized by topics common to the 1L curriculum. It may make sense to dive directly into a later chapter after a review of chapter 1.

While we would love readers to enjoy the book in its entirety, it is organized to allow readers to skip ahead to the subjects which they find most relevant to their teaching. This book includes sections on each of the classes in a traditional 1L curriculum: civil procedure, torts, contracts, property, constitutional law, criminal law, legal writing, and legal research. Each section contains two parts. The first part includes substantive essays on how professors who regularly teach the topic have grappled with diversity issues in their own classrooms. Some pieces take the form of case studies while other paint the topic with a broader brush, suggesting a variety of methods and exercises which demonstrate how these issues can be integrated into a first year class. The second part of each chapter is an annotated bibliography collecting articles, books, videos, and other resources on how to integrate diversity, equity, and inclusion into the classroom in that particular topic. Our intent is to provide several road maps for how to integrate diversity into the traditional 1L curriculum in a way that is approachable and accessible.

---

6. Wendy Leo Moore, Reproducing Racism: White Space, Elite Law Schools, and Racial Inequality 96 (2007).

How did this project come about?

Slowly and with a lot of support from the RWU Law community, law librarians, and professors across the US.

The idea for this book was born of a series of difficult conversations that took place over about a year at my institution, Roger Williams University School of Law (RWU Law). A few years ago, RWU Law formed a committee of faculty, administration, students, members of the board, alumni, and staff to write a diversity and inclusion strategic plan for the law school. This was the first document of its kind that the law school had developed, and it came at a time when the number and percentage of minoritized students were at the highest in the school's history. Serving on the committee, I can attest that the year-long discussions that went into this document were challenging, engaging, thoughtful, difficult, and productive. One of the issues we discussed in our planning meetings was the way in which diversity, inclusion, equity, social justice, equality, religion, race, status, culture, difference, and intersectionality were being taught at the school. There was not much disagreement on whether these issues should be taught; it was a matter of assessing if they *were* being taught, how they were being taught, and how we could further support the teaching of these issues through the new strategic plan. These conversations, among a group in which law faculty constituted a minority, were sometimes challenging. We perceived that offering non-faculty perspectives on what should be taught and how it should be taught could conflict with what faculty viewed as their prerogative, and be viewed as a threat to their academic freedom.[7]

For better or worse, academic freedom prevents a strategic planning committee, no matter how well-intentioned, from dictating what is taught in class. Academic freedom, like tenure, is a core value in law schools but it can also be a bar to change. Academic freedom has been described as a characteristic of academia that is "likely to ground resistance to disruptive changes in legal education."[8] It has more specifically been described as one of the "obstacles facing the institutionalization of race in the curriculum."[9] The students

---

7. The American Association of University Professors (to which the Association of American Law Schools looks for its definition of academic freedom) states in its *Statement of Principles on Academic Freedom and Tenure* that "teachers are entitled to freedom in the classroom in discussing their subject, but they should be careful not to introduce into their teaching controversial matter which has no relation to their subject." Am. Ass'n Univ. Profs., 1940 Statement of Principles on Academic Freedom and Tenure 14 (1940), https://www.aaup.org/report/1940-statement-principles-academic-freedom-and-tenure.

8. Nicholas A. Mirkay & Palma Joy Strand, *Disruptive Leadership in Legal Education*, 22 Rich. Pub. Int. L. Rev. 365 (2019).

9. *See* Forde-Mazrui, *supra* note 3, at 27 ("Academic freedom accords professors substantial discretion over the issues to cover within the courses they teach. Apart from courses where race is virtually unavoidable, many professors will continue to leave race out of their courses to the extent they perceive race as peripheral or too divisive. Unless law school deans or faculties are prepared to press for attention to race over individual professors' preferences, leaving race to the classroom may leave it absent from many.").

on the committee, less familiar with academic freedom and naïve about law school governance, tried to understand why the school could be so committed to diversity, equity, and inclusion in so many areas but could not require faculty to address these important issues in the classroom.[10]

These students, representative of minoritized students at RWU Law, wanted to be understood and have their perspectives heard and reflected in classroom discussions. Based on my experience working with students in this context and others, students perceive that some faculty members shut down or abruptly change conversations when classroom discussions approach the issues of diversity, equity, and inclusion.[11] Some students feel like their voices are not heard and that some faculty choose not to embrace difficult conversations between majority and minoritized students, instead approaching this as "beyond the scope of the class" or a distraction from the large amount of subject matter to be covered in a relatively short amount of class time.[12] In *Teaching Law By Design: Engaging Students from the Syllabus to the Final Exam*, the authors noted that "if you allow free discussion of even one policy issue, your failure to permit discussion of an issue about race or gender or politics, because you are concerned students will be upset, has the potential to send a message that you regard the issues you are ignoring as unimportant."[13] So therein lies the problem and the heart of this aspect of the work of the RWU committee and then this book: bridging the gap.[14]

---

10. *See generally* Committee A on Academic Freedom and Tenure, Am. Ass'n Univ. Profs., Freedom in the Classroom (2007), republished in Academe, Sept.–Oct. 2007, at 54, https://www.aaup.org/AAUP/comm/rep/A/class.htm. Specifically, note the use of the word diversity in the following statement, "Modern critics of the university seek to impose on university classrooms mandatory and ill-conceived standards of 'balance,' 'diversity,' and 'respect.' We ought to learn from history that the vitality of institutions of higher learning has been damaged far more by efforts to correct abuses of freedom than by those alleged abuses. We ought to learn from history that education cannot possibly thrive in an atmosphere of state-encouraged suspicion and surveillance." *Id.* at 61.

11. It is important to note that these conversations are not unique to RWU Law. This book's introduction is about the impetus of the formation of this book and I am in no way unique in having had these conversations at my school. This phenomenon is common in law schools. I am just proud to work somewhere where the conversations are supportive, productive, and include a variety of stakeholders, including staff and students. *See* Leo Moore, *supra* note 7, at 94.

12. Erin C. Lain, *Racialized Interactions in the Law School Classroom: Pedagogical Approaches to Creating a Safe Learning Environment*, 67 J. Legal Educ. 780, 790 (2018) ("Avoiding and minimizing racialized interaction within the classroom is a common response among professors, but this strategy provides little cultivation of psychological safety, and it can be harmful because it provides no learning opportunity.").

13. Michael Hunter Schwartz, Sophie M. Sparrow, & Gerald F. Hess, Teaching Law By Design: Engaging Students from the Syllabus to the Final Exam 196 (2d ed. 2017).

14. As this manuscript goes to publication, I feel compelled to give an update and further muse on these questions. Because of events inside and outside of the law school, the work of integrating diversity into the curriculum at RWU Law was prominent during the summer of 2020. And I am proud to say this story is one of success. The institution and the faculty have committed to addressing the integration of diversity, inclusion, equity, equality, and social justice into the curriculum. And the work that has been done has been exciting and difficult and fraught and challenging. There have

In my office, I have a quote on my wall from author Ijeoma Oluo that states: "do not wait until you are ready to sit down and address race to address race."[15] This quote played on a loop in my brain during our conversations about further integrating discussion of diversity, inclusion, and equity into the law school community, mission, practices, and curriculum. After a meeting one afternoon, when we were discussing resources and trainings available on integrating diversity into the curriculum, I got on the internet and found resources on these topics, just to prove they existed and could be easily accessed. What I found were books and law review articles and blog posts and speeches. What I did not find, however, was any robust compendium of practical resources on teaching diversity, inclusion, and equity in the law school classroom, across the curriculum and in specific courses.

So I did what I always do in this situation: I looked for an annotated bibliography. I didn't find much on teaching diversity, inclusion, and equity in law schools so I did the other thing that I always do—I called another librarian to chat. And then I called another one and then I called another one. Eventually we formed an alliance of sorts. We were going to create a resource for this practical material to help those who teach our students have the resources they need. We believe that faculty should have the freedom to teach as they will. But we also believe law professors should have resources written by their peers and compiled for their convenient use. This was a tall order, but we were librarians and we were built for tall orders.[16]

Law librarians are experts on organizing and presenting legal information. Law librarians are experts in the discovery of, the compilation of, the harmonization of, and the presentation of information. Law librarians are also cooperative, progressive, and trusted.[17] We were the natural choice for compiling and editing this book because we were willing and because we regularly work with faculty on large-scale projects. Finally, librarians are natural collaborators and this book was a project of great collaboration.

---

been community conversations, all-staff/faculty meetings, faculty discussions, a commitment to educating ourselves, a change in curriculum, and a renewed dedication to living our institutional values. As you will read in the next few pages, this book was born of skepticism. But it is being brought to fruition with optimism. RWU Law is engaging in this work and is living its commitment to diversity, equity, equality, and inclusion.

15. Ijeoma Oluo, *I am Drowning in Whiteness*, NPR (Oct. 1, 2017), https://www.kuow.org/stories/ijeoma-oluo-i-am-drowning-in-whiteness.

16. Please notice that one of us isn't a librarian, but instead an experiential professor and pro bono administrator. Because clinical faculty have many resources on diversity and inclusion in the context of experiential education, I approached a member of the RWU community to ask her opinions about our project. She was so enthusiastic about it that she joined the team, for which we are all so thankful. She has survived many discussions which were held in law library jargon and has weathered the storm admirably.

17. *See, e.g.*, PORTLAND RESEARCH GROUP ET AL., MAINE STATE LIBRARY: TRUSTED PROFESSIONALS SURVEY 2016, https://digitalmaine.com/cgi/viewcontent.cgi?referer=&httpsredir=1&article=1100&context=msl_docs (finding librarians to be among the most-trusted professionals).

The editors of this book are indebted to the contributors of the substantive and annotated pieces in this book. Additionally, we owe a debt a gratitude to those legal scholars whose work appears in each chapter bibliography, who have studied and explored these issues for many years. Their work has inspired us and helped us get through the loss and disconnection of living through a pandemic and unprecedented societal discord. This work, this scholarship, and our project has been our balm and our passion project and we are thrilled to finally be able to share this with you all.

Chapter 1

Cross-Curricular Integration of Doctrine and Diversity

Wisdom for Teachers on the Journey to Integrating Diversity in the Law Classroom

Nicole P. Dyszlewski*

"Authentic education is not carried on by 'A' *for* 'B' or by 'A' *about* 'B,' but rather by 'A' *with* 'B,' mediated by the world—a world which impresses and challenges both parties, giving rise to views or opinions about it. These views, impregnated with anxieties, doubts, hopes, or hopelessness, imply significant themes on the basis of which the program content of education can be built."

—Paulo Freire[1]

Introduction

I have been on a journey towards integrating diversity, inclusion, equity, power dynamics, economic class, religion, sexuality, gender, and social justice into my classroom teaching and librarianship. Through this journey, and the shared journeys of my friends and colleagues, I have learned so much. Diversity and inclusion mean

* Nicole P. Dyszlewski, Head of Reference, Instruction, & Engagement, Roger Williams University School of Law. It is so important to me to thank those within and beyond my institution who supported this project and me throughout the past 2 years, but also helped me grow and learn and discover and make mistakes and re-consider and fail and re-imagine and focus and change and improve. Sincere thanks to the RWU Law Friday morning teaching group, especially the leader, Deborah Gonzalez. Thank you to Michael Yelnosky, Jared Goldstein, Raquel Ortiz, Carl Bogus, Lorraine Lalli, Deborah Johnson, Ralph Tavares, Brittany Raposa, Jill Dallaire, Tara Allen, Liza Vorenberg, Laurie Barron, Olivia Milonas, Alisha Hennen, and other members of the RWU Law team past and present. You all had some impact on this project and these ideas and I am grateful. Much gratitude to my family and extended family, including the Pacciones and the Manloves. Thank you to my friend/editor, Lauren, who got to skip editing this book and just enjoy my writing for once. Finally, so many thanks to Suzy Harrington-Steppen. Co-editing this project while working alongside you every day has been a testament to our passion for this topic and our friendship. Thank you for saying yes when I have crazy ideas but thank you more for being such an amazing human being.

1. PAULO FREIRE, PEDAGOGY OF THE OPPRESSED 93 (Myra Bergman Ramos trans., Bloomsbury, 50th Anniversary ed., 2018).

more than reading a book and adding a "diverse" example to a class period. Instead, this is about fully integrating, and sometimes totally re-thinking, how our pedagogical approaches integrate diverse perspectives and about situating social justice into the curriculum where it always should have been. In this essay I will share the wisdom I have learned along the way.

I loosely organized these suggestions into three categories: before class, during class, and within yourself. These ideas come from a variety of places including personal experience, conferences, articles, books, personal conversations, and observation. I present them as recommendations to consider with the caveat that I have no way of knowing where you are on your journey and how these might apply in your classroom.

Before Class:
Create a Safe Space

Update Your Syllabus &
Establish Classroom Guidelines[2]

My conversations with students have allowed me to understand that creating an inclusive space in the classroom is critical to integrating diversity, social justice issues, and equity with doctrine. This is done before class is ever in session and can be done with one of the basic tools of our trade, the syllabus. Review your syllabus and update it with an eye toward the integration of this new content. Consider adding language about what will be expected in classroom discussions. How will racism be addressed in class? How will you handle microaggressions? Will you be open to hearing from students when you have made a mistake or microaggressed against another?[3] Will you bar certain terms or symbols from your class or from student Zoom backgrounds?[4] Adding this type of information to the syllabus signals that that this content related to social justice, diversity, equity, and inclusion is important and welcome. It also may signal to minoritized students that their perspective is valued.

---

2. *See* Shamika D. Dalton, *Teaching Cultural Competency Through Legal Research Instruction*, in Chapter 7 of this book.

3. For more on examining your own mistakes see Bobbi Smith, *Examining Mistakes to Advance Antiracist Teaching in* TEACHING RACE: HOW TO HELP STUDENTS UNMASK AND CHALLENGE RACISM 273 (Stephen D. Brookfield et al., eds., 2019).

4. *E.g.*, Emma Gallegos, *BCHS Student Displays 'Black Lives Don't Actually Matter' as Zoom Background*, BAKERSFIELD CALIFORNIAN (Sept. 2, 2020), https://www.bakersfield.com/news/bchs-student-displays-black-lives-don-t-actually-matter-as-zoom-background/article_6146f676-ed7f-11ea-b3ac-4fa5f738380d.html; *see also* Xanni Brown & Michael W. Kraus, *When the School Mascot Is a Native American Stereotype*, YALE INSIGHTS (Sept. 25, 2019), https://insights.som.yale.edu/insights/when-the-school-mascot-is-native-american-stereotype.

As an example, I have included language from my own syllabus as a starting point to consider:

> Students are expected to treat faculty, staff, and fellow classmates with dignity and respect. Students are responsible for being familiar with and adhering to the published Student Code of Conduct.
>
> This class deals with serious and significant issues which can be difficult to discuss. Here are some basic rules to follow in my class. I adapted them from the UMass Amherst Campus Climate Resources online.[5] I know they are straightforward but I think it is important to state them from the start of class so everyone is aware that they are important. If you think there are other rules we should add, please let me know or we can discuss this in the first class.
>
> Treat all others with dignity and respect.
> Listen to each other but recognize that there may be disagreement.
> Keep discussion and comments on the topic of law, not on each other.
>
> Do not use inflammatory or offensive language.
> Limit sarcasm. It's easy to misread.
> Think before you write. Think before you speak.
>
> Don't use stereotypes, use evidence.
> Be mindful of your own implicit biases.
> Don't make assumptions about your classmates.
> Don't make assumptions about those who are or have been incarcerated.
>
> I am going to try and talk about issues such as race and socioeconomic status in a way which is both candid and respectful. However, I will likely make mistakes. We are all learning to talk about these challenging issues together. If I say something that you think is misguided or offensive, I invite you to email me or meet with me to discuss it. I am trying to foster trust in this class and that means you need to be able to trust me, too. There will also be times where I may point out something that you have written or said that might lead to misunderstandings or be seen as offensive. I will point those comments out to you so that we can all learn how to talk about these issues in a more effective manner.

Make Students Aware of Your Goals[6]

Whether you include your goals in your syllabus or share them at the beginning of class, make sure students are aware that integrating these important issues into

---

5. Univ. of Mass. Amherst, *Promoting Respect in the Classroom* (2018), https://www.umass.edu/diversity/sites/default/files/inline-files/dignity_respect_classroom_umass_2018-ada.pdf (last visited Oct. 5, 2020); *see also* Univ. of Mass. Amherst Center for Teaching and Learning, *Inclusive Syllabus Design*, https://www.umass.edu/ctl/inclusive-syllabus-design (last visited Oct. 5, 2020).

6. Vernellia R. Randall, *Teaching Diversity Skills in Law School*, 54 St. Louis U. L.J. 795, 798 (2010) ("So, teachers need good course planning techniques. That is, they must know what their own goals

your class is a goal.[7] This alerts students that discussions on equity, diversity, and inclusion are not only welcome, but expected. As Vernellia R. Randall explains:

> Teaching diversity skills cannot be happenstance. Don't try to sneak it in by bringing in a case here or a comment there. Doing that is like trying to teach a skill by not approaching the skill straight up and saying that today we're going to learn knitting, but what you are doing is teaching them basketball, but every now and then you throw in something about a stitch.[8]

Be clear in your own mind about your goals but also be clear to share them with the students. This simple step may further engage minoritized students or *any* students who are trying to square their real-world experiences with doctrine. It also keeps you accountable.

Explore Your Own Opportunities for Growth (and Repeat)

One of the experiences I found most helpful to grow my own skills and comfort level in recognizing and discussing diversity issues was to attend a professional development opportunity outside my usual comfort zone in legal academia. I attended a conference, presented by the Rhode Island Coalition for Educators of Color (RICEC),[9] about empowering educators of color and supporting students of color and I listened. I listened to speakers discuss shortcomings in the curriculum, problems with textbook selection, building equitable practices in schools, and decolonizing the classroom. I listened and opened myself up to new points of view and issues I had not considered. This was helpful in becoming aware that there are issues and subtexts that my own privilege has protected me from. My suggestion is to look for opportunities in your own region and explore events where you might not necessarily be the target audience.

Additionally, consider doing an inventory or self-study about your practices, curriculum, and textbooks.[10] Being reflective about the readings you choose and where you draw them from may illuminate areas for future growth. Reflecting on your iden-

---

are and what they are trying to achieve in that classroom. If teaching diversity skills is important, it should be a part of the stated goal for the class. And then the teacher has to make this clear to the student.").

7. *See* Bonny L. Tavares, *Integrating Diversity Through Design of Legal Writing Assignments*, in Chapter 6 of this book; *see also* Bonnie L. Tavares, *Changing the Construct: Promoting Cross-Cultural Conversations in the Law School Classroom*, 67 J. Legal Educ. 211, 226 (2017).

8. Randall, *supra* note 6, at 799–800.

9. Rhode Island Coalition for Educators of Color, *Mission*, https://www.facebook.com/pg/RIed ofcolor/about/?ref=page_internal (last visited Sept. 19, 2020) ("The Rhode Island Coalition for Educators of Color is committed to the empowerment and retention of educators of color. We aspire to elevate their voices by building a strong community of leaders and mentors. We seek to create safe spaces where educators of color can collaborate and engage in honest dialogue.").

10. Also consider doing a self-study of your syllabus. For guidance, see Calif. Cmty. Coll., *Equity in Online Learning, An Equity Syllabus*, https://sites.google.com/view/anequitysyllabus/home?authuser= 0, (last visited Oct. 5, 2020).

tity and your methodologies is key.[11] Consider strategies you can implement to de-colonize or indigenize your curricular practices.[12]

I further recommend making this learning a practice and not a one-time event.[13] In an article which develops a framework for making commitments to racial justice actionable, the authors sagely conclude:

> we have come to realize the care-full, processual, reiterative, and self-reflexive nature of the work for equity and social justice in educational settings.... By continually doing the self-work and work-with-others, we hope to live a recursive theory-practice-theory-practice life allowing us to never stop learning and acting with our local, national, and international communities.[14]

I have continued to attend RICEC events online and in person. I have sought these opportunities and will continue to seek further learning. These opportunities beget growth, which further begets opportunities to make our practices more inclusive and equitable.

Update Your Vocabulary

Using the most respectful means of addressing a student's race, ethnicity, religion, gender, or sexuality is important.[15] It can be emotionally destructive to address a student with incorrect gender pronouns and even the most cautious professor can make mistakes.[16] The preferred way to address racial or ethnic groups can be personal, can be regional, and can change with time.[17] For example, do you call a member of an

---

11. *See generally* Lee Anne Bell, Diane J. Goodman & Rani Varghese, *Critical Self-Knowledge for Social Justice Educators, in* TEACHING FOR DIVERSITY AND SOCIAL JUSTICE 401 (Maurianne Adams, Lee Ann Bell with Diane J. Goodman & Khyati Y. Joshi eds., 2016).

12. *See, e.g.,* Shauneen Pete, *Idle No More: Radical Indigeneity in Teacher Education, in* CULTURALLY RESPONSIVE PEDAGOGY: WORKING TOWARDS DECOLONIZATION, IDIGENEITY AND INTERCULTURALISM 69 (Fatima Pirbhai-Illich, Shauneen Pete & Fran Martin, eds., 2017). For more on decolonization in education, I recommend Carol Azumah Dennis' list of ten defining pedagogic approaches to decolonizing education. *See* Carol Azumah Dennis, *Decolonising Education: A Pedagogic Intervention, in* DECOLONISING THE UNIVERSITY 202 (Gurminder K. Bhambra, Dalia Gebrial & Kerem Nişancıoğlu, eds., 2018).

13. Sharlene Voogd Cochrane, *Who I am in How I Teach, in* CULTURALLY RESPONSIVE TEACHING AND REFLECTION IN HIGHER EDUCATION, 21 (Sharlene Voogd Cochrane, Meenakshi Chhabra, Marjorie A. Jones & Deborah Spragg eds., 2017).

14. Rasha Diab, Thomas Ferrel, Beth Godbee, & Neil Simpkins, *Making Commitments to Racial Justice Actionable,* ACROSS THE DISCIPLINES 10 (2013), https://wac.colostate.edu/atd/race/diabetal.cfm.

15. *See* Nancy Leong, *Naming Them,* in Chapter 5 of this book.

16. Kevin A. McLemore, *Experiences with Misgendering: Identity Misclassification of Transgender Spectrum Individuals,* 14 SELF & IDENTITY 51 (2014) ("Identity misclassification, or the experience of not having one's social identity correctly recognized by others, is psychologically disruptive. These experiences undermine belonging and coherence needs, disrupt the social identity process, and reflect a failure to have one's social identity accurately verified by others." (internal references omitted)).

17. *See* Constance Grady, *Why the Term "BIPOC" Is So Complicated, Explained by Linguists,* VOX.COM (June 30, 2020) https://www.vox.com/2020/6/30/21300294/bipoc-what-does-it-mean-critical-race-linguistics-jonathan-rosa-deandra-miles-hercules.

indigenous tribe in the United States an Indian, a Native American, American Indian, indigenous, aboriginal, BIPOC, by the tribal affiliation, or some other name? It depends. Before trying to introduce new issues of diversity and inclusion into the 1L classroom, it is recommended that you refresh your vocabulary. Even language which you may consider "neutral" should be investigated.[18] Your law school or university will have a diversity office with resources which can help with this. Another option would be to consider speaking directly with your students about how they wish to have their ethnic, social, religious, and gender identification addressed. Finally, consider hosting a faculty educational session on this topic so you can learn from others who are trying to get these issues right.

In Class:
Seeing the Trees in the Forest

Set the Tone from the Beginning

Although we all hope that students pore over our syllabus with the same exactitude with which we wrote it, it is possible that some students may have missed your updated diversity language. One way to reinforce the text of your syllabus, or introduce it to those who failed to read it thoroughly, is to discuss your integration of diversity, inclusion, social justice, and equity issues in your first class. Setting the tone from the start of the semester — that identity matters and has a place in your classroom — is a critical way to make students feel comfortable. Making it clear that respect is critical in these discussions is another step to minimizing harm in future interactions.[19] Some

---

18. *See* Johnny Eric Williams, *The Academic Freedom Double Standard: "Freedom" for Courtiers, Suppression for Critical Scholars*, AAUP J. of Academic Freedom (2018), https://www.aaup.org/sites/default/files/Williams.pdf. Professor Williams explains:

> Language is never neutral because it is inscribed in power relations in terms that shape our thinking and perceptions about our reality. To grasp this dynamic, just ask who has the power to set the parameters for what constitutes "diversity," who determines who is a "minority," and who defines "inclusion" and "equity." Such power queries reveal that overt and timid white supremacists are not serious about eliminating their system of domination. Rather these verbal/linguistic gymnastic schemes legitimize systemic white racism, exonerate self-identified "whites," and normalize racialized cruelty. This is the outcome because "white" as an imagined identity and whiteness as ideology are conditioned by the material systemic practices of white supremacy. The only way to overcome this racialized quagmire is to name and problematize the racial subjectivity of "whites" in order to open up space for abolishing the cultural and structural feedback loops sustaining systemic white racism.

Id. at 8.

19. Teaching Tolerance, *Critical Practices for Anti-Bias Education*, https://www.tolerance.org/sites/default/files/2019-04/TT-Critical-Practices-for-Anti-bias-Education.pdf ("Because many students experience classrooms that do not value shared inquiry and dialogue, it is important for teachers to create a safe environment before asking students to engage in this work. Safety can be established by discussing principles of engagement, demonstrating the teacher's commitment to collective learning or creating a set of discussion agreements.").

faculty use the first class to build out the classroom community guidelines and ask students for input on new rules which should be added to the syllabus or to suggest terms which the class agrees to be stricken from discussions.[20]

Be Willing to Share Personal Stories[21]

Your own experiences are valuable.[22] While this seems obvious, the culture of legal academia may sometimes encourage taking your own perspective or emotions out of the classroom.[23] While this may have some benefits, it may also make you seem less relatable or genuine. This may impact how, or if, students trust you. It may make discussions of identity more difficult, specifically because it may work to obscure your own identity as a woman or Muslim or immigrant.[24] Institutions or traditions that focus on "objective standards" obscure the fact that such standards are based on

---

20. For an example of how some students responded when to an incident where a racial slur was used in an educational context, see this letter: Concerned Black Stanford Students, Opinion, *We Have Waited Long Enough: Black Students' Response to CCSRE Faculty Directors*, STANFORD DAILY (May 31, 2020), https://www.stanforddaily.com/2020/05/31/we-have-waited-long-enough-black-students-response-to-ccsre-faculty-directors/. *See also* Ruth A. Starkman, Opinion, *Dropping the N-Word in College Classrooms*, INSIDE HIGHER ED (July 24, 2020), https://www.insidehighered.com/views/2020/07/24/colleges-should-develop-guidelines-using-n-word-classes-opinion (explaining why institutions should develop policies on this issue).

> Our classrooms and other institutional units already have guidelines that are not legally enforced but shape the parameters for discussion, just as all debate forums have their own guidelines. Guidelines can be written to promote choice, enable better communication and become a helpful discussion tool for instructors and students in tense situations. Beyond the social unrest of this spring, we now live in culturally volatile times, which is all the more reason to equip participants for a mutually respectful conversation that avoids shaming battles in class. Students, like faculty members, have their own legal right to free speech and to speak out in class, but they also have a choice to employ civil and empathetic practices. Guidelines, however they might be written to encourage participants to choose such practices, will benefit both instructors and students.

Id. See also generally MICHAEL HUNTER SCHWARTZ, SOPHIE M. SPARROW & GERALD F. HESS, TEACHING LAW BY DESIGN 196 (2d ed. 2017).

21. *See* Deborah Ahrens, *Centering Race and Diversity in the Criminal Law Classroom*, in Chapter 4 of this book.

22. Teaching Tolerance, *supra* note 19 ("Personal anecdotes — respectfully and thoughtfully shared by teachers — have great power. Stories should be chosen carefully, kept brief, and told at a level that invites appropriate student sharing."); *see also* Susan Hadley, *Teaching Whiteness in Predominantly While Classrooms in* TEACHING RACE: HOW TO HELP STUDENTS UNMASK AND CHALLENGE RACISM 48 (Stephen D. Brookfield et al., eds., 2019).

23. See generally, Angela P. Harris & Marjorie M. Shultz, *"A(nother) Critique of Pure Reason": Toward Civic Virtue in Legal Education*, 45 STAN. L. REV. 1773 (1993).

24. Erin C. Lain, *Racialized Interactions in the Law School Classroom: Pedagogical Approaches to Creating a Safe Learning Environment*, 67 J. LEGAL EDUC. 780, 795 (2018) ("Not only does acknowledging these aspects of self free professors from having to pretend they are superhuman, but it provides a vulnerability to the conversation that allows for others to share. For example, a white female professor telling students 'I have certain privileges that shape my worldview, so it is important for us to hear many perspective' not only liberates the teacher but allows the students to think about how their own identities shape their perspectives.").

a tradition of whiteness and maleness. Additionally, your own "social identities and relative privilege or marginality in different social groups will influence [y]our perspectives on, and awareness of, particular social justice issues and dynamics."[25] As such, your own experiences, shaped by your identity, can be powerful tools in the classroom.

Understand Triggers and Trauma-Informed Teaching

Students do not come to the law school classroom as blank slates. They come with their own experiences which have formed their identities. The experiences of students who occupy a minoritized space, whether because of racism, ableism, homophobia, or other forms of oppression, can be traumatic. In fact, "A 2009 study … found that the typical reactions for students during racialized interactions include fear, anxiety, anger, defensiveness, sadness, crying, leaving the classroom, and withdrawing from the class."[26] While some trauma is violent or physical, students may also have social or emotional trauma that can be triggered or re-triggered in the classroom. For example, a student who was raped may leave the classroom during a conversation in criminal law about sexual assault. In the same way, a student who has experienced the trauma of racism may also be triggered or re-triggered by classroom discussions.[27]

A professor using trauma-informed teaching acknowledges that some students have experienced trauma and seeks to reduce re-traumatization. Likewise, a trauma-informed teacher understands that those students experiencing or re-experiencing trauma may not be able to carry on typically or professionally in the classroom.[28]

---

25. Bell, Goodman & Varghese, *supra* note 11, at 401.

26. Lain, *supra* note 24, at 784.

27. Dottie Lebron, Laura Morrison, Dan Ferris, Amanda Alcantara, Danielle Cummings, Gary Parker & Mary McKay, *Facts Matter! Black Lives Matter! The Trauma of Racism*, McSilver Institute for Poverty Policy and Research, N.Y.U. Silver School of Social Work (2015), https://www.issuelab.org/resources/23698/23698.pdf.

> The invention of race as an ethnological human stratification, and the racism that followed it, created a historical chain of dehumanizing and traumatic events that continue to hinder human progress … The trauma of racism refers to the cumulative negative impact of racism on the lives of people of color. Encompassing the emotional, psychological, health, economic and social effects of multi-generational and historical trauma, trauma of racism relates to the damaging effects of ongoing societal and intra-social-group racial micro aggressions, internalized racism, overt racist experiences, discrimination and oppression within the lives of people of color. When repetitive and unresolved, these experiences rooted in racism can create severe emotional pain and distress that can overwhelm a person's and community's ability to cope, creating feelings of powerlessness.

Id. at 10.

28. Within and beyond law, the concept of professionalism, specifically the appearance of professionalism, has long been a tool of oppression. *See* Elizabeth B. Cooper, *The Appearance of Professionalism*, 71 Fla. L. Rev. 1, 5 (2019) ("Both *de facto* and *de jure* expectations of workplace presentation favor historical norms, which have been created and reinforced by dominant culture. Courts, law firms, government offices, and legislatures have their respective sets of conservative appearance norms that reflect those who have traditionally held powerful positions: White, heterosexual, cisgender

Those students may react with untoward aggression, may retreat from conversation for the rest of the class, and may need to distance themselves physically from conversations that re-trigger trauma. Recognizing that students may have a background of trauma and supporting them within and beyond the classroom is a critical best practice.

Don't Assume Trust

Despite your best intentions and adherence to best practices, some students will not trust you, your class, and their classmates. Don't assume that the classroom is a sacrosanct place of trust for all students.[29] Sometimes students have had many years of bad experiences before they step through the law school doors and your class may not be able to undo what came before.[30] You may be the same race or have the same accent as those who have caused harm in the lives of your students before they even met you. Some students I've spoken with felt that white, cisgender students enjoy a sense of safety in the classroom that can allow them to express offensive opinions without consequence. Creating a safer space for all may start by recognizing that there are those in our classes who do not trust us and treating those students with care.

Manage the Discussion

Discussions of privilege and identity within the context of a first year class may be uncomfortable, but they can also be powerful learning tools, teaching students about the law, inequity, critical thinking, and professionalism. However, these discussions need to be managed to be successful. Erin C. Lain states, "improperly navigated racialized interactions diminish psychological safety for all students, but in particular for students of color."[31] Luckily, Socratic teachers are uniquely talented at managing classroom discussions. You are already skilled at managing discussions on springing executory interests and these discussion management skills are transferable! Facilitating discussion on race, gender, privilege, and identity within and touching the law may be new, but you can reflexively rely on the classroom and discussion

---

males. Yet, with the broader range of identities present in the legal industry, the inability or choice not to conform to appearance expectations can have significant career consequences.").

29. Gabriel "Asheru" Benn, *Relationships and Rapport: "You Don't Know Me Like That!"*, 76 Educ. Leadership 20 (2018), http://www.ascd.org/publications/educational-leadership/sept18/vol76/num01/Relationships-and-Rapport@-£You-Don%27t-Know-Me-Like-That!£.aspx ("A more colloquial way an offended student might describe this misstep is with the blurted-out phrase, "You don't know me like that!" When teachers make assumptions about rapport, they risk damaging relationships—and losing any ounce of authority they've earned up to that point.").

30. Pamela E. Barnett, *Building Trust and Negotiating Conflict When Teaching Race, in* Teaching Race: How to Help Students Unmask and Challenge Racism 112 (Stephen D. Brookfield et al., eds., 2019) ("Why should students trust you? Chances are that their experience of at least some teachers has been in the form of authorities, avoiders, or correctors when it comes to discussions of race.").

31. Lain, *supra* note 24, at 783.

management skills you built in your early years of teaching.[32] Additionally, some professors have found success with assigning reflective writing if managing the discussion on a particular set of issues becomes untenable.[33] Finally, it is also critical to be aware of and manage your own emotional reactions during discussions.[34]

Individuate

We have all heard someone claim they are colorblind and that they don't "see" race.[35] We have also heard people say that they aren't homophobic because they "don't care" who you sleep with. Those statements raise many problems, one of which is that they fail to see people for who they are. We are not all the same. White people are not all the same. White people named Nicole are not all the same. We are individuals with unique, multi-layered, intersecting identities which are vitally important to us. Dismissing part of a student's identity by failing to see their race or failing to care about their sexual identity is not productive. On the other side of the coin, it is helpful to see students as individuals. I cannot speak for all white women named Nicole. Your students should never be put in the position to speak for other members of their gender or immigration status or religion.[36] Conversations about difficult issues like equity, power, and inclusion will be more successful if you require your students to speak from their own perspective and not others who may look like them. Attunement to these multi-layer identities is also key.[37]

---

32. *See generally* Annemarie Vaccaro, *Building a Framework for Social Justice Education, in* THE ART OF EFFECTIVE FACILITATION: REFLECTIONS FROM SOCIAL JUSTICE EDUCATORS (Lisa M. Landreman ed., 2013).

33. HUNTER SCHWARTZ, SPARROW & HESS, *supra* note 20, at 197.

34. *Id.*

35. For more on the problems of colorblindness, see Judith A. M. Scully, *Seeing Color, Seeing Whiteness, Making Change: One Woman's Journey in Teaching Race and American Law*, 39 U. TOL. L. REV. 59, 74 (2007).

36. *See* Kimberlé Williams Crenshaw, *Toward a Race-Conscious Pedagogy in Legal Education*, 11 NAT'L BLACK L.J. 1, 6 (1989).

37. Lain, *supra* note 24, at 793.

> Identifying when a racialized interaction is occurring and understanding that there are likely multiple perceptions in the room allow the professor to facilitate the discussion. Attunement refers to the professor's ability to understand the varying lived experiences of the students. Being aware of these perceptions allows the professor to direct the students to consider different views and, thus, begin the learning process. Attunement does not mean calling on minority students to provide alternative perspectives, as that would diminish psychological safety by exploiting students. Attunement requires the professor to notice implicit interactions, pause the course content, and redirect the dialogue to allow for multiple perspectives to be shared or for the professor herself to share differing views.

Id.

Within Yourself:
Walking Your Own Journey

Accept That You Will Make Mistakes

Does the prospect of acknowledging the identities of 100 students while teaching mutual assent sound tricky? Of course it does. It's important to understand that integrating diversity, inclusion, and social equity into the first year curriculum is challenging for everyone and you will make mistakes. Accept that these mistakes are part of the process and forgive yourself now. Don't be afraid to start the next class with thoughts about a discussion from the previous class. Sometimes processing a discussion that went off track can be a good way to bring a point home or to reflect on the shared experience. Law professors are experts and it can be hard to admit to students that you might not know everything. Know that you learn and grow from mistakes and students will be better off from your efforts.

Be Okay with Being Uncomfortable

This work is uncomfortable.[38] Especially if you are doing a good job at it. Society has constructed privilege and has conditioned us to put up barriers around deconstructing that privilege. Openly discussing religion, race, culture, ability, power, and gender is uncomfortable for everyone. It is very uncomfortable for those who have not ever had to confront their own identity and the privileges it accords. Just because these interactions will be uncomfortable doesn't mean they aren't helpful and important. Acknowledging discomfort is a critical step, and talking through that discomfort with others in the same circumstances may lead to honest discussions otherwise unavailable to you. Finally, humanity can exist within the discomfort, as Rhonda V. Magee states, "[f]rank discussion and common struggle together over difficult issues need not, and indeed must not, require us to leave human kindness at the door. Indeed, the way forward is and must be one which sheds as much warmth as light—one which, at long last, aims consciously at illumination without alienation."[39]

---

38. Additionally, it may be wholly unfamiliar to you at first. You may be learning yourself as you lead the discussions and classes. *See* Randall, *supra* note 6, at 807 ("But you need not have full knowledge or understanding or expert diversity skills. You have to realize that you are going to be teaching a skill that you are learning. You weren't taught it, and so when teaching skills and knowledge that you are learning, you are literally going to be one step ahead of your students in the beginning.").

39. Rhonda V. Magee, *Competing Narratives, Competing Jurisprudences: Are Law Schools Racist? And the Case for an Integral Critical Approach to Thinking, Talking, Writing, and Teaching about Race,* 43 U.S.F. L. Rev. 777, 794 (2009).

Listen

Listen.[40] Listen more than you talk. Especially to your students. This is obvious but important. Just like you are (hopefully) open to allowing students to help you when you have a technology snafu, be open to allowing students to help you navigate interactions with race, gender, identity, social dynamics, religion, and ability. While the burden lies on you to engage your students on these issues, you are not alone. Just like you ask for feedback and assessment on your teaching, ask for feedback and assessment on your integration of these issues into the classroom. Students will likely appreciate being heard even if you choose not to incorporate their suggestions.

Conclusion

This book and the tools within its pages are not something you can read, implement, and check off a list. This is a way of thinking and a framework for making change which is necessary, overdue, and critical. However, these tools can expose your own vulnerabilities as a professor and as a human being. This work requires humility, patience, resolve, and dedication; the same qualities which helped you become a law professor in the first place. This authentic education has you working with students, and this work, however difficult, is the way forward.

---

40. Lain, *supra* note 24, at 799:

When navigating a racialized interaction in the classroom, professors must focus on emotionally supporting students by using nonverbal immediacy skills to invite conversation and help students feel at ease. Using body language that cuts off dialogue, such as not making eye contact or being stiff and rigid, will not help the emotional aspects of the discussion. It is also important that professors focus on communication competency skills such as encoding and decoding the situation. Active-listening techniques, by which the professor helps the conversation by actively listening and providing supportive language to continue the conversation, are essential.

Working towards Equitable Outcomes in Law School— The Role of the ABA Standards

Genevieve Blake Tung[*]

Law schools are the first gatekeepers of the legal profession. They control who may study law and what that study entails. Both of these gatekeeping functions require schools to articulate their vision of what future legal communities should look like and accomplish. Historically, legal education and accreditation has been rife with bigotry, particularly racism.[1] Today's law schools, and the professional organizations that represent them, have established diversity as an imperative for their student bodies, but they have held back from demanding that law schools address issues of diversity and equity in their curricula. This topic falls largely to individual law professors. This essay will describe how the Association of American Law Schools (AALS) and the American Bar Association (ABA) have tried to grapple with diversity in legal education, the limitations of their efforts, and why a broader approach is needed to create and realize a commitment to equality and inclusion in law schools.

The Limits of Demographic Diversity as a Core Value

In 1950, Yale Law School submitted a proposal to the AALS to expel any school which maintained a policy of segregating or excluding qualified applicants or students on the basis of race.[2] Opponents of this proposal argued that it was inappropriate for

[*] Associate Director for Educational Programs, Biddle Law Library, the University of Pennsylvania Carey Law School. I would like to acknowledge each of my co-editors of this volume for their friendship and dedication to bringing this collection to fruition.

1. *See* Judith Areen, *Accreditation Reconsidered*, 96 Iowa L. Rev. 1471, 1486 (2011).

2. Ass'n Am. Law Sch., Proceedings of the 1950 Annual Meeting 22 (Dec. 28, 1950).

AALS to concern itself with what they perceived to be a mere "social issue," and that the association should "confine itself to its traditional function of the promulgation, the encouragement and the attainment of academic standards of legal education."[3]

The committee charged to report on the issue concluded that non-white students would receive superior education at white law schools.[4] White students were at least somewhat likely to benefit from integration, in the committee's view, for three reasons: they would have the opportunity to meet "able and intellectual Negroes" so that they can become professionally acquainted; they could discuss racial issues in class with "Negro" students ("particularly in constitutional law and criminal law") and benefit from their perspectives; and that, eventually, white law graduates would be less likely to tolerate racial discrimination in the future, making them "wiser counselors and leaders in their generation."[5] Equal opportunity, the committee determined, "is beneficial to legal education, and will contribute to the improvement of the legal profession. It is in accordance with our democratic creed and would enhance our nation's influence in world affairs."[6]

It has only been a few decades since law schools began to systematically dismantle their efforts to discriminate in admissions. Today, AALS promotes diversity among its core values,[7] and has argued that diversity, measured among many attributes of a person's lived experience, is essential to legal education.[8] It does so for three reasons: law schools train the future leaders of the United States, who must reflect the nation's diversity if they are to exercise power legitimately; law schools must prepare students to interact with people of a different race as part of a diverse society; and that diversity among students inherently improves education: "Because law school classes are usually discussion-based, much of what students take from their classes depends on the contributions of their peers."[9] These rationales are strikingly similar to those described by the Association in 1951.

The ABA, which is responsible for accrediting law schools in the United States, first addressed non-discrimination in legal education in 1963[10] and has since added

---

3. Ass'n Am. Law Sch., Proceedings of the 1951 Annual Meeting 279–280 (Dec. 28, 1951) (Report of the Special Committee on Racial Discrimination).

4. *Id.* at 280.

5. *Id.* at 281.

6. *Id.* at 282.

7. *See* Ass'n Am. Law Schools, About AALS, https://www.aals.org/about/ (last visited Sept. 1, 2020). AALS made racial non-discrimination mandatory for member schools in 1957. *See* Ass'n Am. Law Sch., Proceedings of the 1957 Annual Meeting 95–109 (Dec. 28, 1957). The Association eventually expanded its policy to discrimination on the basis of sex and religious affiliation in 1970. Ass'n Am. Law Sch., Proceedings of the 1970 Annual Meeting 126–142 (Dec. 28, 1970).

8. Brief for *Amicus Curiae* Association of American Law Schools in Support of Respondents, Fisher v. Univ. of Texas, 136 S.Ct. 533 (2015) (No. 14-981).

9. *Id.* at 8.

10. *See* Am. Bar Assoc., Standards of the American Bar Association for Legal Education 3 (Nov. 1, 1969), https://www.americanbar.org/content/dam/aba/publications/misc/legal_education/Standards/standardsarchive/1969_aba_standards.pdf ("In accordance with the position taken by the

increasingly-detailed requirements for law schools to admit diverse student bodies.[11] In 2014, the ABA completed a comprehensive review of its Standards and Rules of Procedure for Approval of Law Schools and made several changes. Standard 212, "Equal Opportunity and Diversity," was replaced with a revised Standard 206, "Diversity and Inclusion."[12] The title change was reportedly adopted "to emphasize the purpose of the standard," although the ABA's supporting documentation did not explain its understanding of the relationship between "inclusion" and "equal opportunity." In contemporary usage, "inclusion" typically refers to institutional belonging; beyond being merely present, to being socially accepted and respected.[13] The text of revised Standard 206 "continued to focus on providing full opportunities for the study of law and entry into the profession by members of underrepresented groups"[14] and requires law schools to demonstrate "a commitment to having a student body that is diverse with respect to gender, race, and ethnicity."[15] The ABA suggests that a law school *may* demonstrate its commitment to providing full educational opportunities to members of underrepresented groups by, among other things, "programs that assist in meeting the academic and financial needs of many of these students" that may "create a favorable environment" for them.[16] As Professor Ann Mallatt Kil-

---

American Bar Association in 1963, law schools are expected to maintain equality of opportunity in legal education without discrimination or segregation on grounds of race or color.").

11. The ABA incorporated a non-discrimination provision into its Standards in 1973. *See* Am. Bar Ass'n, Approval of Law Schools: American Bar Association Standards and Rules of Procedure 5 (1973) https://www.americanbar.org/content/dam/aba/publications/misc/legal_education/Standards/standardsarchive/1973_standards.pdf (Standard 211: The law school shall maintain equality of opportunity in legal education without discrimination or segregation on the ground of race, color, religion, national origin, or sex.) After the Supreme Court's decision in *Regents of the Univ. of Calif. v. Bakke*, 438 U.S. 265 (1978), the ABA added a new standard further requiring schools to demonstrate a commitment to equal opportunity. Am. Bar Ass'n., Section of Legal Education and Admission to the Bar, Syllabus (Oct. 1980), at 2 (describing consideration and adoption of Standard 212). The ABA updated its standard again after the Court's decision in *Grutter v. Bollinger*, 539 U.S. 306 (2003), requiring schools to commit to creating "a student body that is diverse with respect to gender, race, and ethnicity." Am. Bar Ass'n, Standards and Rules of Procedure for Approval of Law Schools 2006–2007 15 (Standard 212(a)). In its accompanying interpretation, the ABA stated that "a law school shall take concrete actions to enroll a diverse student body that promotes cross-cultural understanding, helps break down racial and ethnic stereotypes, and enables students to better understand persons of different races, ethnic groups, and backgrounds. *Id.* at 16 (Interpretation 212-2).

12. Am. Bar Ass'n, Explanation of Changes from 2014 Comprehensive Review of the Standards 5 (hereinafter 2014 Explanation of Changes), https://www.americanbar.org/content/dam/aba/administrative/legal_education_and_admissions_to_the_bar/council_reports_and_resolutions/201408_explanation_changes.pdf.

13. *See, e.g.*, Pamela Newkirk, Diversity, Inc. 5 (2019).

14. *See* Memorandum from Hon. Rebecca White Berch & Barry A. Currier re: ABA Standards for Approval of Law Schools Matters for Notice and Comment (Dec. 11, 2015) at 6, https://taxprof.typepad.com/files/notice-and-comment-december-11-2015.pdf.

15. Am. Bar Ass'n, Standards and Rules of Procedure for Approval of Law Schools 2020–2021, Standard 206(a). The ABA's Council of the Section of Legal Education and Admissions to the Bar declined to adopt "gender identity, sexual orientation, age, and disability" in this list. *See* 2014 Explanation of Changes, *supra* note 12, at 5.

16. Am. Bar Ass'n, Standards and Rules of Procedure for Approval of Law Schools 2020–2021, Interpretation 206-2.

lenbeck has described, "the ABA does not appear to treat the pursuit of diversity as optional."[17] But the Standards are far less prescriptive when it comes to the pursuit of inclusion.[18]

The ABA's Standards on diversity have always fallen in the chapter on "Organization and Administration," rather than the chapter on the "Program of Legal Education." Even though the core benefits of diverse enrollments in law schools are and have always been grounded in what happens in the classroom (dialogue and discussion) and how students are transformed by their education (ready to lead and work in a diverse world), the ABA structures its requirement in terms of the administrative function of admissions and enrollment, with a nod towards unspecified optional academic support. The organization of the Standards creates a gap between admissions and educational outcomes similar to that identified by Professor Meera Deo in her analysis of *Grutter v. Bollinger*, one that "ignore[s] the practical question of how diversity within a student body would create the expected interactional benefits of learning."[19] The result is that the work of diversity—building a representative student body and using it to generate a better educational experience—falls exclusively to administrators and the students from underrepresented groups that they matriculate. Faculty and "non-diverse" students have no specific obligations, but share in the benefits. This is consistent with broader dynamics in higher education. As Professor Pamela Newkirk writes in the context of racial and ethnic diversity on college campuses, students of color "are left to believe that they, and not the faculty, administrators, and their White peers, are solely accountable for racial harmony. White students, in turn, become proxies for social norms."[20]

The Gap between Inputs and Outcomes

Admissions numbers are fundamentally an input measure: what the law school brings in to its program, like the number of faculty hired, or per-student spending. But educational attainment—whether students are benefiting from their school's investments—is an *outcome* measure. Most fields of professional study began to in-

---

17. Ann Mallatt Killenbeck, *Bakke, with Teeth? The Implications of* Grutter v. Bollinger *in an Outcomes-Based World*, 36 J.C. & U.L. 1 (2009). Professor Killenbeck's work refers to the 2008 version of the standards, then-designated as Standard 212(a) and Interpretation 212-1.

18. It is important to note that compositional diversity, more specifically class cohorts that include a "critical mass" of students from a historically-underrepresented group, can be critical for the inclusion and wellbeing of students in those groups. *See* Dorothy H. Evensen & Carla D. Pratt, The End of the Pipeline: A Journey of Recognition for African Americans Entering the Legal Profession 109–112 (2012).

19. *See* Meera E. Deo, *The Promise of* Grutter: *Diverse Interactions at the University of Michigan Law School*, 17 Mich. J. Race & L. 63, 73–74 (2011) (explaining how the Supreme Court concluded that law school diversity was a compelling state interest despite the respondents' silence about how compositional diversity would translate to desired outcomes, like "engaging classroom conversations.").

20. Newkirk, *supra* note 13, at 90.

corporate outcome-based assessments of their programs in the 1990s.[21] The ABA, however, had customarily looked only to bar passage and job placement statistics to gauge how well schools were performing.[22] As part of its 2014 revision package, the ABA introduced major changes to its Standards which collectively prompted law schools to construct learning outcomes measures for both their J.D. programs and then to systematically assess whether their students are meeting those goals.

Standard 302, in particular, demands that law schools establish a set of learning outcomes for their J.D. programs that shall, at a minimum, include competency in the following:

(a) Knowledge and understanding of substantive and procedural law;

(b) Legal analysis and reasoning, legal research, problem-solving, and written and oral communication skills in the legal context;

(c) Exercise of proper professional and ethical responsibilities to clients and the legal system; and

(d) Other professional skills needed for competent and ethical participation as a member of the profession.[23]

Interpretation 302-1 suggests the types of "other professional skills" that schools might want to specify in their outcomes; these include working with clients, drafting, management skills, and "cultural competency."[24] The ABA has been careful, however, not to recommend that any particular kind of coursework intended to prepare students for competent and ethical legal practice should be required. The Standards continue to "reflect the general principle that law schools should be given considerable discretion to fashion their own curricula, consistent with their varied and diverse missions."[25]

The ABA's Guidance on Standard 302 explains that each law school's outcomes "should identify the desired knowledge, skills and values that a school believes its students should master." As Professor Killenbeck has observed, it is curious that Standard 302 is totally unconnected to the "supposedly essential educational and profes-

---

21. *See* Deborah Maranville, Kate O'Neill & Carolyn Plumb, *Lessons for Legal Education from the Engineering Profession's Experience With Outcomes-Based Accreditation*, 38 WM. MITCHELL L. REV. 1017, 1027 (2012) ("Legal education is ten to twenty-five years behind engineering and other professions in adopting outcomes-based education.").

22. *See* Alexandra Pavlakis & Carolyn Kelley, *Accreditation in the Professions: Implications for Educational Leadership Preparation Programs*, 11 J. RESEARCH LEADERSHIP EDUC. 68, 79 (2016) ("Unlike accreditation processes in other professional fields, until recently, there was little to no emphasis on whether students have acquired the necessary knowledge, skills, and professional legal values.... Output was solely measured by the percentage of graduates that pass the bar exam.").

23. AM. BAR ASS'N, STANDARDS AND RULES OF PROCEDURE FOR APPROVAL OF LAW SCHOOLS 2020–2021, Standard 302.

24. *Id.* at Interpretation 302-1.

25. COUNCIL OF THE AM. BAR ASS'N SECTION OF LEGAL EDUC. & ADMISSION TO THE BAR, 2013–2014 COUNCIL STATEMENTS 151, https://www.americanbar.org/content/dam/aba/publications/misc/legal_education/Standards/2013_2014_council_statements.authcheckdam.pdf.

sional outcomes associated with diversity" described in Standard 206.[26] The Diversity and Inclusion standard uses the mandatory *shall*; the educational outcome of cultural competency is suggested with a *may* (and is mentioned only in an interpretation, not the rule itself).[27] Unlike the accreditation standards used in medicine,[28] education,[29] engineering,[30] and other fields, the ABA's Standards allow law schools to treat cultural competency as a skill which they may or may not think essential to their mission.

The structure of the Standards assumes and ascribes the educational benefits of integrated law school classrooms to a natural reaction catalyzed by a diverse student body. They are an outcome of wise administration, not of wise teaching; educational benefits that demand nothing from the institution beyond judicious gatekeeping. This approach gives law schools, collectively, the option not to substantively grapple with their legacy of social exclusion.

Every ABA-accredited law school now publishes its program-level outcomes on its website.[31] Many law schools have published outcomes that closely track the language of Standard 302, which they may see as the path of least resistance.[32] Today, roughly

---

26. Ann Mallatt Killenbeck, *Ferguson, Fisher, and the Future: Diversity and Inclusion as a Remedy for Implicit Racial Bias*, 42 J.C. & U.L. 59, 107 (2016).

27. Professor Anastasia M. Boles has described the inclusion of cultural competency in Interpretation 302-2 as an "ethical mandate," and identifying law faculties' lack of skills in this area as a roadblock to culturally proficient legal education. Anastasia M. Boles, *Seeking Inclusion from the Inside Out: Towards a Paradigm of Culturally Proficient Legal Education*, 11 CHARLESTON L. REV. 209, 267 (2017).

28. *See* Standard 7.6, LIAISON COMMITTEE ON MEDICAL EDUCATION, FUNCTIONS AND STRUCTURE OF A MEDICAL SCHOOL: STANDARDS FOR ACCREDITATION OF MEDICAL EDUCATION PROGRAMS LEADING TO THE MD DEGREE, 2020–2021, https://lcme.org/wp-content/uploads/filebase/standards/2020-21_Functions-and-Structure_2019-10-04.docx ("The faculty of a medical school ensure that the medical curriculum provides opportunities for medical students to learn to recognize and appropriately address gender and cultural biases in themselves, in others, and in the health care delivery process.").

29. *See* Standard #2, Learning Differences, COUNCIL FOR THE ACCREDITATION OF EDUCATOR PREPARATION, STANDARDS, http://www.ncate.org/standards/standard-1 ("The teacher uses understanding of individual differences and diverse cultures and communities to ensure inclusive learning environments that enable each learner to meet high standards.").

30. Criterion 5 (Curriculum), ENGINEERING TECHNOLOGY ACCREDITATION COMMISSION, CRITERIA FOR ACCREDITING ENGINEERING TECHNOLOGY PROGRAMS, 2019–2020, https://www.abet.org/accreditation/accreditation-criteria/criteria-for-accrediting-engineering-technology-programs-2019-2020/#GC2 ("The discipline specific content of the curriculum must focus on the applied aspects of science and engineering and must ... E.[I]nclude topics related to professional responsibilities, ethical responsibilities, respect for diversity, and quality and continuous improvement.").

31. ABA Standard 302 became fully effective in the 2016–2017 academic year. Am. Bar Ass'n, Section of Legal Education and Admissions to the Bar, *Transition to and Implementation of the New Standards and Rules of Procedure for the Approval of Law Schools* (Aug. 13, 2014), at 2, https://www.americanbar.org/content/dam/aba/administrative/legal_education_and_admissions_to_the_bar/governancedocuments/2014_august_transition_and_implementation_of_new_aba_standards_and_rules.authcheckdam.pdf.

32. *C.f.* Areen, *supra* note 1, at 1482 ("Merely assessing whether a particular institution meets a series of minimum standards on a checklist ... does not encourage institutions to accomplish more than the minimum; nor does it push even the best colleges and universities to ask, 'Is this the best we can do?' ").

a quarter of law schools have elected to specify learning outcomes related to cultural competence.[33] Standard 315 requires schools to continuously evaluate their outcomes and assessment methods; for each additional goal a school sets for itself, there is a concomitant obligation to see that goal met. A school that publicly tasks itself to produce culturally proficient lawyers will need to teach to that goal or grapple with its failure to do so in a semi-public way. A school that does not set such a goal has no obligation to meet it, nor be seen trying.

Overcoming Institutional Barriers

Beyond concerns about overpromising, there are other reasons a law school might be reluctant to create learning outcomes related to diversity, equity, or inclusion. For starters—how to measure success? An outcome-statement should be concrete and ascertainable, describing the knowledge, skill, or behavior the professor (or school) expects students to achieve.[34] An outcome that cannot be assessed is like a question that cannot be answered. Fortunately, legal and education scholars have already documented the virtues and methods of assessing diversity and cultural sensibility education in law school.[35]

Law schools may also take the position that diversity is an administrative issue, not a curricular one. This view, however, is not dissimilar from that sounded to AALS in 1951 from opponents of the Yale resolution: that schools have a "traditional function" of guiding students to meet academic standards through legal education, and that legal education has a core substance that must be prioritized above, and that can be distinguished from, "social issues." Professor Kimberlé Crenshaw has described this belief—that legal discourse can be objective and free from cultural and political attachments—as "perspectivelessness."[36] Perspectivelessness does harm by speaking "a 'truth' about law's neutrality that is plainly untrue for members of disadvantaged communities."[37] The truth remains that the traditional American law school curricu-

---

33. *See* Holloran Center for Ethical Leadership in the Professions, University of St. Thomas School of Law, Learning Outcomes 302(c) and (d), https://www.stthomas.edu/hollorancenter/resourcesforlegaleducators/learningoutcomesdatabase/learningoutcomes302c/ (last accessed July 23, 2020) (reporting outcomes published by 51 U.S. law schools). The ABA currently accredits 203 law schools. Am. Bar Ass'n, ABA-Approved Law Schools, https://www.americanbar.org/groups/legal_education/resources/aba_approved_law_schools/ (last visited July 23, 2020).

34. *See, e.g.,* Anthony Niedwiecki, *Law Schools and Learning Outcomes: Developing a Coherent, Cohesive, and Comprehensive Law School Curriculum*, 64 Clev. St. L. Rev. 661, 679 (2016).

35. *See* Andrea A. Curcio, Teresa E. Ward & Nisha Dogra, *A Survey Instrument to Develop, Tailor, and Help Measure Law Student Cultural Diversity Education Learning Outcomes*, 38 Nova L. Rev. 177 (2014); *see also* Elizabeth Stevens, Heather Douglas, Bridget Cullen-Mandikos & Rosemary Hunter, *Equity, Diversity and Student Engagement in a Law School—A Case Study Approach*, 16 Legal Educ. Rev. 1 (2006).

36. Kimberlé Williams Crenshaw, *Toward a Race-Conscious Pedagogy in Legal Education*, 11 Nat'l Black L.J. 1 (1988).

37. Faisal Bhabha, *Towards a Pedagogy of Diversity in Legal Education*, 52 Osgoode Hall L.J. 59, 72 (2014).

lum has a perspective — white, male, heterosexual, cisgendered, abled, and well-re-sourced, and that "this assumed perspective forms an invisible pedagogical norm."[38] This normative foundation, if unquestioned, is self-replicating.

Law schools, and individual law teachers, may fear "getting it wrong." Administrators may fear pushback from faculty.[39] Faculty may be indifferent, or fear mishandling classroom discussions on topics with which they have little first-hand experience.[40] Such fears may be well-founded in schools that are "culturally pre-competent," to borrow from the framework created by Kikanza Nuri-Robins and Lewis Bundy.[41] A culturally pre-competent organization has brought issues of diversity and difference to the surface, but addresses them in a superficial or haphazard way.[42] Many law schools likely could fall into this category. As Professor Anastasia Boles has pointed out, "awareness of cultural differences does not, in itself, create change."[43] These schools must push themselves to create real accountability, even if Standard 302 does not (yet) make it mandatory.

The solution is unlikely to come from the ABA or AALS. It must come from law schools and, more importantly, their faculties. While compositional diversity remains imperative, law faculty, particularly those teachers who represent historically-included demographics, must do more, including working in the classroom to "ensure that ideas are exchanged, that lawyering skills are developed, and that biases are acknowledged and addressed."[44] Law professors who recognize the moral imperative to build real inclusion in law schools and in the legal profession can assume a role in creating the kind of educational benefits that, today, are assigned to students to generate amongst themselves, and which disproportionally burden "diverse" students. Individual faculty members can work to improve their own cultural proficiency and apply that knowledge to their teaching.[45] Faculties can also work collectively to create accountability and build what Professor Faisal Bhabha has termed a "diversity pedagogy," one that reorients the law school to "produce an institutional and professional culture, reflected in curriculum, that is expressly and comprehensively built on equality-positive assumptions."[46] This will require real work to translate hazy aspirations into meaningful commitments.

---

38. Boles, *supra* note 27, at 221.

39. Law school administrators may also be limited by the absence of an internal policy or process to address complaints or correct mistakes.

40. *See, e.g.*, Deo, *supra* note 19, at 105–106.

41. *See* Kikanza Nuri-Robins & Lewis G. Bundy, Fish out of Water: Mentoring, Managing and Self-Monitoring People Who Don't Fit In 38–39 (2016).

42. *See* Boles, *supra* note 27, at 256.

43. *Id.*

44. Samia E. McCall, *Thinking Outside of the Race Boxes: A Two-Pronged Approach to Further Diversity and Decrease Bias*, 2018 B.Y.U. Educ. & L.J. 23, 59 (2018).

45. *See* Boles, *supra* note 27, at 265.

46. Bhabha, *supra* note 37, at 93.

Starting at the Start: Integrating Race and Reflection for an Antiracist Approach to Professional Identity Development in the First Year Curriculum

Eduardo R.C. Capulong, *
Andrew King-Ries, ** *& Monte Mills* ***

Introduction

Our professional obligations as lawyers demand that we disrupt and end racism.[1] Unfortunately, our approach to developing the professional identity of law students overlooks the racism endemic in the law, legal system, profession, and legal education. While students may take electives in critical race theory or intern in clinics that take racism head-on, law schools generally do not require them to wrestle with how the legal system created and perpetuates racism nor do they develop the values and skills necessary to respond effectively to and ultimately dismantle it. In this chapter, we begin with the premise that antiracism is essential to the profession's responsibility to serve justice and must be a core aspect of legal professional identity.

---

* Professor of Law and Director, Lawyering Program, City University of New York (CUNY) School of Law.

** Professor, Alexander Blewett III School of Law at the University of Montana.

*** Associate Professor and Director, Margery Hunter Brown Indian Law Clinic, Alexander Blewett III School of Law at the University of Montana.

1. *See, e.g.,* MODEL RULES PRO. CONDUCT, pmbl. (AM. BAR ASS'N 1983) ("A lawyer, as a member of the legal profession, is a representative of clients, an officer of the legal system and a public citizen having special responsibility for the quality of justice.") The President of the American Bar Association issued this call: "the country, and indeed the world, is watching and depending on American lawyers to stand up to bigotry, hatred, racism, sexism, homophobia, xenophobia and inequality." Judy P. Martinez, *ABA advances the rule of law to assure fairness, justice, and ultimately, our democracy*, ABA. J. (Sept. 1, 2019), http://www.abajournal.com/magazine/article/aba-advances-the-rule-of-law-to-assure-fairness-justice-and-ultimately-our-democracy.

We develop this argument more extensively elsewhere.[2] Here, our focus is on a practical application of that argument, which we distill into two prescriptions. First, surface and center race by recognizing and injecting critical inquiry into the primary role of the law, legal system, and legal profession in the construction of race and the perpetuation of racism. We offer here ways by which to increase students' understanding of these complex processes. Second, infuse reflective practice with an antiracist ethic. By promoting reflective practice, our purpose is to constructively guide students' exploration of how a deeper, simultaneously more personal and systemic understanding of race and racism shapes their professional identity and commitment.

These objectives are co-extensive. Without reflection and internalization, the study of race and racism is an academic exercise. Given the defining nature of race and racism, in particular the white-normative aspects of legal education and professional identity, academic study, without more, merely perpetuates them, preserving the status quo, advantaging white students, disadvantaging non-white students, and indoctrinating a "bleached out" professional identity.[3] Likewise, an exploration of professional identity divorced from a critical understanding of the constitutive role of race and racism in the law and legal system personalizes and pathologizes a systemic, social reality. Therefore, we begin also with the premise that combatting and ending race and racism require both critical understanding *and* professional commitment.

The remainder of this essay describes our learning goals and strategies to spark further incorporation of this integrated approach across the law school curriculum.

Learning Goals and Strategies

We've described our overall learning objectives in this realm elsewhere.[4] Here, we offer three suggestions. First, devote class time to discussing the law's and legal system's role in creating and perpetuating race and racism. The law school curriculum is woefully inadequate on these issues. Race and racism are viewed as largely extraneous to traditional first year courses, (indeed, the entire curriculum). To the extent they are addressed, inquiry is limited mostly to anti-discrimination doctrine and, with it, the language of diversity and multiculturalism. This isn't enough: we believe that interdisciplinary work demonstrating the pervasiveness — the systemic, social, structural, personal nature — of race and racism is essential reading for every law student.[5]

---

2. Eduardo R.C. Capulong, Andrew King-Ries & Monte Mills, *Antiracism, Reflection, and Professional Identity*, 18 Hastings Race & Poverty L. J. 3 (2020).

3. David B. Wilkins, *Identities and Roles: Race, Recognition, and Professional Responsibility*, 57 Md. L. Rev. 1502, 1511–17 (1998).

4. *See* Eduardo R.C. Capulong, Andrew King-Ries & Monte Mills, *'Race, Racism and American Law': A Seminar from the Indigenous, Black, and Immigrant Legal Perspectives*, 21 Scholar: St. Mary's L. Rev. Race & Soc. Just. 1, 20 (2019).

5. *See, e.g.*, Capulong, King-Ries & Mills, *supra* note 2, at 11–12; Laura S. Abrams & Jene A. Moio, *Critical Race Theory & the Cultural Competence Dilemma in Social Work Education*, 45 J. Soc. Work Educ. 245, 247 (2009); Debra Chopp, *Addressing Cultural Bias in the Legal Profession*, 41 N.Y.U. Rev. L. & Soc. Change 367, 381–87 (2017). *See also* Ian Haney López, White by Law: The Legal

Second, students should be provided multiple opportunities for reflection. These reflections can be brief and need not require extensive additional work for either students or professors; what's essential is sustained, repeated reflective practice. Reflection prompts should alternate between the systemic and substantive and the personal and professional. Alternating prompts in this fashion provides the space for students to develop and exercise personal agency in constructing a professional identity committed to social change.

Here is a list of prompts we've used in our seminar, "Race, Racism, and American Law," a second and third year elective class:[6]

1. What is your first experience with race? When did you first become aware of race?

2. Discuss a policy, action, or law that you identify as racist and why?

3. Reflect on the results of your Project Implicit test(s).[7]

4. Discuss a recent interaction with people of another/other race(s) and how the choices you made during those interactions may have promoted or undermined an antiracist agenda?

5. Write down the names of the first three Native Americans that come to mind. Reflect on why those were the names that came to mind for you.

CONSTRUCTION OF RACE (2006); Russell G. Pearce, *White Lawyering: Rethinking Race, Lawyer Identity, and Rule of Law*, 73 FORDHAM L. REV. 2081 (2005); EDWARD E. BAPTIST, THE HALF HAS NEVER BEEN TOLD: SLAVERY AND THE MAKING OF AMERICAN CAPITALISM (2014); Justin Desautels-Stein, *Race as a Legal Concept*, 2 COLUM. J. RACE & L. 1 (2012); ARIELA J. GROSS, WHAT BLOOD WON'T TELL: A HISTORY OF RACE ON TRIAL IN AMERICA (2008); Cheryl I. Harris, *Whiteness as Property*, 106 Harv. L. Rev. 1707 (1993); WALTER JOHNSON, THE BROKEN HEART OF AMERICA: ST. LOUIS AND THE VIOLENT HISTORY OF THE UNITED STATES (2020); Michael C. Dawson, *Racial Capitalism & Democratic Crisis*, ITEMS, https://items.ssrc.org/race-capitalism/racial-capitalism-and-democratic-crisis/ (Dec. 4, 2018); Cynthia Lee, *Making Black and Brown Lives Matter: Incorporating Race into the Criminal Procedure Curriculum*, 60 ST. LOUIS U. L.J. 481 (2016); DOROTHY A. BROWN, CRITICAL RACE THEORY: CASES, MATERIALS, AND PROBLEMS (3d ed. 2014).

6. *See generally* Capulong, King-Ries & Mills, *supra* note 4. In crafting prompts, we find the work of colleagues from the University of St. Thomas and Regents University particularly useful. *See, e.g.*, Neil Hamilton & Jeff Maleska, *Helping Each Law Student Develop Affirmative Evidence of Cross-Cultural Competency*, 19 SCHOLAR: ST. MARY'S L. REV. RACE & SOC. JUST. 187 (2017); Neil Hamilton & Jerry Organ, *Thirty Reflection Questions to Help Each Student Find Meaningful Employment and Develop an Integrated Professional Identity (Professional Formation)*, 83 TENN. L. REV. 843 (2016); Benjamin V. Madison, III & Larry O. Natt Gantt, II, *The Emperor Has No Clothes, But Does Anyone Really Care? How Law Schools are failing to Develop Students' Professional Identity and Practical Judgment*, 27 REGENT U. L. REV. 339 (2015). These scholars call for the organization of reflection along the lines of students' articulation of values, self-awareness, strengths and weaknesses, recognition of the professional identity "hidden curriculum", cognitive dissonance, and strategies.

7. PROJECT IMPLICIT, OVERVIEW, https://implicit.harvard.edu/implicit/education.html (last visited Sept. 1, 2020). We ask students to complete at least one implicit bias test. Often students will take several different tests to explore their potential biases in different contexts. Interestingly, students report taking the same test multiple times to see if they "improve." The tests can generate feelings of frustration and disappointment for some students, which may be expressed by resistance to the validity of the test. Given the personal nature of these feelings, they are a rich area for reflection and discussion. We find it productive to assign the tests and have the students reflect on them early in the semester.

6. Discuss common threads of race and racism for immigrants, Native Americans, and African Americans.

7. Discuss a personal example of system 1 and system 2 thinking connected to race.[8]

8. Given our discussion of the history and conflict of race, sovereignty, and federal Indian law, what do you think the future holds, whether in terms of the current challenge to the Indian Child Welfare Act (ICWA) or more broadly?

9. Give an example of a lived experience that is different between yourself and a person of another race?

10. What has challenged you in our reflections/course and how will you respond to that challenge as a lawyer?

Third, the professor should provide space in class for structured debrief and discussion of the themes that emerge from the reflections. We have used two different debriefing methods. The first method is for the professor to review the submitted reflections and identify the primary themes. The professor can surface these themes and then ask for comment or input on these themes from the entire class. The second method is to have students break into pairs or triads and discuss the prompt for which they already submitted a reflection. Because they have prepared a reflection on the prompt, their small discussions tend to be engaged and push into more personal experiences with race and racial identity. In the report-backs from the small groups, students generally articulate reflection themes similar to those identified by the professor. The primary advantages of the second method are increased student engagement and greater openness about personal racial identity. We have used both methods and have developed a preference for the second approach. Our preference stems partly from our observation that students engage more deeply and personally with the material. The small group setting also provides students with a more relaxed environment in which to share thoughts or reflections about which they may be self-conscious. We have found that students enjoy hearing similar concerns from their peers and, in a small group, could more easily identify with each other regarding these sensitive issues. Finally, we have observed that the second approach results in students drawing greater connections between substantive, critical inquiry and professional identity.

Challenges

These discussions are challenging. They challenge prevailing post-racial, color-blind ideology and go to the heart of each student's identity and sense of self, place, and value. By definition, the purpose of these conversations is to surface and counter the racialization of law and society and to destabilize students. We want to take ad-

---

8. System 1 and System 2 are terms used by Daniel Kahneman in his book, "Thinking Fast and Slow"; *see* Daniel Kahneman, Thinking Fast and Slow 19–30 (2011). According to Kahneman, System 1 thinking is fast, intuitive, and emotional. System 2 thinking is slower, more deliberative, and more logical. Our self-perception tends to be more associated with System 2.

vantage of the identity crisis that is law school to help students develop an explicitly antiracist professional identity. This is a project of primary importance given the law and legal system's role in racist oppression. The reality is that centering race, challenging the status quo, and destabilizing students is hard work. It is heavy, emotional, and fraught with pitfalls for both students and professors alike. It is therefore equally important to create a safe space that nurtures not just the mind but also the body and heart.[9]

The 1L Year

While developed in an upper-level elective course, we are convinced our approach could be infused throughout the curriculum. Indeed, we believe it should start in the first year, from day one. Law students begin forming their professional identities as soon as they enter their first day of law school—if not earlier. Implicit and explicit messages about performance, competition, expectations, responsibilities, and self-disclosure, to name a few, pervade the entire law student experience. Especially in the opening weeks of the first year, law school can foment intense crises of identity for students. In nearly every instance, however, the white-normative standards of the legal system, the legal profession, and law school are messages that go unmentioned; they are a given. As a result, the first year law student is left to navigate the often entirely foreign terrain of learning how to "think like a lawyer" without being encouraged or provided the tools to critically examine whether what's really expected is how to "think like a (white) lawyer."[10] A systematic approach to antiracist professional identity formation therefore must be rooted as early as possible in the first year curriculum to ensure that every law student has the ability to recognize the role of race and racism in forming their person and profession, which ideally will allow the development of a fuller professional identity rooted in an antiracist approach.

Some of this work is already being done. "Doctrinal"[11] classes—such as constitutional law, property, and criminal law—routinely explore these topics. Indigenous peoples' rights, slavery's role, the history of Jim Crow, immigration, and civil rights are central themes in the development and ratification of the Constitution.[12] Equal

---

9. In facilitating these difficult discussions, we draw on lessons shared by other scholars. *See, e.g.,* Erin C. Lain, *Racialized Interactions in the Law School Classroom: Pedagogical Approaches to Creating a Safe Learning Environment,* 67 J. LEGAL ED. 780 (2018) (discussing *inter alia* need for safety and inclusion, sensitivity to racialized interactions, and attunement, authenticity, and power-sharing); *see also* Jean Koh Peters & Susan Bryant, *Talking About Race* in SUSAN BRYANT, ELLIOTT S. MILSTEIN, & ANN C. SHALLECK, TRANSFORMING THE EDUCATION OF LAWYERS: THE THEORY & PRACTICE OF CLINICAL PEDAGOGY 375–406 (2014).

10. And, we would add: male, hetero, and cis-gendered.

11. We do not accept the skills-doctrinal divide.

12. *See, e.g.,* Nikole Hannah-Jones et al., *The 1619 Project,* N.Y. TIMES (Aug. 14, 2019), https://www.nytimes.com/interactive/2019/08/14/magazine/1619-america-slavery.html; Adam Serwer, *The Fight Over the 1619 Project is Not About the Facts,* THE ATLANTIC (Dec. 23, 2019), https://www.theatlantic.com/ideas/archive/2019/12/historians-clash-1619-project/604093/.

Protection jurisprudence is all about race. Grounded in the theft of Indian land, property is meaningless without the study of the doctrine of discovery.[13] And criminal law's modern origins, the doctrine of self-defense and the disproportionate representation of people of color at all stages in the criminal justice system are staple discussions. More can be done. For example, in constitutional law, discussions could integrate better issues of federal Indian law, including the constitutional bargaining around federalism and federal-tribal-state relations.[14] The Commerce Clause can also elucidate principles of federal Indian law and the role of race in the adoption of that clause.[15] We applaud the sustained efforts of colleagues to center race and racism in these and other "traditional" first year courses.[16] Since doctrinal classes tend to be focused on formal legal rules, the challenge here is to reject the "perspectivelessness" of legal study and connect substantive knowledge and critical inquiry to acquisition of professional skills and development of professional identity.[17]

Here is where the second component of reflection is vital. Doctrinal classes are supposedly uninvolved in professional identity development, which traditionally is the realm of professional ethics — in most schools one separate "professional responsibility" course. Yet doctrinal courses — where students learn how to "think like a lawyer" — are precisely the primary vehicles for construction of professional identity.[18] Without consideration of professional identity in doctrinal classes, the perspectiveless discussion of substantive knowledge simply perpetuates white-normative, "bleached out" professional identity. Coupling substantive knowledge about race and racism and reflective practice into doctrinal classes counteract this built-in bias.

Legal skills courses — such as lawyering and legal writing — are especially primed for an exploration of professional identity. Because they are experiential, these courses already incorporate reflective practice and often professional ethics — and therefore professional values and identity.[19] Spurred by a new ABA accreditation standard,[20]

---

13. *See, e.g.,* Johnson v. M'Intosh, 21 U.S. 543 (1823); *see* K-Sue Park, *Conquest & Slavery as Foundational to the Property Law Course,* in THE OXFORD HANDBOOK OF RACE & LAW IN THE UNITED STATES (DEVON CARBADO, KHIARA BRIDGES & EMILY HOUH EDS., OXFORD UNIVERSITY PRESS, forthcoming).

14. *See, e.g.,* Gregory Ablavsky, *The Savage Constitution,* 63 DUKE L.J. 999 (2014).

15. *See* Gregory Ablavsky, *Beyond the Indian Commerce Clause,* 124 YALE L.J. 1012 (2015).

16. *See* Racial Bias, Disparities and Oppression in the 1L Curriculum: A Critical Approach to the Canonical First-Year Law School Subjects, Boston University School of Law (Feb. 28–29, 2020) (conference on incorporating race and racism in property, contracts, torts, civil procedure, and criminal law), http://www.bu.edu/law/files/2019/12/BU-Symposium-Schedule-February-26th-.pdf.

17. Kimberlé Williams Crenshaw, *Toward a Race-Conscious Pedagogy in Legal Education,* 11 NAT'L BLACK L.J. 1 (1988).

18. *See* Elizabeth Mertz, *Teaching Lawyers the Language of Law: Legal and Anthropological Translations,* 34 J. MARSHALL L. REV. 91 (2000).

19. Indeed, some schools offer first year skills courses or course components that work with actual clients, which is ideal for professional identity formation. *See, e.g.,* THE NEW 1L: FIRST YEAR LAWYERING WITH CLIENTS 83–147 (Eduardo R.C. Capulong, Michael A. Millemann, Sarah Rankin & Nantiya Ruan, eds., 2015).

20. American Bar Ass'n, Standards and Rules of Procedure for Approval of Law Schools, Chapter 3: Program of Legal Education (2019).

the recent proliferation of experiential courses[21] is fertile ground for the professional identity movement to flourish.[22]

Our experience has convinced us that this effort—the combination of substantive knowledge and personal racial identity development—is worth it. It is also vital if we are truly committed to interrupting and eliminating racism and genuinely delivering on the promise of equality in our country's founding documents.

---

21. *Reflecting on Recent Expansions and Experimentations with Experiential Learning*, AALS Clinical and Experiential Law Directors' Workshop, May 4, 2019, San Francisco, California (Professors Eduardo Capulong, Allison Korn, Donna Lee & Lisa Martin); Allison Korn & Laila L. Hlass, *Assessing the Experiential (R)evolution*, 65 VILL. L. REV. ___ (forthcoming 2020).

22. Neil W. Hamilton, Verna E. Monson, & Jerome M. Organ, *Empirical Evidence that Legal Education Can Foster Student Professionalism/Professional Formation to Become an Effective Lawyer*, 10 U. ST. THOMAS L.J. 11 (2012).

Presenting Issues of Diversity and Social Justice in the 1L Curriculum: A Report on a Lecture Series and Seminar

Mark Tushnet[*]

This essay reports on the background and content of a lecture series and accompanying seminar at Harvard Law School. The lectures and seminar focused on how issues of diversity and social justice were—and could be—presented in the standard 1L curriculum. I am typically quite skeptical about reports on successful pedagogic innovations in legal education. Despite that, I believe that the "experiment" described in this essay—the lectures and seminar spread out over two years—was generally successful. The first lectures were extremely well-attended, though the follow-up ones were not. With sufficient administrative support, the lecture series is almost certainly reproducible elsewhere, perhaps on a one-shot basis, perhaps periodically so that at some point in their legal education students have access to a version of the series. The seminar produced some quite interesting materials, and the students thought systematically about both pedagogic and substantive questions. The writing exercise was clearly quite challenging for students, and I wonder how it might be tweaked to make it a bit less challenging while preserving its intellectual benefits; some of the other essays in this book offer promising suggestions.

Section I briefly discusses the rationale for the series and seminar. Section II describes the lecture series, and Section III the seminar. A brief conclusion follows.

[*] William Nelson Cromwell Professor of Law Emeritus, Harvard Law School. I thank Deans Martha Minow and John Manning for supporting the activities reported here, and the faculty members who volunteered for the lecture series and the students in the seminar described in this essay, for their contributions.

Why We Developed the Lecture Series

The background for the lectures and seminar was the "Reclaim Harvard" movement in the spring of 2016.[1] Over the following summer, Dean Martha Minow, reflecting on the events associated with the movement, suggested to a group of faculty members interested in legal history that it might be valuable to present a lecture series on issues of race and diversity in U.S. legal history. I volunteered to organize those lectures, which were quite successful (in the terms I use to assess success—the lecture hall was regularly filled to overflowing).[2] During the same semester I visited the law school at the University of California—Berkeley, and saw a poster announcing a lecture— part of a monthly series—on "Core in Context," which seemed to me interestingly complementary to the series at Harvard I was coordinating.[3] On my return I proposed to continue the theme into the spring semester of 2017 with a series of lectures on how to present issues of diversity and social justice in the 1L curriculum. Dean Minow continued to support the lecture series by providing administrative assistance and— importantly—lunch for students who attended.

What Were the Lectures About?
Contrasting Siloing and Pervasive Presentation of Diversity Issues

The lecture series began with a presentation on tape of a lecture Duncan Kennedy had given at an event organized by a student group that was a predecessor of the Re-claim Movement, followed by a question-and-answer exchange.[4] The series continued with lectures on property, torts, international law, contracts, civil procedure, criminal law, and legislation and regulation—the Harvard 1L curriculum.[5]

---

1. For the movement's self-description, see Reclaim Harvard Law School, *We Reclaim Harvard Because....* https://reclaimharvardlaw.wordpress.com/why/ (last visited Sept. 1, 2020).

2. The lectures can be viewed at *Diversity and Legal History: A Harvard Law School Lecture Series*, YouTube (Aug. 8, 2017), https://www.youtube.com/playlist?list=PL2q2U2nTrWq0KixVOa11h Bv8wOssEtgLu.

3. For brief description of the Berkeley series, see *Social Justice Thursdays*, https://perma.cc/C93H-5Q7X (Mar. 13, 2018).

4. Kennedy's lecture can be found at Harvard Law School, *Diversity and Social Justice Series: Duncan Kennedy, "Hot Cases and Cold Cases,"* YouTube (Feb. 7, 2017) https://www.youtube.com/watch?v=mKqzGpBBHv4. A more extensive version of my introductory remarks, focusing on the idea of "hot" and "cold" cases, can be found at Harvard Law School, *Diversity and Social Justice in First-Year Classes: Mark Tushnet*, YouTube (Feb. 28, 2018) https://www.youtube.com/watch?v=gqX 6623YptE.

5. Not all of the lectures were recorded, but those that were can be found at Harvard Law School, *Diversity and Social Justice Series: Todd Rakoff on Justice and Regulation*, YouTube (Mar. 10, 2017), https://www.youtube.com/watch?v=6jS4q_44aL0; *Diversity and Social Justice Lecture Series: Jeannie Suk Gersen, "Hiding in Plain Sight,"* YouTube (Feb. 23, 2017), https://www.youtube.com/watch?v= W6tkqpqYfds; *Diversity and Social Justice Lecture Series: Oren Bar-Gill, "Contextualizing Contracts,"* YouTube (Apr. 3, 2017) https://www.youtube.com/watch?v=o8mZoWIcya4; *Diversity and Social*

Kennedy's presentation introduced one theme that pervaded the series, sometimes beneath the surface, sometimes overtly: the choice among available legal rules has distributional effects, and those effects can be considered in terms of diversity and social justice.[6] More frequently, though, the lectures offered two pedagogical approaches to issues of diversity and social justice, which participants in the seminar later came to call "siloing" and the pervasive method. Once identified, the content of these approaches is reasonably obvious, as are their advantages and drawbacks.

"Siloing" involves picking several topics scattered throughout the semester and framing the discussion of the specific legal questions raised by those topics around issues of diversity and social justice; the pervasive method raises such issues with respect to every topic covered in the course. Siloing focuses discussion but poses several pedagogic problems. Students may think that the *only* issues in the course that pose questions about diversity and social justice are those considered in these class sessions. And, the classes may take on something of the pejorative tone associated in the past with "women's day"—simultaneously invidiously singling out some issues as "special" and, perhaps more important, leading students (and perhaps instructors) to look to the "targets" of concern (women, racial minorities) for distinctive insights into the issues. The pervasive method avoids those difficulties, but instructors and students reported some concern that the approach had adverse effects on the coverage offered in the course and, again perhaps more important, concern that at some point students would "turn off" as they had to consider once again how this topic, and then that one, raised issues of diversity and social justice. Proponents of the pervasive method argue as well that it finesses the problems sometimes said to be associated with class discussions of "difficult issues": If such issues arise constantly, students basically will have to participate in discussing them.

Justice Lecture Series: Samuel Moyn, "Is Black Lives Matter a Human Rights Movement?," YouTube (Apr. 3, 2017), https://www.youtube.com/watch?v=WkpMDceXtOM; Diversity and Social Justice Lecture Series: Rebecca Tushnet, "Zoning and Race in Property Law," YouTube (Mar. 8, 2017), https://www.youtube.com/watch?v=u-m5XgDX-c4.

The Dean's Office supported a re-run of the series in the spring semester of 2018, but it was much less successful. The reasons are complex. The person in the Dean's office who had helped with administration the year earlier left just before the semester began, and there were gaps in developing publicity for the series. More important, I suspect, is that student "demand" for the series had mostly been satisfied the prior year; only 1L students had not had a chance to hear the lectures, and—unlike the prior year's students—they had not experienced the Reclaim Movement's activities directly. (There is some reason to think that there was some attempt to interfere with publicity for the series; posters advertising it were seemingly randomly removed before they should have been.)

6. Kennedy presented the way he would teach *Coblyn v. Kennedy's Inc.*, 268 N.E.2d 860 (Mass. 1971), a false imprisonment case included in the section on intentional torts in the casebook Kennedy used. The court framed the question presented as offering a choice between a subjective standard of reasonable belief on the part of the company's employee or an objective standard, opting for the latter. Drawing on a note in the casebook, Kennedy posed the alternative of strict liability and then laid out the distributional effects, emphasizing in particular how strict liability would probably benefit racial minorities while raising prices charged to all customers.

A Writing Seminar Devoted to Developing Diversity-Focused Units for First Year Classes

The lecture series had a companion seminar associated with it.[7] Students in the seminar were required to attend the lectures, and for most of the semester class discussion dealt with the immediately preceding lectures, with students particularly attentive to the ways in which what they had heard in the lecture corresponded to or were in tension with what they had experienced in their classes. Students were also required to develop a one-day "lesson" in a 1L course of their choosing, in which they were to present materials dealing with diversity and social justice. As 2L and 3L students, the seminar participants discovered how difficult it was to compile materials for a single day's class session.

Though the papers varied in depth and detail, overall, they produced a quite interesting set of materials.[8] Nearly all attempted to combine more or less standard presentations of cases and comments with questions that focused specifically on diversity and social justice. Some of the latter are sometimes used in existing casebooks, from which the students might have drawn them. Pulling the cases together in a single unit might be a form of siloing, and scattering them throughout a casebook might be seen as a way of using the pervasive approach.[9] In the summaries below, though I focus on the latter features of the materials, I emphasize that the materials did provide coverage of standard questions comparable to that in more conventional materials.[10]

Here are summaries of selected papers and lesson plans students in the seminar developed. I have included references to the principal cases the papers included to show how the lesson plans incorporated components of the "regular" curriculum—that is, how they were sensitive to questions about "coverage."

Civil Procedure

(1) "Pleading": The cases are standard ones—*Dioguardi v. Durning, Conley v. Gibson, Ashcroft v. Iqbal.* The central issues raised in the questions deal with the fact that some plaintiffs lack the resources to generate the kinds of

---

7. The first semester's series on diversity in U.S. legal history had an associated "reading group," a smaller class given fewer credits, in which students discussed the lectures they had attended.

8. No student chose to develop materials for courses on international law and only one student did so for legislation and regulation, perhaps because those courses were the least familiar to students.

9. I thought that the assignment was appropriate as a writing requirement in a course that explicitly discussed the choice between siloing and the pervasive method.

10. I considered but rejected the possibility of compiling the papers into a file that could be accessed upon request. I rejected the possibility because of issues associated with student confidentiality (here, among other things, the facts that some materials were underdeveloped and that students were being asked to do a task with which they were entirely unfamiliar except as consumers of coursebook materials), even with consent of individual students.

complaints skilled advocates can, and with interdisciplinary material raising questions about how formal equality can mask substantive inequality.[11]

One question asks, "How, if at all, might aversive bias be present in the majority's analysis of the plausibility of Iqbal's claims?" Then, "To the extent that aversive bias impacts judicial decision-making, what (if anything) do you think should be done about it?" One suggestion is judicial education, citing a video produced by the ABA Commission on Diversity and Inclusion. The Notes then turn to the possibility that "narrative theory ... would help litigants meet the ... plausibility standard."[12] The Notes conclude with "examples of judges exhibiting distaste or even disgust at certain litigants of their claims."

(2) "Aggregation, Movement Lawyering, and Social Change": The framing question here is whether "the class action device [is] an effective vehicle for advancing social justice agendas." The materials include *Wal-Mart v. Dukes* and excerpts from Derrick Bell's *Serving Two Masters*, which serves as a focal point for the questions. After the materials, the Notes provide short excerpts from Brandon Garrett and Alexandra Lahav arguing that class actions "promote democratic participation" and "achieve some of the key values of a valuable democratic society," and ask whether those views are in tension with Bell's. Similarly, the Notes ask whether *Wal-Mart* and the Fairness in Class Action Litigation Act, both usually understood as hostile to class litigation, can be understood as addressing, perhaps unintentionally, some of Bell's concerns. The Notes then extend the analysis to LGBTQ litigation,[13] and conclude with a discussion of community lawyering as an alternative to class action litigation, and a reference to increased contributions to the ACLU since the election of Donald Trump. In an interesting twist, the Notes end by asking students to "consider your own career goals. What do you want to accomplish and how do you plan to pursue those ends?"

Contracts

(1) "The translation industry"[14] as background for three cases.[15] One deals with consent forms signed, after a conversation with his daughter, at a hospital by "an illiterate, non-English speaking Arabic man" seeking emergency treatment. The second and third are a pair of cases dealing with the enforceability

---

11. The materials quote Victor Quintanilla, *Beyond Common Sense: A Social Psychological Study of Iqbal's Effect on Claims of Race Discrimination*, 17 Mich. J. Race & L. 1 (2011).

12. *Citing* Anne E. Ralph, *Not the Same Old Story: Using Narrative Theory to Understand and Overcome the Plausibility Pleading Standard*, 26 Yale J.L. & Human. 1 (2014).

13. *Citing* Gwendolyn M. Leachman, *From Protest to Perry: How Litigation Shaped the LGBT Movement's Agenda*, 47 U.C. Davis L. Rev. 1667 (2014).

14. Rose Kennedy, *Much Ado About Noting: Problems in the Legal Translation Industry*, 14 Temp. Int'l & Comp. L.J. 423 (2000).

15. Mizyed v. Palos Community Hospital, 2016 Il. App. (1st) 142790.

of arbitration clauses against plaintiffs, neither literate in English, who signed contracts written in English. After the material on problems in translation, the Notes ask, "If law hinges on the precision of words, what is a non-English speaker to do when his language does not provide for precise legalese germane to the English version?" The overall tenor of the questions is that the court is using notice and the possibility that the patient might have been in a position to understand the forms as sufficient to make the contract binding, and that such a conclusion can be questioned. One of the arbitration cases involves a transaction in which the seller interacted with the buyer in Spanish and provided a contract in Spanish, though the Spanish version did not precisely match the English one.[16] The Notes ask the student to compare the contract's inaccuracy with the advice provided by the patient's daughter in the preceding case. The final questions about this case are, "Do these cases all hinge on what side the translator or the translated document is on in the litigation? What if a neutral party is requested to translate the document?" My impression is that these materials go a decent way toward opening up all the standard questions associated with contract formation.

Torts

(1) "Police Negligence Cases": The principal case here is *Baldwin v. City of Omaha*, applying contributory negligence in a case where a college student, depressed about being unable to continue on the Nebraska's football team, had a severe mental breakdown; police officers shot him as they attempted to restrain him during one episode of mental distress, causing permanent paralysis from the chest down.[17] One take-away from the presentation is that cases that seem to be about one person's claim against another might actually exemplify broader problems—or, one might say (though the paper did not), that Lon Fuller's well-known distinction between bipolar cases and polycentric ones fails fully to acknowledge the ways in which the former actually should be understood to be the latter.[18] So, for example, the materials refer to an article by Ian Haney-Lopez discussing "the structural and institutional components of race and racism,"[19] and suggest that Baldwin's actions might be understood not as contributory negligence but as "a sort of self-defense mechanism, flowing from fear of being subjected to racialized police violence?"

The materials present the case's factual background in great detail, again implicitly suggesting the value of narrative jurisprudence. The Notes take up the distributive effects of contributory negligence doctrine in *Baldwin* and similar cases and include a discussion of the Black Lives Matter movement, asking whether, or how, that Movement might affect the development

---

16. Ramos v. Westlake Services LLC, 195 Cal.Rptr.3d 34 (Cal. Ct. App. 2105).

17. Baldwin v. City of Omaha, 607 NW 2d 841 (Neb. 2000).

18. Lon L. Fuller, *The Forms and Limits of Adjudication*, 92 Harv. L. Rev. 353 (1987).

19. Ian F. Haney-López, *The Social Construction of Race: Some Observations on Illusion, Fabrication, and Choice*, 29 Harv. C.R.-C.L. L. Rev. 1 (1994).

of tort law. The questions point in the direction of a radical revision on tort doctrine, similar to that suggested by the materials on crime and the duty of justice discussed below.

(2) "Negligent Infliction of Emotional Distress": The classic case of *Dillon v. Legg* is used to present the basic arguments about the tort of negligent infliction of emotional distress, in the context of an overall attempt to "introduce students to the potentially disparate consequences of facially neutral rules,"[20] with the disparities here being based upon gender. Much of the material is similar to what one would find in standard coursebooks, but the materials also include excerpts from Martha Chamallas's discussion of "the law of fright," which takes an expressly gendered perspective on the doctrine and on cases including *Dillon v. Legg*.[21] The Notes following the excerpt suggest two perspectives on *Dillon*: as a "progressive" decision that treats "the mother's emotional harm" not "as merely idiosyncratic, unreasonable, or hysterical" but as "legally cognizable," but also as embodying a "sentimental emphasis on the plaintiff's role as a mother" that "reflect[s] circumscribed gender roles." The materials quote Elizabeth Handley's suggestion that privileging those who fear only for themselves over those whose primary concern is others' safety "reflects a 'fundamentally masculine world view'"—a reasonably explicit observation about the distributional aspects of facially neutral rules.[22] The Notes conclude with a brief discussion—presumably expandable elsewhere in an imagined set of materials—on the possibility that the "reasonable person" standard is applied, in effect, as a "reasonable man" standard.

Criminal Law

(1) "Crime and the Duty of Justice": As noted above, these materials push toward a radical reconception of what society should use the criminal law for. They consist of extensive excerpts from philosopher Tommie Shelby's book *Dark Ghettoes: Injustice, Dissent, and Reform* (2016). The excerpts present a case for "rejecting the claims of law" through an argument against the proposition that "the ghetto poor have an obligation to respect and abide by the law." The Notes on Shelby's work begin by questioning whether modest reforms in the criminal justice system could make it a just system of punishment even "within an unjust society," using the example of someone "from the marginalized social group" who "'steals' some sort of property from one whom the society privileges." After a general discussion, the Note turns to an example of shoplifting from a local store, presenting the argument, first, that such behavior will increase prices or even lead to disinvestment in the community and, second, that the price increases might not occur (and even

---

20. 441 P.2d 912 (Cal. 1968).

21. Martha Chamallas & Linda K. Kerber, *Women, Mothers, and the Law of Fright: A History*, 88 MICH. L. REV. 814 (1990).

22. Elizabeth Handsley, *Mental Injury Occasioned by Harm to Another: A Feminist Critique*, 14 LAW & INEQ. 391 (1996).

if they do, the thefts might be justified as acts of resistance to the unjust social order). The materials include a brief discussion of Richard Delgado's discussion of "rotten social background" as a defense to criminal liability and Frank Michelman's response.[23]

(2) "The Reasonable Juvenile Standard": These materials pose questions about whether there can be an abstract reasonable "person" in contrast to the gendered and raced and "age-d" real people in courts. They draw upon feminist and critical race theoretical perspectives to focus attention on the way in which the category "youth" is constructed. The Notes suggest the possibility of a "reasonable juvenile" standard, thereby opening up the possibility of a discussion of the ways in which intersectionality might drive toward an even more person-focused approach.[24] After a discussion of whether "other vulnerabilities and disadvantages" such as cultural background, education, and intelligence should be "factor[ed] … into criminal law standard," the materials raise questions about whether changing the reasonable person standard "would actually create a society in which there is significant confusion about behavioral standard (lack of clarity) and unequal treatment of people (lack of consistency)."

(3) "Rape Law—Consent": This set of materials, perhaps the most creative in form of those submitted in the seminar, includes several "Pedagogy Boxes."[25] The first is headed, "The Pervasive Method Meets the Socratic Method," and lays out some of the techniques described in the lecture on criminal law by Professor Jeannie Suk-Gersen. The second refers to Duncan Kennedy's *Legal Education and the Reproduction of Hierarchy: A Polemic Against the System* for the argument that "the most aggressive, adversarial forms of the Socratic Method" "promote disproportionate harm to women and people of color." The third asks, "Should Male Professors Teach Rape Law?," and summarizes Jennifer Denbow's argument for the answer, "Yes."[26] The fourth discusses several articles dealing with "passion and Emotion in the Teaching of Rape Law." And the final Pedagogy Box, headed "The Core, Periphery, and the Case for Strict Liability," uses the possibility of strict criminal liability to illustrate the concepts of "core" and "periphery" in legal doctrine, and the possibility of the inversion of the categories' content.[27]

---

23. Richard Delgado, *"Rotten Social Background": Should the Criminal Law Recognize a Defense of Severe Environmental Deprivation?*, 3 Law & Ineq. 9 (1985); Frank I. Michelman, *"RSB," the Social Contract, and a Bridge Across the Gap: Delgado Talks to Rawls*, 33 Law & Ineq. 417 (2015).

24. The Note points to German law on criminal negligence as one using a more subjective standard.

25. Some of these boxes seem intended to be included in the materials understood to be teaching materials available to students. Others seem to me more inward-looking, directed to non-student readers. I should note that the materials, though quite creative, were also among the more heavy-handed of those developed by seminar students.

26. Jennifer M. Denbow, *The Pedagogy of Rape Law: Objectivity, Identity and Emotion*, 64 J. Legal Ed. 16 (2014).

27. There is also a Pedagogy Box about student assessment.

The organizing principle for the substantive materials here is that rape law implicitly and sometimes explicitly rests upon race, gender, and class distinctions among both aggressors and victims/survivors. The materials are divided into sections on race, gender, and class, but the introduction notes that all three themes "permeate into one another in a way that suggests their omnipresence and interrelatedness." *State of New Jersey in the Interest of M.T.S.* and *Commonwealth v. Fischer*, both of which are what some describe as "acquaintance rape" cases, are the principal cases on gender. The materials ask students to "consider both the pros and cons of the elimination of a force requirement" in favor of one requiring only sexual penetration together with lack of consent, mentioning specifically the effect on "men of color and men of lower socioeconomic status." They also ask what the legal effects of changing "assumptions about dating and 'hooking up'" should be. The Notes conclude with a discussion of the possibility of a requirement of affirmative consent, including an excerpt from Janet Halley's skeptical view of that possibility.[28] The materials conclude with a "student assessment" exercise asking students to address questions raised by Antioch College's "affirmative consent" policy.

Property

(1) "The Impact of Eminent Domain on Low-Income and Minority Residents": The lesson's title accurately describes its content. After presenting a newspaper article on the use of eminent domain to acquire land for an automobile manufacturing plant, "Black Families Resist Mississippi Land Push," the materials turn to *Kelo v. New London*, which, they assert, "poses a similar series of questions" about the "distributive consequences of eminent domain." The Notes on *Kelo* begin with one on eminent domain's "disproportionate impact on the poor and minorities," and include another on "power imbalances" in the case. The materials reflect a modest degree of interdisciplinarity in legal analysis.

(2) "Self-Help Remedies: Repossession and Powerlessness": The materials use the principal case of *Williams v. Ford Motor Credit Co.*, involving "a single mother whose car is repossessed from her at 4:30 in the morning," as a focal point for prodding students to take the perspectives of both the plaintiff and the defendant.[29] The Notes following the case examine both "the majority's view of the facts" and the "dissent's more contextualized view" in determining whether there had been a breach of the peace during the repossession. That examination raises questions about the appropriate level of generality or contextualization, in light of the rule's purposes including its economic rationale. Like others I have described, this focus can both illustrate the value and introduce an explicit discussion of narrative jurisprudence.

---

28. Janet Halley, *The Move to Affirmative Consent*, 42 SIGNS 257 (2016).
29. Williams v. Ford Motor Credit Co., 674 F.2d 717 (8th Cir. 1982).

The Note discusses the usual economic analysis of self-help repossession, thereby ensuring some degree of coverage. Picking up on a dissenting opinion's use of the word "powerless" to describe Ms. Williams, the Notes examine the concept of powerlessness, citing a work on social psychology (another example of interdisciplinarity), and raising questions about how issues of class, race, and gender fit into a framework in which powerlessness is relevant.[30] The materials conclude with a consideration of whether self-help repossession should be abolished or made more difficult, again noting the effects on the price of doing so as well as the distributional effects within the class of low-income purchasers.

* * *

Some of the materials are strongly revisionist with respect to doctrine, while others are more tempered in presenting issues of diversity and social justice as only part of what students should be thinking about. Many students made quite effective use of the facts in the cases they presented, perhaps suggesting their views on the importance of narrative perspectives on the law. More experienced instructors would almost certainly tone down some of the more pointed questions (some of which I have presented above). And, not surprisingly, often the students had not mastered the technique of framing questions in ways that subtly rather than openly convey the author's perspective. But on the whole the materials prepared by the seminar's students are an impressive collection, particularly when one takes into account their unfamiliarity with the way in which teaching materials are compiled.

Conclusion:
Lessons Learned and Transferability

As noted at the outset, I believe that the lecture series and seminar were on the whole successful.[31] I am confident that the lecture series can be reproduced at any law school, provided that the series has sufficient administrative (and to a modest degree financial) support from the Dean. A seminar devoted to student reflections on the lectures is also easily reproducible. Whether writing assignments associated with the seminar should take the form of lesson plans is for me a closer question. The students in the seminar generally did a good job in developing the lesson plans, but it was a quite unfamiliar task for them, and it is not clear to me that what they learned from the writing exercise contributed a great deal to their training as lawyers. It might be better to ask students to satisfy writing requirements a school has for seminars to write substantive papers rather than ones focusing on pedagogy.

---

30. Jojanneke van der Toorn et al., *A Sense of Powerlessness Fosters System Justification: Implications for the Legitimation of Authority, Hierarchy, and Government*, 36 POL. PSYCH. 93 (2014).

31. I have been unable to locate student evaluations of the seminar; apparently I failed to distribute the evaluation materials, or so the Registrar's Office suggests.

The main lesson learned, though, is something like "proof of concept." Each lecture showed not only *that* issues of diversity and social justice can be incorporated into the first year curriculum, but also offered specific examples of *how* that can be done. Reproduced elsewhere, the lecture series would provide the opportunity for faculty members to reflect upon, and students to learn about, how they too might build such issues into their classes through thoughtful consideration of both the pervasive and siloing methods.

Breaking through Silence: The Necessary Space of the Doctrinal Classroom

Kali Nicole Murray[*]

1.

So many silences[1] still the doctrinal classroom.[2]

The pedagogy of the scientific lawyer, famously promoted by Christopher Columbus Langdell, is connected to the ideal that law is a science, and the case method, the review of appellate cases, is to convey that science to law students within the doctrinal classroom.[3] The doctrinal classroom, characterized by an admissions entrance, curved classroom, final examinations, a standardized law school curriculum and most famously, the case method[4]—fosters many silences.

The silence of the "other" student, produced by "relationship of circumstances" such as race, ethnicity, class, gender or sexuality—juxtaposed—even now—against

---

[*] Professor of Law, Marquette University Law School.

1. Here, I draw on Tillie Olsen's seminal feminist text, *Silences.* TILLIE OLSEN, SILENCES vii (1978). In *Silences,* Olsen explores how certain type of writing may never come into being—Olsen notes because "the relationship of circumstances—including class, color, sex; the times, climate into which one is born" cause silences that prevent writers from achieving creative work. *Id.* Olsen names a range of silences: background silences, those silences after a work has been published such as censorship and political silences, foreground silences those silences before a work has been written (like the circumstance of motherhood), and those silences imposed on those whom could have never written at all. *Id.* at 10–15.

2. I refer to the doctrinal classroom in opposition to other learning spaces in law school such as a legal writing class, clinic, workshop, or internship.

3. Laura I. Appleman, *The Rise of the Modern American Law School: How Professionalization, German Scholarship, and Legal Reform Shaped Our System of Legal Education*, 39 NEW ENG. L. REV. 251, 253 (2004) (outlining the approach of legal science and its influence on law school in the early twentieth century).

4. David D. Garner, *The Contemporary Vitality of the Case Method in the Twenty-First Century*, 2000 BYU EDUC. & L. J. 307, 317 (2000) (outlining the different elements of the Langdell method).

a model student is a "white male" gentleman.[5] We can even speak to how the traditional law school classroom silences many professors—themselves faculty of color or women—stilled by teaching cultures that often police difference through teaching evaluations or otherwise.[6] Margaret Montoya, discussing the silencing of racial identity in law generally, and legal education specifically, states that "[t]he silencing of racialized information is largely why the law feels alien and alienating to those for whom race or other identity characteristics are reality defining and often the starting point for legal analysis."[7]

2.

We have tried to disrupt the doctrinal classroom.

In the 1930s, starting with critical frameworks such as legal realism, the doctrinal classroom has been intermittently challenged by critical frameworks such as legal realism and critical legal studies, feminist legal theory, and critical race studies, drawing on philosophy, sociology, psychology, economics, historical, literary, and anthropological frameworks.[8] While this interdisciplinary method has made significant inroads in scholarship, sustained application of interdisciplinary methods in the doctrinal classroom has often been limited.[9]

Two other changes impacted the doctrinal classroom from the 1960s onward. The doctrinal classroom was challenged by a skills model that sought to develop the professional skills of law students by adding elements to the law school curriculum including clinical, legal writing, alternative dispute, transactional, clinical, and workshop

---

5. Lani Guiner, Michelle Fine, Jane Balin, Ann Bartow & Deborah Lee Stachel, *Becoming Gentleman: Women's Experience at One Ivy League Law School*, 143 U. Pa. L. Rev. 1, 46 (1984) (describing the silencing women students feel in the law school classroom).

6. Maritza I. Reyes, Angela Mae Kupenda, Angela Onwauchi-Willis, Stephanie M. Wildman & Adrien Katherine Wing, *Reflections on Presumed Incompetent: The Intersections of Race and Class for Women in Academic Symposium—The Plenary Panel*, 29 Berkeley J. Gender, L. & Just. 195, 215–221 (2014) (discussing the types of silences imposed on female faculty of color).

7. Margaret E. Montoya, *Silence and Silencing: Their Centripetal and Centrifugal Forces in Legal Communication, Pedagogy and Discourse*, 33 U. Mich. J.L. Reform 263, 308 (2000).

8. Kate Kruse, *Getting Real About Legal Realism, New Legal Realism, and Clinical Legal Education*, 56 N.Y. L. Sch. L. Rev. 659, 672–676 (2011) (assessing the curricular reforms, including course sequences, case books, and clinical education, inspired by the Legal Realist Movement); Francisco Valdez, *Barely at the Margins: Race and Ethnicity in Legal Education—A Curricular Study with Lat Critical Commentary*, 13 Berkeley La Raza L. J. 119, 133–136 (2002) (examining syllabus related to critical theory teaching in law school); Francisco Valdes, *Outsider Jurisprudence: Critical Pedagogy and Social Justice Activism: Marking the Stirrings of Critical Legal Education*, 10 Asian L. J. 65, 73 (2003) (examining the basic principles of critical pedagogy, which is an educational theory based the emancipatory functions of law school teaching).

9. Antitrust being a significant exception due to changes in the scholarly and professional field that have emphasized economic method as a central intellectual method. Eleanor M. Fox, *Teaching and Learning Antitrust—Politics, Politics, Casebooks, and Teachers*, 66 N.Y.U. L. Rev. 225 (1991) (analyzing the impact of economic theory on the teaching of antitrust).

experiences. The impact of a skills curriculum faces key limits. Skill-based curriculum does not often fully grapple with the problems of diversity, equity, and inclusivity that will confront lawyers in practice, and moreover, despite significant pedagogical innovation, the techniques of the skill-based curriculum have not been fully embraced in the doctrinal classroom. Additionally, law schools seek to (uneasily) embrace students with more diverse social identities including race, gender, class, sexual orientation, and religion.[10]

3.

A primary lesson from previous reforms: it is not enough to change the *subject-matter* of the doctrinal classroom.

To put it simply, if we want to create diverse, inclusive, and equitable classes—that is to break the silences imposed by the current law school classroom—our methods need to match the need to create diverse, equitable, and inclusive classroom. If we decide that diversity, equity, and inclusion("equality values") is a dedicated goal of teaching, we need to use methods that reflect those goals ("equality methods"). A key change, therefore, is that we need to understand the doctrinal classroom as an experiential space, a space where the student's experience of learning is valued as what they are learning.

Here, I need to be careful about how I use the term "experience" to distinguish my use from reforms based on the pedagogy of professionalism. Experiential curricular design is not simply including practical skills into the law school curriculum. Rather, for educational theorists such as John Dewey, a experiential education means a link exists between the teacher's methods and the classroom experience. As Dewey noted, "the primary responsibility of educators is that they not only be aware of the general principle of the shaping of actual experience by environing conditions, but that they also recognize in the concrete what surroundings are conducive to having experiences that lead to growth."[11]

4.

We can learn through multi-cultural educational theory how to create the necessary space of the law school classroom.

Saundra Murray Nettles, a scholar of environmental psychology and human development, has identified concrete methods based on an ecology of experience within the African American community. In her seminal text, *Necessary Spaces: Exploring the*

---

10. Christopher Chambers Goodman, *Retaining Diversity in the Classroom: Strategies for Maximizing the Benefits that Flow from a Diverse Student Body*, 35 Pepperdine L. Rev. 663, 688–698 (2020) (assessing curriculum design from the standpoint of fostering diversity in the law school classroom).

11. John Dewey, Experience and Education 40 (1963).

Richness of African American Childhood in the South,[12] Nettles examines those experiences "that consistently emerge from the interplay of physical, social, and psychological environments and the convergence of these qualities with contemporary notions of factors needed for the optimal development of Black children."[13] Nettles identifies seven necessary spaces that aid in the educational experience of Black children:

> 1) *Connection*, the experiences of "relatedness" to others, including nature, spiritual communities, and social institutions; 2) *Practice*, the experience of play and rehearsal of skills; 3) *Renewal*, the experience of reflection, play and re-creation of mind, body and spirit; 4) *Exploration*, the experience of discovery, investigation, and novelty; 5) *Design*, the experience of imagining, solution building and getting feedback from others; 6) *Resistance*, the experience of "actions [that seek to] understand, apply critical analysis and oppression, inequality"; 7) Last but not least, "*empowerment* includes experiences that increase the capacity of individuals to manage resources, make decisions, and develop a sense of personal control...."[14]

Nettles' framework of necessary spaces would be useful in breaking the silence of the law school classroom for three reasons.

Initially, the framework of necessary spaces challenges the "default whiteness" and "default maleness" that undergirds the model of doctrinal classroom. Instead, the framework of necessary spaces starts with the lived experiences of students of color and presumes that these experiences can serve as a model for how to teach all students. This is profoundly important because shifting away from teaching methods that reproduce pre-existing social hierarchies benefits all students not just students of color.

What does a method that shifts from "default whiteness" look like in practice? For instance, I provide the students, before each class, a class outline with the major rules discussed for the day, how the cases discussed each rule, and the major take-always associated with our class conversation of the day. When I started to use class outlines, I quickly discovered that the class outline interrupted the silences of the doctrinal classroom in crucial ways: it demonstrated for first generation students how to take notes, it reduced gendered anxiety about making mistakes during on-call and provided students with disabilities ways to access materials. This technique has been controversial. In faculty review of my work, I was often informed that I was "doing the work" for my students. I disagree. This technique, by speaking out loud to students what really matters in the doctrinal class, lets them know upfront: your responsibility as a student is to understand the basic rule at stake, and you need to understand how that rule may shift in light of factual and policy circumstances.

Additionally, Nettles' framework of necessary spaces is holistic insofar that it acknowledges that learning best occurs in multiple spatial contexts. Very often in the

---

12. Saundra Murray Nettles, Necessary Spaces: Exploring the Richness of African American Childhood in the South (2013).
13. *Id.* at xxi.
14. *Id.* at xx–xxi.

first year curriculum I ask my students whether the lecture should be understood as the central learning space in law school. Instead, I explicitly outline two specific necessary spaces that matter in law school: comprehension spaces (that is, those spaces in which students comprehend the material, including initial reading and individual review of material), and collaborative learning spaces, which include lecture, office hours, discussion groups, and team feedback. After we explore these learning spaces, I further explain to my students the different pedagogical techniques that can be used in those contexts. A spatial framework, such as Nettles provides, is consistent with the current literature suggesting learning outcomes improve when law students understand that learning can be self-regulated;[15] it is within the autonomous choice of a given student insofar as it decenters the lecture as the *only* moment for students' acquisition of knowledge.

Finally, on a practical level, Nettles' framework of necessary spaces can foster innovation in pedagogical techniques within the law school classroom. Specifically, by separating out recurring experiences, it helps us map out how innovative pedagogical techniques can be used to foster diversity, equity, and inclusion. For example, in designing my first year property law class, I used the "space" of connection to introduce a weekly session that allowed small groups of students to meet with me to discuss the broader issues raised by my property law class. It has become a space where students can delve deeper into issues raised by seemingly neutral subjects in property law (such as how race can become engrained on the landscape through common, statutory, or constitutional law).[16] Equally, though, it is a place where my students and I can get to know each other, through discussions of their interests, or even bonding over mutual love of coffee. I have noticed that by consciously building opportunities for collaborative connection outside of the confines of the lecture, it makes discussions in my lecture easier to manage because the students have already built a relationship of trust before beginning difficult conversations.

Likewise, by focusing on a principle of practice, I have incorporated a writing technique in class, called the written hypothetical. Instead of the student just reciting the rule and applying it to a given circumstance, I have the student write the hypothetical out on the board. The written hypothetical is an important pedagogical technique (not simply an exercise) because it demonstrates to the student that the exam itself will be written and that the student needs to learn how to manage the rule in writing both on the law school exam and in legal practice. The importance of linking learning the rule to controlling the written analysis is a lesson that is often lost on students because of their intense focus on the use of oral hypotheticals in-class.

---

15. Michael Hunter Schwartz, *Teaching Law Students to Be Self-Regulated Learners*, 2003 Mich. St. DCL L. Rev. 447 (2003) (outlining the method of self-regulated learning and its usefulness in the law school context).

16. Angela Onwuachi-Willis, *Teaching Employment Discrimination*, 54 St. Louis U. L.J. 755, 764 (2010) (outlining the use of a method of using a small group session before a large class).

5.

Here is a map of pedagogical techniques that create the necessary doctrinal classroom.

Necessary Spaces	Pedagogical Technique
Connection: *Building Connection for Hard Discussion*	*Weekly Small Group Discussion:* You can conduct a weekly check-in session to build trust.
Practice: *Allowing Students to Practice Test Skills*	*Written Hypothetical:* You can have students draft a written hypothetical on the board.
Renewal: *Treating Law as Everyday Learning*	*Review Competitions:* You can have a Jeopardy-like competition at the close of each unit to reinforce material.
Exploration: *Building Interdisciplinary Technique into Classroom*	*Interdisciplinary Module:* You can have students explore a unit of the class from an inter-disciplinary perspective. For instance, an evidence law classroom can use materials from anthropology to understand the experience of victims.[17]
Design: *Aiding Student Learning*	*The Self-Regulated Learning:* You can use self-regulation theory to help students to design learning plans that emphasize comprehension strategies and collaboration strategies.
Resistance: *Including New Material and Perspective*	*The Unsilenced Curriculum:* You can introduce students to materials that embody critical perspectives on social identities such as a race, gender, sexual orientation, class, color, national origin, and religion.
Empowerment	*Resilient Empowerment:* You can openly acknowledge diverse student social identities and help them to develop strategies for navigating discrimination in their career.

---

17. Heather R. Hlavka & Sameena Mulla, *"That's How She Talks": Animating Text Message Evidence in the Sexual Assault Trial*, 52 L. & Soc'y Rev. 401 (2018).

6.

To conclude. I am not claiming that many of these strategies are new; indeed, they often reflect pre-existing strategies in the scholarly literature. The new is in how these pedagogical strategies are linked to a coherent worldview of learning. We often underestimate Langdell as an educator by reducing him to "the case study" method. The persistence of his model in legal education, though, is not necessarily linked to this one particular technique. Rather, his model offered a coherent goal—the lawyer as a scientist—and offered techniques that embodied that goal.

This essay, by grounding its reforms in an educational framework—necessary spaces—and then working towards a set of pedagogical techniques, is an attempt to ground reform efforts in a worldview. Hopefully, by doing so, it works toward achieving a sustainable method of legal education reform.

The Critical Case Brief:
A Practical Approach to Integrating Critical Perspectives in the 1L Curriculum

Hoang Pham*

Introduction

One of the primary reasons students go to law school is because they want to bring "real change and impact to their communities, their fields of study, or their future clients."[1] The number of students motivated by these goals is likely to increase, especially given the law and policy issues existing today stemming from the Trump administration and implicated in the ongoing mass Movement for Black Lives.[2]

Professor Meera Deo refers to "diversity discussions" as conversations in class regarding race, gender, and/or sexual orientation, "brought up by either faculty or students that are often used to augment lectures on black letter law."[3] "Critical perspectives" builds on "diversity discussions" by additionally (1) preparing professors

* J.D. Candidate, 2021, University of California, Davis School of Law. The author thanks Professor Meera E. Deo for supervising this project, Professors Irene O. Joe and Lisa R. Pruitt for your model teaching, and Professor Mary Louise Frampton for your encouragement to pursue change. The author also thanks King Hall students, past and present, who have organized tirelessly around building more inclusive and equitable spaces in law school. Above all else, the author thanks his wife Brooklynn for the countless hours of discussion, and his daughter Marvel for her patience—both of which contributed to this project.

1. *Five Reasons Why Students go to Law school*, Orange Law Blog: Syracuse University College of Law (Sep. 22, 2016), http://law.syr.edu/news_events/orange_blog/five-reasons-why-students-go-to-law-school1.

2. Spencer Rand, *Social Justice as a Professional Duty: Effectively Meeting Law Student Demand for Social Justice by Teaching Social Justice as a Professional Competency*, 87 U. Cin. L. Rev. 77, 77 (2018); Larry Buchanan, Quoctrung Bui & Jugal K. Patel, *Black Lives Matter May Be the Largest Movement in U.S. History*, N. Y. Times (Jul. 3, 2020), https://www.nytimes.com/interactive/2020/07/03/us/george-floyd-protests-crowd-size.html.

3. Meera Deo, *Faculty Insights on Educational Diversity*, 83 Fordham L. Rev. 3115, 3125 (2015).

and students before class to effectively facilitate and participate in the discussion; (2) shifting pedagogical practices to improve facilitation of critical conversations; and (3) normalizing a critical lens on issues of race, gender, class, and/or sexual orientation as an expectation for competent lawyering.

However, critical perspectives are largely missing from a student's first year in law school. As a student who went to law school to pursue social change, I had the expectation that because justice is innate in law, I would learn about how the law can perpetuate and alleviate social justice issues as part of how it is applied. Yet, while I had amazing professors who greatly cared about students and are incredibly knowledgeable about their content area, race and gender issues are rarely discussed in class even when it is apparent they exist within the cases we read. Those professors who do infuse critical perspectives in their pedagogy are predominately women. Still, approaching their teaching with a more critical lens is not always welcomed, as some of their student evaluations reflect the dissatisfaction students have with their pedagogical philosophy.[4]

Naturally, I became disengaged in some of my classes because traditional law school pedagogy failed to help me see myself—a first generation, Vietnamese American from a low-income community—both personally in classroom discussions and as a future advocate who seeks to use the law to serve his community.[5] The 1L curriculum primarily requires students to study cases and read textbooks without addressing the prevalent social justice issues related to race, gender, class, sexuality, and other identifying characteristics.[6] Students who are either acutely impacted by these issues or aware of them through other experiences often leave class feeling at the very least frustrated; while students not impacted often leave unaware and ill-equipped to serve their future clients.[7]

Yet, the first year curriculum remains largely the same.[8] The materials taught and pedagogy used center around whiteness norms, pursue a "think like a lawyer" approach to learning substantive law, and remain neutral, or even worse, colorblind in assessing issues of race as they arise in case law.[9] While many law schools continue to practice a traditional approach to legal education, law students are rapidly diversifying, no longer reflecting a predominately white, male, heterosexual upper-class institution that law school once was.[10]

---

4. Richard L. Abel, *Evaluating Evaluations: How Should Law Schools Judge Teaching?*, 40 J. LEGAL EDUC. 407 (1990).

5. Chris K. Iijima, *Separating Support from Betrayal: Examining the Intersections of Racialized Legal Pedagogy, Academic Support, and Subordination*, 33 IND. L. REV. 737, 740 (2000).

6. Meera Deo, Maria Woodruff & Rican Vue, *Paint by Number? How the Race and Gender of Law School Faculty Affect the First-Year Curriculum*, 29 CHICANO-LATINO L. REV. 1, 10 (2010).

7. Iijima, *supra* note 5, at 753–54.

8. R. Michael Cassidy, *Reforming the Law School Curriculum from the Top Down*, 64 J. LEGAL EDUC. 428, 430 (2015).

9. Iijima, *supra* note 5, at 757.

10. John O. Sonsteng, Donna Ward, Colleen Bruce & Michael Petersen, *A Legal Education Renaissance: A Practical Approach for the Twenty-first Century*, 34 WM. MITCHELL L. REV. 303, 315–16 (2007).

These changes should prompt every law school to reevaluate their first year curriculum. Not only can the first year of law school be indicative of how students approach the rest of their law school career and profession, it is the one time in law school where all students are required to take classes together. Professor Deo's research tells us that "a majority of law students from all racial/ethnic backgrounds 'not only appreciate diversity discussions, but also wish that they were included more often as a standard part of the first year curriculum.'"[11] While some students may eventually self-select into courses providing critical perspectives, other students will miss out on the opportunity to challenge their thinking as it relates to issues they will undoubtedly face in their legal careers.[12]

In this essay, I introduce a practical approach professors can adopt to integrate critical perspectives in the 1L curriculum: the Critical Case Brief (CCB) framework. While many professors may already integrate critical perspectives in their classroom, this approach hopes to inspire more professors and schools to include critical perspectives by offering an easy to use tool based on traditional teaching methods.

The Critical Case Brief

Traditional Case Briefing and the Need for a Critical Case Brief Framework

Traditional case briefing is considered to be a "structured form of note-taking about the content of a judicial opinion."[13] Case briefs may be different depending on the student, however, the common case brief format is: (1) the title of the case; (2) the facts; (3) procedural history; (4) the legal issues; (5) the court's analysis; (6) the conclusion/holding of the case; and (7) notes on any dissenting or concurring opinions.[14] While this framework may be efficient for teaching and communicating Black Letter law, it may not be effective at reaching all students and generally fails at providing any critical perspectives regarding a case.

The traditional case brief is efficient because it complements the case and Socratic teaching methods used in most law school classrooms. Students are expected to brief assigned cases to adequately prepare for class discussion (case method). When called upon, they will usually recite the facts and dialogue about the holding and the court's rationale (Socratic method). This efficient process is presumed to ensure students will know most if not all subject content necessary to pass the bar exam.

However, efficiency is not synonymous with effectiveness. Marginalized students often leave class feeling disengaged, disaffirmed, and alienated when critical perspec-

---

11. Deo, *supra* note 3.

12. *Id.* at 3126.

13. Valerie J. Munson, *Orienting the Disoriented: The Design and Implementation of an Optimal Law School Orientation Program*, 44 W. St. L. Rev. 73, 74 (2017).

14. *Id.* at 75.

tives are ignored.[15] While students may still understand the doctrinal points, feeling engaged, affirmed, and included improves their understanding and retention of information discussed. Furthermore, although students in the majority may not personally identify with social justice issues arising from cases read for class, a discussion providing critical perspectives would also help them better understand the applicable law, retain information discussed, and challenge them to critically think about various ways in which the law can be interpreted. These outcomes help build a more effective generation of attorneys who will serve our ever-diversifying world.

There are two primary components of traditional case briefs that can be supplemented to integrate critical perspectives: (1) the facts of the case; and (2) the judicial analysis. First, facts in the casebook are typically included insofar as it is necessary to establish the law. Most casebook excerpts do not provide facts regarding race, gender, class, or sexuality as it relates to the case—*i.e.* critical facts. While this information is not required to learn *what* the law is, it could have likely been a factor in *how* the law was made. A student who critically understands both the "what" and the "how" of legal precedent will likely better understand the law.

Likewise, critical analysis is largely missing from many judicial opinions. Although the court's rationale in the casebook will provide students with one perspective regarding "how" the case was decided (even when the dissent is included), it is a disservice to students if other perspectives are completely omitted and not discussed in class. These additional perspectives can develop students' critical thinking skills by challenging them to analyze whether rules were correctly applied based on critical facts. Furthermore, a lack of critical analysis means students generally do not see themselves validated in the learning they are doing in law school. Missing critical facts and analysis from case briefing means critical perspectives are fundamentally not included in the 1L curriculum.

The Critical Case Brief: Easing into Critical Perspectives

Foundationally, the CCB focuses on critically preparing, reading, briefing, and discussing a case while guided by the traditional case brief. CCBs address the shortcomings of the traditional case brief by adding two components: (1) critical facts; and (2) critical analysis. Critical facts are those which indicate the race, gender, class, sexuality, and other identifying characteristics of individuals involved in a case and how those characteristics may have factored into events leading up to, during, and after trial. Critical analysis utilizes the same rule(s) the court applied but with the additional critical facts to provide critical perspectives on the case.

The CCB framework utilizes a scaffolding approach to make integration of critical perspectives easy for all faculty, regardless of their prior experience integrating critical perspectives in to their course. For professors who are new to discussing critical per-

---

15. Deo, Woodruff & Vue, *supra* note 6, at 11.

spectives, the CCB framework retains the traditional case and Socratic methods as central in teaching law. For professors who are already comfortable with critical perspectives and different pedagogical practices, CCBs provide additional structure to enhance student engagement and discussion in their classroom. This two-tiered scaffolded approach lowers the barrier for all professors to integrate critical perspectives in their curriculum by meeting professors where they are and giving them tools to help move toward critical perspectives.

Tier one of the CCB framework is tailored for professors who are more comfortable with critical perspectives. Under tier one, professors would: (1) choose their own cases which they know have implications of race, gender, class, and sexuality issues; (2) research the missing critical facts in these cases; (3) assign a supplemental reading providing those critical facts and corresponding discussion questions; and (4) using their pedagogy of choice, discuss the case in class with an emphasis on the critical facts and critical analysis of the case.

Tier two of the CCB framework is for professors who are less comfortable but are interested in bringing critical perspectives to their classroom. Tier two provides a toolkit that supplements tier one so professors can spend more time on teaching critical perspectives and less time on researching it. First, instead of choosing their own cases, tier two would provide professors with pre-selected cases for their content area. Professors are provided the critical facts from each case, in addition to a supplemental reading assignment for students accompanied by discussion questions. Finally, tier two professors may choose to stick with the case and Socratic methods when facilitating their discussion.

Ideally, professors should feel free to utilize the CCB framework however they see fit in order to successfully integrate critical perspectives in their 1L course. Additionally, and most importantly, professors should continually seek feedback from their students, and approach the process as one which requires collaboration between professor and student for integration to truly be successful. Professors should set the expectation for critical perspectives on the first day of class, and seek to build a strong classroom environment at the very beginning of instruction by allowing everyone to get to know each other. These foundations in establishing relationships will build trust and foster a cooperative learning environment where critical conversations not only occur, but flourish.

Application of the CCB Framework

Students are responsible for three things in a CCB framework regardless of which tier the professor chooses: (1) reading the case as presented in the casebook; (2) reading the supplemental materials and answering corresponding discussion questions; and (3) writing a CCB. As mentioned above, a CCB includes all components of a traditional case brief except it adds critical facts and critical analysis sections. Critical facts and critical analysis components challenge students to engage in critical perspectives of the case and allow students to compare and contrast information included and excluded from the casebook. CCB will hopefully normalize race, gender, class, and sexual orientation so it is not an additional task, but becomes part of each thought a student has when reading a case or participating in classroom discussion.

Below, I apply the CCB framework to *Ashcroft v. Iqbal*—a seminal first year case in civil procedure—to illustrate how the framework can be used both by the professor and the student. Specifically, I show the importance of providing critical perspectives in 1L doctrinal courses through my juxtaposition of casebook information and missing critical facts and analysis. I want to underscore that CCB is intended to provide students with critical perspectives on the cases they study. Although CCB may prompt students to come to a different conclusion than the court, the focus is less on the outcome of the case and more on the student's analytical process. Critical facts for *Iqbal* were discovered through brief research, and because the critical analysis component of CCB is student-formulated, the critical analysis below is my own.

Civil Procedure:
Iqbal Using a CCB Framework

<u>Case Title</u>: *Ashcroft v. Iqbal*, 556 U.S. 662 (2009).

<u>Casebook Facts</u>: After the September 11 terrorist attacks, Iqbal, a Pakistani Muslim was arrested on criminal charges and detained by federal officials.[16] Following his release, Iqbal sued numerous federal officials—specifically, United States Attorney General John Ashcroft and FBI Director Robert Mueller—alleging the government defendants designated him a person "of high interest" on account of his race, religion, or national origin, violating his First and Fifth Amendments.[17] He also alleged the FBI detained thousands of Arab Muslim men as part of its September 11th investigation and the defendants "knew of, condoned, and willfully and maliciously agreed to subject Iqbal to harsh conditions of confinement" because of his race.[18]

<u>Critical Facts</u>: Javaid Iqbal immigrated to the United States in 1992, on a false passport, by immigration smugglers.[19] He settled in New York and worked for part of his time using a false identity.[20] Eight weeks after September 11, 2001, law enforcement searched his apartment and found a U.S. Immigration & Naturalization Service (INS) letter indicating an appointment he had in lower Manhattan the morning of September 11, a *Time* magazine cover featuring the burning World Trade Center, and a Pakistani newspaper

---

16. David Crump, William V. Dorsaneo III, Rex R. Perschbacher & Debra Lyn Bassett, Cases and Materials on Civil Procedure 276 (6th ed. 2012).

17. *Id.*

18. *Id.*

19. Shirin Sinnar, *The Lost Story of Iqbal*, 105 Geo. L.J. 379, 394 (2017).

20. *Id.* at 395.

reporting on the attacks.[21] These items made the officers suspicious that Iqbal helped the hijackers in the attacks.[22] They then questioned him about a second ID he used, and ultimately arrested him for providing false identification.[23] Iqbal was charged with making a false statement and held at the Metropolitan Detention Center (MDC).[24] By November 2001, he was labeled as being of interest to the terrorism investigation.[25]

In January 2002, Iqbal was transferred to the K Unit at MDC, which housed eighty-four inmates arrested in connection with the September 11 investigation.[26] On the evening of the day he was transferred, several officers kicked and beat him, called him a "terrorist," punched him in the face, and threw him against the wall.[27] After physical abuse which left him bleeding from his mouth and nose, the officers cuffed his arms and legs and forced him to strip and undergo an extensive search.[28] On March 20, 2002, prison guards conducted three strip and body-cavity searches of Iqbal and when he protested, guards punched him in the face and kicked him, causing him to bleed.[29] Despite requests for help, Iqbal did not receive medical care for two weeks.[30] Due to these conditions, Iqbal lost over forty pounds in detention.[31]

Upon release, Iqbal sued numerous federal officials alleging the government defendants designated him a person "of high interest" on account of his race, religion, or national origin, violating his First and Fifth Amendments.[32] He also alleged the FBI detained thousands of Arab Muslim men as part of its September 11th investigation and the defendants "knew of, condoned, and willfully and maliciously agreed to subject Iqbal to harsh conditions of confinement" because of his race.[33] Iqbal's allegations align with findings by the Justice Department Inspector General: (1) MDC detainees were confined to cells for at least twenty-three hours a day; (2) exercise was offered on the exposed top floor of the MDC on cold winter mornings; (3) nearly twenty-four hours each day of illumination in the cells caused lack of sleep, depression, and panic attacks among the inmates; and (4) access to counsel was sometimes blocked.[34]

---

21. *Id.* at 397.
22. *Id.*
23. *Id.*
24. *Id.*
25. *Id.*
26. *Id.* at 399–400.
27. *Id.* at 400.
28. *Id.*
29. *Id.*
30. *Id.*
31. *Id.*
32. *Id.*
33. *Id.*
34. *Id.* at 402.

Procedural History: The District Court and Court of Appeals held the complaint sufficient to give "fair notice."[35] The government appealed and the Supreme Court granted certiorari.

Legal Issue: Whether Iqbal's complaint meets the pleadings standards of Federal Rule of Civil Procedure 8.

Rule: Rule 8 requires sufficient factual matter, accepted as true, to "state a claim to relief that is plausible on its face."[36] A claim has facial plausibility when the pleaded factual content allows the court to "draw the reasonable inference" that the defendant is liable for the misconduct alleged.[37] Mere conclusory statements are not enough to meet Rule 8 standards.[38]

Casebook Analysis: Iqbal's allegation that the defendants acted "on account of his race, religion or national origin" was insufficient under the applicable standard.[39] The pleading was a mere conclusion, unsupported by facts making any inference of a claim "plausible," and the same was true of his allegations of knowledge, condonation, willfulness, and malice.[40] Furthermore, the court found that because the September 11 attacks were perpetrated by nineteen Arab Muslim hijackers, it should be "no surprise that a legitimate policy directing law enforcement to arrest and detain individuals because of their suspected link to the attacks would produce a disparate, incidental impact on Arab Muslims."[41]

Critical Analysis: Given the additional critical facts, arguments can be made for Rule 8 being met and not being met. One could argue Rule 8 was not met because these additional facts do not help the court draw a reasonable inference the government defendants are liable for the misconduct alleged. The actual harm against Iqbal was committed by individual law enforcement and corrections officers. No facts indicate Ashcroft or Mueller was directly involved in subjecting Iqbal to the harms he suffered. Even while one could argue the pleadings are not mere conclusory statements due to these additional facts, it would likely not be sufficient to meet the Rule 8 facial plausibility standard.

However, the critical facts illuminate unspeakable harms against Iqbal, and one could also argue Rule 8 was met. First, there was no reason to suspect Iqbal was involved in the September 11th attacks. Except for policy directing "law enforcement to arrest and detain individuals because of their suspected link to the attacks," it is unclear why police targeted Iqbal in the first place.

---

35. Crump et al., *supra* note 16, at 276.
36. *Id.* at 277.
37. *Id.*
38. *Id.*
39. *Id.*
40. *Id.*
41. *Id.*

The INS appointment letter, *Time* magazine cover, and Pakistani newspapers are all innocent facts insufficient to corroborate reasonable suspicion to determine Iqbal was part of the terrorist attacks. While the agents should have left at this point, it was only because Iqbal had false identification that justified any detainment. One would suspect top law enforcement officials in the United States—like Ashcroft and Mueller—would have at the very least some part in drafting and carrying out such a policy. Absent any other reasons, it is likely Iqbal's race and religion was used to target and detain him.

Second, Iqbal was transferred to the K Unit with no explanation. One could only make the inference that because the unit was specifically for terror suspects, he was transferred due to his race and religion because of the "incidental impact on Arab Muslims" the court mentioned in the opinion. When he was there, he was subject to inhumane conditions where officers referenced his race and religion as justification for his treatment. Additionally, these conditions were corroborated by the Attorney Inspector General. Therefore, it is likely he was subject to harsh conditions of confinement solely on account of his race and religion. Similar to the conclusion above, a unit dedicated to terror suspects and the subjection of individuals in that unit to harsh treatment had to at the very least be implicitly approved by top law enforcement officials—those with the authority to do so would be Ashcroft and Mueller.

Conclusion: While arguments could be made for either side, given the critical analysis above it is more likely Iqbal's pleading does meet Rule 8 standards because accepted as true, the critical facts help him establish his allegations are facially plausible.

Side Effect: Retraumatization on Marginalized Students

There are many concerns whenever introducing sensitive topics into any conversation, let alone a law school classroom. Critical perspectives often carry emotions of pain, anger, frustration, sadness, and angst. One reason why so many professors avoid discussing issues of race, gender, class, or sexual orientation is for fear of poorly handling a discussion such that students become upset, or worse, offended. Still, even if a professor does do a great job of facilitating a diversity discussion, it does not change the fact that some marginalized students, by discussing topics in which they have personally experienced, will be re-traumatized—thus having the opposite effect of the CCBs' originally intended purpose: engage and improve the learning experience for students.

Re-traumatization may occur multiple times: re-traumatization from reading a case and then re-retraumatization from discussing it in the classroom. The very real experiences of our students should prompt all schools and professors who adopt the CCB framework to first think about creating safe classroom environments for students to exist in. Many schools already implement various types of programming to accomplish this, such as implicit bias trainings and community norms. Additionally, some professors who are experts in teaching critical perspectives have their own techniques on creating safe spaces for students to engage in.

While there are countless approaches to developing safe spaces, a simple way professors can do this is by taking time to build relationships with and among students from the very first day of class (as mentioned above). Implicit bias trainings, though important, tend to be one-off trainings that come and go with the trainer, and not nearly consistent enough for the concepts to solidify with students and staff such that all students feel safe in the classroom space. Community norms also tend to present a similar issue in that they are typically not reinforced throughout the classroom space by professors, but instead taught to students during orientation or sent in an email as a reminder to students when issues arise on campus.

Although re-traumatization undoubtedly will occur, it is the job of professors, schools, and fellow classmates to do the heavy lifting of supporting those students who are most impacted by critical perspectives in class. For example, schools could build a support framework through academic support, student services, or even a diversity ombudsperson. When in doubt about how to create safer spaces, remember that you can always ask the students — they tend to always know the best answers when it comes to their own needs in learning.

Conclusion

Because the law directly impacts people, it is impossible to avoid how race, gender, class, and sexuality influences the making of law, both through statute and litigation. What has been missing is the integration of these perspectives into legal education. The CCB framework is a practical next step in moving toward critical perspectives. It lowers barriers for professors to facilitate diversity discussions in their classroom and does not detract from the traditional legal education approach. If law schools seek to be responsive to the diversifying law student population and develop professionals who will competently serve their clients, critical perspectives must be integral in the 1L curriculum.[42]

---

42. For future research, I will expand on the CCB framework tiers and address how professors can shift their pedagogical practices to improve facilitation of critical conversations. By providing a complete CCB framework supplement for all 1L doctrinal courses, I hope it becomes easier for more professors to engage students in critical perspectives, particularly at a time when our country is in great need of deeper understanding. Additionally, I will build on research arguing how normalizing critical perspectives as an expectation for competent lawyering and advocacy can transform law school, the legal profession, and ultimately, outcomes for justice and equality in the United States.

Selected Bibliography for Inclusive Critical Legal Pedagogy

*Margaret "Meg" Butler**

Introduction

Compiling and annotating a bibliography about legal pedagogy, particularly focusing on critical pedagogy which has at its heart interests of equity and inclusion, presented multiple challenges. Many resources individually address the topics of legal pedagogy, equity, inclusion, and their components, while fewer reflect on all of those topics at the same time. Distinctions between types of materials (books, articles, podcasts, etc.) that appear in this bibliography reflect the challenge of identifying resources that carefully address each of the subjects that are integral to the focus of this bibliography. Possibly, the emphasis on print materials reflects my own preference for print, rather than other forms of media. Given the audience, the materials included in this bibliography largely address pedagogy, at a minimum in a higher education context, and preferably in a law teaching context. To be included, entries also incorporate some discussion of oppression, social categories and their effects in the classroom, or similar content. My position as a white woman, leaving aside other aspects of my identity, no doubt affected the choices I made. I hope that I have succeeded in reflecting the diversity of resources despite my biases and needs.

The needs of the reader also present a challenge in determining eligibility for inclusion. Based on positionality, experience, and other factors, readers may have significantly different needs and interests. For example, an economically privileged white, heterosexual woman law professor at the mid-point of her career may have different needs and interests as she is considering critical legal pedagogy than a first-generation, Latino, gay male law professor just entering the profession. Readers of this bibliography may find, thus, that some entries are just what they need, but others are for other readers in other places. Perhaps this will make the bibliography worth revisiting over time.

* Associate Director for Public Services, Georgia State University College of Law Library. Many thanks to the editorial team for inviting me to work with them on this bibliography and sharing their thoughtful feedback.

Allow me to explain the criteria I have applied to keep some resources "out" and others "in" this bibliography. Resources mostly about pedagogy and race or inclusion that focus on the elementary and secondary teacher and learner are generally "out." Also, I omitted those resources that focused more intently on the experiences of faculty of color within the law school institution or the higher education system than on their experiences in the classroom. The omitted resources often reflect the impact of institutional racism and related issues. Professor Derrick A. Bell raised those issues in his book *Confronting Authority: Reflections of An Ardent Protester,* describing his protest of Harvard Law School's failure to hire an African-American female in a tenure-track position.[1] Institutional and systemic racism absolutely influence a professor's experience and perceived authority in the classroom. Books, such as Meera E. Deo's *Unequal Profession: Race and Gender in Legal Academia,* are a starting point for those interested in learning more. The materials in this bibliography rely on a narrower definition of pedagogy that focuses on teaching strategies and techniques and the relationship between the teacher and the student. Thus, the articles and books which focus more on the lived experiences of students and faculty of color within law school or higher education are just outside of the scope of this bibliography. The epistolary exchange between Robert S. Chang and Adrienne D. Davis, considering race, gender, and sexual orientation in the classroom, is included in this bibliography, however, because the authors directly address the effects of bias in the classroom and how that bias affects student learning. Readers wanting to follow that vein of scholarship would do well to consult the many secondary sources that have cited the article.

Attentive readers may note that many of the resources directly addressing intersectionality focus on the dual identities related to race and gender. Although Kimberlé Crenshaw's groundbreaking work first posited intersectionality at the junction of race and sex,[2] intersectionality conceptually implicates other identities or social groups as well. Because the resources addressing other forms of intersectionality are rarer, there may be opportunities for our voices to contribute to the scholarship of critical legal pedagogy.

Finally, when I selected items for inclusion, I privileged materials that included some sort of action that the reader would be able to take. As a teaching law librarian, I find it very fulfilling that, in my work, I am able to both help people find resources and take appropriate action, whether they are members of the public trying to help themselves or whether they are law students trying to make the grade. I wanted to provide readers opportunities to do more than talk about how to make our classrooms reflect the just world we seek to create. Some actions relate to specific teaching practices, such as creating assignments, while others relate to the creation of an inclusive classroom environment. The unification of theory and action is important, and op-

---

1. *See* DERRICK A. BELL, CONFRONTING AUTHORITY: REFLECTIONS OF AN ARDENT PROTESTER (1994).

2. *See* Kimberlé Crenshaw, *Demarginalizing the Intersection of Race and Sex: A Black Feminist Critique of Antidiscrimination Doctrine, Feminist Theory and Antiracist Politics,* 1989 U. CHI. LEGAL F. 139.

timally it should be part of an ongoing conversation. Some pieces may foster a sense of connection, as we read each other's experiences working with students. Hopefully, this bibliography and its associated chapter encourage us in our work to the continued development of an inclusive critical legal pedagogy.

Books

Brookfield, Stephen D., and Associates, eds., *Teaching Race: How to Help Students Unmask and Challenge Racism*. Newark: John Wiley & Sons, 2018.

Presented through the metaphor of cooking and adapting rather than prescribing ingredients or actions, *Teaching Race* presents a variety of considerations for instructors who want to advance anti-racist teaching ideals in their classrooms. In addition to providing basic definitions for racism, microaggressions, etc., the contributors explicitly address teaching techniques to build trust, teach intersectionality, and build community in the classroom. They suggest "Guidelines for Whites Teaching About Whiteness" in one chapter, and in another address "Teaching Whiteness in Predominantly White Classrooms." Perhaps because this book is not also trying to address complications of teaching law, it is well-able to focus on teaching race in a post-secondary context.

Freire, Paulo. *Pedagogy of the Oppressed: 30th Anniversary Edition*. New York: Bloomsbury Academic & Professional, 2014.

Originally published in 1968, *Pedagogy of the Oppressed* is central to many theorists' analysis of ways instructors may create and engage in critical pedagogy.[3] In addition to providing criticism of the banking model of education, Freire argues that educational systems perpetuate the inequities existent in our societies. He proposes instead a changed relationship between student and instructor, with both student and instructor experiencing agency and subjective power in the teaching and theorizing jointly about the epistemological goal. Ultimately, both student and instructor are positioned to make real, through theory and praxis combined, a new social order. The text is informed by Freire's Marxist thinking, though the criticisms raised and theory suggested are not explicitly limited to considerations of class.

Gannon, Kevin M. *Radical Hope: A Teaching Manifesto*. Morgantown: West Virginia University Press, 2020.

Written for a general audience of university-level instructors, Professor Gannon presents an argument for the role of hope in the development of one's pedagogy. To that end, and interspersed with analysis of Paolo Freire, bell hooks, Stephen

---

3. Paulo Freire continued his scholarship for many years, though *Pedagogy of the Oppressed* remains his most commonly cited work. More information about Freire and his philosophy may be found at "Paulo Freire, 1921–1997)," by Kim Diaz, *Internet Encyclopedia of Philosophy*, https://iep.utm.edu/freire/.

Brookfield, and others, Gannon includes examples of teaching choices in action. Each chapter has a specific focus and ends with a suggestion or question of what an instructor could do to extend the focus of the reading "Into Practice." This book provides an accessible entry point and practical suggestions for those who would like to begin engaging.

Kernahan, Cyndi. *Teaching about Race and Racism in the College Classroom: Notes from a White Professor.* Morgantown: West Virginia University Press, 2019.

The audience for this book is white instructors who teach (or plan to teach) race in their classrooms. As a psychology professor who is also assistant dean for teaching and learning, Kernahan brings significant experience to the guidance. Written in an accessible voice, Kernahan includes both practical teaching suggestions and explanation about how to meet student resistance. Some might find particularly helpful her chapter on developing a secure teacher identity. Others may find the appendix of readings for historical understanding especially helpful.

Öztok, Murat. *The Hidden Curriculum of Online Learning: Understanding Social Justice Through Critical Pedagogy.* London: Routledge, 2019.

Critical pedagogy is a useful approach to teaching in the online environment, according to Professor Öztok. In the online context, this means considering the intersections of power and agency, how the analyses of the material world are reflected in online environments. New questions considered include "How are the oppressive forms of power created in online spaces?" (ix). Readers may find the chapter addressing the hidden curriculum particularly interesting, as they are developing or teaching their own online courses.

Quaye, Stephen John, Shaun R. Harper, and George D. Kuh. *Student Engagement in Higher Education: Theoretical Perspectives and Practical Approaches for Diverse Populations.* Second edition. New York: Routledge, 2015.

Research has shown that students who are engaged in their educational experience are more likely to interact with their teachers and fellow students, devote their time and energy toward educational activities, seek feedback, and more. This collection focuses more on student engagement than it does on classroom pedagogy. The essays focus on engagement of students based on designated statuses, including race, sexual orientation, gender identity, class, etc. Additional groups considered include athletes, returning learners, and veterans. Intersectionality is considered in some chapters. Each chapter includes discussion of needs of the respective groups, as well as considerations the groups may have in navigating campus and classes. Specific suggestions for improving student engagement are included in each chapter.

Ríos, Raquel. *Teacher Agency for Equity: A Framework for Conscientious Engagement.* London: Routledge, 2017.

As a teacher educator, Professor Ríos saw a need to support teachers who work for equity. Ríos positions herself and her interests in critical pedagogy, describing the Conscientious Engagement framework that helps teachers "develop teacher agency for equity" (xix). After positioning herself, Ríos guides the reader through consideration of each principle of the framework, focusing on ways to nourish efforts and vision of equity, the tension between human 'belonging' and building equity, and the direction of energy toward equitable practices. Though the readership may include teachers of children and teens, the core of the author's suggestions apply to law instructors. Chapters include reflection questions.

Teaching with Tension: Race, Resistance, and Reality in the Classroom, edited by Philathia Bolton, Cassander L. Smith, and Lee Bebout. Evanston, IL: Northwestern Univ. Press, 2019.

Positioned in the pedagogical context of scholar/authors who consider "the ways in which race, gender, and class influence" academic experiences, the authors and contributors consider the ways in which "we teach and talk about race" (8) through the lenses of theory, anecdote, and pedagogy. The collection is organized in three parts: Teaching in Times and Places of Struggle, Teaching in the Neoliberal University, and Teaching How to Read Race and (Counter)Narratives. Though researched and scholarly, the authors' tone approaches conversational, directly describing experiences teaching explicitly about race and the discussing the construction of authentic classroom relationships. For those wishing to include explicit discussion of the role race plays in the development and function of the law, this collection may be guiding.

Tobin, Thomas J., and Kirsten Behling. *Reach Everyone, Teach Everyone: Universal Design for Learning in Higher Education*. Morgantown: West Virginia University Press, 2018.

The authors advocate for the broad adoption of the Universal Design for Learning (UDL) framework in higher education, based on the underlying supposition that the UDL approach will benefit all learners by using multiple means to create learner experiences and interactions. The book begins with historical context about how UDL came to be and notes that UDL is most effective when adopted enthusiastically, rather than merely as a means to avoid litigation. Following their argument for adoption of UDL, the authors provide examples of ways in which instructors can improve their courses by adopting UDL changes and offer suggestions for encouraging the commitment to UDL at the institutional level.

Vulnerable Populations and Transformative Law Teaching: A Critical Reader. Edited by the Society of American Law Teachers and Golden Gate University School of Law. Durham, N.C.: Carolina Academic Press, 2011.

This collection is the product of a law teaching conference examining the ways in which "race, gender, sexual identity, nationality, disability, or outsider status generally are linked to poverty." In three parts, the book first includes three essays described as foundational, providing background, context, challenging basic assumptions about poverty and attorney responsibilities, and calling for students to be engaged both inside and outside the classroom. The remainder of the chapters fall into two categories: Inside the Classroom and Outside the Classroom. In each category, the contributors provide suggestions for ways in which law teaching is enriched by actively including social and economic justice considerations.

Articles

Alleva, Patti, and Laura Rovner. "Seeking Integrity: Learning Integratively from Classroom Controversy." *Southwestern Law Review* 42, no. 2 (2013): 355–420.

Classroom controversy presents opportunity for law students to learn how to think, perform, and value like a lawyer. The authors suggest ways in which discussions of sensitive subjects including, but not limited to social identity categories, may offer particularly valuable opportunities for learning. The opportunities for students to synthesize what they know and build connections that they can apply to new situations are promoted through the strategies described by the authors. To facilitate lesson planning, they include a framework of questions that can also be used to develop instructional objectives.

Brooks, Kim, and Debra Parkes. "Queering Legal Education: A Project of Theoretical Discovery." *Harvard Women's Law Journal* 27 (2004): 89–136.

Professors Brooks and Parkes describe a goal of queer legal pedagogy as one recognizing multiple consciousnesses of queer students and professors and yet speaks to individuals in their entirety. The authors describe the contributions of outside scholars to legal education and propose eight principles of pedagogy, inviting conversation about queer legal pedagogy. After considering the queering of law school curriculum, the authors address the transformative power of queer legal pedagogy.

Cedillo, Christina V. "What Does It Mean to Move?: Race, Disability, and Critical Embodiment Pedagogy." Composition Forum 39 (Summer 2018), http://composition forum.com/issue/39/to-move.php.

Critical embodiment pedagogies strive for inclusivity and accessibility by both recognizing and foregrounding bodily diversity. With a context of rhetoric and composition, Professor Cedillo describes ways that rhetoric treats bodies and fosters institutionalized oppression. She argues from an intersectionalized position based on her race and invisible disabilities that critical embodiment pedagogies create conditions fostering inclusivity. The sections addressing biases arising from use of objective voice in writing and the call for critical embodiment pedagogies may be of particular interest to law instructors. Licensed under a Creative Commons Attribution-Share Alike License, Cedillo generously includes in the appendix a literacy narrative writing project, encouraging students to practice rhetorical devices and strategies including identifying and writing to the audience, using sensory detail to enliven the writing, and considering alternate perspectives and the effect of positionality on knowledge.

Crenshaw, Kimberlé Williams. "Toward A Race-Conscious Pedagogy in Legal Education," *National Black Law Journal* 11 (1989): 1–14.

This issue of the *National Black Law Journal* was the culminating project of Professor Crenshaw's seminar course, with the seminar students contributing articles to the issue and Professor Crenshaw contributing this Foreword. She describes the "norm of perspectivelessness" (2), in which the dominant beliefs are 'color-blind' and presented as though they do not privilege any perspective or group. She further describes situations in which students of color are placed in a double-bind, either "think[ing] like a lawyer" ignoring their identity and experience as a student of color (5) or raising questions of race and being judged by their peers as not on point and emotional. Instead, Crenshaw calls for professors to broaden class discussion and include a greater variety of perspectives when teaching. Instructors are exhorted to not rely upon minority students to provide their perspectives as experts related to their race(s). Crenshaw concludes by describing choices she made in her seminar to implement critical and constructivist approaches to the course.

Darling-Hammond, Sean, and Kristen Holmquist. "Creating Wise Classrooms to Empower Diverse Law Students: Lessons in Pedagogy from Transformative Law Professors." *Chicana/o-Latina/o Law Review* 33 (2015): 1–90; also published in *La Raza Law Journal* 25 (2015): 1–67; *National Black Law Journal* 24, no. 1 (January 2015): 1–90; *Berkeley Journal of African-American Law & Policy* 17, no. 1 (2016): 47–115.

Recognizing that students who are from underrepresented groups are also subjected to stereotyping and may lack a background in the law, Darling-Hammond and Holmquist observe that inclusive pedagogy that supports students from underrepresented groups serves to support success for all students. The authors demonstrate the effects of race and gender on student learning and classroom experience, relying on results from student surveys from UC Berkeley Law School. Most helpful are the practices identified through the authors' legal pedagogical study, practices which the "transformative professors"—as identified by law students—implement in their own classrooms "to encourage students from all backgrounds to thrive." The guidance includes: use great care in selecting a textbook or teaching materials, learn from others, include discussion of modern cases and political and social issues, engage in "compassionate cold calling" (48), and assess students regularly and give feedback to facilitate self-correction.

Bhabha, Faisal. "Towards a Pedagogy of Diversity in Legal Education." *Osgoode Hall Law Journal* 52, no. 1 (2015): 59–108.

Beginning with the premises that diversity pedagogy in law schools is "thin" and that law schools have had "incomplete results" with their institutional diversity initiatives (63), Professor Bhabha promotes a diversity pedagogy and argues that its implementation with both "hands on experience and structured critical reflection" would meet the twin goals of increasing lawyer competence and reduction of barriers for practitioners (64). Diversity pedagogy is based on "equality-positive assumptions" (93). To implement diversity pedagogy, not only does representation of minority students and faculty need to improve, but also inclusion should be meaningfully implemented. Bhabha calls for an increase in learning by doing, for example including greater opportunities for experiential education.

Chang, Robert S. and Adrienne D. Davis. "Making Up Is Hard To Do: Race/Gender/ Sexual Orientation in the Law School Classroom," *Harvard Journal of Law and Gender* 33, no. 1 (2010): 1–57.

Professors Chang and Davis make clear their friendship and mutual commitment to teaching as they compare their classroom experiences and how their respective positionalities affect their success in the classroom. Through their "conversation," the professors consider bias, as it affects teaching evaluations, student learning, and their own learning, as well institutional response to bias. The authors describe "projected stereotype threat" which reflects that the attribution of accent or incompetence by student also adversely affects student comprehension (55). The letters call for continued excellence on the part of instructors, as well as institutional changes, with the goal of creating conditions that minimize projected stereotype threat and ultimately improve student learning and comprehension.

Freeman, Alexi Nunn, and Lindsey Webb, "Positive Disruption: Addressing Race in a Time of Social Change Through a Team-Taught, Reflection-Based, Outward-Looking Law School Seminar." *University of Pennsylvania Journal of Law and Social Change* 21, no. 2 (2018): 121–152.

The authors suggest that the Critical Race Reading Seminar (CRRS) they jointly teach would serve well as a template for other law schools to address questions of race and social justice. First, the authors argue for inclusion of race in the law school curriculum and note the urgency of that need. The authors describe the pedagogical goals for their course, as well as their teaching philosophy. The goals and philosophy dovetail with details regarding the structure and management of the course.

Kupenda, Angela Mae. "Making Traditional Courses More Inclusive: Confessions of an African American Female Professor Who Attempted to Crash All the Barriers at Once." *University of San Francisco Law Review* 31, no. 4 (1996): 975–92.

The metaphor of swimming is used throughout the article, which describes Professor Kupenda's experiences as a professor crashing through barriers. Reflecting her own internal development as a professor, as well as the experiences of her students, Kupenda offers insight into the changes she made to her contracts course, as well as to her classroom environment. In conclusion, Kupenda notes that diversity and substantive goals may coexist and offers encouragement for others.

Lain, Erin C. "Racialized Interactions in the Law School Classroom: Pedagogical Approaches to Creating a Safe Learning Environment." *Journal of Legal Education* 67, no. 3 (2018): 780–801.

The hierarchy of needs for education to be successful includes at its most basic level that the student must feel included and safe, with safe including physical, emotional, and psychological components. Professor Lain notes that professors may fail to recognize racialized interactions in their classrooms, minimize or miss such interactions, or control such interactions by stopping them or correcting them. Lain offers alternative pedagogical approaches to racialized interactions including attunement, authenticity, and power-sharing. Professor Lain shares her own experience handling a racialized interaction in a summer institute she led.

Lopez Torres, Arturo, and Mary Kay Lundwall. "Moving beyond Langdell II: An Annotated Bibliography of Current Methods for Law Teaching." *Gonzaga Law Review* 36 (2000): 1–62.

Scholarship on pedagogy from June 1993 to December 1999 is the focus of this article, and annotations are organized topically for ease of discovery. Topics of interest include Critical Legal Studies, Critique, Diversity, Feminist Legal Theory, Gender, Learning, Race, and Torts. The methodology used in identifying included articles provides the reader assurance that the articles included are worth consideration.

Magee, Rhonda, V. "The Way of ColorInsight: Understanding Race and Law Effectively Through Mindfulness-Based ColorInsight Practices." *Georgetown Journal of Law and Modern Critical Race Perspectives* 8, no. 2 (2016): 251–304.

Professor Magee suggests bringing together the "theory and practice supporting inclusive and identity-safe classrooms" with the "theory and practice of mindfulness in teaching and learning" (253). The practice of mindfulness would, Magee argues, provide meaning and connection in the classroom, in fulfillment of the imperative of inclusivity. The argument includes discussion of goals of and challenges to inclusivity in the classroom, as well as suggestions for fostering inclusivity across a variety of social identity categories. Contemplative pedagogy, a pedagogy of mindfulness, is reflected in equal detail including benefits and suggestions. Includes an Appendix with suggested contemplative practices.

McMurtry-Chubb, Teri A. "The Practical Implication of Unexamined Assumptions: Disrupting Flawed Legal Arguments to Advance the Clause of Justice." *Washburn Law Journal* 58, no. 3 (2019): 531–76.

Legal writing programs are often described as peripheral to the curriculum, and thus the writing classroom can be "a place of liberation" that "provide[s] opportunities for students to grapple with the inequities that context creates," according to Professor McMurtry-Chubb (535). The writings produced by first year law students in the second semester of the year formed the basis of Professor McMurtry-Chubb's study of her students writing demonstrates that students must be actively taught skills necessary to effectively advocate for marginalized and/ or underrepresented groups. Her proffered solution includes advocacy for critical pedagogies and the various critical pedagogical practices that she has employed, thereby creating a liberatory educational space as well as improving her students' understanding of power and privilege.

Aníbal Rosario-Lebrón, "If These Blackboards Could Talk: The Crit Classroom, a Battlefield." *Charleston Law Review* 9, no. 2 (2015): 305–333.

Critical pedagogy uses dialogue to focus on identifying social injustice and the promotion of actions which may transform oppressive relationships or institutions. Professor Rosario-Lebrón suggests that conflict or confrontation should not be diminished in the classroom but treated as a pedagogical strategy. At the same time, Rosario-Lebrón offers suggestions useful for "the development and implementation of a critical didactic methodology" (320).

Rush, Douglas K., and Suzanne J. Schmitz. "Universal Instructional Design: Engaging the Whole Class." *Widener Law Journal* 19, no. 1 (2009): 183–214.

Advocating for universal instructional design, Professors Rush and Schmitz note that law schools have seen increases in disabled students and that universal instructional design supports all learners. The two include design principles in the contexts of higher education and law school, providing strategies that may be used in a higher-education context and more detailed guidance about incorporating universal design principles in law classrooms. The authors include a collection of online resources that would be helpful to professors seeking to implement universal design. Some included resource also address diversity and inclusion issues.

Sedillo Lopez, Antoinette. "Beyond Best Practices for Legal Education: Reflections on Cultural Awareness — Exploring the Issues in Creating a Law School and Classroom Culture." *William Mitchell Law Review* 38, no. 3 (2012): 1175–1184.

Law students receive cultural norms of professional behavior while they are learning to be lawyers, and the values the lawyer brings to a client representation affects that representation. Also affective are the judgments the lawyer may make about the culture of the client. Professor Sedillo Lopez suggests that cross-cultural awareness be included in the process of training student lawyers. Professor Sedillo Lopez notes that law school classrooms provide opportunities for students to explore their biases. Further, she champions traits of humility and respect, modeled by instructors and encouraged in students, for the ultimate benefit of students, clients, and others in the professional community.

Solorzano, Daniel G., and Tara J. Yosso. "Maintaining Social Justice Hopes within Academic Realities: A Freirean Approach to Critical Race/LatCrit Pedagogy." *Denver University Law Review* 78, no. 4 (2001): 595–622.

Professors Solorzano and Yosso consider both Paolo Freire's *Pedagogy of the Oppressed* (elsewhere in this bibliography) and critical race theory to describe elements of critical race pedagogy. Elements, or techniques, include counterstorytelling, as described by Richard Delgado. The authors note that counterstorytelling serves multiple pedagogical functions. Following that description of critical race theory, the authors continue the article in the form of a narrative conversation between a tenured male professor and an untenured female professor beginning with the question of how critical educators maintain their integrity when working for social change from within the academy (602) and considering related issues such as how critical race pedagogy appears in the classroom.

Strand, Palma Joy. "We Are *All* on the Journey: Transforming Antagonistic Spaces in Law School Classrooms." *Journal of Legal Education* 67, no. 2 (2017): 176–210.

An advocate for equity and inclusion in the classroom, Professor Strand identifies teaching strategies that can be used toward that goal, particularly seeing people and creating space for differences. Strand recognizes differences among groups and structural inequalities as a call to action for law professors, with examples from the context of professional responsibility, as well as state and local government law. After defining antagonistic spaces in opposition to the safe spaces described by Darling-Hammond and Holmquist, Strand identifies ways in which different types of microaggressions play out in the law school classroom and the ways in which professors may instead practice microinclusive strategies.

Tavares, Bonny L. "Changing the Construct: Promoting Cross-Cultural Conversations in the Law School Classroom." *Journal of Legal Education* 67, no. 2 (2017): 211–241.

After demonstrating that cross-cultural communication in the classroom is beneficial for student and professor alike, Professor Tavares describes several "best practices" for professors to consider implementing in their classrooms. In addition to proactive steps professors may take, Tavares also describes the actions a professor may take in the face of resistance or incivility. Tavares positions the need for students to improve their cross-cultural awareness as a professional duty, in light of the American Bar Association Standards for law schools.

Vélez Martínez, Sheila I. "Towards an Outcrit Pedagogy of Anti-Subordination in the Classroom." *Chicago-Kent Law Review* 90, no. 2 (2015): 585–613.

Power and privilege in society are reflected in the law school classroom, and outcrit scholars extend critical legal scholars' criticism of power and hierarchy to call for an anti-subordination agenda. Professor Vélez Martínez addresses teaching practices that may reinforce systemic discrimination, exclusion, and oppression and also proposes that collaboration serve as the basis for the teacher-student relationship. The analysis describes and critiques traditional Langdellian pedagogy and highlights Professor Derrick Bell's Outcrit scholarship on pedagogy. Vélez Martínez concludes with the proposition that teaching should be a collaboration and "there is a non-oppressive dialectic relationship between students and professors" (588).

Wlodkowski, Raymond J., and Margery B. Ginsberg. "A Framework for Culturally Responsive Teaching." *Educational Leadership* 53, no. 1 (September 1995): 17–21.

The authors describe a pedagogy called culturally responsive teaching, that engages learners' intrinsic motivation by a unified and meaningful approach. Fundamentally, motivation and culture are united. To encourage engagement of sustained intrinsic motivation, teachers are encouraged to establish inclusion, develop a positive attitude toward the learning by increasing relevance, enhance meaning by including student perspectives and values, and building competence among students, so they understand they are learning something valuable.

Podcasts

Friend, Chris. *HybridPod*, https://hybridpedagogy.org/tag/podcast/.

The podcast is hosted by Professor Chris Friend and is associated with the online peer-reviewed journal *Hybrid Pedagogy*. Though the episodes may not always directly address pedagogy as manifest in the classroom, the themes considered on the podcast mirror critical pedagogy considerations, including connection, asking questions, and access. Episodes are an interview format, and guests vary. Transcripts of episodes are available.

Frye, Bryan L. et al. *Ipse Dixit: A Podcast on Legal Scholarship*, https://shows.acast.com/ipse-dixit/.

Episodes of this podcast feature guest speakers who are interviewed by a member of the crew of nine hosts. There are many episodes available on the podcast home, however, the site lacks a search functionality. The easiest way to try and find podcasts addressing pedagogy is to use a web search engine such as Google and include "ipse dixit" and your desired topic in the search box.

Kane, John, and Mushtare, Rebecca. *Tea For Teaching*, http://teaforteaching.com/.

The podcast hosts run the Center for Excellence in Learning and Teaching at the State University of New York at Oswego. With over 150 episodes complete, the interviews cover a variety of topics including those related to diversity, inclusion, uniform design for learning (UDL). The episodes typically involve a guest interview, and the episodes also include transcripts. Show notes include a variety of external resources ranging from book recommendations to software/apps to video or audio content. Episodes are tagged, which helps locate interviews on a particular topic. However, listeners can only find tags from within the entry to an episode—there is no list of tags that is searchable separate from the episodes.

Stachowiak, Bonni. *Teaching in Higher Ed Podcast*, https://teachinginhighered.com/episodes/.

A weekly podcast with a general higher education audience, Bonni Stachowiak interviews different guests each week. Among the topics addressed include cultural competence, digital pedagogy, and others. The site includes search tools facilitating a search by guest or by topic Searches for race, equity, and critical pedagogy presented multiple episodes each. However, searches for sexuality, sexual orientation, and transgender retrieved no results. The site also hosts a related blog.

Chapter 2

Property

Everyone Should Have Some: Inclusion & Equity in Property Law

*Joseph William Singer**

Robert Montgomery was a liberal economics professor at the University of Texas. John Kenneth Galbraith tells us those liberal views "made him unpopular with the Texas legislature" which decided to interrogate him. "When he was asked if he favored private property, Montgomery replied, 'I do—so strongly that I want everyone in Texas to have some.'"[1]

Property law, it turns out, is not just about keeping what you have but getting property, that is, the freedom and power to acquire property. In a society that treats each person as equal, this means every person must have a realistic opportunity to acquire property that is both sufficient to live a full and flourishing life and that respects the person's dignity and autonomy.

A free and democratic society that aspires to treat every person with equal concern and respect does not recognize different statuses like noble and commoner, free and unfree, racially superior and racially inferior. Moreover, such a society constructs property laws with the goal of promoting widespread distribution of ownership: the freedom to buy and sell without discriminatory exclusion from the marketplace, liberty from servitude or other forms of arbitrary hierarchical power that would deny individuals equal concern and respect, and social relationships that promote respect for each person as well as prohibit powers over others that are illegitimate or unjust.

These matters are commonplace in many property law courses that teach the origins of the system of estates in land and future interests. That history explains how feudalism was established in England and how, over time, legal rules were developed to protect peasants from the arbitrary power of lords, eventually promoting the fee simple form of property rights that gives the owner autonomy, freedom from lordly

---

* Bussey Professor of Law, Harvard Law School. Thanks and affection go to Martha Minow and Mira Singer.
    1. THE LITTLE, BROWN BOOK OF ANECDOTES 395 (Clifton Fadiman ed., 1985).

prerogatives, the power to move away and sell the land without the lord's consent, security of land tenure, and the freedom to use one's property as one sees fit, subject to legitimate regulations. The antifeudal property system achieved these goals by rules that promoted the alienability of land while protecting owners from loss of their homes, consolidated powers in owners, and limited future interests that might unduly hamper the freedom of individuals to run their own lives, and regulated the powers of landlords. From lords, vassals, and serfs, we moved to a political-legal system that values free and equal citizens; property law both reflected and enabled that change to occur. While those changes in law were imperfect and had limitations—especially with regard to race and gender—there is no doubt that they significantly shifted from norms of hierarchy and servitude to norms of equality and liberty.

This means that the estates system, which serves as the core of many property law courses, teaches us some valuable lessons about inclusion and equity. To move from feudal property relations to democratic ones, laws limited the powers of lords and increased the powers of those who lived on the land. The laws redistributed property rights downwards from lords to peasants and converted a hierarchical system with only a few "owners" to one which had widespread access to ownership as well as freedom to use one's land as one saw fit, subject to laws that applied to all. If property law is built on law reforms that opened access to property to those who had been locked out of the system in the past—or relegated to a subordinate position in it and in social relations—then we can see how fair housing and public accommodation laws further the same values and norms. They open up property to people who were previously excluded from home ownership and full and equal enjoyment of the goods and services offered in public accommodations. Property should be available to all rather than hoarded by a privileged class. Property law changed over time to promote these norms.

This does not mean that either English or American property law was perfect or that either was a model for a property system that included everyone. It is important for students of property law to understand the ways that U.S. law does, and does not, adequately promote inclusion and equity. American property law is filled with acts of oppressive dispossession—through conquest of Native nations, slavery, racial segregation, discriminatory denials of access to housing, public accommodations, employment, and failures to fairly divide income and wealth through economic institutions that actually promote equal opportunity. Property law also fails to recognize and reward the unpaid work done in the home—most often by women—such as cleaning, cooking, and caretaking of children and the elderly.

This suggests that a core topic of property law is the way that it does—and does not—achieve the norms of equality that it embraces. Treatment of the estates system as an antifeudal, pro-egalitarian structure can be reinforced by teaching other subjects that show how these issues play out in modern times. Property law abounds with issues related to discrimination, wealth and poverty, and access to housing affordable by all. My own property law casebook integrates these topics into sections that teach basic property law rules.[2] Possible topics that can easily be included in a first year property course include:

Public Accommodations Law

- Federal and state statutes seek to ensure access to the marketplace of goods and services by prohibiting discrimination in places of public accommodation. These laws apply to certain types of markets and certain types of discrimination, but they allow other forms of discrimination to continue to exist. For example, no general federal statute prohibits discrimination on the basis of sex in public accommodations. While most (but not all) states have state laws that do so, half those states do not prohibit discrimination on the basis of sexual orientation or gender identity, and despite the recent case of *Bostock v. Clayton County, Georgia*, 140 S. Ct. 1731 (2020), those states may continue to interpret their state laws to deny full and equal enjoyment to public accommodations for LGBTQ persons.

- Public accommodation laws include, for example:
  - Title II of the Civil Rights Act of 1964 (the Public Accommodations Act of 1964), 42 U.S.C. §2000a.
  - Civil Rights Act of 1866, 42 U.S.C. §1981 & §1982.
  - Americans with Disabilities Act of 1990, 42 U.S.C. §12102 et seq.
  - State public accommodation statutes like Mass. Gen. Laws ch.151B.
  - Common law cases like Uston v. Resorts Intl, 445 A.2d 370 (N.J. 1982) (holding that all places open to the public have a duty to serve the public unless they have a good reason not to).

Fair Housing Laws

- Both federal and state laws prohibit discrimination on the basis of race, sex, disability, religion, and against families with children. Many state laws also prohibit discrimination on the basis of age, marital status, sexual orientation, and gender identity.[3] Each of these types of discrimination has different parameters, and proving discrimination will be a little different for each type. It is valuable to teach examples in some or all of these categories to get a sense of how discrimination plays out in the real world and the ways existing law does and does not help.

---

2. This may seem self-serving, but my own casebook—although not perfect—does cover all these topics. Joseph William Singer, Bethany R. Berger, Nestor M. Davidson, & Eduardo Moisés Peñalver, Property Law: Rules, Policies, and Practices (7th ed. 2017).

3. After the 2020 *Bostock* decision, it is likely that federal courts will interpret the federal Fair Housing Act to prohibit discrimination in housing on the basis of sexual orientation and gender identity.

- These laws prohibit both intentional discrimination and disparate impact discrimination. They include:
  - ° The Fair Housing Act, 42 U.S.C. §§ 3601 to 3631.
  - ° The Civil Rights Act of 1866, 42 U.S.C. § 1982.
  - ° State fair housing laws like N.J. Stat. § 10:5-12.

Homelessness

- The law of trespass gives owners the freedom to exclude non-owners, but several courts have limited those rights when homeless persons need a place to be.
- Recent cases include:
  - ° *Commonwealth v. Magadini*, 52 N.E.3d 1041 (Mass. 2016) (holding that a homeless person cannot be criminally prosecuted for trespass if he entered land because of necessity to protect his life when he had no reasonable alternative).
  - ° *Martin v. City of Boise*, 902 F.3d 1031 (9th Cir. 2018) (holding that it violates the 8th Amendment to prosecute a homeless person for sleeping in public if the shelters are full and there is no other place to sleep).

Migrant Farmers

- People who live in precarious housing, like migrant farmers living in barracks, may have rights to visitors and charitable and governmental aid; those rights limit the powers of the farmer to exercise the right to exclude.
- See, e.g., *State v. Shack*, 277 A.2d 369 (N.J. 1971) (allowing migrant farmworkers to receive visitors in their barracks on the farmer's land despite his objections, including services from doctors, lawyers, and activists).

Exclusionary Zoning

- This issue has rocketed into public debate in the last few years as housing becomes more and more expensive and incomes do not keep pace. Zoning laws shape municipal environments to achieve various legitimate government goals, but they also have the effect of making it illegal to build affordable housing in many cities and towns.
- Laws in some states require local zoning laws to make room for the construction of affordable housing, see *Southern Burlington County NAACP v. Township of Mount Laurel*, 336 A.2d 713 (N.J. 1975).
- Both the Equal Protection Clause and the Fair Housing Act prevent private exclusionary practices by prohibiting the enforcement of racially restrictive covenants,

Shelley v. Kraemer, 334 U.S. 1 (1948), and even writing such restrictions in leases or deeds, Fair Housing Act, 42 U.S.C. §3604(c).

- Because the Fair Housing Act prohibits unjustified acts that have a disparate impact on protected groups by denying them access to housing, and because those laws apply to local zoning and land use permitting decisions, a useful topic to cover is the extent to which local zoning laws that exclude multi-family housing (and hence affordable housing) have a disparate impact on groups that are relatively poor and disproportionately in need of lower cost housing. Those groups include African Americans, Latinos, and American Indians, women of all races, children, and persons with disabilities.

Marital Property

- It is helpful for students to learn the history of increasing rights granted to married women and fact that they were denied legal autonomy until the second half of the nineteenth century.

- It is also helpful to understand the power imbalance that came from women working in the home without any salary and how both community property and equitable distribution statutes were passed over time to ensure that married women earn a fair share of the marital assets.

- Those laws have not erased inequalities in access to property because of sex. Women still take more time than men away from paid employment to take care of children and the elderly; disparities in wages still hamper the ability of women to accumulate property; and both discrimination and sexual harassment remain serious social problems.

Tribal Property and the History of Conquest

- Many property casebooks describe first possession as the origin of title, and then note the fact that conquest of Indian nations means that much of the land in the U.S. is based on dispossession or denial of first possession rather than protection for first possession.

- On the other hand, most of the land was acquired through treaties that were coercive but in which tribes did reserve some lands and bargained for certain rights that they retain to this day, including inherent sovereignty and property.

- Indian nations are not just historical relics, but flourish today and their property rights are a unique estate in land not usually covered in first year property classes. It is important to understand accurately what tribal property rights are and how they continue to exist.

- Case law both protects tribal property rights and justifies taking it without tribal consent and sometimes without compensation. Examples include:

  ○ *Johnson v. M'Intosh*, 21 U.S. 543 (1823) (land owned by Indian nations cannot be transferred in fee simple without the consent of the United States).[4]

  ○ *Lone Wolf v. Hitchcock*, 187 U.S. 553 (1903) (treaties can be unilaterally abrogated by the United States, and tribal property rights can be abrogated without the consent of the tribe even when the treaty provided otherwise).

  ○ *Tee-Hit-Ton Indians v. United States*, 348 U.S. 272 (1955) (property owned by Indian nations can be taken by the United States without compensation if that title is not recognized by a federal treaty or statute).

  ○ *United States v. Sioux Nation of Indians*, 448 U.S. 371 (1980) (tribal property recognized by the U.S. cannot be taken without compensation but the U.S. is only required to show a "good faith effort" to provide compensation rather than obligated to pay fair market value as is the case with other property rights).

In conclusion, given the topics traditionally covered in the property law course and the very nature of property itself, the property law course may be one of the easiest first year courses to use to promote inclusion and equity in the first year curriculum. Antifeudal background principles like rules limiting restraints on alienation are based on an historical process designed to combat and contain the inegalitarian aspects of feudalism. For this reason, then, these modern topics of discrimination and inequality fit neatly with core principles in the field, and can be incorporated into the basic property course in ways that illuminate the basic principles and rules of property law.

---

4. In my view, this case is often misunderstood. For my take on how it should be understood and taught by property professors, see Joseph William Singer, *Indian Title: Unraveling the Racial Context of Property Rights, or How to Stop Engaging in Conquest*, 10 ALBANY GOV'T L. REV. 1 (2017).

Zoning and Race, from Ladue to Ferguson

Rebecca Tushnet[*]

With Jeremy Sheff, Mike Grynberg, Steve Clowney, and James Grimmelmann, I have written a property casebook that is open and free for students (except the cost, if any, of printing a copy).[1] We believed that the ever-rising price of law school casebooks had become unacceptable for our students, and that we could provide an alternative that would allow teachers to teach property without the guilt of assigning an expensive book, often only partially used. Where we offered an alternative perspective to those often found in property casebooks, as in our foreclosures and zoning chapters, professors could incorporate whatever they liked in addition to traditional casebooks without additional costs to students.

Our zoning chapter, for example, has a very strong point of view. It comes in what we call "plain vanilla" and "director's cut" versions, but both versions are designed to tell the story of how the built environment reflects a series of deliberate public and private choices that were influenced by and often deliberately in support of racial stratification. The chapter focuses on St. Louis and its surrounding suburbs, specifically the wealthy, nearly all-white Ladue; the now-heavily Black Ferguson; and the New Urbanist Wildwood, all of which represent different attempts to implement zoning to achieve broader social and economic goals, and all of which can only be fully understood when race is a major part of the story of property law.

To a first approximation, all issues in the U.S., especially all legal issues, are racialized. Our casebook focuses on St. Louis, not because it's unusual, but because decisions in and around St. Louis are typical of issues nationwide. Missouri allows particularly easy formation of municipal governments on unincorporated land, so some of the issues are heightened there, but it's still representative of the types of land use choices that Americans have made. This essay briefly summarizes the story that students find in our casebook and offers some of my hopes for what they can learn from it.

---

* Frank Stanton Professor of the First Amendment, Harvard Law School. I would like to thank my coauthors and students for their feedback on the materials discussed in this essay.

1. *See* OPEN SOURCE PROPERTY: A FREE CASEBOOK (Stephen Clowney, James Grimmelmann, Michael Grynberg, Jeremy Sheff & Rebecca Tushnet, eds., 2015), opensourceproperty.org.

Background:
Zoning Arrives and Thrives

St. Louis's current racial segregation has a history. In 1916, the St. Louis Realtors Association backed a ballot referendum to prohibit Blacks from moving onto blocks where at least 75 percent of existing residents were white, and vice versa. This referendum passed, but the Supreme Court quickly invalidated a similar ordinance in Louisville, Kentucky (not on equal protection grounds, but because it infringed on owners' property rights). A few years later, the Supreme Court blessed zoning in *Euclid v. Ambler*.[2] Although the Court didn't allow explicitly racial zoning, race, ethnicity, and poverty were on the Court's mind. Richard Chused points out that the Court's analogy between apartment houses and nuisances allowed it to paper over ugly prejudice with polite words: regulators would be allowed to zone to keep presumptively white kids away from disorderly, noisy, slovenly slum-like districts. That is, they could use "Euclidean" zoning to keep middle- and upper-class white children away from contact with poor immigrant or Black culture.[3]

Until early in the twentieth century, suburbs were routinely absorbed into expanding cities. After courts blessed zoning, suburban residents decided that they could go it on their own. Safe in their enclaves, they would provide their own schools, police, and other services, and they would pay relatively low taxes.

But zoning tends to become more and more restrictive over time, especially favoring larger single-family houses. William Fischel, who studies zoning around the U.S., points out that zoning began with just a few zones: single family, then multi-family, commercial, and industrial. Today, it's quite common for there to be twenty or even fifty zones and zonelets of different things. Fischel argues that zoning tightened because of homeowners' fear for the value of their houses, their single largest asset.[4]

As Fischel explains, people who live near where they work have to balance their interests as homeowners with their interests as business owners, as employers, or as employees. People who vote where they work are thus more likely to support growth and new construction. But suburban residents generally don't do that, so they support restrictive zoning. Most homeowners don't have much in the way of assets other than their homes. This makes them very nervous and very politically active locally. So they vote in ways that they hope will keep the neighbors wealthy and the services cheap.[5] And while courts have generally been hostile to racial discrimination since

---

2. Euclid v. Ambler Realty Co., 272 U.S. 365 (1926).

3. Richard H. Chused, *Euclid's Historical Imagery*, 51 Case W. Res. L. Rev. 597, 599 (2001).

4. William A. Fischel, *An Economic History of Zoning and a Cure for Its Exclusionary Effects*, 41 Urban Stud. 317 (2004).

5. Although much of the discourse surrounding home values has to do with schools, there is no evidence that state-level equalization of school funding, which makes property taxes less important, has reduced exclusionary zoning. California equalized school finance and imposed a limit on property taxes that meant that homeowners didn't need to worry that low-income housing would increase their taxes, but exclusionary zoning didn't diminish and even intensified.

the mid-20th century, they have mostly accepted facially neutral economic discrimination that just happens to preserve racial lines. (It is worth noting that nearly all-white states like Vermont and New Hampshire have also implemented ever more restrictive zoning, suggesting that class may be independently sufficient to drive much of this dynamic.[6])

When minorities and working people followed wealthier whites to the suburbs, those wealthier whites moved further out, leaving suburban ghettos in their wake.[7] Without enough density to support robust public transportation, suburban residents—rich or poor—needed cars if they were going to get to work. Suburbs could not easily be reconfigured as residents' demographics changed.

Specifics In and Around St. Louis

St. Louis started its first city planning division in 1911 and developed rules to protect white, single-family neighborhoods by blocking denser, multi-family or commercial buildings. Its zoning ordinance was adopted in 1919. Without making explicit racial categorizations, it still consigned areas with or near substantial Black populations to future industrial development.[8]

Once the Federal Housing Administration (FHA) was established during the New Deal, the zoning then rendered Blacks ineligible for mortgage guarantees: federal underwriting guidelines considered "inharmonious" uses, that is, mixed uses, to threaten the security of property values. Thus, the government deliberately didn't invest in homes occupied by Blacks, while enabling white suburban families to build wealth through mortgage financing. Between 1943 and 1960, St. Louis County, which was mostly white, received five times as many federally guaranteed FHA loans as the city of St. Louis, which was racially mixed. Racial exclusivity was enforced by whites through persistent economic discrimination and sporadic violence.[9]

As whites moved further out, the state and the federal government expanded roads to serve them. Unsurprisingly, homes in Black neighborhoods deteriorated; those neighborhoods later became eligible for federal "slum clearance" or "urban renewal" (or, as St. Louis civil rights activist Ivory Perry said, "black removal with white approval").[10] St. Louis destroyed some of the city's oldest Black neighborhoods, replacing them with office buildings for middle class suburban workers, who came into the city via the federally funded highway.

---

6. Fischel, *supra* note 4, at 331.

7. Reihan Salam, *How the Suburbs Got Poor*, SLATE (Sept. 4, 2014), https://slate.com/news-and-politics/2014/09/poverty-in-the-suburbs-places-that-thrived-in-the-era-of-two-parent-families-are-struggling-today.html.

8. RICHARD ROTHSTEIN, ECONOMIC POLICY INSTITUTE, THE MAKING OF FERGUSON: PUBLIC POLICIES AT THE ROOT OF ITS TROUBLES 8 (2014), https://files.epi.org/2014/making-of-ferguson-final.pdf.

9. Walter Johnson, *Ferguson's Fortune 500 Company*, ATLANTIC, Apr. 26, 2015, at https://www.theatlantic.com/politics/archive/2015/04/fergusons-fortune-500-company/390492/.

10. *Id.*

Federal and local attempts to re-house the mostly Black families displaced by urban renewal, and to help people in general find more affordable housing, intensified segregation because of the ability of small municipalities to keep poor and nonwhite people out. Whites in St. Louis County adopted restrictive covenants; they ran whites-only real estate markets; they bought empty property to keep it out of the "wrong" hands; and they bought out Black homeowners. But perhaps the most important thing they did was to create new municipalities so that they could zone.[11] Where they could, they banned multi-unit housing, which made it impossible to build federally subsidized housing.

Our zoning chapter introduces the mechanics of zoning through actual zoning codes, starting with the wealthy suburb of Ladue and continuing to Ferguson, which drew national attention after the death of Michael Brown.

Ladue

Ladue is the wealthiest suburb of St. Louis, with a Black population of 1 percent and per capita income of $88,000.[12]

Ladue's zoning relies on single-family residences on large lots, often up to one acre (that is, a substantial portion of an American football field). Businesses are allowed in only a few places; multiple-family dwellings and condos are expressly banned in every zone. Many businesses, including car dealerships and funeral parlors, are also expressly banned. Ladue's non-domestic workers must, therefore, generally drive out of town in order to get to work, as is the case for many St. Louis suburbs. Ladue's most recent zoning plan identifies one of its most significant challenges as the problem of McMansions: big houses that look tacky to the neighbors.[13]

Ladue has been the source of several important cases about aesthetic zoning and family composition zoning, both of which serve to put further controls on who can live in a municipality and how they may live. As it turned out, Ladue's economic and racial homogeneity didn't stop conflict between landowners: they still wanted to control each other's behavior.

Among other things, Ladue banned signs other than tiny "for sale" signs on residential properties, and it fined a resident who put up a sign opposing the first Gulf War. A unanimous Supreme Court held that given the importance of the home in

---

11. *Id.*

12. A few years back the city sought to cover a $300,000 budget shortfall through traffic tickets rather than by raising taxes on its millionaire homeowners. In 2006, Blacks made up 25% of traffic stops by Ladue police. Though the percentage had decreased a little by 2014, Blacks were still sixteen times more likely to be stopped than their percentage of the population would predict. Walker Moskop, *Traffic enforcement report: Black drivers in Missouri still stopped at higher rate*, St. Louis Post-Dispatch, June 2, 2015, at A1.

13. City of Ladue, Missouri, Comprehensive Plan Update (Sept. 27, 2006), reprinted at https://opencasebook.org/casebooks/510-open-source-property/resources/29.1.3.3.1-city-of-ladue-missouri-comprehensive-plan-update-september-27-2006/.

providing a uniquely cheap and convenient way of expressing oneself, the ban was unconstitutional.[14]

However, Ladue retains a number of continuing restrictions on things you can do with your house, and many of them have survived. For example, another case upheld Ladue's general architectural standards as not violating substantive due process or the First Amendment.[15] A modernist architectural plan was rejected because its design was inconsistent with that of the other houses in the neighborhood; the neighbors believed that it would interfere with the value of their colonials. (Mrs. Joan Stoyanoff, whom we managed to contact, was one of the people trying to build the proposed house. She believed that the opposition was actually due to the fact that they were perceived as being Jewish, although they were not.)

Apart from use zoning and architectural controls, Ladue has what's called family status regulations, designed to keep too many unrelated people from living together; for example, two or more unrelated law students would be such a prohibited group. Ladue said that single family zones, which is to say the entire town, a family has to be "[o]ne or more persons related by blood, marriage or adoption, occupying a dwelling unit as an individual housekeeping organization."

The only exception was, of course, for servants.

The stated purpose of Ladue's ordinance was to promote health, safety, and general welfare. The Missouri Court of Appeals upheld this restriction as applied to a heterosexual family where both adults had children from a previous relationship. The Court said that Ladue had a legitimate concern for land use guidelines addressing family needs. Zones where "family values, youth values, and the blessings of quiet seclusion and clean air make the area a sanctuary for people."[16] How an unmarried couple interferes with this is left as an exercise for the reader.

Up until 2006, Ladue was still denying people the right to live in Ladue if either member of an unmarried couple had children.[17] Before same-sex marriage was the law of the land, that meant that Ladue excluded all gay and lesbian couples with children.

Ladue's exclusion of people who can't afford to buy big houses on big lots can be contrasted with the example of Ferguson, eleven miles (and a world) away.

Ferguson

Ferguson used to be a "sundown town"—where whites threatened the lives of Blacks who remained after dark—but, over the later 20th century, the majority of

---

14. City of Ladue v. Gilleo, 512 U.S. 43 (1994).

15. State ex rel. Stoyanoff v. Berkeley, 458 S.W.2d 305 (Mo. 1970).

16. City of Ladue v. Horn, 720 S.W.2d 745 (Mo. Ct. App. 1986).

17. Nancy Larson, *Gay Couples Keep Out!*, ADVOCATE, Jul. 18, 2006, at 34 (discussing lesbian couple and daughter who were warned by real estate agents that Ladue would prevent them from living together).

St. Louis' Black population took up residence in a corridor running northwest towards Ferguson. About two-thirds of Ferguson's population is now Black, and its per capita income is approximately $21,000.[18]

Although Blacks are represented in Ferguson's government (albeit underrepresented), the city government has limited powers. Under the Missouri constitution, municipalities can't raise taxes on their own. To raise money without a referendum, they can fine their citizens, or they can tax utilities. In Ferguson, 60% of the city's revenue comes from regressive taxes on electricity and heat (paid by renters). Property taxes make up under 12%. Huge parcels of valuable corporate property in Ferguson have been given tax exemptions.[19]

Ferguson's most recent land use planning document is from 1998 and was designated "Vision 2015," which may say something in and of itself about the resources available. It shows the same embrace of Euclidean zoning as Ladue but with a different economic context.[20]

Ferguson, too, would like more suburban development, albeit at four single family houses per acre. But residential land use doesn't generate much in the way of taxes, either property or sales taxes. Plus, Ferguson had a rental property problem. Its plan said that some owners of rental property, particularly absentee owners who didn't live in the community, didn't maintain the property as well as owners who occupied properties. The planners recommended requiring inspection of rental property for any change in occupation, pushing the city more towards fine-based policing. The land use plan also recommended reducing the number of properties that were rented, but the plan didn't provide resources to do that.[21]

The legacy of Euclidean zoning, favoring separate houses and car-based transportation, is a built environment that contributed to the poverty and social isolation in Ferguson, underlying the protests surrounding Michael Brown's death. Brown was initially stopped, according to police, for walking in the street.

One person, discussing the location of the shooting, pointed out:

> The buildings are auto-oriented—parking minimums force that logical adaptation—and so they present a rather despotic front to people not in a car. There are no eyes on the street; the buildings all orient towards the parking lot. And nobody even cared enough when this was built to plant some shade trees next to the sidewalk so people could walk in a modest amount of comfort.

---

18. *See* U.S. Census, QuickFacts, Ferguson city, Missouri, https://www.census.gov/quickfacts/fergusoncitymissouri (describing population estimates as of July 1, 2019).

19. Johnson, *supra* note 9.

20. Richard Shearer & Assoc., City of Ferguson Vision 2015 Plan Update (Aug. 1998), https://www.fergusoncity.com/DocumentCenter/View/536/2015-Vision-Plan-Comprehensive-Plan-1998-2015-.

21. *Id.*

Are we surprised that two men would be walking in the street here? If they were going to be on the sidewalk, they would need to march single file.[22]

Ferguson also has a family composition ordinance, though it's less strict than Ladue's. To enforce the family composition ordinance and other land use regulations, Ferguson also has a permit system. Residents need an occupancy permit, and they need to pay a fee every time the occupancy of a dwelling unit changes. They need birth certificates for children, photo IDs for adults, and an inspection with a separate $40 fee with each change. The Department of Justice review of policing in Ferguson concluded that this regulatory scheme became part of the disparate treatment of poor Blacks. For example, one woman who called the police for domestic violence was arrested for violating her occupancy permit because the call revealed that she had a boyfriend on the premises.[23]

Even though residents couldn't have been jailed for violations themselves, Ferguson's municipal court routinely issued warrants so that residents were arrested and locked up for failing to pay related fines and fees. In 2011, the judge responded to the city's instructions to increase revenue from the court by touting his plans to substantially increase fines, especially for housing violations. Ferguson requires anyone who's cited for a housing violation to appear in court, whether or not they contest the charges. Failure to appear brings additional charges and an arrest warrant.[24]

This is a zoning story. It's not a conventional zoning story, but it's a story about how land use decisions constrain other decisions and reinforce structures of discrimination that persist without need for conscious malice (though there is also that).

New Urbanism

One response to the current situation is the rise of New Urbanism, a land use planning philosophy that rejects many of Euclidean zoning's premises.[25] A fundamental question our chapter asks is whether zoning, born in sin, can be redeemed by better purposes—and particularly by purposes that are not centrally focused on racial justice. New Urbanists often decry white flight, but sometimes their proposals are gentrification by another name. And New Urbanists can have the same desires to interfere with others' use of their own property as the politically conservative homeowners who are often associated with Euclidean zoning.

---

22. Charles Marohn, *Stroad Nation*, Strong Towns, Aug. 25, 2014, https://www.strongtowns. org/journal/2014/8/25/stroad-nation.html.

23. U.S. Dep't of Justice, Civ. Rts. Div., Investigation of the Ferguson Police Department 81 (Mar. 2015), https://www.justice.gov/sites/default/files/opa/press-releases/attachments/2015/03/ 04/ferguson_police_department_report.pdf.

24. *Id.* at 57.

25. For an introduction to the principles of New Urbanism from an organization devoted to promoting the movement, see Congress for the New Urbanism, *What Is New Urbanism?*, available at https://www.cnu.org/resources/what-new-urbanism (last visited Aug. 11, 2020).

Map of Wildwood: note traditional cul-de-sacs immediately outside town line.

New Urbanism values mixed use and increasing density: residences mixed with businesses and multi-family dwellings mixed with single-family houses. The St. Louis suburb of Wildwood, incorporated in 1985, rejects the cul-de-sacs of the traditional suburbs around it, trying to have its residents walk and bike instead of driving.[26]

Unlike an Euclidean zoning code segregating businesses from single-family houses from apartment buildings, Wildwood's code focuses extensively on the appearances of buildings but approves mixed uses. However, unlike experiments in some states with "inclusionary zoning," which prioritizes building affordable houses or units, often mixed in with market-rate housing, Wildwood has given no particular priority to affordability.

What Is To Be Done?

We hope students learn from studying zoning that decisions in individual municipalities have powerful effects on those around them, mostly in the form of externalizing costs. Decisionmakers have used racialized zoning to produce a built environment that supports suburbanites with cars to the exclusion of other ways of life. Along with the unwalkable sidewalks of Ferguson, the green spaces of Ladue, and the mildly mixed uses of Wildwood, central cities like St. Louis are also shaped by suburban zoning. The negative effects of this focus on single-family houses insulated from poor people include pollution, diminished city revenues, and enhanced white flight and deterioration of school districts.

---

26. CITY OF WILDWOOD, WILDWOOD TOWN CENTER DEVELOPMENT MANUAL 4 (2004), https://www.cityofwildwood.com/DocumentCenter/View/39/Town-Center-Development-Manual-PDF.

Given the chapter's strong point of view, it can generate outrage or cynicism in some students and resistance in others. Students often arrive in law school with general ideas about unconscious bias and structural racism, but zoning provides them with concrete (pun intended) examples of how small rules do the work of power. Many students have been eager to apply what they learned to zoning in their hometowns, using examples from their own lives to reflect on how the law affected the environments with which they are most familiar. During these discussions, I emphasize that all the decisions reflected in zoning codes and court cases reflect *choices*—choices that could still, for all the overhang of Euclidean zoning's century of dominance, be made differently. I find it striking that, while my students understand why Euclidean zoning persists, many of my students find family status rules almost incomprehensible. How could anyone think that the law should define a family in order to regulate who can live together? (They do understand why a municipality might want to limit the number of college students who can live together off-campus, many of them having recently been such students.) Their incredulity is a sign of how fast the legal imagination can change, if we change it.

The zoning chapter has no easy answers for students. While inclusionary zoning fits many progressive priorities, it too can raise costs for developers and may end up helping those who are only moderately below the average income in a given area. Very poor people can rarely afford to buy housing, or even to rent it in a stable way. But zoners have shaped the country, and lawyers need to understand how the law can ensure that hierarchies are literally set in stone. Zoning interacts with other racialized regulatory regimes, from policing to transportation systems, in ways that need to be understood to be improved.

Who Are These People and What Are They Doing in My Casebook? Teaching Inclusion and Diversity in First Year Property

*Todd Brower**

First year real property cases are almost always about families or neighbors—none of whom ever seem to be people you would want to have living next-door[1] or sitting across the table from you at Thanksgiving.[2] That should not surprise us. In order to make it into a casebook[3] the litigation has to generate a groundbreaking, well-written appellate opinion[4] or a poorly reasoned judgment that can be pedagogically useful for explaining an important doctrinal point[5] in the first year curriculum. Moreover, the actual litigants have to maintain a sufficiently strong stake in the controversy to pay court costs and attorney fees to appeal to a state's highest court over *e.g.,* (a) a $4 per year homeowner's fee that was due to expire in 5 years,[6] (b) trespass across a fallow field so frozen that it could support the weight of a flatbed truck and mobile home without damage,[7] or (c) an undivided 1/18 interest in a house that you don't

---

* Professor of Law, Western State College of Law, Irvine, California. Judicial Education Director, The Williams Institute, UCLA School of Law, Los Angeles, California. A.B. 1976, Princeton University; J.D. 1980, Stanford University Law School; LL.M. 1990, Yale University Law School.

1. *See, e.g.,* the neighbor who chased your children off his property with an iron pipe screaming "I'll kill you!" and whom you subsequently had thrown in jail, Jesse Dukeminier, et al., Property, 77 (9th ed. 2018) (discussing the record in Van Valkenburgh v. Lutz, 106 N.E.2d 28 (N.Y. 1952)).

2. *See, e.g.,* the wife who secretly destroyed her husband's survivorship interest in their joint property and then willed her now-severed share to someone else. Riddle v. Harmon, 162 Cal. Rptr. 530 (1980).

3. Virtually all cases discussed here appear in Dukeminier, *supra* note 1.

4. Boomer v. Atlantic Cement Co., 257 N.E.2d 870 (N.Y. 1970).

5. *See, e.g.,* the court's miscalculation of present value of future property appreciation in *Baker v. Weedon,* 262 So. 2d 641, 643 (Miss. 1972).

6. Neponsit Property Owners' Ass'n, Inc. v. Emigrant Industrial Sav. Bank, 15 N.E.2d 793 (N.Y. 1938) (discussed in Stewart E. Sterk, *Neponsit Property Owners' Association, Inc. v. Emigrant Industrial Savings Bank* in Property Stories, 301, 308 (Gerald Korngold & Andrew Morriss eds., 2004)).

7. Jacque v. Steenberg Homes, Inc., 563 N.W.2d 154 (Wis. 1997).

want to live in, that even a prior buyer no longer wanted to purchase, and that could eventually be sold for only $10,000.[8]

But then, that's the point. Who are the people in these cases and what do they want? And why do they care enough to litigate for so long? Maybe law students don't need to know who Shelley was[9] to understand the rule in his case.[10] But understanding litigants and their needs is important. We should discuss Jessie Lide and her relationship with her sister-in-law, Evelyn and her niece, Sandra; and why Jessie would rather leave her house and personal effects to them instead of to her two living sisters or other relatives.[11] We should explore what John Weeden likely told the lawyer hired to write his will, what follow up questions a good lawyer should have asked to best plan John's estate, and how to avoid the problem that spawned the lawsuit.[12]

John almost certainly never said, "I'd like to devise a legal life estate to my third wife with a contingent remainder over in fee simple absolute to her potential children. And in default of issue, I grant my farm to my grandchildren in a contingent remainder as tenants in common in fee simple absolute. Also, I want to disinherit my two pretermitted heirs from my first marriage." He simply wanted to take care of his wife. She was 38 years younger and he undoubtedly wanted to ensure she could remain on the land after he died.[13] Like Jessie Lide, John Weedon sought to provide for the people he loved and needed a lawyer to translate those desires into action. The hierarchy of estates and future interests, easements by estoppel, and termination of residential covenants, conditions, and restrictions are not just rules to memorize; they are tools to help people do specific things like care for their family,[14] ensure continued access to the house they just built,[15] or live in a condo with their three indoor cats.[16]

To do so students must understand the strains in litigants' marriages,[17] squabbles among relatives,[18] or how neighborhood friendships[19] and landlord/tenant relationships turn sour[20] because these issues spur people to hire property lawyers. Lawyers are in the thick of people's lives because their problems involve parties who cannot easily exit the ties binding them to their adversaries: they are family or neighbors. As at-

---

8. White v. Brown, 559 S.W.2d 938 (Tenn. 1977); DUKEMINIER, *supra* note 1, at 271 (letter from Sandra White Perry regarding the house in *White*).

9. Sir William Shelley, an English judge. *Shelley, Sir William (1480?–1549?)* 52 DICTIONARY OF NATIONAL BIOGRAPHY 41–43 (Smith, Elder & Co. 1897).

10. Shelley's Case (1581) 76 Eng. Rep. 206; 1 Co. Rep. 93b.

11. *White*, 559 S.W.2d at 938.

12. *See Baker*, 262 So. 2d at 642.

13. *Id.*

14. *Id.*; *White*, 559 S.W.2d 938.

15. Holbrook v. Taylor, 532 S.W.2d 763 (Ky. 1976)

16. Nahrstedt v. Lakeside Village Condo. Ass'n., 33 Cal. Rptr. 2d 63 (1994)

17. Sawada v. Endo, 561 P.2d 1291 (Haw. 1977).

18. Delfino v. Vealencis, 436 A.2d 27 (Conn. 1980).

19. Othen v. Rosier, 226 S.W.2d 622 (Tex. 1950).

20. Berg v. Wiley, 264 N.W.2d 145 (Minn. 1978).

torneys we need to understand all types of relationships and families in order to best serve our clients. That knowledge must extend to both conventional and nontraditional relationships, communities and people, familiar to us or not. We should explore those connections where we might expect to find them, and also where we might overlook them because of our implicit biases.

Implicit biases not only affect how we perceive people, but also doctrine. We should examine the cultural and societal assumptions underlying legal rules. For example, in *Van Valkenburgh v. Lutz* the majority and dissent split over whether the Lutzes sufficiently improved the land to satisfy adverse possession requirements.[21] Those requirements mandated that property claimed by adverse possession either be "protected by a substantial inclosure" [sic] or "usually cultivated or improved."[22] Thus, the statute and both judicial interpretations assumed that rewarding productive land use by adverse possession demanded exploitation of assets rather than other, non-consumption uses.[23] Although often ignored by casebooks, non-consumption uses comport better with the values of some indigenous American communities and consequently generate divergent doctrine.[24]

Diverse communities and values appear throughout our casebooks and sometimes during classroom discussions. Naturally we explore issues of race, racism, and exclusion when discussing private racially restrictive covenants in *Shelley v. Kraemer*.[25] To understand state action in *Shelley* we must explore how private covenants, Jim Crow, and redlining affected/affect real estate transactions[26] — and not only against Blacks.[27] But we might also discuss race in *Moore v. City of East Cleveland*[28] where a predominantly Black city enacted a zoning ordinance to address concerns about Black

---

21. *Compare* Van Valkenburgh v. Lutz, 106 N.E.2d 28, 29–30 (Dye, J.) *with* 106 N.E.2d at 30–33 (Fuld, J. dissenting).

22. *Van Valkenburgh,* 106 N.E.2d at 29 (quoting the New York code).

23. *See* 7 Richard R. Powell, The Law of Real Property 1012[1] (P. Rohan rev. ed., 1986); Roger A. Cunningham, et al., The Law of Property § 11.7, at 764 (1984).

24. *E.g.,* Nome 2000 v. Fagerstrom, 799 P.2d 304, 308 (Alaska 1990) (Despite customary element of exclusive use, court grants adverse possession through claimants' use of the disputed parcel consistent with traditional, non-exclusive Native Alaskan system of land use: a stewardship in which other members of the claimant's social group may share in the resources of the land without obtaining permission, so long as the resources are not abused or destroyed).

25. 334 U.S. 1 (1948).

26. Katie R. Eyer, *The New Jim Crow Is the Old Jim Crow,* 128 Yale L.J. 1002 (2019) (book review); Brentin Mock, *Remember Redlining? It's Alive and Evolving,* Atlantic, (Oct. 8, 2015), https://www.theatlantic.com/politics/archive/2015/10/remember-redlining-its-alive-and-evolving/433065/.

27. *See, e.g.,* Christopher Ramos, *The Educational Legacy of Racially Restrictive Covenants: Their Long Term Impact on Mexican Americans,* 4 Scholar: St. Mary's L. Rev. on Minority Issues 149, 149–184, 159–166 (2001) (Mexican-Americans); Garrett Power, *The Residential Segregation of Baltimore's Jews: Restrictive Covenants or Gentlemen's Agreement?* Generations (Baltimore), Fall 1996, at 5. https://digitalcommons.law.umaryland.edu/fac_pubs/254 (Jews); Bob Haye, *Keizer family sues HOA, says RV is necessary for mentally challenged daughter,* KATU2 News (Portland, Ore.)) (Jan 13, 2016) [https://web.archive.org/web/20160116054731/https://katu.com/news/local/keizer-family-sues-hoa-says-rv-is-necessary-for-mentally-challenged-daughter] (people with disabilities).

28. 431 U.S. 494 (1977).

family structure.[29] Just because Justice Powell's plurality opinion avoids the issue does not license teachers to do likewise.[30] The parties in *Moore* are Black; that matters.

Teachers should challenge the default assumption that property litigants do not have race (or are white). Blacks sue and are sued over abandonment of a lease and affirmative waste,[31] over problems with intestate succession,[32] or over temporary licenses to cross private property.[33] After all, racial discrimination is not the sole issue bringing Blacks into courtrooms or lawyers' offices. We should prepare our students for law practices that include diverse communities, no matter their specialty.

This preparation may entail questioning judicial language or factual descriptions and raising diversity and inclusion when and where students and teachers may not expect it.[34] For example in the Dukeminier casebook,[35] *Harms v. Sprague*[36] addresses severance of joint tenancy interests by mortgage hypothecation. The Illinois Supreme Court held that the grant of a mortgage by only one joint tenant did not sever the joint tenancy; modern mortgages should be analyzed as liens and not as title transfers.[37] Thus, the right of survivorship still attached to the mortgaged interest in land. On the joint tenant/mortgagor's death, the surviving joint tenant became the sole property owner.[38] Consequently, the mortgagee's security evaporated because the estate to which the mortgage attached no longer existed.[39] Similarly, the deceased joint tenant's will could not pass title to his devisee.[40] *Harms* and its subsequent notes are typical casebook materials; they resolve a doctrinal point and then elaborate its consequences to reach dependent or analogous legal claims.

The court's facts:

---

29. Robin A. Lenhardt & Clare Huntington, *Forward*: Moore *Kinship*, 85 FORDHAM L. REV. 2551 (2017).

30. *Accord, Moore*, 431 U.S. at 508–11 (Brennan, J., concurring).

31. Mike Vulpo, *Tyga Ordered to Pay $186,000 Towards Another Landlord After Allegedly Failing to Pay Rent and Causing Damage*, E!NEWS, (Aug. 23, 2016), https://www.eonline.com/news/789647/ tyga-ordered-to-pay-186-000-towards-another-landlord-after-allegedly-failing-to-pay-rent-and-causing-damage.

32. Andrea Mandell & Lorena Blas, *7 legendary stars who died without wills: Prince, Aretha Franklin and more*, USA TODAY, (Aug. 22, 2018), https://www.usatoday.com/story/life/people/2018/08/22/ legendary-stars-who-died-without-wills-aretha-franklin/83550424/.

33. Ny Magee, *Oprah Winfrey opens private road at her home to help evacuations during Maui brush fire*, THEGRIO, (July 13, 2019), https://thegrio.com/2019/07/13/oprah-winfrey-opens-private-road-at-her-home-to-help-evacuations-during-maui-brush-fire/.

34. Alternatively, some teachers substitute readings specifically referencing race and culture instead of casebook authors' traditional introductory material on foxes (Pierson v. Post, 3 Cai. R. 175, 2 Am. Dec. 264 (1805)) or Blackstone (2 WILLIAM BLACKSTONE, COMMENTARIES ON THE LAWS OF ENGLAND *2 (Oxford, 1765)). *E.g.*, Alfred L. Brophy, *Integrating Spaces: New Perspectives on Race in the Property Curriculum*, 55 J. LEGAL EDUC. 319, 319–21 (2005).

35. DUKEMINIER, *supra* note 1, at 398.

36. Harms v. Sprague, 473 N.E.2d 930 (Ill. 1983).

37. *Id.* at 933–934.

38. *Id.* at 934.

39. *Id.* at 934–35.

40. *Id.* at 934.

Plaintiff, William Harms, and his brother John Harms, took title to real estate located in Roodhouse, on June 26, 1973, as joint tenants. The warranty deed memorializing this transaction was recorded on June 29, 1973, in the office of the Greene County recorder of deeds.

Carl and Mary Simmons owned a lot and home in Roodhouse. Charles Sprague entered into an agreement with the Simmonses whereby Sprague was to purchase their property for $25,000. Sprague tendered $18,000 in cash and signed a promissory note for the balance of $7,000. Because Sprague had no security for the $7,000, he asked his friend, John Harms, to co-sign the note and give a mortgage on his interest in the joint tenancy property. Harms agreed, and on June 12, 1981, John Harms and Charles Sprague, jointly and severally, executed a promissory note for $7,000 payable to Carl and Mary Simmons. The note states that the principal sum of $7,000 was to be paid from the proceeds of the sale of John Harms' interest in the joint tenancy property, but in any event no later than six months from the date the note was signed. The note reflects that five monthly interest payments had been made, with the last payment recorded November 6, 1981. In addition, John Harms executed a mortgage, in favor of the Simmonses, on his undivided one-half interest in the joint tenancy property, to secure payment of the note. William Harms was unaware of the mortgage given by his brother.

John Harms moved from his joint tenancy property to the Simmons property which had been purchased by Charles Sprague. On December 10, 1981, John Harms died. By the terms of John Harms' will, Charles Sprague was the devisee of his entire estate. The mortgage given by John Harms to the Simmonses was recorded on December 29, 1981.[41]

Notice what's missing: why would John Harms, the deceased joint tenant, behave like that? John and his brother deliberately purchased a house in joint tenancy apparently intending to live there together. Eight years later, however, John moved from that house and to another not far away[42] that John shared with Charles Sprague. John cosigned a promissory note for almost a third of the purchase price for a house solely in Sprague's name and mortgaged his joint tenancy property. Sprague and John lived together in Sprague's house until John died, willing everything to Sprague.

It is impossible to know definitively—the court calls them friends[43]—but John Harms and Charles Sprague were probably gay life partners. If that assumption is true, then John's actions can be seen as financial transactions taken to further and support his life together with his partner. In 1981, their legal options for relationship recognition were limited; they could not have married in Illinois or elsewhere.[44] Their

---

41. *Id.* at 932–33.

42. Roodhouse, Illinois has a total area of 1.13 square miles according to Wikipedia. *See Roodhouse, Illinois,* Wikipedia, https://en.wikipedia.org/wiki/Roodhouse,_Illinois (last visited Aug. 11, 2020).

43. *Harms*, 473 N.E.2d at 931–32.

44. United States v. Windsor, 570 U.S. 744, 752, 763 (2013).

relationship may not have changed the outcome of the case, but it might have influenced how the court valued their relationship and wrote its opinion.

The Illinois court only mentioned Sprague while summarizing the facts and proceedings below. Although he was a named party, the sole devisee under John's will, and his house purchase triggered this litigation, he's treated as insignificant; the opinion never mentions him again. In contrast, the other party, William Harms, and his property interests appear throughout.[45] Moreover, the court specifically mentioned that the Simmons's mortgage no longer burdened the joint tenancy property after John's death.[46] Sprague's devise and the Simmons' mortgage were affected by the same legal doctrine and same factual events, yet the court mentions the effect on the mortgagees but not on the defendant, Sprague.[47]

After discussing severance doctrine in *Harms*, I often ask students what motivated John's behavior. Students are usually puzzled. I then ask them to change Sprague's name from Charles to Charlene. Almost immediately, they posit that John and Charlene were a couple. I sometimes ask students why they saw the possible relationship with a different-sex couple, but not a same-sex one.[48] This begins a conversation about baselines and how 'neutral'/'default' often assume heterosexual, white, able-bodied, cisgendered, etc. protagonists.[49] My students take Property at the same time as they study Constitutional law, so the concept of baselines is not unfamiliar.[50] But some are surprised that unexamined baselines or assumptions may also affect ostensibly "noncontroversial" opinions as well as how those baselines influence their own perspectives and reasoning about cases.

We might explore whether being same- or different-sex partners would make a difference in the case. At the time, it certainly would have affected their choices. Although John cosigned the loan with Charles, only Charles's name was on the title. Why? Given that decision, what could John have done to continue to live in the house

---

45. *Harms*, 473 N.E.2d at 931–32, 934.

46. *Id.* at 934–935.

47. *Id.* at 934.

48. *See, e.g.*, Todd Brower, *Social Cognition 'At Work:' Schema Theory and Lesbian and Gay Identity in Title VII*, 18 Law & Sexuality 1, 6–7 (2009); Amos Tversky & Daniel Kahneman, *Judgment Under Uncertainty: Heuristics and Biases*, 185 Science 1124–31 (1974).

49. *E.g.*, Daniel Wickberg, *Heterosexual White Male: Some Recent Inversions in American Cultural History*, 92 J. Am. Hist. 136, 136–157 (2005); *accord*, Plataforma SINC, *Medical Textbooks Use White, Heterosexual Men as a 'Universal Model*, ScienceDaily, (Oct. 17, 2008), www.sciencedaily.com/releases/2008/10/081015132108.htm.

50. *See e.g.*, Romer v. Evans, 517 U.S. 620 (1996) (declaring unconstitutional a Colorado constitutional amendment prohibiting all state or local nondiscrimination protections for lesbians, gays and bisexuals). In *Romer*, Justice Kennedy's majority opinion saw the appropriate baseline for judging the changes wrought by Amendment 2 as the state of existing federal and state law before the amendment—a world in which some groups already had legislative protections against discrimination. Thus, the Amendment imposed a "special disability" on lesbians, gays and bisexuals. *Id.* at 631. In contrast, Justice Scalia's dissent viewed the original tabula rasa as no group having any protection in law against discrimination. Accordingly, the withdrawal of sexual minorities' ability to have government create those protections was merely a bar to "preferential treatment." *Id.* at 638–39 (Scalia, J., dissenting).

had Charles predeceased him and died intestate, or if they had split up? What options were available to same-sex couples then and now to protect the other partner's rights in shared residences?

Moreover, as Sprague's lawyer, would you have counselled him to mention the relationship or closet it? What if they were in Chicago and not in small-town, conservative, downstate Illinois? Would your answer change if Charles or John were not out as gay prior to the lawsuit or before John's death? Finally, remember that the court barely mentioned Sprague and the effects of its decision on him. Would the court's opinion have emphasized that relationship if Sprague had been a woman in a heterosexual relationship? Does that say something about same-sex relationships and law?

Some might question spending time on hypotheticals that create few or no doctrinal differences. Indeed, our students themselves may doubt that approach preferring to focus on what will be tested in class or on the bar exam. One response is that hypotheticals are law professors' stock in trade.[51] Part of the purpose of hypos is to explore implicit assumptions and limitations.

More importantly, classroom discussions should be relevant beyond the close of the semester or end of law school, but be valuable well into students' legal careers. Students must realize that diverse people and relationships are part of the legal world. By engaging solely with what judicial opinions choose to make visible, we sometimes ignore the real people behind case captions. The tendency to forget actual litigants in casebooks is exacerbated because textbooks primarily use appellate court decisions[52]— a world in which clients have limited roles, usually relegated to the audience.[53] Even if they are not noted in the opinion, litigants in cases and casebooks have race, economic status, gender, religion, ethnicity, sexual orientation, physical or mental abilities, gender identity, or some combination of these and other dimensions. Clients will also have these salient characteristics, just as students, their classmates, and teachers do.[54]

---

51. *See, e.g.*, Ashley Thorne, *Hypotheticals in the Criminal Law Classroom: An Interview with Lawrence Connell*, Nat. Ass'n Scholars, (Feb. 18, 2011), https://www.nas.org/blogs/dicta/hypotheticals_in_the_criminal_law_classroom_an_interview_with_lawrence_conn; James A. Henderson, Jr., *A Defense of the Use of the Hypothetical Case to Resolve the Causation Issue—The Need for an Expanded, Rather Than a Contracted, Analysis*, 47 Texas L. Rev. 183 (1969).

52. *See* Amy R. Mashburn, *Can Xenophon Save the Socratic Method?*, 30 T. Jefferson L. Rev. 597, 599 (2007).

53. *See, e.g.*, United States Court of Appeals for the Fourth Circuit, Courtroom Protocol for Counsel, (2018), https://www.ca4.uscourts.gov/oral-argument/courtroom-protocol-for-counsel; Appellate Courts Comm. of the Los Angeles County Bar Ass'n, Basic Civil Appellate Practice in the Court of Appeal for the Second District 10 (2003), https://www.courts.ca.gov/partners/documents/BasicPractice.pdf.

54. *See generally, e.g.*, C. Neil Macrae & Galen V. Bodenhausen, *Social Cognition: Thinking Categorically About Others*, 51 Ann. Rev. Psych. 93 (2000) (describing social categories or characteristics as salient descriptors of people); Ryan M. Stolier & Jonathan B. Freeman, *Neural Pattern Similarity Reveals the Inherent Intersection of Social Categories*, 19 Nature Neuroscience 795 (2016) (same, focusing on brain patterns).

Finally, I suspect that all of us have had students approach us after class, in our offices or by email to relate how something said during class spoke to them personally or resonated with their own backgrounds or experiences. Students share these confidences because the topics we discuss and the language we use signal to them our openness or awareness of things that law school sometimes ignores. These bridges between student and teacher are not inconsequential. Scholars have noted the phenomenon of perceptive divergence, whereby outsiders are more likely than insiders to be self-conscious of that difference between themselves and the majority, to view their outsider status as relevant to others' perceptions of them, and to state that their difference contributed to their treatment in a particular situation.[55] That heightened perception of dissimilarity may produce alienation and stress in those students that their classmates do not experience and that may impose barriers to student success.[56] The student-teacher connections we build can ameliorate that isolation.[57] By making the real people behind cases visible and seeing them as individuals who have gender, race, sexuality, and other characteristics even when those aspects seem doctrinally insignificant, we remind our students that perceptual divergence can shape clients' options and expectations and possibly their treatment within legal institutions, just as it may affect their own or their fellow law students' experiences.

Perceptual divergence can also mean that people can observe the same event but experience it differently,[58] or can read the same case but see different things in it. Our classrooms should not disregard those divergent perspectives; we should embrace them. If we bring these issues up only when they are explicit in cases, this suggests that sexuality, race and gender, etc. are not present in casebooks, classrooms or germane to legal discussions. That conclusion is not only false, but may conflict with our students' personal history and background.[59] Their life experiences and our own, as well as those of the litigants in our casebooks should be brought forward in the

---

There is a significant literature on implicit bias and legal decision-making. *E.g.*, Andrew J. Wistrich & Jeffrey J. Rachlinski, *Implicit Bias in Judicial Decision Making: How It Affects Judgment and What Judges Can Do About It*, in ENHANCING JUSTICE REDUCING BIAS 87, 90 (Sarah Redfield ed., 2017); Jerry Kang et al., *Implicit Bias in the Courtroom*, 59 UCLA L. REV. 1124 (2012); Jeffrey J. Rachlinski et al., *Implicit Bias in the Courtroom: Does Unconscious Racial Bias Affect Trial Judges?*, 84 NOTRE DAME L. REV. 1195 (2009).

55. Jonathan Feingold & Doug Souza, *Measuring the Racial Unevenness of Law School*, 15 BERKELEY J. AFR.-AM. L & POL'Y 71, 86–88 (2013) (discussing the effects of racial minority status on law school performance).

56. *Id.*

57. *Cf. Id.* at 115 (discussing hiring and assessing faculty who are attuned to combatting racial unevenness in the law school experience).

58. *Cf.* Claude M. Steele, *A Threat in the Air*, 52 AM. PSYCHOL. 613, 613 (1997) (giving the example of a Black and a white student in the same classroom with the same teacher and books but who experience the classroom differently because of race, thus affecting their performance).

59. *Cf.* Valerie Purdie-Vaughns, et al., *Social Identity Contingencies: How Diversity Cues Signal Threat or Safety for African Americans in Mainstream Institutions*, 94 J. PERS. SOC. PSYCH. 615 (2008) (discussing the issue in the context of race).

classroom. Doctrine is important, but it is neither abstract nor does it exist in a vacuum. After all, John Harms did not mortgage Blackacre; he mortgaged 220 E. Clay St., Roodhouse, Illinois.[60] We should insist our students see law affecting real people and shaping the diverse communities of which they are a part.

---

60. Harms v. Sprague, 476 N.E.2d 976, 977 (Ill. 1983).

Deconstructing Discrimination within Common Interest Communities: *Hill v. Community of Damien of Molokai*— A Case Study on Combatting AIDS Panic in Your Neighborhood

*D.O. Malagrinò**

Neighborhoods erect "walls" between themselves and others—undesirable people, stigmatized for their difference and rejected from the community. Persons with AIDS are often stigmatized on multiple levels: first by having the serious disease, then compounded by being (or wrongly thought to be) in a disenfranchised group already, such as being a racial minority, gay, a drug addict, and/or someone in poverty.[1] This fear of AIDS continues to cause people and neighborhoods to panic. *Hill v. Community of Damien of Molokai*, 911 P.2d 861 (N.M. 1996), shows how to combat housing discrimination derived from AIDS panic by honing in on covenant construction and enforcement.

In my 1L property course, students first study housing discrimination at about the half-way mark in the course materials when we discuss the selection of tenants in landlord/tenant law. We revisit housing discrimination when we cover discriminatory covenants much later in the course. I assign *Hill* because it serves as a great capstone case, showing how concepts covered earlier in the course are still relevant tools for disputes we study later in the materials. *Hill* is a great example for my 1L students to model their own legal analyses. Plus, this case provides opportunities for

* Associate Professor of Law, Charleston School of Law, Charleston, S.C. Thanks are due to Nancy Zisk, Allyson Haynes Stuart, and AshleyAnn Sander for their contributions to this essay.

1. Gwendolyn Barnhart, *The Stigma of HIV/AIDS: HIV/AIDS-related Stigma Exerts a Direct Negative Impact on the Health of Those Who Have HIV*, American Psychological Association, In the Public Interest Newsletter, Dec. 2014 [https://web.archive.org/web/20200628113851/https://www.apa.org/pi/about/newsletter/2014/12/hiv-aids].

the students to see a court use case law comparisons, private law construction, and statutory analysis, all while resolving one dispute.

The *Hill* decision remains important for integrating diversity into property doctrine because the court provided a well-reasoned and organized judicial opinion for courts to use when analyzing the validity of a single-family, residential-use-only private restrictive covenant under the Fair Housing Act (FHA),[2] when such covenants are specifically designed to exclude undesirables from the neighborhood.[3] There has been a great deal of litigation concerning disputes over group homes in neighborhoods that restrict property to "single-family" and/or "residential" use.[4] These cases often raise questions about what constitutes "residential" use because group homes often provide substantial medical assistance to residents with nonresident medical professionals providing those services daily in-home, whether group homes constitute "single families" when the residents are often unrelated, and whether public policy or statutory regulations prohibit enforcing a covenant specifically intended to have the effect of excluding a group home.

First, this essay will provide a synopsis of *Hill*. When discussing this case study in property class, I try to get the students to identify all facts relevant to the outcome of the case and any helpful background facts that place this dispute between the parties in context. For example, we are talking about a home for four people. We should not lose sight of what the concerns are for them relative to the complainants' concerns. The objectives of the parties and why they are seeking relief in court become key to uncovering what is really at stake in this dispute and to identifying the legal tools available to combat housing discrimination, while balancing the importance of protecting one's private property rights.

Then, this essay identifies the sources of law and a series of questions the court in *Hill* used to resolve this dispute. The court organized the material in an effective way so that readers of the full opinion will clearly see the comprehensive analysis required to mediate that balance between preventing housing discrimination and protecting private property rights. Students are often quick to see for themselves the potential argument for housing discrimination based on violations of the Fair Housing Act. I have found that students later realize the potential for preventing housing discrimination through generally accepted rules of construction for interpreting covenants.

---

2. 42 U.S.C. §§ 3601–3631.

3. *See generally* South Kaywood Community Ass'n v. Long, 56 A.3d 365 (Md. Ct. Spec. App. 2012); Eldorado Community Improvement Ass'n v. Billings, 374 P.3d 737 (N.M. Ct. App. 2016); Valencia v. City of Springfield, 883 F.3d 959 (7th Cir. 2018).

4. *See generally* Malcolm v. Shamie, 290 N.W.2d 101 (Mich. Ct. App. 1980); Crane Neck Ass'n v. New York City/Long Island County Servs. Group, 460 N.E.2d 1336 (N.Y. 1984); Westwood Homeowners Ass'n v. Tenhoff, 745 P.2d 976 (Ariz. 1987); Hagemann v. Worth, 782 P.2d 1072 (Wash. Ct. App. 1989); Deep East Tex. Regional Mental Health Mental Retardation Servs. v. Kinnear, 877 S.W.2d 550 (Tex. Ct. App. 1994).

Consider the facts of *Hill*. In December 1992, the Community of Damien of Molokai (the Community)[5] leased the residence at 716 Rio Arriba, S.E., Albuquerque, New Mexico, located in a planned subdivision called Four Hills Village, for use as a group home for four individuals with AIDS. The Community was a private, nonprofit corporation, which provided homes to people with AIDS, as well as other terminal illnesses. The four residents, who moved into the Community's group home were unrelated, and each person required some degree of in-home nursing care.

Living in the subdivision on the same street as the group home were neighbors William Hill III, Derek Head, Charlene Leamons, and Bernard Dueto (the Neighbors). Shortly after the Community opened the group home, the Neighbors noticed an increase in traffic on Rio Arriba.

In August 1993, the Neighbors sued the Community seeking an injunction to enforce a private restrictive covenant, and to prevent the Community from using the house as a group home. The Neighbors argued that the Community using its lot as a group home violated one of the covenants applicable to all lots in the subdivision, namely that: "No lot shall ever be used for any purpose other than *single family residence purposes*."[6] The Community defended that the covenant did not prohibit the group home and, in the alternative, that enforcing the covenant against the Community violated the Fair Housing Act.

The trial court held that the covenant prohibited the Community from using the house as a group home, and it issued a permanent injunction against the Community. The Community appealed, and the Supreme Court of New Mexico granted a stay of the permanent injunction pending the appeal. The court considered two primary questions: (1) whether four unrelated residents using a house within a subdivision as a group home for persons living with AIDS was a "single family residence" for the purposes of the private covenant on the property; and (2) whether the private covenant, if enforced against the group home residents, would violate Section 3604(f) of the Fair Housing Act.

Construction of the
Restrictive Covenant

First, the court concluded that a group home for four unrelated residents qualifies as a "single family residence" as required by the covenant. At issue in this case was

---

5. The Community organization is named for a 19th-century Belgian-born priest, Jozef De Veuster, known as Father Damien, who worked with lepers in Hawaii. Father Damien died of leprosy in 1889 after years tending to the sick on the island of Molokai. In October 2009, U.S. President Barack Obama said in a statement at Father Damien's canonization: "In our own time, as millions around the world suffer from disease, especially the pandemic of H.I.V./AIDS, we should draw on the example of Father Damien's resolve in answering the urgent call to heal and care for the sick." Rachel Donadio, *Benedict Canonizes 5 New Saints*, N.Y. Times, Oct. 11, 2009, at A9.

6. Hill v. Community of Damien of Molokai, 911 P.2d 861, 865 (N.M. 1996).

the proper interpretation of the restriction, "[n]o lot shall ever be used for any purpose other than *single family residence purposes.*" There are two variables that needed construction: "residence purposes" and "single family." The court considered each.

Residence Purposes

Operating a house for group-home use constitutes residential purposes because the purpose of a group home is to provide the residents with a traditional family structure and atmosphere.[7] The court held, as a matter of law, that this group home, by design, provided the four individuals living in the house a traditional family setting and that those individuals used the home as would any family with a disabled member.[8] For example, the four residents shared communal meals; they provided support for each other socially, emotionally, and financially; and they also received spiritual guidance together from religious leaders, who visited the group home weekly.

Single Family

Residents of a group home can meet a "single-family" requirement when they are a relatively permanent functioning family unit, exhibiting the kind of stability, permanency, and functional lifestyle equivalent to the traditional family unit.

The court noted that the covenant did not define the word "family" and that nothing in the covenant itself indicates an intent to limit the term to a discrete family unit comprised only of individuals related by blood or by law. Accordingly, the court held that the term "family" in the covenant is ambiguous, so the court, favoring the free enjoyment of the property and against restriction, concluded that the term "family" encompasses a broader group than just related individuals.

Then, the court observed that the local municipal zoning ordinance itself provided a definition of "family" that included the residents of the group home being a "single family." The Albuquerque zoning ordinance includes within the definition of the term "family" "[a]ny group of not more than five [unrelated] persons living together in a dwelling."[9] The court stated that, because the Albuquerque zoning ordinance would include the residents of the group home within its definition of a "family," it was persuasive evidence for the proper construction of the ambiguous term in the covenant.

Next, the court recognized a strong public policy favoring small group homes within the definition of the term "family" because there are government policies encouraging locating group homes in single-family residential areas, treating them as if they constituted traditional families, and opposing barriers to these goals. For example, the federal government has expressed a clear policy in favor of removing bar-

---

7. *See* Jackson v. Williams, 714 P.2d 1017, 1022 (Okla. 1985); *see also* Rhodes v. Palmetto Pathway Homes, Inc., 400 S.E.2d 484, 485–86 (S.C. 1991).

8. 911 P.2d at 866.

9. *Id.* at 867–68 (citing Albuquerque, N.M., Rev. Ordinances, art. XIV, § 7-14-5(B)(41) (1974 & Supp.1991)).

riers preventing individuals with physical and mental disabilities from living in group homes in residential settings and against restrictive definitions of "families" that exclude congregate living arrangements for the disabled,[10] including individuals with AIDS.[11] Additionally, the court remarked that in New Mexico, too, the Developmental Disabilities Act expresses a clear state policy of integrating disabled individuals into communities.[12]

Here, the individuals living in the Community's group home operated as a family unit. Much of the activities of the residents were communal in nature. The residents provided moral support and guidance for each other and, together, created an environment that assisted them in living with their disease.

Further, the court accepted that other jurisdictions consistently have held that restrictive covenants mandating single-family residences do not bar group homes, wherein the occupants live as a family unit.[13]

Discrimination on the Basis of a Disability under the Fair Housing Act

Second, the court concluded that, even if having four unrelated residents living in a group home violates the private restrictive covenant [which the court already reasoned it does not], such a covenant would be discrimination on the basis of a disability, violating the Fair Housing Act as applied to individuals living with AIDS because it creates a disparate impact on a protected group of people.[14] Further, because refusing to enforce the covenant against the group home would impose no undue hardship on the neighbors, those neighbors could reasonably accommodate the group home.

The FHA helps provide disabled individuals the opportunity to live in traditional community settings by removing obstacles that hinder their quest for independent living. The FHA clearly prohibits intentional housing discrimination motivated by big-

---

10. *See* United States v. Scott, 788 F. Supp. 1555, 1561 n. 5 (D. Kan. 1992) *stating* "[t]he legislative history of the amended Fair Housing Act reflects the national policy of deinstitutionalizing disabled individuals and integrating them into the mainstream of society."

11. *See* Support Ministries for Persons with AIDS, Inc. v. Village of Waterford, 808 F. Supp. 120, 129 (N.D.N.Y. 1992) (stating "[t]he legislative history of the 1988 amendments to the FHA reveals that Congress intended to include among 'handicapped' persons those who are HIV-positive.").

12. 911 F.2d at 868 (citing Developmental Disabilities Act, NMSA 1978, §28-16A-2 (Cum. Supp. 1995), providing that the purpose of the legislature is to promote opportunities for all persons with developmental disabilities to live, work, and participate with their peers in New Mexico communities).

13. *See* Jackson v. Williams, 714 P.2d 1017, 1023 (Okla. 1985); *see also* Welsch v. Goswick, 181 Cal. Rptr. 703 (Cal. Ct. App. 1982); Maull v. Community Living for the Handicapped, Inc., 813 S.W.2d 90, 92 (Mo. Ct. App. 1991); Montana ex rel. Region II Child Family Servs., Inc. v. District Court, 609 P.2d 245, 248 (Mo. 1980).

14. Although the 1996 *Hill* opinion uses the term "handicap" to describe the effects of the residents' disabilities, I have chosen to use the term "disability" in an effort to be "person-first," and to be consistent with the current text of federal laws. *See* U.S. Dept. of Justice, A Guide to Disability Rights Laws (Feb. 2020), https://www.ada.gov/cguide.htm.

otry or misunderstanding of an individual's disabilities. However, the FHA also helps disabled individuals overcome the subtle effects of unintentional, facially neutral, or even well-meaning restrictions that consequently deny housing to those individuals.

The court reviewed the trial court finding that a facially-neutral restriction, which is equally applicable to both disabled and able-bodied individuals, does not implicate the FHA and ruled that the trial court's view was incorrect because it is well established that the FHA prohibits enforcing restrictive covenants that discriminate or have the effect of discriminating on the basis of a disability.

Section 3604(f)(1) of the FHA provides in relevant part that it is unlawful "[t]o discriminate in the sale or rental, or to otherwise make unavailable or deny, a dwelling to any buyer or renter because of a handicap of … a person residing in or intending to reside in that dwelling after it is sold, rented, or made available."[15] Section 3604(f)(3)(B) states, "[f]or purposes of this subsection, discrimination includes … a refusal to make reasonable accommodations in rules, policies, practices, or services, when such accommodations may be necessary to afford such person equal opportunity to use and enjoy a dwelling."[16] The court interpreted these provisions as creating three distinct claims for violations of Sec. 3604(f) of the FHA: discriminatory intent, disparate impact, and reasonable accommodation.[17] The court addressed each of these three claims because the Community raised each of these claims in response to the Neighbors' lawsuit.

Discriminatory Intent

The Court began by stating that a discriminatory-intent claim focuses on whether a defendant has treated disabled individuals differently from other similarly situated individuals. The claimants need only show that the disability of the residents of a group home, as a protected group under the FHA, was in some part the basis for the restrictive covenant being challenged, or the basis for the enforcement thereof.

The Community argued that the Neighbors were aware the Community was using the property as a group home and decided to enforce the covenant, in part, because of antagonism to that use. The Community presented evidence that the Neighbors' traffic complaints began a few days after a newspaper published an article describing the group home, and that the Neighbors asked if the group home could be relocated outside of the subdivision. The Community also identified several covenant violations by other landowners in the neighborhood that were not being enforced. However, the court held that this evidence was equivocal at best; absent further evidence of an intent to enforce the covenant because of some animus toward residents with AIDS, the Community's allegations are insufficient to support a claim for discriminatory intent.

---

15. 42 U.S.C. § 3604(f)(1).

16. *Id.* at § 3604(f)(3)(B).

17. 911 P.2d at 871; *see* Stewart B. McKinney Found., Inc. v. Town Plan Zoning Comm'n, 790 F. Supp. 1197, 1210–11, 1221 (D. Conn. 1992).

Disparate Impact

Next, the court explained that for a violation of the FHA under the disparate-impact analysis, a claimant need only prove that the defendant's conduct actually or predictably results in discrimination or has a discriminatory effect.

The court recited four factors for evaluating a discriminatory-impact claim: 1) the strength of the claimant's showing of discriminatory impact; 2) whether there is any evidence of discriminatory intent; 3) the defendant's interest in taking the challenged action; and 4) if the claimant is seeking to compel the defendant to affirmatively provide housing to disabled persons or merely to restrain the defendant from interfering with individual landowners who wish to provide this housing.[18]

The court held the Community proved that enforcing the covenant as the Neighbors interpreted it would violate the FHA. First, the covenant, which attempted to limit group homes, had the discriminatory effect of denying housing to disabled individuals. A covenant that restricts occupancy only to related individuals or that bars group homes has a disparate impact not only on the current residents of the Community's group home who have AIDS, but also on all disabled individuals, who need congregate living arrangements to live in traditional neighborhoods and communities.

Second, the court acknowledged that the evidence the Community presented regarding the Neighbors' discriminatory intent was equivocal at best. However, the court recognized that this intent factor is the least important of the four factors in a disparate-impact claim, and a lack of evidence of intent is not detrimental to a disparate-impact claim.

The third factor is the defendant's interest in enforcing the covenant. An important consideration in evaluating this factor is the nature of the interest at issue. Here, the Neighbors' interest is to eliminate the increased traffic that the trial court found had detrimentally altered the residential character of the neighborhood. The court accepted that this is a legitimate interest, which weighed in the Neighbors' favor.

Finally, the court considered the nature of the relief sought. The Community was not attempting to force the Neighbors to provide housing for the disabled. It sought to prevent the Neighbors from interfering with its operation of the group home. The court saw this factor strongly favoring the Community. Accordingly, the court balanced the Neighbors' interest in avoiding increased traffic against the Community's interest in providing housing to disabled individuals and concluded that the FHA factors weigh in favor of the Community, because the Community's interest in maintaining its congregate home for individuals with AIDS outweighed the negative effects of increased traffic, without any additional harms to the Neighbors.

Thus, because the Community proved a disparate impact under the FHA, the court concluded that the Neighbors could not enforce the covenant against the Community.

---

18. Metro. Housing Dev. Corp. v. Village of Arlington Heights, 558 F.2d 1283, 1290 (7th Cir. 1977), *cert. denied*, 434 U.S. 1025 (1978).

Reasonable Accommodation

Nevertheless, the court considered the Community's third claim under the FHA: that the Neighbors failed to make reasonable accommodations under section 3604(f)(3)(B). The court explained that a restriction need only serve as an impediment to an individual claimant, who is disabled and is denied access to housing to implicate the "reasonable accommodation" requirement of the FHA.[19] "Reasonable accommodation" includes changing some rule that is generally applicable to make its burden less onerous on the disabled individual.[20]

The court explained that "an accommodation is not reasonable (1) if it would require a fundamental alteration in the nature of a program, or (2) if it would impose undue financial or administrative burdens on the defendant."[21]

In *Hill*, the Neighbors' interpretation of the covenant had the effect of denying housing access to the disabled residents. Accordingly, Section 3604(f)(3)(B) of the FHA was implicated, and the Neighbors must reasonably accommodate the group home, provided it would not require a fundamental alteration in the nature of the restrictions or impose undue financial or administrative burdens on the Neighbors.

The Neighbors admitted that allowing the group home to operate did not impose any financial or administrative burdens on them. For instance, the Neighbors neither were responsible for operating or maintaining the group home in any way, nor must they have paid any additional costs associated with the group home. Further, not enforcing the single-family residence requirement against the Community's group home did not fundamentally alter the nature of the restriction because the covenant was to regulate the structural appearance of houses and to prevent the business use of the lots within the subdivision. The Community's group home did not affect the structural appearance of the house and was not a business use. The residents used the house like a traditional residential home and acted as a family for one another.

Indeed, the Neighbors' stated reason for enforcing the covenant was not because of the nonresidential nature of the occupancy, but because of the traffic generated by the group home; however, the court held that traffic regulation is not a fundamental aspect of the Four Hills restrictive covenants as there were no traffic-specific restrictions among the private covenants;[22] and, the traffic generated by the group home was no greater than the traffic that a traditional family unit would generate if it had a disabled member needing in-home care.[23]

Accordingly, the court concluded that not enforcing the covenant against the Community's group home would not have imposed an undue hardship or burden on the Neighbors and would not have interfered with the plain purpose of the covenants.

---

19. 911 P.2d at 875.

20. *Id.* (citing North Shore-Chicago Rehabilitation, Inc. v. Village of Skokie, 827 F. Supp. 497, 508 (N.D. Ill. 1993)).

21. U.S. v. City of Philadelphia, 838 F. Supp. 223, 228 (E.D. Pa. 1993).

22. 911 P.2d at 876.

23. *Id.* at 870–71.

The court bluntly concluded that a reasonable accommodation in this case would have been for the Neighbors simply to not enforce the covenant against the Community.

When integrating this case into the classroom, I am sensitive to the possibility students themselves or their loves ones might be among the community targeted; I remind the class always to be respectful. Recently, I have realized, over the years, students have become more surprised there would still be negative treatment of persons living with AIDS. Some of the class discussion highlights the relevance of this case today: that common interest communities still seek to keep out "others" with actions cloaked in enforcing restrictive covenants. Whether these "others" are residents of a home for victims of domestic violence, or a sober home for residents receiving treatment to stay clean and healthy, or group homes for people with mental impairment, neighbors will have some negative associations that will require good lawyers to know how to combat such discrimination. *Hill* provides an effective case study.

Property, Ownership, and the "Other": A Selected Annotated Bibliography of Sources for Addressing Issues of Diversity in the First Year Property Law Course

*Clanitra Stewart Nejdl**

Perhaps more than any other course taught in the first year of law school, property law lends itself to a frank discussion of the wide-ranging and long-lasting negative effects[1] that the development of U.S. law in this area has had on minority Americans. Slavery, the conquest of land belonging to indigenous peoples, racially discriminatory ordinances and covenants, and restrictions on the ownership and use of land are all issues that could, and should, be addressed in a property law class. In addition to discrimination based on race and ethnicity, discrimination based on gender, sexual orientation, and other traits is tied to the history of U.S. property law; this connection that has been written about extensively.[2] However, many law professors may feel hes-

---

* Clanitra Stewart Nejdl serves as Head of Professional Development and Research Services Librarian at the Alyne Queener Massey Law Library at Vanderbilt University. The author would like to thank Associate Dean Larry R. Reeves, Director of the Alyne Queener Massey Law Library and Associate Professor of Law at Vanderbilt University, for his support. She also thanks her husband, Bryan, and their son, Miles, for their continued love and support.

1. These effects may be due to the text of the laws themselves or due to the application of seemingly neutral laws.

2. *See* Sally Ackerman, *The White Supremacist Status Quo: How the American Legal System Perpetuates Racism as Seen through the Lens of Property Law*, 21 Hamline J. Pub. L. & Pol'y 137 (1999); Gretchen Arnold & Megan Slusser, *Silencing Women's Voices: Nuisance Property Laws and Battered Women*, 40 Law & Soc. Inquiry 908 (2015); Brenna Bhandar, *Property, Law, and Race: Modes of Abstraction*, 4 U.C. Irvine L. Rev. 203 (2014); Margaret E. Johnson, *A Home with Dignity: Domestic Violence and Property Rights*, 2014 BYU L. Rev. 1; John D. Johnston, Jr., *Sex and Property: The Common Law Tradition, The Law School Curriculum, and Developments Toward Equality*, 47 N.Y.U. L. Rev. 1033 (1972); Arlene S. Kanter, *A Home of One's Own: The Fair Housing Amendments Act of 1988 and Housing Discrimination Against People with Mental Disabilities*, 43 Am. U. L. Rev. 925 (1994); Priscilla A. Ocen, *The New Racially Restrictive Covenant: Race, Welfare, and the Policing of Black Women in Subsidized Housing*, 59 UCLA L. Rev. 1540 (2012); Laura M. Padilla, *Gendered Shades of Property: A*

itant or ill-prepared to attempt to address these issues into their own property law courses.

This selected annotated bibliography highlights several resources that delve into the rationales and methods for incorporating diversity-related issues into a first year property law course. In selecting these resources, particular emphasis is placed on resources that provide practical guidance on selecting cases and other class materials, effectively framing the class discussion, and helping students to feel comfortable with discussing these issues. Although there are many relevant materials available on this topic, readers are encouraged to consider these resources as a starting point.

Books

Bender, Steven W. "From Sandoval to Subprime: Excluding Latinos from Property Ownership and Property Casebooks." In *Vulnerable Populations and Transformative Law Teaching: A Critical Reader*, edited by the Society of American Law Teachers and Golden Gate University School of Law, 111–124. Durham, N.C.: Carolina Academic Press, 2011.

Bender's chapter details his concerns about the failure of property law casebooks to include information about housing problems unique to Latinos. He asserts that too frequently "property casebooks tend to adhere to the Black/White paradigm that emphasizes the civil rights gains in recent decades on several fronts" (112) while ignoring Latinos' housing problems such as lack of access to safe and affordable housing, problems with subprime mortgages, and loss of land. Bender notes that such problems are not tied just to ethnicity, but also to discrimination based on language and immigrant status. Bender argues that new lawyers need to be exposed to these concerns because they will need to be ready to help remedy the problems in the future.

Brophy, Alfred, Alberto Lopez, and Kali Murray. *Integrating Spaces: Property Law and Race.* Austin, TX: Wolters Kluwer Law & Business, 2011.

Alfred Brophy has authored multiple works exploring the intersection of property law and race,[3] but this book, co-written with Alberto Lopez and Kali Murray, may be the definitive guide on the topic. The authors note that the purpose of the book is to "help to 'integrate' talk of the salience of race and ethnicity with traditional property law and theory." (xvii) Throughout the book they emphasize

---

Status Check on Gender, Race, & Property, 5. J. Gender Race & Just. 361 (2002); Isaac Saidel-Goley, *The Right Side of History: Prohibiting Sexual Orientation Discrimination in Public Accommodations, Housing, and Employment*, 31 Wis. J. L. Gender, & Soc'y 117 (2016); Joan C. Williams, *Married Women and Property*, 1 Va. J. Soc. Pol'y & L. 383 (1994).

3. *See* Alfred L. Brophy, *Integrating Spaces: New Perspectives on Race in the Property Curriculum*, 55 J. Legal Educ. 319 (2005); Alfred L. Brophy, *[Re]Integrating Spaces: The Possibilities of Common Law Property*, 2 Savannah L. Rev. 1 (2015). *See also* Alfred L. Brophy, *When More Than Property Is Lost: The Dignity Losses and Restoration of the Tulsa Riot of 1921*, 41 Law & Soc. Inquiry 824 (2016).

the links between the history of the acquisition and control of property in the United States and the harm suffered by some because of their status as racial or ethnic minorities.

The first part of this book discusses dispossession, slavery, and the connection between property rights and civil rights. The second part explores the race-related aspects of zoning and nuisance cases, as well as housing discrimination based on race and ethnicity. The final part examines the role of race in contemporary property law issues, such as environmental justice, takings, gifts, and partition cases. Within in each chapter of the book, the authors examine key cases that illustrate the issues addressed in the chapter. In addition to the case discussions, "Note and Questions" sections are placed throughout the book to aid the reader in closely analyzing the material and discussing the material with students. A "Table of Cases" and a "Table of Statutes" are provided at the end of the book.

Rose, Carol M. "Property Stories: Shelley v. Kraemer." In *Property Stories*, edited by Gerald Korngold and Andrew P. Morriss, 189–220. New York: Thomson Reuters/ Foundation Press, 2009.

In *Property Stories*, each chapter discusses a major court decision on a topic that would be covered in a first year property law class. The text differs from similar texts, however, in that it uses storytelling as a mechanism to delve into the social policies and political context that led to the issues and outcomes in the cases. The authors do not shy away from detail in an attempt to help students better understand the issues at play in each case and the impact each case has had on current law. Rose's chapter focuses specifically on the U.S. Supreme Court case *Shelley v. Kraemer*,[4] which held that the enforcement of racially restrictive housing covenants violated the Equal Protection Clause of the Fourteenth Amendment. Because of the amount of detail in this chapter, property law professors may find it helpful to use it in their property law classes for its discussion of the case itself or its more general explanation of residential segregation mechanisms and common law.

Articles

Bobroff, Kenneth H. "Indian Law in Property: Johnson v. M'Intosh and Beyond." *Tulsa Law Review* 37, no. 2 (Winter 2001): 521–538.

Encouraging first year property law professors to use materials about American Indian law in their courses, Bobroff makes three important suggestions. First, he suggests that property law students be taught the case *Johnson v. M'Intosh*,[5]

---

4. 334 U.S. 1 (1948).

5. 21 U.S. (8 Wheat.) 543 (1823). *Johnson* involved a dispute over title to land purchased from the Piankeshaw Indians in the 1770's. *Johnson* emphasizes the doctrine of discovery and supports the federal government's claim to Native American land over claims from private individuals.

in conjunction with two other cases related to the transfer of land: *United States v. Percheman*[6] and *Tee-Hit-Ton Indians v. United States*.[7] Bobroff asserts that this combination of cases not only reinforces the doctrinal principles of property law, but also allows students to more fully consider the varied rationales behind the outcomes of the cases and the degree to which those outcomes might be tied to "assumptions about race and culture." (528) Secondly, Bobroff suggests supplementing a discussion of the seminal property law case *Pierson v. Post*[8] with a selection from the novel "Ceremony"[9] by Leslie Marmon Silko that discusses hunting and preparation of a deer by Laguna Pueblo Indians in order to give students the opportunity to compare the values presented in the Court's opinion with those in Silko's work. Finally, Bobroff advises American Indian philosophies should be included in any analysis of the philosophies behind ownership and property. While Bobroff recognizes that there is no single view of property held by all American Indians, he argues that including perspectives from multiple tribes will enrich students' awareness of differing viewpoints about property. He specifically references the beliefs of the Lakota peoples and the Hopi tribe in the article.

Gilmore, Angela. "Incorporating Issues of Sexual Orientation into a First Year Property Law Course: Relevance and Responsibility." *Nova Law Review* 32, no. 3 (Summer 2008): 595–608.

In this article, Gilmore asserts that issues related to sexual orientation are prevalent throughout property law and should therefore be addressed in the property law curriculum. Gilmore stresses that property laws need not be explicitly biased to negatively affect others because of their sexual orientation. To illustrate this in her own property course, Gilmore includes a discussion of leasehold laws, concurrent ownership, and land use controls. She presents students with hypotheticals that challenge their assumptions about the sexual orientation of the parties involved and in which the sexual orientation of the parties is relevant to the legal issue being discussed. Gilmore suggests that anyone who is considering whether to address issues related to sexual orientation in property law courses take several steps in preparation. First, she suggests the careful selection of the text that will be used, to ensure that it will be helpful for this type of discussion. She also suggests a determination be made about the use of personal stories in the classroom. Also required is a consideration of how the students in the class should be involved

---

6. 32 U.S. (7 Pet.) 51 (1833). In this case, Percheman held title to land in Florida granted to him by Spain that was later surrendered to the U.S. by Spain via treaty. Percheman argued that despite the surrender, he still held valid title to the land. The Supreme Court ultimately upheld Percheman's title to the land.

7. 348 U.S. 272 (1955). This case involved a claim by the Tingit Indians for compensation under the Fifth Amendment for timber cut on their lands. The U.S. Supreme Court ruled that compensation was not due where there was no ownership claim recognized by Congress.

8. 3 Cai. R. 175 (1805). *Pierson v. Post* addressed ownership in a fox that was hunted by Post but ultimately killed by Pierson.

9. Leslie Marmon Silko, Ceremony (1977).

in the discussion. Finally, the professor must assess comfort levels and make sure that the class is ready to have a discussion on these issues before raising them.

Harris, Cheryl I. "Whiteness As Property." *Harvard Law Review* 106, no. 8 (June 1993): 1707–1791.

This frequently cited article provides substantial background and a unique perspective useful for property law professors on the relationship between racial identity and property by examining how property rights in the U.S. are intertwined with the racial domination of Native Americans and Blacks. Harris argues that "whiteness" itself has become a form of property in both theoretical and functional senses, especially since slavery monetized the subjugation of non-whites and limited who was considered as having legal rights. (1714) Using *Plessy v. Ferguson*[10] and the *Brown v. Board of Education*[11] decisions as examples, Harris also focuses on how "whiteness" as a property interest has been reflected in U.S. case law. The author asserts that affirmative action, because "[i]t exposes the illusion that the original or current distribution of power, property, and resources is the result of 'right' and 'merit,'" (1778) can be used to help counter the effects of "whiteness" as property.

Lee, Brant T. "Teaching the Amistad." *St. Louis University Law Journal* 46, no. 3 (Summer 2002): 775–789.

The author suggests using the U.S. Supreme Court case *The Amistad*[12] to teach first year law students property law. The case directly addresses slavery, constructive possession, title, and rules related to salvage. The author also uses it in his classroom to emphasize the basic principles of property law and to teach legal analysis and reasoning. He suggests supplementing the discussion of the case with shorter relevant readings, such as current articles about modern-day slavery.

Roisman, Florence Wagman. "Teaching About Inequality, Race, and Poverty." *St. Louis University Law Journal* 46, no. 3 (Summer 2002): 665–690.

Roisman, an esteemed housing law scholar and champion of housing rights for low-income communities, argues that students must first understand the history of property control in the U.S. and the racial disparities caused by that history to truly see how property law has evolved over time. She provides salient statistics and extensively recounts the history of actions taken by federal agencies to directly exclude minorities from homeownership programs. Roisman then suggests specific cases to incorporate into property law courses to better explain these issues, including *Levitt & Sons v. Division Against Discrimination*[13] and *Jones v. Alfred H. Mayer Co.*[14] The article ends with a suggested list of "Social Justice Supplemental Materials" (687–690) that could be used for or incorporated into property law courses.

---

10. 163 U.S. 537 (1896).
11. 347 U.S. 483 (1954) and 349 U.S. 294 (1955).
12. 40 U.S. (15 Pet.) 518 (1841).
13. 363 U.S. 418 (1960).
14. 392 U.S. 409 (1968).

Sealing, Keith. "Dear Landlord: Please Don't Put a Price on My Soul: Teaching Property Law Students that 'Property Rights Serve Human Values.'" *New York City Law Review* 5, no 1 (Summer 2002): 35–108.

Sealing asserts that there is a relationship between human values and property rights and advocates for addressing social justice and diversity-related issues in the property law classroom. His article extensively details many ways in which property law intersects race, ethnicity, gender, sexual orientation, disability, and familial status. He clearly explains the need to use a textbook to address these issues, arguing that a textbook will provide "a sense of legitimacy to the materials that a homemade supplement might lack." (36) Sealing then discusses fifteen textbooks and how useful each textbook might be for this purpose. While the information about the textbooks may be outdated today, the criteria that he considers when determining the usefulness of a textbook for his purposes can be applied to any property law textbook currently available. Sealing also recommends supplementing the materials in the textbook with various court opinions, dissents, and articles. To that end, he discusses the holdings of nearly fifty cases in which the diversity of at least one party is an issue, categorizing each under the property law topic that could best be explained using that case. Given the large number of topics Sealing covers, this article is a critical resource for anyone who is looking for a broad understanding of these issues.

Singer, Joseph William. "Re-Reading Property." *New England Law Review* 26, no. 3 (Spring 1992): 711–730.

In this article, Singer (co-author of the casebook "Property Law: Rules, Policies, and Practices"[15]) focuses on how property law would be taught if race and gender issues were at the heart of the subject. Referencing the work of the late Mary Joe Frug, Singer suggests that if such were the case, it would be evident that there is a difference between the theory and the reality of how property is acquired, especially to the extent that labor, possession of land, and the distribution of wealth are considered in the equation. He argues that "every single important area of property law has been historically structured by both race and gender" (724) and uses land use regulation as an example to support this assertion. Singer also considers how property law courses would need to change in order to incorporate diversity-related issues and determines that they would likely need to be broadened to include these issues and to allow for the discussion of related issues like anti-discrimination laws as part of the course.

Williams, Joan C. "Gender As A Core Value: Teaching Property." *Oklahoma City University Law Review* 36, no. 2 (Summer 2011): 551–553.

Williams' brief article highlights her process for teaching the relationship between gender and property. Williams first explains her use of three views of property as the basis for her course: the feudal view, the republican view, and the liberal

---

15. Joseph William Singer, Bethany R. Berger, Nestor M. Davidson, & Eduardo Moisés Peñalver, Property Law: Rules, Policies, and Practices (7th ed. 2017).

view. Within that framework, she subtly infuses the effects of gender into the discussion of property law. Examples Williams provides include addressing the effects of domestic violence on property-related legal claims, addressing the link between poverty and gender, especially with regard to landlord-tenant and fore-closure cases, and focusing on marital property and how gender roles might affect it.

Websites

Murray, Kali. "Teaching From Narrative in Property Law—Part I of II." Law and Po-litical Economy. February 4, 2019. https://lpeblog.org/2019/02/04/teaching-from-narrative-i-of-ii/.

Murray, Kali. "Teaching From Narrative in Property Law—Part II of II." Law and Po-litical Economy. February 5, 2019. https://lpeblog.org/2019/02/05/teaching-from-narrative-in-property-law-part-ii-of-ii/.

In these two posts, Murray shares her experiences shaping her property law course using narratives and storytelling. Murray, who co-authored the book "Integrating Spaces: Property Law and Race,"[16] references several sources that helped her with this process. She notes that using narratives cannot only allow students to see legal issues from new perspectives, but also shed light on topics related to property law that are less frequently discussed, such as the Thirteenth Amendment. Murray also points out how using narrative to teach property law can provide relatable frameworks for topics that are often misunderstood, such as dispossession, dis-ruption and spatiality. In this way, property issues related to race and other di-versity-related areas can be understood from a larger context.

---

16. Alfred Brophy, Alberto Lopez & Kali Murray, Integrating Spaces: Property Law & Race (2011).

Chapter 3

Contracts

Uncovering Bias:
Teaching Contracts Critically

*Jeremiah A. Ho**

At initial glance, the idea of teaching implicit bias awareness to first year law students while espousing the doctrine of American contract law seems like a tall and difficult order. Intrinsically, the pedagogical demands that the traditional program of American legal education places in the first year curriculum—the objectives we put on the mastery of Black Letter, the recognition of theoretical and historical perspectives behind the rules of law, and the skills of legal analysis in first year courses—make the idea of adding an introduction of implicit bias within the law daunting. Nevertheless, because of the hierarchical nature of the profession and the pursuit of justice through law itself are often limited by unconscious bias, I argue that placing students—future lawyers—directly on notice of this phenomenon from the start is imperative during the first year. And surprisingly, it can be done in a contracts course.

After all, unlike other law subjects, one way to reduce contract law to a sound-bite phrase is to call it a set of procedural rules of agreement-making and by doing so raise an apparent image of neutrality. In fact, such a view about contract law is an illusion that has pervaded many sensibilities in the legal academy, especially where contract law has become the facilitator of modern capitalism.[1] Unlike courses on criminal law and procedure or property law, a contract law course can be taught merely with a focus on doctrine—the rules of making and enforcing agreements. In fact, one could set that as the goal of the course and as an imprimatur of quality to teaching the course; students can just analyze cases under this simple theory and glean the rules without regard for the context of these agreements. In this way, students can master contract law in its purest, distilled form, internalize the rules for doctrines

* Associate Professor of Law, University of Massachusetts School of Law. Many thanks to my law librarians, Jessica Almeida and Emma Wood, for their research assistance. I also thank the editors involved in this project for this opportunity to share my teaching and their editorial efforts on this chapter: Nicole P. Dyszlewski, Raquel J. Gabriel, Suzanne Harrington-Steppen, Anna Russell, and Genevieve B. Tung. Lastly, this chapter is dedicated to my students and the wonderful teachers who have influenced me.

1. Critical legal scholars have observed and critiqued that illusion. *See, e.g.,* Jay M. Feinman, *The Significance of Contract Theory,* 58 U. Cin. L. Rev. 1283 (1990); Duncan Kennedy, *Form and Substance in Private Law Adjudication,* 89 Harv. L. Rev. 1685 (1976).

such as manifesting mutual assent or consideration, answer bar examination questions adequately, and successfully enter the profession.

But inequality—racial, gender, economic, or otherwise—is structurally built into our laws of modern contracting.[2] The relational nature of agreement-making and the dynamics of power are always present when two private parties engage in the meeting of minds. Thus, teaching contract law without context misses the mark about the realities of contracting. It ignores the opportunity to explore descriptive observations premised on contributing to a fair and just society and consequently, normative ideas about contracts that further democratic values.

The Case Method

Concurrently, the traditional method of law teaching assumes such faith and perfection in the rules of law, which further obscures the institutional biases and inequalities that the law potentially carries. Since the rise of law schools in American universities in the late nineteenth century, American law teaching has relied on the Case Method as its primary teaching methodology.[3] At its core, the Case Method relies on the reading of appellate judicial opinions in law courses to dissect and consequently tease out the doctrinal rules and principles of a particular subject.[4] The traditional in-class lecture presentation uses Socratic inquiry, in which the professor creates a rigorous dialogue by constantly asking students questions about the law of a judicial opinion in order to get students to comprehend the legal principles.[5]

Beginning with its inception and development in the 1870s, the Case Method was eventually adopted by law schools nationwide and is still used as the predominant teaching methodology of American legal education.[6] Centrally, the Case Method's creators used judicial opinions and Socratic dialogue, in part because they believed that the law was an objective phenomenon that could be discovered through a scientific and empirical inquiry.[7]

Despite its genuine ability to instill rigor in legal studies, the Case Method has been critiqued numerous times over the years. Many of the critiques have settled

---

2. *See* Deborah Zalesne, *Racial Inequality in Contracting: Teaching Race As A Core Value*, 3 COLUM. J. RACE & L. 23, 25–26 (2013) ("Contract is an area of private ordering, but it is courts that invalidate or legitimize the allocation of power between or among parties to a contract. Unspoken assumptions about power—who has it, who may use it, and how it may be used—are embedded in contract law and theory. These assumptions may conceal bias, the impact of stereotypes, and cultural preferences in a court's final decision.").

3. LAWRENCE M. FRIEDMAN, A HISTORY OF AMERICAN LAW 468 (3d ed. 2005).

4. *See* ROBERT STEVENS, LAW SCHOOL: LEGAL EDUCATION IN AMERICA FROM THE 1850S TO THE 1980S 52–53 (1983).

5. PHILIP C. KISSAM, THE DISCIPLINE OF LAW SCHOOLS: THE MAKING OF MODERN LAWYERS 37–50 (2003).

6. *See* STEVENS, *supra* note 4, at 64.

7. *See id.* at 54, 61–63.

around a few common observations of the Case Method. First, the teaching of judicial opinions in a laboratory-like dissection, after the legal dispute has occurred and been resolved, tends to emphasize legal knowledge over practical training.[8] The law, studied in that context, is purely descriptive rather than performative. Second, many have observed that the philosophy embodied in the Case Method and its instructional aspects have become obsolete.[9] Obsolete because that philosophy considered that the law could be perfected internally within a body of judicial opinions over time and thus is scientifically discoverable. It reflects notions regarding scientific objectivity that were prevalent in the nineteenth century. However, from a more modern-day perspective, that conception of the law purposely eschews the subjects and authors of the law and any discussion about what social or political vantage points such "objectivity" might actually represent.[10]

Objectivity

As a natural corollary from that observation, there is a third critique of the Case Method: the method itself relies on an antiquated notion of objectivity, shaped by legal minds of a particular generation, predominately upper class, white, and male.[11] Some legal academics have observed that teaching students in this way replicates a social hierarchy that allows students from dominant groups to prevail and succeed over those from marginalized groups.[12] Objectivity, from that perspective, thus raises implicit bias issues.[13] Some have found that this hierarchy inhibits authenticity and

---

8. Jerome Frank, *Why Not a Clinical Lawyer-School?*, 81 U. Pa. L. Rev. 907, 907–08 (1933) (painting the developer of the Case Method, Langdell, as misguided in his practice of law, and how that translated to some of his development of the case method, and why, "[d]ue to Langdell's idiosyncrasies, *law school law came to mean 'library-law'*" (emphasis in the original)).

9. The literature is replete with such critiques of the Case Method. I offer a shortly sampling here spanning over the last half-century. *See generally, e.g.,* Sheila I. Vélez Martínez, *Towards an Outcrit Pedagogy of Anti-Subordination in the Classroom*, 90 Chi.-Kent L. Rev. 585 (2015); Julie M. Spanbauer, *Using a Cultural Lens in the Law School Classroom to Stimulate Self-Assessment*, 48 Gonz. L. Rev. 365 (2013); Ruta K. Stropus, *Mend It, Bend It, and Extend It: The Fate of Traditional Law School Methodology in the 21st Century*, 27 Loy. U. Chi. L.J. 449 (1996); Paul F. Teich, *Research on American Law Teaching: Is There a Case Against the Case System?*, 36 J. Legal Educ. 167 (1986); Arthur D. Austin, *Is the Casebook Method Obsolete?*, 6 Wm. & Mary L. Rev. 157 (1965).

10. *See* Gary Minda, *One Hundred Years of Modern Legal Thought: From Langdell and Holmes to Posner and Schlag*, 28 Ind. L. Rev. 353 (1995).

11. *See* Marcia Speziale, *Langdell's Concept of Law as Science: The Beginning of Anti-Formalism in American Legal Theory*, 5 Vt. L. Rev. 1, 29 (1980) ("Langdell's return to original sources—the cases, his activization of the classroom, and his preference for principles over maxims parallel nineteenth-century empiricist and evolutionist thinking.").

12. *See* Duncan Kennedy, *Legal Education as Training for Hierarchy, in* The Politics of Law: A Progressive Critique 54, 54–75 (David Kairys ed., 3rd ed. 1998).

13. Renee Nicole Allen, Deshun Harris, *#socialjustice: Combatting Implicit Bias in an Age of Millennials, Colorblindness & Microaggressions*, 18 U. Md. L.J. Race, Religion, Gender & Class 1, 18 (2018) ("Legal training with its emphasis on objectivity, thus puts lawyers and law students in a position to be susceptible to implicit bias."); Elizabeth L. MacDowell, *Law on the Street: Legal Narrative*

empowerment in law students with negative consequences for their ultimate professional identities.[14]

In the first-year contracts course, the dominance of this notion of objectivity is still very prevalent; it is very often subsumed into the way in which American contract law is taught and learned. The word "objectivity" and its clinical, scientific variants poses an extremely impermeable standard. It poses a challenge for teaching contracts critically. But like the word "perfect," the imperviousness of objectivity is debunked once we realize that objectivity is only to be framed through human experience and perspective. The question that I want my students to ask always when they hear the word "objectivity" in the practice of law is: whose objectivity are we talking about?

In the first semester of my contracts course, I pose this question when I teach the objective theory of contracting, which is the way in which all of contracting is interpreted. And through this, I am able to teach contract law and inform students about the law's tendency to favor a particular perspective over others: in essence I show them how important it is to be wary of the law's tendency to further unconscious bias. This lesson appears at the very beginning of the semester and course.

Embry v. Hargadine, McKittrick Dry Goods Co.

First, we look at the most prevalent iteration of the rule for objectivity in contract law, as espoused by one of the most widely taught cases on the subject, *Embry v. Hargadine, McKittrick Dry Goods Co.*[15] Under that version of the rule, objectivity is used to judge and interpret contractual negotiations by placing objectivity within a qualified reasonable person standard: a common viewer who is placed in the shoes of the recipient of a particular communication in order to discern whether a communication is an offer or perhaps something else.[16] In *Embry*, the plaintiff Embry worked for a dry goods company in a written service agreement that expired in December 1903.[17] Several days after the agreement expired, Embry alleged that he informally spoke with defendant McKittrick, who verbally agreed to hire him for an additional year.[18] Yet, shortly after this alleged conversation, Embry was let go.[19] In a breach of contract

---

and the Street Law Classroom, 9 Rutgers Race & L. Rev. 285, 317–18 (2008) ("[W]ithin the guise of objectivity, these assumptions are both hidden in fact, and hidden as assumptions. The subjective—personal experience, for example—is unwelcome in the typical law school classroom. Moreover, objectivity-as-epistemology creates the illusion that critique itself is subjective; only contributions that reflect the law's dominant assumptions are without viewpoint. In this way, law school polices against the formation of counter-hegemonic consciousness.").

14. Grant Gilmore, The Death of Contract 13 (1974).

15. 105 S.W. 777 (Mo. Ct. App. 1907).

16. *Id.* at 779.

17. *Id.* at 777.

18. *Id.* at 777–78.

19. *Id.*

lawsuit, Embry would need to establish the existence of a contract and the way to do so would be to examine how a contract could have formed through the informal verbal exchange Embry had with McKittrick.[20] In order to do so, the court ruled that an objective lens through a reasonableness standard, as qualified by the recipient's position, must be used to interpret the informal verbal exchange between Embry and McKittrick.[21]

The informality of that verbal exchange lends itself greatly to interpretation—not merely for determining the case's outcome (contract or no contract?) of the communication that Embry, the recipient, received from his employer Hargadine, but how agreements are created within a relational context—the history of the parties, the business norms of that industry. At first, the omission of most of Embry's identifying characteristics in Judge Goode's opinion could prove to be problematic. But in a class discussion of the case, that omission allows me to pose factual questions about Embry's personal characteristics that may change the outcome of relying on the objective standard in this case.

I ask: But what if the plaintiff wasn't Mr. Embry? What if the plaintiff was Mr. Liu? Or Ms. Liu, who is a recent immigrant to the United States? What other facts would this qualified reasonableness standard of objectivity prompt us to view? In other words, would we need to know more about plaintiff's position? (Yes, indeed.) And what would we want to know in order to utilize objectivity more precisely? Whether or not we would ultimately reach the same conclusion with the switch in the plaintiff's personal characteristics from that of Mr. Embry is not as relevant. We're not using Ms. Liu's characteristics alone to determine a subjectivist interpretation. What this new inquiry provokes in a class discussion is what would a legal thinker need to make sure we approach the interpretation of a verbal employment agreement that tries earnestly to avoid applying reasonableness with some level of implicit bias.

One could read the communication between Employer and Ms. Liu in a way that neglects the business practices and social norms of someone from Asia. Is that appropriate and just under the rule? Or is that detrimental because it potentially shifts application of the rule by implicitly adopting the viewpoint of a native English speaker or a person accustomed to business practices in the United States? Is that an impulse? Is that our subjectivity and our biases coming through the law and into the facts of the case?

What if Asian business etiquettes demanded some nuances in interpreting Hargadine's words? What if the bargaining power between the parties has changed because of Ms. Liu's immigration status? What about race? And gender? Or age? What would an interpretation of the reasonable person in her shoes reveal? The ultimate outcome might be the same judicially—which again is not the point of this class exercise— but the inquiry *must be different*. I want my students to understand that if they me-

---

20. *Id.* at 778–79.
21. *Id.* at 779.

chanically subsumed Judge Goode's analysis and interpretation of the Embry case onto variations for Ms. Liu, injustice emerges because the proper perspective of the litigant is not accurately and sensitively accounted for.

I don't expect to solve everything in one lesson. But it serves as an introduction to bias in contracts and the type of structural inequality within the legal profession that a cursory understanding of the reasonable person standard and objectivity might replicate in practice.

This lesson also has implications for teaching contracts for the remainder of the year. When we cover doctrines where equity lurks into contract law, for instance, the discussion can be more robust and contextual, and students are more likely to see how the traditional rules of contracting could effectuate harsh and unequitable results. As an illustration with the teaching of the unconscionability defense later in my first semester of contracts with my students, students grapple more easily with the implicit bias that arises with the rules of contract-making in its lack of regard for unfairness, and how such disregard within contract law ignores some realities of contracting that affect lives and pocketbooks of parties who are less enfranchised in society than others — especially when more sophisticated parties or parties with more leverage take advantage of them in the bargaining process. That first lesson on objectivity is revisited in a larger context in terms of who gets to create and enforce the rules of contracting and why doctrines such as unconscionability are needed. Using the seminole case taught widely here in this doctrine, *Williams v. Walker-Thomas Furniture Co.*,[22] I find that students more readily note the socio-economic, race, and gender status of Williams who purchased several items of furniture from Walker-Thomas Furniture through installment contracts that contained harsh forfeiture and cross-collateralization clauses.[23] On the one hand, we discuss how contract law could help create contracts that have certain imbalances and how such contracts could be tolerated in the marketplace and in society. Along those lines, the furniture company here might have some justification to protect itself with clauses that allow some recourse when it takes on higher risk customers. But what is the tipping point? And how could clauses that are too one-sided prove to be pernicious and continue to help perpetuate race, class, and/or gender inequality?

Parker v. Twentieth Century Fox, Co.

Another meaningful example of setting the course with implicit bias awareness in mind appears further along in a course's study of contractual remedies, when we examine the avoidability doctrine through the famous Shirley MacLaine case, *Parker v. Twentieth Century Fox, Co.*[24] The film studio, Fox, and Shirley MacLaine entered into a contract for her to play a female lead in a film called "Bloomer Girl," for which

---

22. 350 F.2d 445 (D.C. Cir. 1965).
23. *Id.* at 447.
24. 474 P.2d 689 (Cal. 1970).

she was to receive a minimum salary of $750,000.[25] But before the film's production, Fox repudiated the contract and offered her the opportunity to play a female lead in another film for the same compensation.[26] Having refused the substitute lead, MacLaine sued Fox for contract breach.[27] Without disputing liability, Fox asserted that that MacLaine had failed to make reasonable efforts to avoid damages.[28]

In teaching the case, one could analyze the original film role with the substitute role in a mathematical breakdown. Both were female lead roles in big Hollywood productions for the same salary; therefore, as the dissent in the case would deemed, the roles are comparable enough for MacLaine to have a duty to avoid damages for Fox's contract breach. This approach—although not incorrect—again allows us to see how contract law's apparent neutrality could be skewed to disregard the subtleties of MacLaine's case—subtleties that the majority did examine in favor of MacLaine. With students familiarized to the possibility of unconscious bias in the law, they grapple less adversely with seeing how MacLaine's gender played a role in determining how different the two offered roles were. Fox's offered substitute role was qualitatively of a different kind, given the diminishment of creative control in the production, the switch from a dramatic lead to a musical role, and the feminist themes in Bloomer Girl versus the dated female stereotypes in the substitute film. Despite the salary and major Hollywood production, students, with an awareness of implicit bias can see how much deeper an analysis of the original and substitute roles is required. Whether they agree with the majority decision or not (MacLaine indeed prevailed), students understand that a fuller and more methodical analysis would take account of MacLaine's gender with heavier regard.

Odorizzi v. Bloomfield School District

Finally, teaching awareness of implicit bias has its rewards when students encounter an example of contract law and enforcement of explicit bias—for instance, in teaching the classic undue influence case, *Odorizzi v. Bloomfield School District*.[29] In *Odorizzi*, a schoolteacher Odorizzi had been arrested for criminalized same-sex intimacy in the 1960s.[30] When he returned from arrest and interrogation, and lacking sleep for several days, Odorizzi was confronted at his home by school officials.[31] Claiming that they had his best interests in mind, warning him of the adverse consequences of not resigning, and telling him that an attorney could not be consulted in time, the officials got Odorizzi to resign immediately.[32] The trial court found that Odorizzi's agreement

---

25. *Id.* at 690.
26. *Id.* at 690–91.
27. *Id.* at 691.
28. *Id.*
29. 54 Cal. Rptr. 533 (Cal. Dist. Ct. App. 1966).
30. *Id.* at 537.
31. *Id.*
32. *Id.* at 537–38.

to resign, indeed, had been procured through undue influence. But the case is a good example of how contract law, by extension, law itself is used to further the then-prevalent bias against sexual minorities. Already able to see how the law can harbor implicit bias, students often note how the trial court here avoided homophobic attitudes of the day to only focus on the contractual injustice against the rule of freedom of contracting. Further, students often find that in analyzing undue influence here, the court missed the opportunity to discuss the significance that Odorizzi's arrest had for perceptions about his sexual identity that then would enhance undue influence. The subtleties of marginalized LGBTQIA identities then rise to the surface from this contracts case. How did the potential perceptions of Odorizzi to the school district as a gay man (whether he was or wasn't) add to the pressures from the school officials to influence his choice to resign in addition to the physical and emotional challenges stemming from his arrest and confrontation with his employers? Not only does this stretch the difference in leveraging potential between Odorizzi and his employers but also reveals the emotional impact on his ability to make a healthy and justified bargain. Helping students tease out how such questions could be placed on Odorizzi's sexuality and future well-being allows students to understand the empathic role that his attorney might have had to play in order to select the correct contract doctrine for rescinding his resignation.

Conclusion

Ultimately, it is imperative that law faculty lead students into the profession in a way that helps them see not just the mere possibilities of law but also its tendencies to further inequality. This notion soars beyond courses that might have more overt social justice experiences and themes, but also to courses that are standardized throughout the curricula at American law schools, especially courses at the beginning of students' careers. In my experience, a more nuanced inquiry into objectivity at the very beginning of contract law is helpful to uncover law's tendency to carry implicit bias. Doing so effectively sets up a critical mindset at the very beginning and is worth the potential of more empathetic and mindful justice-centered legal competency.

A Law and Political Economy Approach to Race, Gender, and Power in Contracts[*]

Noah D. Zatz[**]

If forced to choose, I might pick *Bailey v. Alabama*[1] as my favorite 1L contracts case. That is, if it even counts as contract law. Raising that question is pretty much my point in teaching it.

Decided in 1911, *Bailey* is a criminal case—Lonzo Bailey was convicted for fraud. It is also a constitutional case—the Supreme Court struck down the conviction as violating the Thirteenth Amendment's prohibition of involuntary servitude. A labor case, too—the criminal statute specifically targeted workers who took advances on wages and then later quit before paying off this debt to the employer. And a race case, though the Court denied it—Alabama's "false pretenses" law was one cog in the wheel of Jim Crow neoslavery.[2] But yes, also a contracts case, one that appears in a prominent libertarian's casebook, no less.[3] Not only does the case arise from a labor contract, but the Court used *Bailey* to erect a boundary between criminal and civil consequences for breach of contract.

Bailey's overflowing of conventional doctrinal boundaries makes it a perfect vehicle for presenting a Law & Political Economy approach to contracts, perhaps the quintessential "private law" topic. This approach treats private law as a study in public

---

* This essay draws heavily from material the author previously published on the Law & Political Economy blog (lpeblog.org) as *State Power and the Construction of Contractual Freedom: Labor and Coercion in Bailey v. Alabama* (Nov. 24, 2017); *Colorblindness and Liberal Racial Paternalism in Bailey v. Alabama* (Apr. 19, 2018); *Is 'the Market' the Enemy?: Racial Exploitation in Bailey v. Alabama* (Jan. 17, 2018); and *The Public Law of Private Promising, And Not Even That: LPE 101 for Contracts* (Feb. 26, 2019).

** Professor of Law, UCLA School of Law.

1. 219 U.S. 219 (1911).

2. Douglas A. Blackmon, Slavery by Another Name: The Re-enslavement of Black Americans from the Civil War to World War II (2009); Dennis Childs, Slaves of the State: Black Incarceration from the Chain Gang to the Penitentiary (2015); Sarah Haley, No Mercy Here: Gender, Punishment, and the Making of Jim Crow Modernity (2016).

3. Randy E. Barnett & Nathan B. Oman, Contracts: Cases and Doctrine (6th ed. 2016).

power, and one in which questions of race and inequality are fundamental.[4] Doing so also links substantive analysis of cases and doctrine to the creation of an inclusive classroom environment, one where race matters rather than being treated as distracting from or intruding on a whitewashed understanding of "thinking like a lawyer."

Randy Barnett's casebook positions *Bailey* within remedies, and, like quite a few others, it positions remedies at the beginning of the course. In my telling, starting with remedies centers the exercise of state power. Ultimately, the question is whether a government institution (a court) will render a judgment and back it up with the threat of publicly authorized violence: seizing property to satisfy a judgment or throwing someone in jail for contemptuously defying a court order.

I underline this point on the very first day of class by assigning a recent ACLU report on incarceration for nonpayment of private consumer debt.[5] Anticipating *Bailey*, this reading challenges conventional field boundaries, enabling students to follow a thread of debt and poverty that connects their contracts class to Ferguson, racialized policing, and mass incarceration. The link to criminalization immediately challenges, as I make explicit, the common conflation of all things "economic" with the outcomes of "markets," a framing that generally treats race and racism as extraneous, a topic for another course.

The publicness of contracts goes beyond the brute fact that it is law. Rather, the field reflects policy judgments about *when* to make the force of law available to private parties. Although invocations of party intent typically submerge this point, it actually appears on the surface of the most conventional place to start contracts: the very first section of the Restatement (Second) of Contracts. "A contract is a promise or a set of promises for the breach of which the law gives a remedy, or the performance of which the law in some way recognizes as a duty."[6] Well then, when and how does "the law" (speaking for we, the people) choose to transform private promises into legal duties?

There are two subsidiary points here. First, when the law *does* transform promises into contracts, it delegates public power to private entities. Those entities then choose how to exercise that power, but this space of empowered private discretion is the creation of public choices. Such choices require justification in terms of public values. Those values might well counsel the establishment of zones of decentralized ordering, structured by individual promising. But we can only have an honest conversation about whether and how to do so after recognizing that the public constructs the private.

A second point underlines the first: the law draws distinctions among the promises it renders as contracts. Promise-ness alone does not command the law's backing.

---

4. David Singh Grewal, Amy Kapczynski & Jedediah Purdy, *Law and Political Economy: Toward a Manifesto*, Law & Political Economy (Nov. 6, 2017), https://lpeblog.org/2017/11/06/law-and-political-economy-toward-a-manifesto/.

5. American Civil Liberties Union, The Criminalization of Private Debt (2018), https://www.aclu.org/issues/smart-justice/mass-incarceration/criminalization-private-debt.

6. Restatement (Second) of Contracts § 1 (Am. L. Inst. 1981).

This substantive point underlies that most notorious and abstruse of contracts topics, the doctrine of consideration. Consideration can seem only marginally relevant because ordinary commercial cases rarely dispute it. But that is precisely the point: consideration becomes uninteresting only *after* bracketing out the full range of real-life promissory practices to commercialize contracts. Indeed, one can flip the point. Arguably, applying contract law or not is precisely how we *constitute* a domain *as* commercial in character and distinguish it from other realms — realms where legal duties are allocated by noncontractual means, even when they affect "economic" matters.[7]

What best illustrates this constitutive role are the family relationships that, by no coincidence, populate many classic boundary-drawing cases around consideration. These, as well as thick relationships of solidarity, reciprocity, and human concern in employment settings, dominate cases like *Hamer v. Sidway*[8] (uncle-nephew), *Ricketts v. Scothorn*[9] (grandfather-granddaughter), *Webb v. McGowin*[10] (saving the boss' life), and *Feinberg v. Pfeiffer Co.*[11] (supporting the devoted long-term employee). These cases trouble the notion that consideration tracks a pre-existing line between the market sphere of bargains (enforceable) and a nonmarket sphere of gifts (unenforceable). Instead, we see a messy reality of "nonmarket" relationships structured through exchange and of "nonmarket" values governing relationships among commercial actors.

Perhaps most provocative and revealing are those cases where the law overrides its formal categories in order to preserve distinctions among purportedly separate spheres. It does so in classic cases like *Sonnicksen v. Sonnicksen*[12] and *Borelli v. Brusseau*[13] where all the consideration in the world cannot get a wife paid, as promised, for her caretaking labor. The boundary-drawing around markets both draws upon and reanimates gendered and raced distinctions among people and forms of interaction. In these cases in particular, situating them in a gendered world is the only way to make them legible and coherent, rather than hopelessly ad hoc; again, this runs contrary to many students' assumption that gender is some kind of extraneous consideration located outside "legal doctrine" in a separate and suspicious world of "policy arguments."

The family labor cases also reveal another way that public and private interact in contracts: public judgments are regularly masked by an authorizing discourse of private-ness. Rather than openly relying on policy judgments about the appropriate

---

7. Elsewhere, I have developed an analogous argument with regard to employment law, and in particular its invocation that employment's fundamentally contractual nature ties it to market relations. Noah D. Zatz, *Working at the Boundaries of Markets: Prison Labor and the Economic Dimension of Employment Relationships*, 61 VAND. L. REV. 857 (2008).

8. Hamer v. Sidway, 27 N.E. 256 (N.Y. 1891).

9. Ricketts v. Scothorn, 77 N.W. 365 (Neb. 1898).

10. Webb v. McGowin, 168 So. 196 (Ala. Ct. App. 1935).

11. Feinberg v. Pfeiffer Co., 322 S.W. 2d 163 (Mo. Ct. App. 1959).

12. Estate of Sonnicksen, 73 P.2d 643 (Cal. Dist. Ct. App. 1937).

13. Borelli v. Brusseau, 16 Cal.Rptr.2d 16 (Ct. App. 1993).

basis for differentiating—and differently regulating—relationships, contract doctrine often draws the boundary of the market by invoking the intentions it ascribes to the parties regarding legal enforcement. People in family or social settings are deemed to have intended not to be legally bound (or to have expected no compensation), while the opposite presumption is applied to settings deemed commercial, as in Restatement § 21[14] or *Roznowski v. Bozyk*.[15]

This general technique of ventriloquizing policy in the voice of party intent is ubiquitous. We see it also in Cardozo's declaration in *Jacob & Youngs v. Kent* that "[i]ntention not otherwise revealed may be presumed to hold in contemplation the reasonable and probable,"[16] and in the legal fictions of "implied" or "quasi" contracts that overcome the absence of consideration (*Webb*[17]) and even the absence of any promise at all *(Cotnam v. Wisdom*[18]). Indeed, such cases raise the tantalizing prospect that not just consideration, but even promise, is more of a fetish than a firm foundation.

The core ideological function of the promise requirement is to enact freedom *from* contract, freedom *from* legal obligation. In this framework, a promise may not be sufficient to enlist the machinery of law in enforcement, but it surely is necessary. A private party must invite the state in. And yet. . . .

One startling omission from standard contracts curricula is anti-discrimination law. Correcting that provides another concrete way to incorporate questions of diversity and inclusion into the contracts course and, by doing so, reframe student interest in those topics as an interest *in contracts*, not just a reason to look forward to 2L year.

The standard omission partly reflects the anachronistic distinction between the common law of contracts and various specialized statutory domains that sound in contract, whether IP licenses or labor law collective bargaining agreements. But even setting aside statutes specific to housing, employment, or public accommodation discrimination, what about Section 1981?[19] It guarantees a general right to "make and enforce contracts" without race (or alienage[20]) discrimination. Derived from the Civil Rights Act of 1866, its dusty historical pedigree rivals that of other statutory mainstays of "common-law" contracts, like abolition of the seal[21] and (ahem) statutes of frauds, not to mention the newfangled 1952 Uniform Commercial Code.

The ban on discriminatory contracting means that some "private" promises are legally obligatory. This makes sense if *all* contractual promising ultimately serves some public purpose (such as allocating access to important resources)—public pur-

---

14. Restatement (Second) of Contracts § 21 (Am. L. Inst. 1981).

15. Roznowski v. Bozyk, 251 N.W.2d 606 (Mich. Ct. App. 1977).

16. Jacob & Youngs, Inc. v. Kent., 129 N.E. 889 (N.Y. 1921).

17. Webb v. McGowin, 168 So. 196 (Ala. Ct. App. 1935).

18. Cotnam v. Wisdom, 104 S.W. 164 (Ark. 1907).

19. 42 U.S.C. § 1981.

20. *See* Anderson v. Conboy, 156 F.3d 167 (2d Cir. 1998).

21. Note, *Contracts without Consideration; The Seal and the Uniform Written Obligations Act*, 3 U. Chi. L.Rev. 312 (1936).

poses that ultimately trump the mere presence or absence of promising. The discrimination context in particular highlights the deep connection between contract and "civil rights," both in its older[22] and newer senses. The "private" field of contract is a public forum for belonging as equals, to paraphrase Patricia Williams.[23]

Anti-discrimination law's neglect within contracts curricula also exemplifies the broader bracketing off of power relations that is enabled by fetishizing the private promise. Racism and all manner of inequality simply are pushed offstage, to be addressed alongside the regulatory intrusions of other professors' upper-division courses. But just as there is no natural, pre-legal core to "regular" contracts, nor can the constituting context be kept entirely at arm's length.

In the classic common-law cases of refusal-to-contract, discrimination appears as purely private preference, however misguided. Refusal may be grounded equally in the "cut of his coat or color of his hair [or] the color of his skin," among which the law will not distinguish;[24] private parties may be racist, but the law's refusal to recognize that constitutes evenhandedness.

Law's role can be elusive when it merely refuses to obligate, in contrast to its much more visible enforcement of "private" promises. But rather than accepting this passive/active distinction, I push my students to see the law at work through the interconnection of contract and property. In *Bowlin v. Lyon*, the nineteenth-century opinion just quoted, the proprietor of a skating rink refuses to sell a ticket of admission.[25] The proprietor's resulting non-obligation, however, becomes meaningful only because it sits atop a legally constituted property baseline in which the Black skater is legally obliged not to enter the premises without the owner's consent. The hands-off posture with respect to contract is meaningless without the prospect of the police laying hands on the skater and dragging him away—or worse.

These points—about the public constitution of private power and how it is obscured by the fetish of private intentions and by legal claims to colorblindness—allow me to show the potential synergy between insights from Legal Realism and Critical Race Theory. That brings me back to *Bailey*, the Supreme Court's pathbreaking 1911 peonage decision.[26]

Bailey shows how understanding power and freedom *within* a contractual relationship requires some account of the surrounding circumstances. The Court had to decide whether to treat the consequences of breach as the responsibility that comes with freedom, or instead as a device of enslavement. The spectre of the latter arose because *the state's* threat to punish the worker handed power *to the employer*. It was the functional equivalent of "authoriz[ing] the employing company to seize the

---

22. T.H. Marshall, CITIZENSHIP AND SOCIAL CLASS, IN CITIZENSHIP AND SOCIAL CLASS, AND OTHER ESSAYS 1–85 (Cambridge Univ. Press, 1950).

23. PATRICIA J. WILLIAMS, THE ALCHEMY OF RACE AND RIGHTS 148 (1991).

24. Bowlin v. Lyon, 25 N.W. 766, 768 (Iowa 1885).

25. *Id.* at 767.

26. Bailey v. Alabama, 219 U.S. 219 (1911).

debtor."[27] The worker would be bound to the employer without anything turning on whether "private" or "public" violence was at issue. A subsequent case put the point even more vividly, with the Court explaining, "When the master can compel and the laborer cannot escape the obligation to go on, there is no power below to redress and no incentive above to relieve a harsh overlordship or unwholesome conditions of work."[28]

This assessment of compulsion depended on considering the full range of legal consequences, including those formally outside contract law: here, exposure to criminal prosecution on account of breach. The contractual relationship's constitution through criminal law was, in turn, thoroughly shaped by the *racial* relationship among Bailey, a Black agricultural laborer, the white farmer who employed him, and the state and local political institutions committed to upholding white supremacy. The law was specifically, though not explicitly, targeted at Black workers.[29] So, too, with the murderous harshness of the potential sentence to "hard labor" in Alabama's convict leasing system that operated under the brutal principle of "One Dies, Get Another."[30]

This racial constitution of the "market" order also operated through contract formation, not solely breach. Assessing whether the contract was freely formed required understanding the legally-structured bargaining position of Black agricultural laborers under Jim Crow. Bailey's Christmastime deal was forged in the shadow of an array of laws, including vagrancy, which paradigmatically criminalized Black laborers' mobility between jobs and any intervening unemployment; some specifically required being employed as of a date in January.[31] These labor regulations complemented racialized systems of land tenure and debt[32] that, through exclusion from capital ownership, produced the economic need, not only for subsistence wages, but for the wage advances that indebted Bailey to his employer.

Despite all this, the Court protested mightily that racial context was irrelevant:

> We at once dismiss from consideration the fact that the plaintiff in error is a black man.... The statute, on its face, makes no racial discrimination, and the record fails to show its existence in fact. No question of a sectional character is presented, and we may view the legislation in the same manner as if it had been enacted in New York or in Idaho.[33]

---

27. *Id.* at 244.

28. Pollock v. Williams, 322 U.S. 4, 18 (1944).

29. *See* HALEY, *supra* note 2; BLACKMON, *supra* note 2; PETE DANIEL, THE SHADOW OF SLAVERY: PEONAGE IN THE SOUTH, 1901–1969 (1972).

30. *See* MATTHEW J. MANCINI, ONE DIES, GET ANOTHER: CONVICT LEASING IN THE AMERICAN SOUTH, 1866–1928 (1996); sources cited *supra* note 2.

31. W.E.B. DU BOIS, BLACK RECONSTRUCTION: AN ESSAY TOWARD A HISTORY OF THE PART WHICH BLACK FOLK PLAYED IN THE ATTEMPT TO RECONSTRUCT DEMOCRACY IN AMERICA, 1860–1880 (1st ed. 1935); MICHAEL J. KLARMAN, FROM JIM CROW TO CIVIL RIGHTS: THE SUPREME COURT AND THE STRUGGLE FOR RACIAL EQUALITY (2006).

32. ROBIN D. G. KELLEY, HAMMER AND HOE: ALABAMA COMMUNISTS DURING THE GREAT DEPRESSION, (25th anniv. ed., 2015).

33. Bailey v. Alabama, 219 U.S. 219, 231 (1911).

This denial provides what may be the most important pedagogical opportunity of the case. That is the occasion to engage directly with an assertion—from the Court itself—of a divide between legal analysis and racial analysis that contributes to so much unequally distributed alienation in the 1L experience. In advance of this session, I charge students with scrutinizing the Court's claim to colorblind reasoning and with searching for evidence *internal to the opinion itself* that the Court doth protest too much.

That evidence can be found late in the opinion, where the Court explains that Alabama's "false pretenses" statute operates as "[a]n instrument of compulsion peculiarly effective as against the poor and the ignorant, its most likely victims."[34] Although still not acknowledging race explicitly, the Court finds it necessary to embed its heretofore rather abstract analysis of compulsion in the practical constraints of the context that gives life to the case, one embedded in the particularities of the Jim Crow South, as the Court and any reader well knew.

To help guide students to this insight, I ask them why someone like Bailey would have signed such a disadvantageous and dangerous contract in order to obtain an advance on wages. They know enough about the period to get the gist, and then I ask them to find the Court's textual gesture in this direction, which someone usually can do. This exercise does triple duty: an exercise in close reading, in pushing back against a court's own account of its reasoning, and, most importantly, in recognizing and undermining the trope of colorblind legal reasoning.

Part of the richness of this exercise lies in the tension between the Court's invocations of poverty and of ignorance. The former shores up the opinion's primary emphasis on legally constructed inequality of bargaining power, while the attribution of ignorance does just the opposite. The whole point of the Court's coercion analysis had been to present the worker as having lacked a meaningful choice, such that a rational, well-informed person would have been backed into a corner. And yet here, the suggestion becomes that a better informed, smarter chooser might have escaped the dilemma. Rather than serving as a bulwark against exploitative abuse of power by the white-dominated legislature, criminal legal system, and landowning class, the Court engages in a rescue fantasy directed at Black people it deems pathetic.

In this fashion, *Bailey* also illustrates how even results that reach toward justice may still reinforce a broader sleight of hand, one by which contracts purports merely to ratify the smooth operation of a pre-legal sphere of market exchange among private parties. As Robert Gordon has written, where contract doctrine does internalize explicit concern for power and inequality, it often shunts them off into exceptional defenses articulated so as to reinforce the rule.[35] This also occurs, for instance, in the law of contracts of adhesion.

Today, analysis of contracts of adhesion largely has been corralled into the defense of unconscionability. That doctrinal location marks unconscionability as operating

---

34. *Id.* at 244–45.
35. Robert W. Gordon, *Unfreezing Legal Reality: Critical Approaches to Law*, 15 Fla. St. U. L. Rev. 195 (1987).

outside "normal" contract doctrine. (Justice Alito did something similar in a bizarre opinion[36] that treated the common-law doctrine of good faith as some kind of external regulatory intrusion into pure common-law contract law, and thus subject to pre-emption, unlike the latter.)

But another way to view adhesive contracts is through the lens of ordinary contract interpretation. There, the general objective test makes one party, especially the drafter, responsible for the meaning reasonably attached to the agreement by the other party. As the Restatement itself provides in section 211,[37] this principle applies to circumstances in which one reasonably expects the other party not to read and understand a text. And those circumstances might include conditions of power imbalance (among other things) that make it seem futile to read the fine print with an eye toward rene-gotiating or seeking a better deal elsewhere. In such circumstances, the drafting party ought reasonably to treat the other party as attaching its reasonable expectations, not a parsing of fine print, to the agreement. Yet such considerations typically are shunted off into "procedural unconscionability."

What, then, are the contents of "reasonable expectations"? The gist of "substantive unconscionability" is that consumers do not reasonably expect harsh and exploitative terms. And yet, internal to objective analysis, one might respond that, no, in a society like ours, it should be no surprise that the powerful exploit and abuse the powerless. The powerless ought to know and expect that when they click "I agree." That would be a refreshingly candid, if morally embarrassing, explanation for binding signatories to adhesive contracts, more so than the fictional, fetishizing claim—contrary to objective analysis—that the signatory agreed to the specific meanings of words that no one expected them to read.

If nothing else, such an analysis would direct our attention to the pervasiveness of inequality, and its pervasive legal relevance. Contract law may well be ill-equipped to remedy that inequality, but neither the doctrine nor our teaching of it ought to obscure and legitimize it. In my experience, women, students of color, those from working-class backgrounds, and others who often find law school especially unwelcoming and alienating frequently express that centering such questions in the classroom helps to affirm their belonging in it and to multiply avenues for academic engagement, including by bringing legally relevant experience to bear. In this fashion, critical analytic substance can function as one mode of inclusive pedagogy.

---

36. Seana Valentine Shiffrin, *Common and Constitutional Law: A Democratic Legal Perspective*, in 37 The Tanner Lectures on Human Values (Mark Matheson ed., 2018) (discussing Northwest, Inc. v. Ginsberg, 572 U.S. 273 (2014)).

37. Restatement (Second) of Contracts § 211 (Am. L. Inst. 1981).

Teaching Contracts to Promote Inclusivity

Kerri L. Stone[*]

Many privileges are attendant to teaching first semester 1Ls, and contracts professors at my school have this teaching opportunity. Foremost among the derived privileges are drawing focus to issues of race, sex, and other protected classes that students previously may never have had the occasion to do in an academic setting. This is best done, of course, by addressing these issues not as "add-ons" or "special topics," but rather as they are—organic, integral aspects of the cases that we study, no matter when or how the cases were decided. This essay will discuss just some of the many and varied themes that speak to sex and gender inequality that naturally arise in the course of a first year contracts course as the class reviews cases, learns and applies legal principles and concepts, and engages in policy and other discussions. I urge that these and other themes, and all of the dimensionality that they bring to a mastery of the law and the cases surveyed, be aerated and permitted, usually in the course of a question-guided discussion, to seamlessly insinuate themselves into students' understanding of the law and its evolution.

A really good contracts class approaches teaching on three levels. At one level, students must learn the Black Letter law that their future practice, and, more immediately, the bar exam will call upon them to know. A thorough survey of case law, statutory law, and restatements of law will go a long way toward imparting and solidifying knowledge and facility. At a second level, students should be permitted to go "underneath" the law that they learn and at least get a "grassroots" glimpse of issues like discovery, settlement, and other facets of practicing law that require its understanding, but are less visible to the readers of a case. Finally, classes should go "above" the Black Letter law to discuss issues of policy, jurisprudential trends and analyses, and theory that, sometimes invisibly, shape and impel the law forward.

A first year contracts class is tasked with serving as a sampler of sorts, whether it comes to the array of bar-covered legal principles and concepts, or the range of socio-

---

[*] Kerri Lynn Stone, Professor of Law, Florida International University College of Law. J.D., New York University School of Law; B.A., Columbia College, Columbia University. I would also like to thank my research assistants, Devon Hoffman and Yina Cabrera, for all of their able assistance, as well as Josh, Dylan, and Marlee for all of their support.

political issues to which students of the law ought to be exposed. But it is not that simple. Shallow coverage of concepts will not produce students with the facility and agility that a school or a state bar would want them to have with the law. They need to be able to discern the presence of a live issue and perform applications of rules in a host of contexts and against a variety of factual backdrops. Similarly, exposure to issues of racial or gender diversity and equality, while essential for students, must not be fleeting or hollow. The breadth and depth of exposure that students get to these issues must be capacious enough to pique students' interest while giving them ample understanding and insight—even over the course of a single semester. This optimization is tricky, as students are simultaneously learning to brief cases, anticipate the types of questions and exercises they may be called upon to do in class, and think critically. However, it is important because the sex, racial, and other diversity of the people who are affected by the law, those who interpret the law, and those who frame and argue the law, is inextricable from the resultant doctrine.[1]

The themes discussed below are far from an exhaustive list of those which may emerge in a thoughtfully-planned contracts course. Each theme is discussed with reference to some case law that my course encounters, but these themes are pervasive throughout the jurisprudence and subject matter of the course and many cases will prove illustrative. The themes are: sex and agency; intersectionality; and historical sex inequality and contextualizing present inequality.

Sex and Agency

The question of agency as it pertains to women and other underrepresented groups is invoked frequently through the cases in casebook chapters that deal with policing contracts, and with unconscionability, specifically.[2] On one hand, the law should operate to alleviate unfairness, like the overbearing of one's will through heightened coercion coupled with undue susceptibility. On the other hand, is there not something paternalistic about the judicial "rescue" of someone from her own decisions and premised on her identity? Professors should be transparent about their wariness that they might portray outsiders as "perpetual helpless victims denied of all agency who are not quite smart enough to protect themselves."

The newest edition of the contracts book that I am lucky enough to use, *Contracts: Making and Doing Deals*, by Epstein, Markell, and Ponoroff, uses a case that addresses the legality and parameters of a contract for surrogate motherhood to introduce the book[3]—and so I use it to introduce and lay the framework for the course. The case

---

1. *See generally* Lenora Ledwon, *Storytelling and Contracts: (Casebook Review Essay), Contracting Law, 2d ed. By Amy Hilsman Kastely, Deborah Waire Post, and Sharon Kang Hom. Durham, N.C.: Carolina Academic Press, 2000,* 13 Yale J.L. & Feminism 117, 121 (2001).

2. *See* Williams v. Walker-Thomas Furniture Co., 198 A.2d 914 (D.C. 1964).

3. David G. Epstein, Bruce A. Markell & Lawrence Ponoroff, Cases and Materials on Contracts: Making and Doing Deals 2 (5th ed. 2018).

is rich with topics and facets that set the stage for a beginning law student: an issue of first impression; the question of the enforceability and possible policing of a contract; the issue of technology engendering the ripening and need for the resolution of ethical questions; and the need to marshal persuasive precedent and public policy concerns to synthesize a proper rule with ample contours. And yet, at its heart, is an issue that compels students to think about the role of sex equality and the agency of women through the lens of the law.

The facts of this case are relatively straightforward. A woman executed a surrogacy agreement whereby she agreed to undergo artificial insemination with the sperm of a man who was part of a couple who wanted children and to carry the child until its birth, at which point, the father would possess "the full legal parental rights of a father," and she would allow the father "to take the child home from the hospital to live with [him] and his wife."[4] The agreement provided that the surrogate would not permanently relinquish her parental rights, and it recited that no monies were paid to the plaintiff pertaining to the adoption of the child or the termination of parental rights.[5] It did, however, say that if she ever sought to have these rights enforced in court and to obtain custody or visitation rights, her rights under the agreement would be forfeited, and she would have to repay the father all of the fees and expenses he had paid her under the contract.[6]

The surrogate changed her mind while still pregnant and returned the last payment that had been made to her, at which point the father sought a declaration of his rights under the agreement, placing its enforceability at issue before the court.[7] This case becomes the perfect vehicle to introduce students to the layers of arguments that can stack up in any contracts case. In the first place, the enforceability of surrogacy agreements in Massachusetts, where the case was brought, is an issue of first impression.[8] This necessitates recognizing that the threshold issue in this case will be the theoretical viability of any such contract. And it is in the course of this discussion that students will invariably touch upon issues of sexual agency, paternalism in the regulation of reproduction, and reproductive rights.

Should women who want to enter into surrogacy agreements be barred from doing so in order to prevent their own exploitation? Would this regulation be paternalistic? Are such agreements inherently coercive? More so than other agreements? Are women viewed through a different lens because of their sex in the regulation and/or policing of these contracts, and is this proper? Ought the socioeconomic status of the parties matter? Haven't women, among other groups, historically been seen as having less agency and denied the ability to contract and own property? As the conversation takes shape, students wind up entering into a policy discussion that introduces them to how the law contours regulation, but also to the ideas that 1) protected class identity

---

4. R.R. v. M.H., 689 N.E.2d 790, 792 (Mass. 1998).
5. *Id.*
6. *Id.*
7. *Id.* at 793.
8. *Id.* at 795.

is an integral consideration to legal analysis and ought not be invisible when public policy informs regulation; 2) historical racial, sex, and other inequality has shaped the legal landscape; and 3) jurisprudence should never evolve in a vacuum divorced from history. Professor Carol Sanger has written of how she starts her contracts class with the famous "Baby M" surrogacy case, and exhorts students to question whether the holding is "good or bad for women," when evaluating policy arguments.[9]

The law of contracts is premised on the notion of volitional agreement to undertakings, but the agency of parties may be questioned as contracts are policed. As students work through the court's analysis in its successive layers—will surrogacy contracts even be viable in this state? If they are, what will their requirements be? Do the facts of this case comport with these requirements?—they begin to understand how much of the substance of the law being debated and contoured centers around consent—and the consent of women, in particular. The notion of there being a "market" for something that only women—and often women who lack traditional wealth and currency—can provide, injects fascinating backdrop against which policy discussions and debates can occur. Students get to see how to broach an issue of first impression, as they trace the court's integration into the analysis of related, but resolved issues, such as the regulation of sperm donation and adoption and the guiding principles that have shaped the law in these areas. This invariably generates a rich discussion about consent to relinquish parental rights, and the significant disparity between the sexes when it comes to this issue.

These considerations all make for a full first day or week of class; it is enough to stoke interest and lay the foundation for fluency when it comes to clear reasoned analysis in judicial decision making. And the case enables students to see how the law may and ought to be seen through critical lenses as it develops.

Intersectionality

As this project shows, diversity and protected class identity is not a layer or an addendum to the law or the way one learns law, but an inextricable, essential consideration of the law and the study of the law. While my class discussions vary somewhat from one year to the next, I make it a point each year to introduce the concept of intersectionality to first year students. Professor Kimberlé Crenshaw, coined the term to explain how the "intersectional identity," of women of color situates them "within discourses that are shaped to respond to one or the other," resulting in their "marginaliz[ation] within both."[10] Her point, she later recounted, was "to illustrate that many of the experiences Black women face are not subsumed within the traditional boundaries of race or gender discrimination as these boundaries are currently un-

---

9. Carol Sanger, *(Baby) M Is for the Many Things: Why I Start with Baby M*, 44 St. Louis U. L.J. 1443, 1464 (2000).

10. Kimberlé Crenshaw, *Mapping the Margins: Intersectionality, Identity Politics, and Violence Against Women of Color*, 43 Stan. L. Rev. 1241, 1244 (1991).

derstood, and that the intersection of racism and sexism factors into Black women's lives in ways that cannot be captured wholly by looking at the race or gender dimensions of those experiences separately."[11]

There are many cases that bring to the forefront issues of protected class identity and intersectionality, but one widely-read case that does so in many casebooks, including the one I use, is *Williams v. Walker-Thomas Furniture Co.*[12] *Williams* is often presented to illustrate the policing of a contract for unconscionability, with both its trial and appellate-level decisions presented.[13] This case presents a request for the court to police an agreement formed by a rent-to-own company with questionable, predatory sales and pricing practices, by a Ms. Williams, described by the court in its opening lines as "a person of limited education separated from her husband," who "is maintaining herself and her seven children by means of public assistance."[14]

Though the Court of Appeals determines that "when a party of little bargaining power, and hence little real choice, signs a commercially unreasonable contract with little or no knowledge of its terms, it is hardly likely that his consent, or even an objective manifestation of his consent, was ever given to all the terms," it is what is not explicit in the opinions that is perhaps most ripe for discussion.[15] As Professor Amy H. Kastely recites, "By failing to include further detail ... [the]opinion allows—even invites—the reader to use raced tropes linking poverty, lack of education, single parenthood, and lack of capacity with black women and to disregard the connection between white racism and exploitative pricing and collection practices."[16] She continues:

> If the reader does not translate the text to mean that Williams is black, living in highly segregated, racially exploitative Washington, D.C., then the grounds for finding unconscionability are vague and so broad as to reach most contracts, or at least most involving a printed form. To conclude that Williams is black, however, and that her life is constrained by racially determined barriers and burdens, the reader must accept and think within these raced tropes. Having taken this step, the reader is left with the vague impression that the unconscionability doctrine operates to relieve those who are socially and economically disadvantaged; but, at the same time, Judge Wright's opinion invites the reader to anticipate lack of understanding, education, and sophistication as significant factors. In this way, the opinion leads readers to see Williams and other members of subordinated groups as defective and to ignore the fact of racism and other systems of social oppression.[17]

---

11. *Id.*

12. *See* Williams v. Walker-Thomas Furniture Co., 198 A.2d 914 (D.C. 1964); Williams v. Walker-Thomas Furniture Co., 350 F.2d 445 (D.C. Cir. 1965).

13. *Williams*, 198 A.2d at 915; *Williams*, 350 F.2d at 448–49.

14. *Williams*, 198 A.2d at 915.

15. *Williams*, 350 F.2d at 449.

16. Amy H. Kastely, *Out of the Whiteness: On Raced Codes and White Race Consciousness in Some Tort, Criminal, and Contract Law*, 63 U. Cin. L. Rev. 269, 306 (1994).

17. *Id.*

Viewed through this lens, the opinion and the considerations surrounding it take on a new dimension. A productive discussion may then be had about not only the doctrine of unconscionability as a policing mechanism, but about systemic racism and the role of codes in upholding it; the ability of the courts to uphold or combat subordination; and the dynamic generated intersectionality in this and other cases, among other worthwhile topics. Indeed, it is useful to explore with students the many assumptions that reading the opinion may engender. There is, of course, the assumption that Ms. Williams is Black. There is also, as Professor Muriel Morisey Spence observes, the assumption that as a woman with seven children and on public assistance, Ms. Williams ought not be buying a stereo to begin with; as she notes, this assumption is truly disturbing, because, among other things, readers tend to disregard the fact that she had been paying 10% of her income in consistent installments over the course of five years.[18] Students must confront prejudicial and paternalistic assumptions. Is it really Ms. Williams's lack of formal education that students ought believe led to a misunderstanding of the financing structure at bar? Or shouldn't students understand, instead, that the predatory and deceptive nature of the structure itself, as well as the way in which it advanced, is what we should be concerned by?

Professor Angela Mae Kupenda suggests another exercise that I find very useful surrounding this material; she contrasts this case, which she identifies as containing "unconscionable behavior that affects less than all of us," with another that she describes as containing "unconscionability that affects the masses."[19] In this way, she is able to posit to students that might be better able to relate to the plaintiff in the latter case "because we could see ourselves in her position, but many of us could not see ourselves in the position of the plaintiff in *Williams*."[20]

Historical Sex Inequality and Contextualizing Present Sex Inequality

A final theme for consideration when teaching contracts is that of historical and present inequality of women and other minorities. Here, too, several popular cases stand out as great catalysts for a discussion that provides historical context and vital policy considerations. First year law students soon learn that American common law is largely derived from English law. However, they may not be aware of the fact that until 1839 and the advent of states' first enactments of the Married Women's Property Acts, the American colonies, and later the United States, lived under coverture, an English common law system that deprived women of their ability to earn money,

---

18. Muriel Morisey Spence, *Teaching* Williams v. Walker-Thomas Furniture Co., 3 Temp. Pol. & Civ. Rts. L. Rev. 89, 95–96 (1994).

19. Angela Mae Kupenda, *Making Traditional Courses More Inclusive: Confessions of an African American Female Professor Who Attempted to Crash All the Barriers at Once*, 31 U.S.F. L. Rev. 975, 987–88 (1997).

20. *Id.* at 988.

own property, and undertake contractual obligations.[21] These rights of a woman were subsumed under those of her father or husband. And, of course, the Property Acts failed to ameliorate things for so many women of color; slavery and the so-called "Black Codes," among other abominable laws and institutions, would deprive African Americans and others of basic human rights for decades more.[22]

Moreover, impediments on women's abilities to contract persist today, whether they manifest in the form of predatory sales techniques used on women or as wage inequality. Structural discrimination pervades modern life, with rules framed as if to apply evenly to all, even as situational differences between the sexes operate to systemically disadvantage women. As one scholar has noted, "Because of the dual burden of raising children as well as maintaining a job, few women in the business world achieve the same success as men. Yet, contract casebooks ignore women's situation. Commercial actors are childless, nonpregnant persons unhampered by family responsibilities."[23]

Numerous cases can be used as vehicles to remind and educate students about historical sex inequality in the law and society. For example, many casebooks conveniently place the classic cases of *Kirksey v. Kirksey* and *Hamer v. Sidway* alongside one another. These are both familial cases, but in the former, the reliance of a widow on her brother-in-law's offer to relocate herself and her family to his property so that they could have a place to stay is deemed misplaced—or, at least, insufficient to render the promise enforceable.[24] As one article devoted to this case puts it: "There is only one woman in this legal tale, and everywhere she turns she is at the mercy of the male-dominated culture and legal system. It may be coincidence that the loser of the case was a woman, or not, but either way, Angelico's life is bound up in a patriarchal worldview."[25] In the latter case, a promise made by a now-deceased uncle to his nephew is enforced.[26] When my class covers these cases, I try to raise Professor Debora L. Threedy's hypothesis, conveniently quoted in our casebook, that the respective sexes of the parties may have influenced the cases' results: "Bargaining, like beauty, is in the eye of the beholder and judges may be less likely to perceive contract bargaining between the sexes in a family context."[27]

Professor Threedy also raises the issue of how sex discrimination feeds into courts' analyses of promissory estoppel, noting that women have historically been more likely to demonstrate that they relied to their detriment when they have performed acts that

---

21. *See generally* Richard H. Chused, *Married Women 's Property Law: 1800–1850*, 71 Geo. L. J. 1359 (1983).

22. *See Black Code*, Encyclopaedia Britannica, https://www.britannica.com/topic/black-code (last visited Aug. 20, 2020).

23. Beverly Horsburgh, *Decent and Indecent Proposals in the Law: Reflections on Opening the Contracts Discourse to Include Outsiders*, 1 Wm. & Mary J. Women & L. 57, 66 (1994).

24. Kirksey v. Kirksey, 8 Ala. 131 (1845).

25. William R. Casto & Val D. Ricks, *"Dear Sister Antillico …" The Story of Kirkesy v. Kirksey*, 94 Geo. L.J. 321, 326 n.13 (2006).

26. Hamer v. Sidway, 27 N.E. 256 (N.Y. 1891).

27. Debora L. Threedy, *Feminists & Contract Doctrine*, 32 Ind. L. Rev. 1247, 1252 (1999).

are not domestic in nature, and more likely to have had claims of detrimental reliance rejected when they performed acts considered to be "women's work," and therefore expected of them anyway.[28] Along these lines, many classes, including mine, read a case in which a court debates the viability of "palimony." Palimony refers to monies paid, akin to alimony, after the dissolution of a relationship in which a couple never formally married, but held themselves out as such and/or functioned as such. These cases are useful vehicles for debating whether form or substance ought to prevail when a court is trying to effectuate the will of the parties. In the context of these discussions, it is enlightening and useful to raise (if a student does not) the notion that many in society have historically believed that it was a woman's duty, upon becoming a "wife," to eschew making her own living and tend to the household so that her spouse could earn money for the household.[29] Indeed, Professor Marjorie Maguire Shultz recounted that a female student observed that the law of contracts sees "everything that women do and value as donative or illusory, as being a moral obligation or a pre-existing legal duty, or as being in some other way noncognizable and unenforceable."[30]

Conclusion

There are innumerable cases that could have been included here as rich vehicles for sparking realizations and discussions relating to women and the law of contracts. At the end of the day, just getting students to consciously think about women as parties and the lens through which they are seen is a good springboard. In the popular case of *Wood v. Lucy, Lady Duff-Gordon*, none other than Justice Cardozo, himself, implied a duty in order to construct reciprocal obligations for and thus render enforceable an agreement between a well known socialite (and Titanic survivor) and the man upon whom she had conferred the exclusive right to market fashions bearing her endorsement, after she reneged on it.[31] As one scholar remarked upon Cardozo's characterization of the defendant as one who "styles herself a creator of fashions," "it could easily be read as implying that she alone had the belief, or as a reference to days when the 'little women' were responsible for house and home and nothing further. Such a characterization ... grossly misrepresents the magnitude of her accomplishments as a woman operating a business at the time."[32]

In another often-taught case from 1968, *Vokes v. Arthur Murray, Inc.*, a female dance student took courses from Arthur Murray, later alleging undue influence and

---

28. *Id.*

29. *See* Marjorie Maguire Shultz, *The Gendered Curriculum: Of Contracts and Careers*, 77 Iowa L. Rev. 55, 59 (1991); *see generally* Orit Gan, *Anti-Stereotyping Theory and Contract Law*, 42 Harv. J. L. & Gender 83 (2019).

30. Marjorie Maguire Shultz, *The Gendered Curriculum: Of Contracts and Careers*, 77 Iowa L. Rev. 55, 64 (1991).

31. Wood v. Lucy, Lady Duff-Gordon, 118 N.E. 214, 214–15 (N.Y. 1917).

32. Celia R. Taylor, *Teaching Ethics in Context:* Wood v. Lucy, Lady Duff-Gordon *in the First Year Curriculum*, 28 Pace L. Rev. 249, 261–62 (2008).

misrepresentation for being induced through flattery and encouragement to spend in excess of $31,000.[33] An appellate court held that her case could proceed because the parties were not dealing at arms' length, and that she did not have an ample chance to seek outside aid in assessing the veracity of the statements made to her that she was a beautiful dancer with much promise.[34] Again, it is useful to have students consider the lens through which the plaintiff was seen as a woman seeking to be excused from her choices. Professor Miriam A. Cherry asks readers to contemplate the dynamics of sex and social class, asking what "if it had been a wealthy businessman who had been sold thousands of hours of lessons, would the court have been so willing to step in and protect him from his own bargain?"[35]

These are but a few themes that will organically work themselves into a thoughtful teaching of this first year course. Diversity and inclusivity are not peripheral or satellite topics when teaching legal doctrine; they are woven into its very fabric.[36]

---

33. 212 So.2d 906, 907 (Fla. Dist. Ct. App. 1968).

34. *Id.* at 909.

35. Miriam A. Cherry, *Exploring (Social) Class in the Classroom: The Case of* Lucy, Lady-Duff-Gordon, 28 Pace L. Rev. 235, 242 (2008).

36. Kerri Lynn Stone, *Teaching Gender As A Core Value in the First-Year Contracts Class*, 36 Okla. City U. L. Rev. 537, 539–43 (2011).

Select Annotated Bibliography on Teaching Diversity in Contracts

Alisha Hennen* & Jessica Almeida**

This bibliography is a selection of resources for teaching diversity in the contracts classroom. The curated list includes books, articles, and videos that discuss issues of race, gender, class, and sexual orientation in contracts law. Many of the resources encourage educators to include discussions of diversity in the classroom; some are a "how to" for teaching diversity through discussion and activities, and others can be used as supplemental readings for students.

Books

Baird, Douglas G., and Lea S. VanderVelde. "The Gendered Origins of the Lumley Doctrine: Binding Men's Consciences and Women's Fidelity." In *Contracts Stories*, 235–71. New York: Foundation Press, 2007.

The book chapter discusses how the case of *Lumley v. Wagner*[1] became a catalyst for a shift in legal doctrine based on "unarticulated gender biases." (269) Author Lea VanderVelde takes an in-depth look at employment cases in the nineteenth century that involved contracts between actresses and theatre managers. Starting with *Lumley* and *Ford v. Jermon*[2] to *Daly v. Smith*[3] and *Duff v. Russell*,[4] her analysis finds that "not only did women performers lose more cases than men did, women performers were sued more often than men were." (264) She contributes this to the perception of gender roles in nineteenth century culture and gender discrimination within the court system. VanderVelde argues that what makes the history of *Lumley* and subsequent rulings on women performers so important is they

---

* Research & Instructional Librarian, Mitchell Hamline School of Law.

** Associate Librarian, University of Massachusetts School of Law.

1. (1852) 42 Eng. Rep. 687; 1 De G. M. & G. 604.
2. 6 Phila. 6 (Dist. Ct. 1865).
3. 49 How. Pr. 150 (N.Y. Sup. Ct. 1874).
4. 14 N.Y.S. 134 (N.Y. Sup. Ct. 1891), *aff'd* 31 N.E. 622 (N.Y. 1892).

"have influenced the selection of legal rules for the treatment of all other employees under similarly restrictive contracts, even for free working men." (269)

Ertman, Martha M. *Love's Promises: How Formal & Informal Contracts Shape All Kinds of Families*. Boston: Beacon Press, 2016.

> Written by Martha Ertman, Professor of Law at University of Maryland's Carey School of Law, *Love's Promises* is part memoir and part law treatise. The book examines how contracts and deals help both common or what the author calls "Plan A" families, children raised by their straight, married, genetic parents, and uncommon or "Plan B" families, which include a variety of families "from repro tech and adoption to cohabitation." (xiv) The first part of the book focuses on parenthood with stories from the author's life, including chapters on reproductive technology and open adoption contracts. The second part of the book focuses on adult partnership-relationships, also with stories from the author's life, and talks specifically about cohabitation and marriage. The later chapters examine property prenups, pair-bond exchanges, and reconciliation agreements.

Mulcahy, Linda, and Sally Wheeler, eds. *Feminist Perspectives on Contract Law*. Portland, OR: Glass House Press, 2005.

> This book looks at contract law through a feminist lens and argues that "feminist analysis of contract law allows us to identify what dominant discourse has left unsaid about the nature of contractual relationships, and to question the credibility of dominant paradigms."(1) This edited volume has chapters on a feminist look at the history of shopping, equality in heterosexual relationships, gendered conception of bilateral consent, undue influence on restitution, contracts in cyberspace, and binding prenuptial agreements. The chapters can be used as supplemental readings to create discussion about gender roles in contracts.

Post, Deborah Waire, and Deborah Zalesne. "Vulnerability in Contracting: Teaching First-Year Law Students About Inequality and Its Consequences." In *Vulnerable Populations and Transformative Law Teaching: A Critical Reader*, edited by the Society of American Law Teachers and Golden Gate State University, 89–110. Durham, N.C.: Carolina Academic Press, 2011.

> This book chapter lays out the teaching technique Post and Zalesne have developed to help first year students learn the meaning of contract law and its cultural, structural, and social significance. They believe that law students should be taught three key things: 1) that the law creates, supports, and reinforces inequality; 2) that the law can and occasionally does make up for the social and economic differences in our current social system; and 3) that social change can happen when the law recognizes the agency of individuals who are part of these vulnerable populations. Throughout the chapter, Post and Zalesne provide exercises intended to help prompt meaningful classroom discussions about the law and issues of race, gender, disability, class, and sexual orientation, as well as provide practical guidance and specific examples for professors to use while teaching various themes and cases.

Articles

Cherry, Miriam A. "Exploring (Social) Class in the Classroom: The Case of Lucy, Lady Duff-Gordon." *Pace Law Review* 28, no. 2 (2008): 235–47.

In *Exploring (Social) Class in the Classroom,* author Miriam A. Cherry tackles social class stereotyping by using specific cases in the contracts classroom. Cherry gives examples of cases, such as *Wood v. Lucy, Lady Duff-Gordon,*[5] *In re Baby M,*[6] and *Hamer v. Sidway,*[7] that educators can use to promote critical thinking about economic stratification and prompt questioning of inequality and bargaining in contracts. Each case provides interesting facts that professors can use to develop classroom discussion around race, gender, and social class. The author discusses her experiences in leading such discussions and the effect it has on students to open up about their own backgrounds. Cherry ends the article with an examination of a new social class amongst law students. She determines that the support some students receive from a family member or mentor in the legal profession can give them an advantage and that educators need to keep in mind the variety in their student backgrounds.

Florestal, Marjorie. "Is a Burrito a Sandwich? Exploring Race, Class, and Culture in Contracts." *Michigan Journal of Race & Law* 14, no. 1 (2008): 1–59.

In 2006, Marjorie Florestal, an Associate Professor of Law at University of the Pacific McGeorge School of Law, was looking for a fact pattern that would be of interest to first year law students in her contracts class. The question "Is a Burrito a Sandwich?" formed the basis for an interesting hypothetical for the class to discuss. The hypothetical was based on the "Burrito Brouhaha," a contractual dispute at the heart of *White City Shopping Ctr. v. PR Rest.,*[8] in which the court ruled that the definition of a sandwich does not include burritos. In this article, Florestal examines the history of class, race, and culture in contract law and scrutinizes the *White City* ruling to "unveil the hidden and unconscious manifestations of race, class, and culture that help explain the outcome." (8)

Harrison, Jeffrey L. "Teaching Contracts from A Socioeconomic Perspective." *Saint Louis University Law Journal* 44, no. 4 (2000): 1233–1246.

This article, written as part of a symposium issue on teaching contract law, discusses how Harrison incorporates themes of socioeconomics into his contracts classes. Harrison defines socioeconomics and dives into three themes he uses in class: 1) the difference between the objective and subjective, or what he calls the "everyone is average" assumption; 2) how one's sense of entitlement and one's

---

5. 118 N.E. 214 (N.Y. 1917).
6. 537 A.2d 1227 (N.J. 1988).
7. 27 N.E. 256 (N.Y. 1891).
8. 21 Mass. L. Rptr. 565 (Sup. Ct. Mass. 2006).

sense of justice are developed and how it can apply to the goals of contract law; and 3) examining opinions as pieces of advocacy. (1236–37) One of the most helpful additions to this article is the section on materials that Harrison uses in his class that may differ from traditional resources, including: results from experiments dealing with fairness and entitlement; the stages of moral development; Ian Ayres's car buying experiments; and Russell Weintraub's study on actual business practices versus formal rules of contracts.

Miles, Veryl Victoria. "Raising Issues of Property, Wealth and Inequality in the Law School: Contracts & Commercial Law School Courses." *Indiana Law Review* 34, no. 4 (2001): 1365–1375.

In this article, Miles discusses how to bring the "rights of the poor and under-represented" into law school classroom discussions. The author notes how many law students start their law school careers believing that the law is always neutral and emphasizes these discussions can help students learn how to effectively represent future diverse clients by considering their different circumstances and needs. Miles highlights how to introduce topics of wealth and inequality into a law school course, examples of discussion points on these topics, and how conversations with clinical professors can incorporate real-life examples into classroom discussions. Miles notes that conversations with clinical professors may be of particular interest to students because they can provide real-life case observations that are usually very topical. While many of the examples in this article seem to be geared toward upper-level contracts course topics, the general ideas could readily be incorporated into first year course discussions.

Morant, Blake D. "The Relevance of Race and Disparity in Discussions of Contract Law." *New England Law Review* 31, no. 3 (1997): 889–939.

In this 1997 article, Morant discusses his use of "avoidance strategy" early in his career, teaching contracts in an objective manner while avoiding discussions of race, gender, and discrimination. After years of teaching Supreme Court cases such as *City of Richmond v. J.A. Croson Co.*,[9] he began to believe that it was "disingenuous" to ignore these issues. (893–894) Instead, he began exploring how issues of race, gender, and class can make an impact when analyzing cases and rules. The author also examines the motivations of contractual parties and the possible issues of disparity that arise. The author also discusses the topic of unconscionability which can bring issues of race and class into the discussion. Overall, Morant points out that teachers and scholars have an obligation to discuss these issues if applicable to the contractual rules.

Sanger, Carol. "(Baby) M Is For the Many Things: Why I Start with Baby M." *Saint Louis University Law Journal* 44, no. 4 (2000): 1443–64.

---

9. 488 U.S. 469 (1989).

In this article, author Carol Sanger explains the "pedagogical advantages" of using *In the Matter of Baby M*[10] as the first case discussed in her first year contracts class. (1451) Sanger gives a detailed breakdown of the court's decision, its use in class discussion, and how it pushes students to read critically. A section of the article explains how class discussion can sometimes lead to questions about the role of income disparity and bargaining inequalities. When scrutinizing feminism and jurisprudence, Sanger encourages educators to use *Baby M* to "introduce issues concerning the relevance of sex because the court itself does it first." (1459)

Shultz, Marjorie Maguire. "The Gendered Curriculum: Of Contracts and Careers." *Iowa Law Review* 77, no. 1 (1991): 55–71.

In this article, Marjorie Shultz examines gender bias in both the formal and informal aspects of law school curriculum. Written in 1991, the article examines how the line between contract and family law has been divided by stereotypical gender traits and "gendered spheres of influence." (56) Shultz determines that contract law changes once the idea of family is introduced. Courts are not interested in dealing with matters in the home, making family life "lawless" which affects women more than men. (59) In turn, the family sphere which is associated with women is less important than the commerce world more closely associated with men. Shultz then transitions into a discussion of career placement where the gendered roles of the formal curriculum bleed into the informal curriculum. This permeates the job searches of female law students, who apply for and accept more public service jobs, versus male students who are finding success in big law. The author reminds the reader that being aware of the gender roles in both the formal and informal curriculum is the first step to eliminating sexist content in the formal curriculum and restructure the informal messages we send to students.

Spence, Muriel Morisey. "Teaching Williams v. Walker-Thomas Furniture Co." *Temple Political & Civil Rights Law Review* 3 (1994): 89–105.

Spence dissects how to teach *Williams* and the unconscionability doctrine as it relates to race, gender, and class. While encouraging educators to include the experiences of culturally diverse people, the author specifically examines the facts, assumptions, and stereotypes of the *Williams* case. She also notes the pedagogical challenges of teaching *Williams* and warns that if taught incorrectly, "we may perpetuate assumptions and stereotypes about the people whose perspectives we seek to incorporate." (89) The appendix includes discussion points that can be used in the classroom.

Stone, Kerri Lynn. "Teaching Gender as a Core Value in the First-Year Contracts Class." *Oklahoma City University Law Review* 36, no. 2 (2011): 537–543.

---

10. 537 A.2d 1227 (N.J. 1988).

This article, part of a symposium issue, discusses the value of incorporating topics of gender and identity into first year contracts courses. Stone describes how she ties in gender to various topics throughout her course and encourages beginning these discussions at the start of the semester. Stone also provides examples of cases that can help foster discussion on various themes, including: the trial and appellate decisions in *Williams v. Walker-Thomas Furniture Co.*[11] for issues relating to gender and consent; *Kirksey v. Kirksey*[12] and *Hamer v. Sidway*[13] to show how gender can affect bargaining and reliance principles; and *Wood v. Lucy, Lady Duff-Gordon*[14] to see how historically courts have depicted women. This piece offers some good advice for those looking to start including topics of gender and identity into their contracts course.

Testy, Kellye Y. "Whose Deal Is It? Teaching about Structural Inequality by Teaching Contracts Transactionally." *University of Toledo Law Review* 34, no. 4 (2003): 699–704.

This essay is an edited version of a talk Testy gave at the January 2003 AALS Annual Meeting. In the essay, Testy encourages law professors to teach contracts using a simple transactional approach by including exercises and simulations into classwork. By using a transactional teaching method, educators can open the door to daily inequalities that are scrubbed from traditional contract courses. Through the transaction, students see that "identities matter in terms of bargaining power" preparing them for clients from differing socio-economic backgrounds. (700) Testy also gives examples of how to incorporate inequality issues into transactional learning, from supplementing casebook readings, to having students interview clients and draft contracts with complex issues based on identity.

Zalesne, Deborah. "Racial Inequality in Contracting: Teaching Race as a Core Value." *Columbia Journal of Race and Law* 3, no. 1 (2013): 23–47.

In this article, Zalesne focuses on how professors can introduce and teach concepts of race in first year contracts courses. One of the overall goals for teaching is to empower students to take narrow legal problems and apply broader social and political conditions to uncover the "concealed racial dimensions in contract law." (24) After a brief introduction to critical race theory, Zalesne dives into discussions on the effect of race on various issues in contract law. Some of these discussions include racial discrimination in the marketplace; issues of assent and the use of the objective test; alternative reproductive technology contracts; and specific performance and negative injunctions. Zalesne gives detailed examples of case law and thoroughly describes how each discussion point can address issues of race in American contract law. Zalesne also notes how the strategies used in the article can be applied to broader discussions about identity.

---

11. 198 A.2d 914 (D.C. 1964); 350 F.2d 445 (D.C. Cir. 1965).
12. 8 Ala. 131 (1845).
13. 27 N.E. 256 (N.Y. 1891).
14. 118 N.E. 214 (N.Y. 1917).

Videos

Harvard Law School, "Diversity and Social Justice in First Year Classes." YouTube. https://www.youtube.com/watch?v=4VLJRBYBzmk.

This talk by Todd Rakoff is part of the Diversity and Social Justice in First Year Classes lecture series at Harvard Law School. The eight-part series aims to combine classroom teaching with lectures that examine how issues of diversity and social justice can be integrated in first year law school classes.[15] In his session, Rakoff focuses on the topic of fair dealing in contract law as a matter of justice. He looks at four justice principles in contract law: that exchanges should be equal, that exchanges should represent honest bets on the future, the justice of dessert, and the justice of not taking advantage. Rakoff details how, as a society, we believe in all four principles, but we believe in some concepts more than others. Throughout his lecture, he uses unnamed case examples to illustrate each of the principles.

Harvard Law School, "Contextualizing Contracts." YouTube. https://www.youtube.com/watch?v=o8mZoWIcya4.

This talk by Oren Bar-Gill was recorded at the Harvard Law School as part of the Diversity and Social Justice in First Year Classes series in 2017. Bar-Gill discusses gender, race, and class in the context of analyzing contracts cases. He examines gender issues in *Parker v. 20th Century Fox*,[16] in which the court opinion did not take gender into consideration. He points to historical doctrine in employment law where negative injunctions were first used against female plaintiffs. He discusses race in the context of *Williams v. Walker-Thomas Furniture Co.*,[17] where once again race is not discussed but has major implications on future cases. Bar-Gill also examines social class and its effect on access to contracting and bargaining power. Lastly, the talk discusses the implications of bias, the effect contracts have on different groups of people, and the variety of legal instruments that address bias and discrimination in contracts.

---

15. *See* Mark Tushnet, *Presenting Issues of Diversity and Social Justice in the 1L Curriculum: A Report on a Lecture Series and Seminar*, in Chapter 1 of this book.

16. 474 P.2d 689 (Cal. 1970).

17. 350 F.2d 445 (D.C. Cir. 1965).

Chapter 4

Criminal Law

A Bronx Tale: Integrating Music, Practical Skills, and Values to Introduce First Year Law Students to Race and the Criminal Law

*Brooks Holland**

Every year since I started full-time law teaching in the fall of 2005, I have taught criminal law to first-semester, first year law students. Teaching new law students in a large doctrinal class is both rewarding and challenging. These rewards and challenges are amplified when the professor incorporates issues of race, gender, sexual orientation, and poverty into a curriculum that is first introducing students to the law and legal methods. This essay shares brief reflections on prioritizing "diversity values" in criminal law,[1] and presents *A Bronx Tale*, a case study exercise I have developed to address ways in which race intersects with criminal law.[2]

---

* Professor of Law and J. Donald and Va Lena Scarpelli Curran Professor of Legal Ethics and Professionalism, Gonzaga University School of Law. The author has practiced criminal law as a public defender in state and federal courts for 26 year, and is a member of the Board of Governors for the Society of American Law Teachers. Xavier Fox, a law student at Gonzaga, provided valuable research assistance. The author also thanks Professor Olympia Duhart for her comments on this essay.

1. I employ this imperfect phrase, "diversity values," both to capture the importance of *values* in legal education, *cf.* Beverly I. Moran, *Disappearing Act: The Lack of Values Training in Legal Education—A Case for Cultural Competency*, 38 S.U. L. Rev. 1 (2010), and to emphasize the unique value of *diversity*. *Cf.* Okianer Christian Dark, *Incorporating Issues of Race, Gender, Class, Sexual Orientation, and Disability into Law School Teaching*, 32 Willamette L. Rev. 541, 542,n. 2 (1996) (coining phrase "diversity issues," despite its imperfection and "political implications").

2. I named this case study exercise "A Bronx Tale" because it draws on a case from the County of Bronx that was decided when I practiced and lived there. *See People v. Douglas*, 680 N.Y.S.2d 145 (Bronx Co. Sup. Ct. 1998). The title also honors the Robert DeNiro movie that presents challenging historical themes about race in this beautiful and complex borough. *See* A Bronx Tale (Tribeca Prod. 1993).

Introduction

Experts have written for years about the need for law schools to incorporate diversity values more effectively in the curriculum.[3] Law schools still have not fulfilled this responsibility,[4] particularly in the first year curriculum.[5] The current widespread attention to anti-racism and anti-subordination values throughout society reinforces both this need and this deficit.[6]

I will not pretend that one case study exercise offers any panacea for this deficit in legal education. On the contrary, I share this case study exercise with a strong sense of humility for my own privileges and limitations as an educator. Yet, I have practiced criminal law for 26 years, almost exclusively as a public defender. This experience of working with thousands of clients, their families, and their communities has allowed me to witness first-hand the lived reality that race, gender, and poverty make a serious difference in how the criminal law is written, enforced, and experienced. If I care about my students learning *this* criminal law, the criminal law of our reality rather than of some preferred neutral construct, I have a duty to expose students to diversity values in the criminal law.[7]

I am not contributing anything new with this claim. Yet, a values aversion can creep quickly into first year law courses, even in a subject such as criminal law with its obvious connection to values. And students do arrive to law school with a tableau of criminal law values already in place. Some of these students are deeply cynical of the criminal law system as unfair and even violent, especially to persons of color. Students arrive to criminal law with *names* on their mind:

Rayshard Brooks

George Floyd

Breonna Taylor

Ahmaud Arbery

Philando Castile

Tamir Rice

---

3. *See generally* Alexi Nunn Freeman & Lindsey Webb, *Positive Disruption: Addressing Race in a Time of Social Change through a Team-Taught, Reflection-Based, Outward-Looking Law School Seminar*, 21 U. Pa. J.L. & Soc. Change 121, 122, 124–28 (2018); Dark, *supra* note 1, at 542–45, 554–56; Frances Lee Ansley, *Race and the Core Curriculum in Legal Education*, 79 Calif. L. Rev. 1512, 1515 (1991).

4. *See* Freeman & Webb, *supra* note 3 at 123 ("[D]espite multiple innovations in the legal curriculum, the decades-long discussion regarding racial inclusion in law schools has led us to the same, largely race-avoidant, place" (internal footnote omitted)).

5. *Cf.* Johanna K.P. Dennis, *Ensuring a Multicultural Educational Experience in Legal Education: Start with the Legal writing Classroom*, 16 Tex. Wesleyan L. Rev. 613, 614 (2010) (commenting that "aside from upper-level course offerings, it is unclear how law schools are achieving that goal"); Moran, *supra* note 1 at 19–20.

6. *See* Freeman & Webb, *supra* note 3 at 124; *see also Law Deans Antiracist Clearinghouse Project*, Ass'n Am. Law Schools, https://www.aals.org/antiracist-clearinghouse/ (last accessed Aug. 17, 2020).

7. *Cf.* Dark, *supra* note 1 at 542, 544–45, 554–56.

Michael Brown

Eric Garner

Trayvon Martin

Michael Stewart

And many more …

Students justifiably treat faculty silence on diversity values as tacit acceptance of the criminal law *status quo*.[8] As one group of law students recently wrote:

The curriculum choices that professors make communicate to future lawyers what knowledge is necessary and valuable in the practice of law. Relegating comprehensive discussions of racism in the law to elective courses indicates that understanding racism in the law is elective. It is not.[9]

At the same time, values discussions in the classroom can be challenging and create vulnerability for both the professor and students.[10] People typically do not have strong personal feelings about how to construct an IRAC or define the elements of a statute. Values, however, can be quite personal, and diversity values can touch student identity deeply.[11] Faculty further cannot always claim the same expertise over values. My training permits me confidently to judge whether a student's statement of a case is accurate, but not so easily whether a student's views on racism or sexism are valid.[12]

Moreover, criminal law itself is a uniquely complex course in the first year curriculum. Unlike the traditional "common law" first year courses, such as torts, contracts, and property, criminal law is heavily statutory. The common law instead plays a complicated role, depending on whether a jurisdiction has codified the common law or employs a common law of statutory interpretation. From this amalgam of statutes and case law, students learn a *lot* of criminal law concepts and rules, including punishment theory, *mens rea*, *actus reus*, substantive crimes, inchoate crimes, and defenses. Students further learn that the truthful answer to most criminal law

---

8. *See* Freeman & Webb, *supra* note 3, at 124 and n. 8 ("Academic silence regarding race does not mean that race is invisible or absent; rather … the void left by this silence contains the presumption that the law is for and about white people or is somehow racially 'neutral'").

9. Tyler Ambrose, Zarinah Mustafa & Sherin Nassar, *Law Schools' Complicity on Racism Must Be Challenged*, The Appeal (June 24, 2020), https://theappeal.org/law-schools-racism/.

10. *Cf.* Freeman & Webb, *supra* note 3, at 122 (observing that "addressing race in the classroom can be a disruptive, even professional hazardous, act"); Dark, *supra* note 1, at 542 (noting that diversity issue discussions "can challenge a professors ability to maintain the focus of the discussion, maintain a supportive and open classroom environment, and, generally, prevent the discussion from degenerating into a brawl").

11. *Cf.* Olympia Duhart, *Education and Pedagogy—On Identity and Instruction*, 48 Cal. W. L. Rev. 453 (2012). These classroom dynamics can impact a faculty member's sense of identity, too. *See* Jeffrey Omari, *Seeing Red: A Professor Coexists with 'MAGA' in the Classroom*, A.B.A. Journal (July 3, 2019), https://www.abajournal.com/voice/article/coexisting-with-maga-in-the-classroom.

12. *Cf.* Dennis, *supra* note 5, at 632 (commenting on experiential expertise of "[l]egal educators of color").

problems is "whatever the jury decides to do." A lot of challenging territory for students to learn, and typically in fewer credit hours than in other first year doctrinal courses.

The challenges of this educational task can make *status quo* pragmatists out of students and professors. The incentives are strong: Treat preexisting law and methods as established, even *neutral*. Teach objective bar examination Xs and Os to sharp IRAC analysis of legal problems. Leave exploration of diversity values to seminar courses or clinics, or to a few discrete conversations about "policy" or "theory." This sterile approach to criminal law, however, deprives students of a full understanding of the law, including how it impacts some people inequitably.

The integration of diversity values does not supplant the core curriculum. Rather, diversity values augment and amplify that curriculum. Bar examination Xs and Os still are important, and I teach them. Policy and theory questions are also important, and I ask them. But discrete policy and theory questions do not typically position diversity values anywhere in a first year law student's IRAC of a legal problem. Students thus can perceive values inquiries as a *separate* and *subjective* discussion that consumes bandwidth from the *objective* world of "law" and legal analysis.[13] As a result, I have thought long and hard about how to de-compartmentalize and synergize "law" and diversity values, so that students can better appreciate the importance of these values to "practical" legal analysis. Or, as Professor Beverly Moran has characterized this pedagogical goal, to educate "in holistic rather than atomistic terms."[14]

A Bronx Tale:
A Case Study Exercise

A Bronx Tale is one case study exercise I have developed for this holistic purpose of integrating doctrine, practical skills, and diversity values. Values exercises, however, are not always easy to deliver top-down. A values icebreaker I thus employ in most of my courses is to open each class with music. Music is all about values, and so many genres offer ample selections that speak to the criminal law. I play thematic music for four to five minutes as students arrive and take their seats. I also invite students to review our textbook table of contents to recommend music for class, and to discuss the music when we begin. In the process, I hope to engage students proactively in class topics, build a sense of community around music, and calm first year classroom anxiety, especially in discussing values.

I want to engage the law-values dichotomy early, so I introduce *A Bronx Tale* on the second day of class. This exercise follows a tutorial on burdens of proof and the

---

13. *See* Moran, *supra* note 1, at 18 (observing that "the modern law school creates an unspoken understanding that in order to develop cognitive skills students must disconnect from their sense of morality, the need to work for justice, and their own observation that gender, race, ethnicity, and class help shape legal rules and legal outcomes").

14. *See id.* at 17.

jury system that leads to the concept of jury nullification.[15] This introduction showcases for new law students that important decision makers affect the outcome of criminal cases other than an omnipotent judge: the lawyers and the jury. *A Bronx Tale* transitions this introduction to a diversity values discussion that informs five course-long learning objectives:

1. Experience with how legislators weigh competing values to enact policy in a criminal statute

2. Competence in expressing a statutory rule

3. Diligence in identifying relevant sources of law

4. Knowledge of lawyer role-differentiation in the adversary system

5. Skill in applying the law to facts and arguing in the alternative

At a meta-level, I also hope this exercise adds a few bricks to students' foundation for appreciating and engaging diversity values in the law.

I typically break this exercise into two parts to sequence the experience for students, each part consuming about half a class session. To conserve in-class time, especially in 50-minute sessions, students can complete some work remotely prior to class. This asynchronous student work can be especially conducive to conducting the rest of this exercise through remote synchronous instruction due to the COVID-19 pandemic or other circumstances.

A Bronx Tale begins with Professor Paul Butler's well-known proposal for race-based jury nullification.[16] In my view, Professor Butler's proposal is so effective for this exercise precisely because it is decidedly not cautious about mixing race and law. On the contrary, to counter the racism and structural white supremacy that are built into in the criminal law system, Professor Butler proposes that juries should nullify certain criminal charges if the defendant is Black. To provide a 360° view of this proposal, I supplement with a few additional materials:

1. An excerpt of a 60 Minutes interview with Professor Butler about his proposal[17]

2. Selected data demonstrating racial disparities in police investigation practices and punishment[18]

---

15. I use the Dressler & Garvey criminal law textbook, which begins with these materials. *See* JOSHUA DRESSLER & STEPHEN P. GARVEY, CRIMINAL LAW: CASES AND MATERIALS 1–25 (8th ed. 2019).

16. *See* Paul Butler, *Race-Based Jury Nullification: Case-in-Chief.* 30 J. MARSHALL L. REV. 911 (1997); Paul Butler, *Racially Based Jury Nullification: Black Power in the criminal Justice System*, 105 YALE L.J. 677 (1995). For faculty who also use the Dressler and Garvey textbook, this textbook excerpts Professor Butler's proposal to close the first chapter. *See* DRESSLER & GARVEY, *supra* note 15, at 25–26.

17. *See* Brooks Holland, *Paul Butler*, YOUTUBE (Oct. 29, 2012), https://youtu.be/0xHa8IZ152A.

18. Criminal law textbooks typically include data about racial disparities in the criminal law system. For other sources of data, *see* Ashley Nellis, *The Color of Justice: Racial and Ethnic Disparities in State Prisons*, THE SENTENCING PROJECT (June 14, 2016), https://www.sentencingproject.org/publications/color-of-justice-racial-and-ethnic-disparity-in-state-prisons/;, and *State-by-State Data*, THE SENTENCING PROJECT, https://www.sentencingproject.org/the-facts/#map (last visited Aug. 17, 2020).

3. Video excerpts from Michelle Alexander[19] and Senator Rand Paul[20] discussing the phenomenon of racialized mass incarceration

4. Excerpts from Professor Andrew Leipold's critique of Professor Butler's proposal,[21] as well as an excerpt of Professor Randall Kennedy's critical comments on 60 Minutes[22]

This assignment primes students for some terrific music to begin this class session. Student recommendations often have focused on hip-hop for its rich and raw themes of racism, mass incarceration, and police brutality, but music from a range of genres and eras can jump-start this exercise.

Some selected tracks:

Beyoncé and Kendrick Lamar, *Freedom*

Common and John Legend, *Glory*

Lauren Hill, *Black Rage*

Public Enemy, *Black Steel in the Hour of Chaos*

Public Enemy, *Fight the Power*

Gil Scott-Heron, *The Revolution Will Not Be Televised*

KRS-One, *Sound of da Police*

Gang Starr, *Conspiracy*

Rage Against the Machine, *Killing in the Name*

Rage Against the Machine, *Take the Power Back*

Rage Against the Machine, *Voice of the Voiceless*

Joel Thompson, *The Seven Last Words of the Unarmed*

Nina Simone, *I Wish I Knew How It Would Feel To Be Free*

Nina Simone, *Mississippi Goddamn*

Marvin Gaye, *What's Goin' On*

Charles Mingus, *Freedom*

Daye Jack & Killer Mike, *Hands Up*

Tom Morello, Shea Diamond, and Dan Reynolds, *Stand Up*

Johnny Cash, *San Quentin*

Bikini Kill, *Double Dare Ya'*

---

19. *See* Brooks Holland, *Is There Racial Bias In Our Criminal Justice System*, YouTube (Sept. 8, 2014), https://youtu.be/HzxbMa7yThM.

20. *See* Brooks Holland, *Rand Paul Testimony*, YouTube (Sept. 8, 2014), https://youtu.be/QRYyiip6PVY.

21. *See* Andrew D. Leipold, *Race-Based Jury Nullification: Rebuttal (Part A)*, 30 J. Marshall L. Rev. 923 (1997); *see also* Dressler & Garvey, *supra* note 15, at 26.

22. *See* Holland, *supra* note 17.

Paul Ochs, *Outside of a Small Circle of Friends*

Sepultura, *Refuse, Resist*

These tracks inspire reflection on a range of relevant themes: anti-racism, anti-subordination, resistance, marginalization, mass incarceration, police violence, the duties of allies, and intersectionality. These themes, in turn, have inspired some thoughtful and animated discussions to begin this exercise.[23]

After this thematic introduction, I invite students to debate the pros and cons of Professor Butler's proposal: the need to resist historical racism in the criminal law system, the symbolic role of Black jurors in countering "democratic domination," the risks of empowering juries to make *ad hoc* racial justice decisions with incomplete information, and the anti-democratic nature of jury nullification. At that point, I tell students: "You are the State of Gonzaga Senate. This proposal is a bill that would require a new jury instruction in criminal cases. How will you vote?" This vote can be taken by individual online survey, which has the benefit of anonymity. Students alternatively can form into groups and report the recommendation of each group.

In Fall 2019, I surveyed the entire class anonymously, with generalized prompts to guide their answers into one of three options:

Question 1: Select the position on Professor Butler's race-based jury nullification proposal with which you agree most strongly:

1. I agree that racial bias in criminal justice causes unfairness, but Professor Butler's proposal is an unproductive solution.	42
2. I agree that racial bias in criminal justice causes unfairness, and Professor Butler's proposal is a reasonable response.	14
3. I do not agree with Professor Butler's description of the problem of racial bias in the criminal justice system.	5

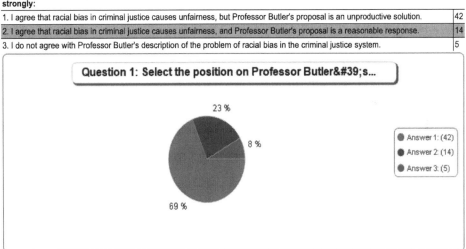

Question 1: Select the position on Professor Butler's...

23 %
8 %
69 %

Answer 1: (42)
Answer 2: (14)
Answer 3: (5)

These data points do not permit broad conclusions, but are consistent with results from previous classes. The exercise, however, gives students a modest experience

---

23. I sometimes have declined to play music that a student recommends. N.W.A. is an example. N.W.A.'s music is quite relevant to some of the themes in *A Bronx Tale*, and I personally have a complete discography of N.W.A.'s music. But some of the sexist and violent themes in this music and very strong language could undermine my educational goals in a large room of first year students, especially when being played by a 50-something white male professor. The goal of this music exercise is not necessarily to make students comfortable, but I also do not want to alienate numerous students before we even have taken much time to work together.

with the legislative process—"this is how the criminal law sausage gets made," I tell them. The responses, moreover, permit students and the professor, none of whom know each other very well yet, to visualize where the class might be on values questions that will surface repeatedly during the term. For example, in this Fall 2019 class, only 8% of students disagreed with Professor Butler's description of the problem of racial bias in the criminal law system. Yet, 77% disagreed with Professor Butler's nullification proposal as a solution to this problem.

At this point, the Butler bill normally would have failed to pass. But I tell students we instead will presume the bill did pass, and they now are Senate staff lawyers who are assigned draft to the statute's text. This part of the exercise requires students to transform *policy* into a *rule statement*, perhaps one of their first law school experiences in drafting a rule statement. Professor Butler's proposal excels for this exercise because, when dissected, it can be expressed as a racial condition precedent that authorizes a three-prong jury instruction. Students can work in groups on this exercise, or the professor can crowdsource the necessary elements from the class as a whole. Either way, the students should be guided to these elements in one form or another:

1. If the defendant is Black, *and*

2. The charge is a non-violent crime that has no victim, the jury should nullify the law and find the defendant not guilty; *or*

3. The charge is a non-violent crime that has a victim, the jury may, but need not, nullify the law, depending on whether nullification is fair; *or*

4. The charge is a violent crime, the jury should not nullify the law.

This exercise showcases for new students the importance, and challenges, of crafting clear and precise rule statements when attempting to apply policy to discrete cases as a legal rule. Furthermore, the exercise can expose the role of interpretative questions in the law. For example, I may ask, "In Professor Butler's proposal, are a certain number of Black *jurors* also a precondition for this jury instruction to apply? How does the law define whether someone is Black? Who decides this question, and from what evidence?" I do not expect correct answers from students. The goal instead is to illustrate how lawyers can interrogate rule statements, and how race can fit into, and complicate, these interpretative questions.

The exercise culminates in part two by transporting students to the County of Bronx, New York with the case of *People v. Douglas*.[24] In *Douglas*, the defendant was charged with unlawful possession of a firearm following a traffic stop. The defendant also allegedly possessed handcuffs. The defendant and the other vehicle passenger were Black, and the police officers were white.[25] In a suppression motion, the defendant challenged the traffic stop as the product of racial profiling, but the judge rejected this claim.[26] At trial, the case turned on the credibility of police officers. The defense

---

24. 680 N.Y.S.2d 145 (N.Y. Sup. Ct., Bronx Co. 1998).

25. *Id.* at 146.

26. *Id.*

lawyer argued to the jury that the defendant "was 'set up,' "[27] and " 'they [the police] stopped the car because they did not like something about the people in the car.' "[28] The trial judge interpreted these arguments as playing the "race card," and inviting jury nullification.[29]

I like the *Douglas* case for this exercise for a variety of reasons. First, the case openly intersects race and criminal law decision-making. Students will see that the judge even cites to Professor Butler. Second, I was a public defender in the Bronx Legal Aid Society when this case was tried, and my colleague was the defense lawyer. I was aware of the case, the issues, and the client. I also worked with the prosecutor and appeared in front of the judge. I thus can share brief narratives to help students appreciate that their "objective" textbook cases involve real people who care about, and who are directly affected by, legal decisions.

Finally, the case presents a great opportunity for students to practice applying the Butler rule to a fact pattern in the role of lawyers. To facilitate this exercise, I give students an edited version of the *Douglas* opinion that omits the judge's final decision based on traditional nullification law.[30] Instead, I instruct students that the Butler proposal is the *law* in this jurisdiction. As part of the assignment, I also give students two statutes—New York Penal Law § 265.03(3) and Penal Law § 70.02(b). I further give students an IRAC template as a handout with directions to draft *arguments* for both the prosecutor and defense counsel:

_____

Prosecutor:

What Issue or Issues Does the Prosecutor Want to Argue?

What Legal Rule or Rules Govern?

Do the Facts Satisfy The Rule?

What Decision Do You Want?

Defense Counsel:

What Issue or Issues Does the Defense Want to Argue?

What Legal Rule or Rules Govern?

Do the Facts Satisfy The Rule?

What Decision Do You Want?

_____

This instruction understandably can confound students a bit this early in their first term, and it can require some care to explain. Students want to analyze legal

_____

27. *Id.*

28. *Id.*

29. *Id.*

30. For an edited version of the *Douglas* opinion, *see* Brooks Holland, *People v. Douglas,* https://gonzagau-my.sharepoint.com/:b:/g/personal/hollandb_gonzaga_edu/EUmKs60cbyZPt2WVLAq7o yEBPV9tEZHf4tuJa9iIPO1cTg?e=hVur1T (last visited Aug. 17, 2020).

problems objectively. But the criminal law is premised on an adversary system. I thus want to reinforce that this system is not nearly as objective as the IRAC model suggests, and that lawyers adopt partisan roles in criminal cases. This partisan advocacy is devoted to advancing the interests of an individual client, whose interests the lawyer must prioritize.[31]

I typically will assign a few students to a prosecution team, a few students to the defense, and three students to be judges. I remind everyone of the context for our exercise, and ask the judges to prepare to decide the argument, with an explanation. I turn to the defense team and say, "The prosecutor objected to your closing argument. What is the issue you want to argue?" I will give that team a chance to kibitz before responding. If the team struggles with the issue, I will take suggestions from students in the audience. And I work back-and-forth between teams until we conclude the exercise and submit the case to the judges to decide.

This process hopefully will unfold several analyses, although naturally with the professor's guidance:

Issue 1: *Whether the Butler rule even applies to this case?* Students struggle with issue, because it turns on the race of the defendant and also, potentially, jurors. Students want to presume these facts because the judge in *Douglas* tells us the defendant and a majority of jurors are Black. But how do lawyers and a judge legally classify someone else by race, I ask, or by gender or sexual orientation? The judge in *Douglas* did not disclose his method for determining everyone's race. To give the question broader relevance, I preview for students that they will need to think about these classifications when analyzing *Batson* challenges in criminal procedure and equal protection challenges in constitutional law. The prosecution team nevertheless often is reticent to argue that the defendant and jurors are not Black, and with good reason. With nudging, the prosecution team may concede the defense team's representation that their client is Black. A good example for students that the adversary system does not mean you die on every hill, especially if the fight means asserting a position in which you are not confident.

Issue 2: *Which Butler rule governs the case?* This issue can be fun and enlightening for students. Many students presume that if the Butler rules applies, the defendant must win. The Butler rule establishes three contingent rules, however, that depend on whether the crime has a victim or is violent. Many students expect that this possession crime is non-violent because the defendant did not use or brandish the gun, although some students may focus on the alleged handcuffs as evidence of intent to harm someone in the *future*. But students who diligently explore their class "library" find a nugget of gold for the prosecution team: New York classifies the unlawful possession of a

---

31. *See e.g.*, Model Rules of Pro. Conduct, Preamble ¶¶ 2, 8, and 9, and r. 1.2(a), r. 1.3, and r. 4.4 comment 1 (Am. Bar Ass'n, 2020). I regularly share relevant Rules of Professional Conduct with students in criminal law to illustrate these professional obligations.

loaded firearm as a violent felony offense.[32] If this classification controls, the prosecution may be able to opt out of the Butler rule altogether. This issue, however, presents a good opportunity to introduce interpretative arguments. For example, does the Butler rule's reference to "violent" crimes defer to statutory classifications, or does it mean violent in *fact*? Where should a lawyer look for this answer? Professor Butler's intent? What a reasonable reader of the Butler rule would understand? Or only the literal text of the statutes?

Decision: *What 'C' in the IRAC do students want from the judge?* Students not surprisingly struggle with articulating their legal ask. Students need to remember that this exercise does not determine guilt. The jury still judges that question. This exercise instead determines the instructions the judge will give to the jury to inform that decision. Moreover, theses instructions will guide and constrain the closing arguments each lawyer properly may make to the jury.

To conclude, I sometimes add a bonus question: Even if the judge finds that this crime is a violent crime and the Butler rule does not apply, can the defense still argue to the jury that the traffic stop was motivated by improper racial profiling? This question understandably stumps many first year students, because it invites them to argue in the alternative, a critical but advanced skill. The answer emerges, however, from what students already learned is a fundamental and exclusive function of the jury: assessment of witness credibility.

The *Douglas* case turns on whether the jury believes the testimony of the police that they found this gun on the defendant during the traffic stop. I thus ask students, if the jury believes that the officers racially profiled the defendant, would the officers be less *credible* as witnesses *to the alleged gun possession itself*? Does a racist act legally make someone less believable? This inference is debatable on this record, however, and we have some fun with it to close the exercise by distinguishing "inferences" from "speculation." But I share with students a lesson I learned early as a lawyer: "Sometimes your audience won't be persuaded by what you think is your best argument. Have a backup plan."

Conclusion

A Bronx Tale is not meant to be an easy or comfortable exercise for new law students. Rather, the exercise is meant to preview a journey in store for students, a journey that will require them to engage diversity values as a part of the law itself. These values are not merely grist for abstract policy or theoretical discussion. Diversity values instead are central to practical lawyering on behalf of a client. In the process, the exercise also illustrates how legal analysis and advocacy must be evidence-based,

---

32. *See* N.Y. PENAL §§ 265.03(3) and 70.02(b) (McKinney 2020).

including in the sources on which a lawyer relies. These legal sources can empower—but also constrain—a lawyer's ability to raise diversity values in a particular case. Holistically, I hope this exercise prepares students for inclusive and respectful, but also rigorous, classroom engagement with the diversity values that will inform their study of criminal law.

Centering Race and Diversity in the Criminal Law Classroom

*Deborah Ahrens**

All hail the podcast. When I get students for their first day of their 1L year of law school, many of them have spent the past several years with podcasts as their sound-tracks for schoolwork, long runs, and commutes. Among those popular podcasts have been several, like *Serial*, that famously focus on criminal law issues. In the fall of 2018, a flight of students came in familiar with *Flowers v. Mississippi*[1]—not nec-essarily because of news coverage, although there had been some of that thanks to the Supreme Court's decision to grant certiorari in the case[2]—but because it had been the subject of the second season of the podcast *In the Dark*.[3] Curtis Flowers was, at the time, on death row for a quadruple murder that took place at the Tardy Fur-niture store in small-town Winona, Mississippi. He had been tried not once, not twice, but six times for the murders; the jury was unable to reach a unanimous verdict twice, but three of those reversals stemmed in part from the prosecutor's conduct—most notably, his conduct during voir dire. Over the course of six trials, the prosecutor had used almost all of his peremptory strikes against Black jurors in a case that involved a Black defendant and three (of four) white victims. Flowers is as of this writing on bond after the Supreme Court reversed the conviction from his sixth trial.[4] The Supreme Court reversed based on its determination that the prosecutor in *Flowers* had violated *Batson v. Kentucky*,[5] noting that the prosecutor had used peremptory strikes against 41 of 42 Black jurors across Flowers' trials; had used strikes against

---

* Professor of Law, Seattle University School of Law. I would like to thank Andrew Siegel for helping me recall some of the things that I have done for years but have never written down, as well as my students who have always been my best teachers.

1. 139 S. Ct. 2228 (2019).

2. Justice Thomas, dissenting in *Flowers*, lamented that media attention to the case may have prompted the Court to grant certiorari in the first place. *See id.* at 2254 (Thomas, J., dissenting).

3. APM Reports, *In the Dark: Season 2* (2019), https://www.apmreports.org/in-the-dark/season-two.

4. *See* Wilson Stribling, *Out on Bond After Six Trials, What's Next for Curtis Flowers?*, WLBT.Com (Jan. 16, 2020, 5:30 AM), https://www.wlbt.com/2020/01/16/out-bond-after-six-trials-whats-next-curtis-flowers/.

5. 476 U.S. 79 (1986).

five of six Black jurors at the sixth trial; had engaged in much lengthier questioning of Black jurors; and had struck at least one Black juror similarly situated to white jurors permitted to remain in the pool.[6] The students who have heard the podcast come in primed to find out exactly how things went sideways in this case; the students who did not know about the case are astonished when we address it. Both groups are incensed that the jury—the body of people which is supposed to serve as a protective layer interposed between the vulnerable criminal defendant and the awesome power of the state—was so unrepresentative of the community from which Curtis Flowers came, particularly because that lack of representation was engineered. This case, and juries in general, have been the jumping-off point in my criminal law course for addressing diversity in concrete, accessible ways for the diverse students enrolled.

The Centrality of the Jury

When I first began teaching criminal law as an adjunct professor in 2003, I spent a great deal of time giving students basic statistics about the criminal legal system. I would have them guess, auction-style, what number of Americans currently were incarcerated in prison or jail. We'd look at graphs illustrating that crime rates have been plummeting since I graduated from high school alongside the rising rates of incarceration. Students always underbid on the number of persons incarcerated, sometimes by millions of persons. They would rarely guess that the United States had the highest reported incarceration rate in the world. We would look at the rise in female incarceration rates and the differences in incarceration rates by race. This correlation would generally seem to be brand-new information to incoming students; that changed several years ago, for reasons that are difficult to pinpoint. Perhaps it is the efforts of criminal justice reform advocates and Black Lives Matter advocates, who have highlighted inequality and brutality in policing, prosecution, and punishment. Perhaps it is a shift in the focus of media—many students have binged those podcasts or documentaries like *Making a Murderer*[7] or *The Kalief Browder Story*[8] in recent years and come into law school with more information about how the criminal legal system does and does not work. Whatever the reason, the starting point that I have with students is different than it used to be, in ways that permit us to have a better and richer course. I have gradually incorporated the jury as a vehicle for encouraging discussion of diversity in class discussion, as well as for ensuring that diverse perspectives are heard in class. Juries provide a portal to discuss more abstract ideas about diversity, as well as to get students comfortable expressing perspectives that their classmates do not share and that might represent the diversity of their own experiences. Juries represent some of the most aspirational and troubling aspects of

---

6. *See Flowers*, 139 S. Ct. at 2235.

7. *Making a Murderer* (Netflix released Dec. 18, 2015) (written and directed by Laura Riccardi and Moira Demos).

8. *Time: The Kalief Browder Story* (Bravo/Spike television broadcast Mar. 1, 2017) (written by Rose Schlossberg and Mark Konko, directed by Jennifer Furst).

criminal law and are the literal importation of the lay community into an arena otherwise dominated by repeat-player professionals. Substantive criminal law focuses more on the elements of specific offenses than on the process of adjudication, but using juries as a teaching tool that threads through the semester encourages participation and discussion. My goal is for that participation and discussion ultimately to raise the level of competency students will have, regardless of the background they bring to law school, in addressing criminal law clients and issues in their careers.

Instructions and Nullification

We open my criminal law class using an exercise that I have students write out before they arrive in class: drafting a jury instruction that explains the concept of "beyond a reasonable doubt" to a jury. I tell the students not to do any outside research but to rely on the two or three pages in the textbook that explain the concept of reasonable doubt in *In re Winship*[9] and various formulations that courts have considered since then to define "reasonable doubt."[10] While part of the point of this exercise is to get them to actively engage and apply course materials from the first day of class, the actual goal of the exercise is to get them to think concretely about how criminal law gets applied in practice. After we read through the first few student submissions—inevitably, beautifully written, substantively reasonable, and reflective of effort and understanding, we ease into a discussion of the intended audience for these words. They have tried to impress one another (and their professor) with their ability to put things into the legal vocabulary they have enrolled to learn. But how are those words received and understood by the persons who serve on a jury and will have to apply the concepts? Do they understand them? What education, experience, and expectations do jurors bring to the courtroom? Who are they? How representative are they? What do we expect them to do? What is the role of a jury in general, and individual jurors in particular?[11] These are the questions with which we open the course and which we carry through the semester. The information the jurors bring with them is critical to their decision-making, but the information they receive about law is largely in the form of the jury instructions the students have just struggled to draft; for the students, realizing this dichotomy, is illuminating. It is also, to some extent, empowering. Students realize that the people to whom they will explain the law probably look more like their pre-law-school-selves and that the experiences and understandings the students bring with them to law school are important.

---

9. 397 U.S. 358 (1970).

10. *See, e.g., Victor v. Nebraska*, 511 U.S. 1, 5 (1994) (discussing constitutionality of "moral certainty" language included in a reasonable doubt jury instruction).

11. There is robust academic and popular literature explaining how badly the general public misconstrues many traditional legal instructions. Some of the best examples are collected and presented clearly by the Plain Language Action and Information Network at https://www.plainlanguage.gov/examples/brochures/jury-instructions/ (last visited Aug. 17, 2020).

We think critically that first week about the ability of juries to nullify, using both juries like the one that acquitted the men who murdered Emmett Till in 1955,[12] as well as juries like the more recent one that could not reach a unanimous verdict in the case of a man who had assisted Central American migrants in an Arizona desert by giving them sustenance and shelter.[13] When students become concerned about the race-based nullification that seemed to occur in the Emmett Till case, we think about whether or not, given the statistics we examine that demonstrate racial disparities in drug cases, it would be a legitimate exercise of juror discretion to refuse to convict Black or Latinx defendants in drug cases.[14] We discuss how the experiences of the jurors—and the composition of the jury—would affect the outcome at trial. These discussions in the first days of class have multiple purposes. One, the students are primed from day one of class to understand that criminal law does not self-execute, but reflects the discretionary decisions of a huge number of actors throughout the process. Victims (where there are any), police, prosecutors, judges, defense attorneys, probation officers, corrections officials, parole boards, and executives with commutation and pardon authority all bring their perspective and power to the table. Two, the students learn that the discretionary authority in the United States historically has excluded (and continues to marginalize) a lot of groups, and that people's experiences may be different based on demographics, particularly color and class. Three, the students come to understand that we will be talking about these issues throughout the semester and that their critical perspective is not just welcome, but encouraged. Finally, the students hopefully learn that they are connected to the jurors—that the juries are intended to be representative of communities, even if that does not execute perfectly in practice, and that the classroom is going to represent divergent viewpoints as well.[15]

Race and Other Jury Biases

We return to juries repeatedly throughout the semester as a way to understand the verdicts we generally are reviewing (my textbook, like most textbooks, is nearly all appellate- and Supreme-Court-level cases) as well as the ways in which the stories the

---

12. *See* Sam Johnson, *AP Was There: 2 Men Acquitted of Murder in Emmett Till Case*, ASSOCIATED PRESS (Jul. 12, 2018), https://apnews.com/f6e82e2661424204b0f1920c313fa307/AP-Was-There:-2-men-acquitted-of-murder-in-Emmett-Till-case (reprinting a prior article noting that an all-white jury acquitted two white men of murdering fourteen-year-old Emmett Till as part of coverage of revelation that the woman who allegedly motivated the murder by reporting that Till had whistled at her had lied about the encounter).

13. *See* Miriam Jordan, *An Arizona Teacher Helped Migrants. Jurors Couldn't Decide if It Was a Crime*, N.Y. TIMES, (June 11, 2019), at A12, https://www.nytimes.com/2019/06/11/us/scott-warren-arizona-deaths.html.

14. *See* Paul Butler, *Racially Based Jury Nullification: Black Power in the Criminal Justice System*, 105 YALE L.J. (1995) (famously arguing in favor of such nullification).

15. In my Criminal Procedure class, where we also spend the semester looking at the course materials through a variety of perspectives, I assign perspective pieces for the first day—we read everything from Justice Thomas' pro-police dissent in *City of Chicago v. Morales*, 527 U.S. 41, 67 (1996) (Thomas, J., dissenting), to Robin D.G. Kelley, *Slangin' Rocks... Palestinian Style: Dispatches from the Occupied Zones of North America*, in POLICE BRUTALITY: AN ANTHOLOGY 21 (Jill Nelson, ed., 2000).

state and defendants tell may have been received by people from the community. There are cases we cover that highlight race, including cases common to many textbooks, like *People v. Du*,[16] in which a Korean immigrant store owner in Los Angeles shoots to death a Black middle-schooler who is in her market, and *People v. Goetz*,[17] in which a white New York subway rider shoots four Black teenagers.[18] Students often have difficulty talking directly about the race issues in those cases, and I have found it helpful not only to get them to speak from the roles of the defense attorneys and prosecutors in those cases (to provide the distance of advocacy), but also to speak about what jurors might have perceived about the stories the advocates were presenting. We think about how prosecutors and defense attorneys might address juror perceptions in cases that involve defendants and victims from different races, as well as how the jurors' own backgrounds might affect those perceptions. By speaking from the perspectives of jurors, rather than directly from their own perspectives, students have a few opportunities: the opportunity to see events from the viewpoint of people who might be dissimilar from them as well as to voice possibly unpopular thoughts without worrying about the repercussions of being personally tied to those perspectives.

We also talk in depth about how juries discuss cases and about the role of race in those discussions. While I started teaching the case in my evidence course, I soon exported *Pena-Rodriguez v. Colorado*[19] into criminal law. In *Pena-Rodriguez*, two jurors approached the defendant's attorney after delivering a guilty verdict; they reported that a fellow juror had made a number of comments that evinced bias, including that he "believed the defendant was guilty because, in [his] experience as an ex-law enforcement officer, Mexican men had a bravado that caused them to believe they could do whatever they wanted with women"; that he thought "he did it because he's Mexican and Mexican men take whatever they want," and "nine times out of ten Mexican men were guilty of being aggressive toward women and young girls."[20] The *Pena-Rodriguez* case underscores for students that the Court accords racial bias a unique place in the criminal justice context, requiring extra vigilance given the history of such bias and the dangers for the legitimacy of the system posed when racial bias is alleged.[21] In *Pena-Rodriguez*, the Court explains that "[p]ermitting racial prejudice in the jury system damages both the fact and the perception of the jury's role as a vital check against the wrongful exercise of power by the State."[22]

The case is also a great entry into discussing how attorneys can or cannot minimize the role of bias in the trial process,[23] in particular through the jury selection process.

---

16. 7 Cal. Rptr. 2d 177 (Cal. Ct. App. 1992).

17. 497 N.E.2d 41 (N.Y. 1986).

18. I use JOSHUA DRESSLER & STEPHEN P. GARVEY, CASES AND MATERIALS ON CRIMINAL LAW (8th ed. 2019).

19. 137 S. Ct. 855 (2017).

20. *Id.* at 862.

21. *Id.* at 867–68 (detailing a history of race discrimination in American criminal law).

22. *Id.* at 868 (internal quotations and citations omitted).

23. The *Pena-Rodriguez* court was skeptical that the voir dire process can adequately address race, noting that jurors might not answer questions about racial bias truthfully. *Id.* at 869.

We brainstorm questions in class that we might use in voir dire to try to root out racial bias specifically, and other kinds of bias more generally, and to interrogate whether or not we think jurors would answer our questions honestly, or whether even if they attempted to do so, they might recognize implicit bias.[24] I present to them Washington State's evolving opening jury instructions that educate jurors on conscious and unconscious bias,[25] and we evaluate whether or not we think such an instruction will be effective.

The Death Penalty

The Supreme Court's jurisprudence on the death penalty offers a final doctrinal opportunity to discuss race and criminal justice. We cover the *McCleskey v. Kemp*[26] and *Buck v. Davis*[27] cases in our death penalty unit, both of which focus expressly on juries and race, reaching divergent conclusions. In *McClesky*, the Court rejected the notion that even highly compelling statistical evidence of racial differences in capital sentencing could constitutionally invalidate a death sentence; the Court reasoned that juries were permitted to review a wide range of aggravating and mitigating evidence in death penalty cases and that variance was to be expected.[28] In *Buck*, on the other hand, the Court was concerned that the defense counsel's elicitation of express testimony that a defendant would be more likely to reoffend because he was Black had poisoned the entire trial—as the Court argued, "some toxins can be deadly in small doses."[29] I use this pair of cases, as well as the Washington Supreme Court's determination that the death penalty statute in this state is unconstitutional,[30] to lead class discussions on the role of race in sentencing, particularly in the odd world of capital sentencing where juries rather than judges make decisions. We discuss the voir dire process in capital cases and the bifurcated guilt/sentencing phases through the lens of how representative or unrepresentative capital juries are of the defendants and the community. I give them statistics from the Capital Jury Project that illustrate

---

24. Some of the kinds of questions students generate on a fairly regular basis include questions that ask a potential juror directly whether their views of particular incidents would be changed if the races of the participants were switched, questions that ask whether the potential jurors think that people of different races tend to view particular kinds of situations differently, and questions that ask about whether differences in the life experiences of different groups of people might lead them to view the world in different ways.

25. *See* Washington Supreme Court Committee on Jury Instructions, Washington Pattern Jury Instruction-Criminal 151.00 (West 2018).

26. 481 U.S. 279 (1987).

27. 137 S. Ct. 759 (2017).

28. *McCleskey*, 481 U.S. at 285.

29. *Buck*, 137 S. Ct. at 777.

30. *See* State v. Gregory, 427 P.3d 621, 626–27 (Wash. 2018) (holding that Washington's death penalty statute violates the state constitution because it is imposed in "an arbitrary and racially biased manner").

the effects of different jury compositions on the likelihood that the jury sentences a defendant to death.[31] We discuss the extent to which the death-qualification rules[32] require that all jurors be willing to impose the death penalty, and how that might shape a jury's willingness both to convict and to impose a death sentence. It is a great context for discussing how rules that are ostensibly neutral might exclude some viewpoints and experiences—in particular, it permits some people with some kinds of deeply-held religious beliefs to consider how those beliefs might affect their ability to serve on a capital jury. Student interest in the death penalty outpaces its importance to most practitioners—I have been appreciative of how that interest has permitted us to use the death penalty in class to explore issues that permeate criminal law and practice.

Taking Gender and Other Differences Seriously

While race issues are at the historical center of criminal law in the United States, the role of gender in criminal law[33]—and the experiences of a majority-female classroom—mean that gender, sexual orientation, and gender identity are also issues I want to encourage students to engage. We read cases carefully to parse how women are described, thinking about why judges choose particular words, and how those words push us to view the facts of the case.[34] We consider self-defense and provocation through gender lenses, looking at statistics about how stand-your-ground laws have worked for men and women, as well as historical expectations for women that might affect how juries view their decisions.[35] Do we think women might respond differently

---

31. For an overview of the literature reporting and building upon the Capital Jury Project's work, see John H. Blume, *An Overview of Significant Findings from the Capital Jury Project and Other Empirical Studies of the Death Penalty Relevant to Jury Selection, Presentation of Evidence and Jury Instructions in Capital Cases* (Fall 2018), https://www.lawschool.cornell.edu/research/death-penalty-project/upload/Empirical-Studies-Summaries-revised-spring-2010.docx (last visited Aug. 17, 2020).

32. *See* Wainwright v. Witt, 469 U.S. 412 (1985); Witherspoon v. Illinois, 391 U.S. 510 (1968).

33. While there are still more men incarcerated than women in the United States, the rate of increase for women has outpaced that for men over the past few decades. *See Incarcerated Women and Girls*, THE SENTENCING PROJECT (June 6, 2019, https://www.sentencingproject.org/publications/incarcerated-women-and-girls/ (demonstrating that the rate of incarceration for women and girls increased more than 750% between 1980 and 2017); *Incarceration Rate of Women is Growing Twice as Fast as that of Men*, EQUAL JUSTICE INITIATIVE (May 11, 2018), https://eji.org/news/female-incarceration-growing-twice-as-fast-as-male-incarceration/.

34. Two cases that always draw robust discussion are State v. Norman, 378 S.E.2d 8 (N.C. 1989) (involving the failure to instruct a jury on the "battered wife syndrome") and People v. Beardsley, 113 N.W. 1128 (Mich. 1907) (involving a married man's liability for failing to come to the aid of his mistress who died of an overdose).

35. I have used different news stories and articles over the years for these issues, but an excellent recent article that provides both statistics illustrating that women have more difficulty than men asserting Stand your Ground defenses and a lengthy narrative of one woman's self-defense claim is Elizabeth Flock, *How Far Can Abused Women Go to Protect Themselves*, NEW YORKER (Jan. 13, 2020), at

to particular situations? Is that because women might on average be smaller, or is it because of how women are socialized to act? Partially as an exercise in role-reversal, I close out the homicide materials by showing the students "Cell Block Tango," a clip from the musical *Chicago*[36] in which a variety of female murder defendants attempt to justify and excuse their killings, as a review problem.[37] The gender-role reversal (most of the textbook cases involve male defendants) makes for interesting class discussion.

We also spend the last week of class discussing sexual assault. I have spoken to criminal law professors who avoid the topic, and I find that students are anxious about covering it, but I have noticed for several years that there is a segment of my female students that ordinarily does not volunteer in class that becomes very interested in entering the discussion. These students are often women who during their college years have, often through their activism, been forced to confront in a detailed way the complicated dynamics of preventing and punishing sexual assault. One thing I have the students do that promotes open discussion — as well as consideration of personal experience and the role of law in shaping or reflecting social norms — is to look at some non-criminal sexual conduct codes (such as the Antioch campus policy from the 1990s[38]) and discuss whether we think those codes are desirable, enforceable as criminal law, aspirational, unrealistic, or problematic.

Some issues of background and personal experience map less clearly onto race or gender, and more onto the general diversity of personal experience. Last year, I started playing a segment from the third season of the *Serial* Podcast (which, as I have noted, often some students already have heard) that narrates a fight on a public bus that ends with one man shooting another to death.[39] The incident allows the students to see how much their own experiences shape how they view the incident and how they expected people to act — people who ride the bus regularly, for example, often have strong ideas about what people who feel threatened on a bus should do, and people's views on the legitimacy of firearms very much shapes their reaction to the incident. (One of the men involved in the incident at one point refers to a "CCW" or concealed carry permit that he claims to but does not have.) Depending on how students view and have experienced guns, some students view that statement as an attempt to de-escalate the situation (by telling the other person that he can protect himself), while others read it as a provocation. Cold text in a casebook can be used to the same effect,

---

20, https://www.newyorker.com/magazine/2020/01/20/how-far-can-abused-women-go-to-protect-themselves.

36. Chicago (Miramax Films 2002).

37. I discuss my use of this clip and other musical theater scenes to teach difficult criminal law topics in Deborah Ahrens, *Giving Tough Criminal Law Topics the Musical Theater Treatment*, in, The Media Method: Teaching Law with Popular Culture 117 (Christine A. Corcos, ed., 2019).

38. The current version of the policy is available along with a discussion of its history at Sexual Offense Prevention Policy (SOPP) & Title IX, https://antiochcollege.edu/campus-life/sexual-offense-prevention-policy-title-ix/ (last visited Aug. 17, 2020).

39. Sarah Koenig, *Serial, Pleas Baby Pleas*, https://serialpodcast.org/season-three/5/pleas-baby-pleas (Season 3, episode 5).

but the rich and immersive narrative in the podcast permits the students to listen to the events unfold and get an initial read.

Towards an Inclusive Classroom

Finally, on a more mundane level, I have found smaller-scale classroom-management decisions to be helpful. I have students fill out index cards on the first day of class, and ask them for a phonetic pronunciation of their names, as well as for the pronouns that they use. I also encourage them to let me know on the card if there are things that I should know about them in order to best teach them, and offer examples such as "I sometimes take a minute to collect my thoughts when I am called on in class." I use the cards to call on students randomly,[40] and I call on a large number of students (usually 10–15) each class period in the early days of the semester, because, at least in my experience, I hear from fewer students overall if I rely on volunteers or panels of participants, and students who are invited into the classroom conversation early on feel more comfortable participating later. I have drafted a number of short problems that students are expected to engage in advance of class—some of which, like the jury instruction exercise with which I open class, require students to submit a short written draft. Some of these assignments—like an exercise where I have them list questions they would have in determining the sentencing that would be appropriate for a defendant they know nothing about, including questions about the person's demographics and social history—simply require them to come to class prepared for discussion. By giving them the chance to think about issues and problems in advance, I find students are more likely to engage in difficult topics when they arrive.

While I was leery in the early days of my career about mentioning much about my non-professional life or background, I've made the conscious decision to share aspects students might find helpful as they are finding their place in law school and the legal community. I let them know that I am a first-generation college-student (and first-generation law student, as a consequence). Knowing that I come from a similar background helps some students feel more comfortable approaching me as a professor. That comfort is particularly important to me since, as I share with the students, I had no idea I could even go to see my college or law professors, and thought that doing so was a burden to them and would reveal my inadequacies. I want them to know that professors are there to support their learning. I also let students know that I had children while in practice. The majority of entering students at my law school has been female for many years, and, this past fall, the entering class was 61% female. Students would often like to talk with people who have practiced law (but who are not trying to persuade them to work for a particular office) about experiences managing practice and family responsibilities.

---

40. Ruthann Robson describes doing this as well, for similar reasons. See Ruthann Robson, *Educating the Next Generations of LGBTQ Attorneys*, 66 J. LEGAL EDUC. 502 (2017).

That openness—and openness is uncomfortable for many of us who became lawyers in part because it is much easier to advocate for and speak about others than about ourselves—is something students value. It makes them more comfortable inside and outside of the criminal law classroom, and makes it more likely that they will forgive you, themselves, and one another as we all inevitably misstep in discussing difficult topics. Criminal law is not unique in presenting those difficult topics, but it is clear that those issues are central, not peripheral, to criminal law.

Taking Up Space in the Criminal Law Classroom

Thea Johnson[*]

Introduction

The first year classroom can be an overwhelming place. Students are learning new and complicated material, getting to know their classmates (who will likely be their future colleagues in the law) and becoming accustomed to the Socratic method. For many, this combination of factors can make participating in the classroom petrifying. Beyond the typical challenges of law school, many students face additional struggles that complicate their relationship with the classroom experience. Empirical research confirms that first-generation law students, students of color, and women all feel less inclined to voluntarily participate in class,[1] which mirrors what I have seen in the classroom. With this in mind, I am always on the lookout for ways to encourage students to reflect on how they and others are "taking up space" in the classroom, to use a term I borrow from Professor Angela P. Harris.

Taking up space is important in all law school classes, but especially in the 1L classroom where students are beginning to develop their professional identities as law students and lawyers. I start the first day of every criminal law class with a plea that

[*] Thea Johnson is an Associate Professor of Law at Rutgers Law School. Thank you to Beth Colgan and Kaipo Matsumura for their insightful comments on this chapter. And many thanks to Cheryl Saniuk-Heinig for her terrific research assistance.

1. *See, e.g.*, Alice Sheh, *Yale Law School Faculty & Students Speak Up About Gender: Ten Years Later*, Ms. JD (Apr. 24, 2020), https://ms-jd.org/blog/article/yale-law-school-faculty-students-speak-about-gender-ten-years-later; Michele J. Eliason & Ruby Turalba, *Recognizing Oppression: College Students' Perceptions of Identity and its Impact on Class Participation*, 42 Rev. of Higher Ed. 1257 (2019); Jonathan Feingold & Doug Souza, *Measuring the Racial Unevenness of Law School*, 15 Berkeley J. Afr.-Am. L. & Pol'y 71 (2015); Celestial S.D. Cassman & Lisa R. Pruitt, *A Kinder, Gentler Law School? Race, Ethnicity, Gender, and Legal Education at King Hall*, 38 U.C. Davis L. Rev. 1209, 1248 (2005); Adam Neufeld, *Costs of An Outdated Pedagogy? Study on Gender at Harvard Law School*, 13 Am. U.J. Gender Soc. Pol'y & L. 511 (2005); Lani Guinier, Michelle Fine, Jane Balin, Ann Bartow & Deborah Lee Stachel, *Becoming Gentlemen: Women's Experiences at One Ivy League Law School*, 143 U. Pa. L. Rev. 1, 2 (1994).

students be mindful about whether they are taking up space in the classroom in an effective way. I want them to think about how much they have talked or not talked in class, including in full-class discussions, small-group sessions (which I break out into frequently in my classroom), and in conversations with me after class or in office hours. Are they taking up a lot of space? No space at all? Or something in between? I ask them to constantly reassess their space in the classroom. One purpose of this is to encourage participation from some students, but it is also meant to provide language for addressing students who take up a lot of space in the classroom. The term "gunner" is a compliment or an insult depending on whom you ask, but either way—the term doesn't account for the effect of one's behavior on others. Framing the conversation as taking up space allows us to talk about those students who may—with no ill intent—be crowding out others from the room.

Of course, one way to regulate how students take up space in the classroom is to stick strictly to the Socratic method.[2] And while I do lean heavily on what I think of as a "gentle" Socratic method,[3] I also want to encourage students to learn to speak up, in a thoughtful way, in front of large groups. They should be thinking not just about the answer they are giving, but also how they communicate that answer. But asking people to self-assess can only get one so far.[4] I want then to encourage students to think about and discuss "space" in the classroom, the courtroom, and the legal world they are about to enter. To that end, I use several exercises that allow students to interrogate how they and others take up space.

Here, I will focus on one such exercise I use to help students become more mindful of how they communicate with one another, with the goal of making them think about the way lawyers communicate with each other, their clients and the broader community. The exercise I use provides students a great introduction to the law of self-defense, while also helping them discuss the way they "take up space" in the classroom. What I describe below is an exercise on the doctrine of self-defense that was inspired by an idea I heard about from Professor Ronald Wright (who, in turn, borrowed the exercise from Professor Sara Sun Beale. You may detect a theme: I borrow, steal, and filch from my brilliant colleagues in the field early and often—and you should too!). I will outline here my spin on that self-defense exercise.

---

2. Although the Socratic Method also has its pitfalls. *See, e.g.,* David D. Garner, *Socratic Misogyny—Analyzing Feminist Criticisms of Socratic Teaching in Legal Education,* 2000 B.Y.U. L. Rev 1597 (2000).

3. I use two modifications to the traditional Socratic method. First, I use a panel system, rotating between 4 panels over the course of the semester. A single panel will be "on call" for each class. That group must have read the material deeply and be able to discuss every aspect of the reading. Second, I usually call on students in pairs-switching between them in case one of them gets in a tough spot with the material. I find that these modifications ease some of the pressure of the Socratic method, while still keeping students accountable for the material.

4. I should note that I offer the students to check in with me anytime about the space they're taking up in the class and on a few occasions students have come for a check-in.

Self-Defense Exercise

Self-defense is one of the most complicated concepts in criminal law. It is intuitively easy to understand, but the law has created many layers of inquiry that require the fact-finder to ask a series of questions—almost like a choose-your-own-adventure novel—that gets them to the "right" answer. Because it's so difficult, I take several class periods to go over the concepts of self-defense, defense of others, and defense of the home.

But before launching into the study of self-defense, I have the students act as jurors in a self-defense case that I put on during one class period. This means the students have not yet been exposed to these difficult back-and-forth inquiries required by self-defense law. For the most part they have the actual understanding of the law that a real juror might. Which is to say, zilch. (Well, perhaps, not entirely. They have by this point in the semester been introduced to certain related concepts, like the analysis for reasonableness under criminal law.)

There are a few purposes to introducing them to self-defense through a mock jury trial. First, it is an engaging way to dive into the topic, which gives them a sense of how the real world functions. Second and relatedly, it allows us to have a conversation about how the criminal law, in theory, is meant to be applied by lay fact-finders (at least some of the time) and how we can understand the role of the jury when the law—as I'll describe below—is written in such a complicated way. Third, it lets us have some important conversations about how each student takes up space in the classroom and beyond. Generally, most students will agree that each juror in a real-life trial should have the opportunity to express their views of the evidence for discussion by the full jury. A juror's expertise is not based on whether they got good grades in college, but the life experience and common sense that they bring to the jury, regardless of their background. The exercise then allows students to interrogate their own behavior during mock jury deliberations and what it might tell them about larger class dynamics.

The first question is what case to choose. I had the benefit of having the crime-beat reporter for the local newspaper as a student in my class the first time I taught criminal law. He introduced me to a self-defense case that posed some tricky questions about the "reasonableness" of the defendant's actions.[5] Through my connection with this student and the local DA who tried the case, I was able to get many of the exhibits that were used at the actual trial. But you can choose any self-defense case, and there are many that will lead to difficult and important conversations about the issues that arise in self-defense cases. For instance, Professor Wright uses the Bernie Goetz case,[6]

---

5. *Maine v. Kimball*, 2016 ME 75, 139 A.3d 914.

6. For more on the Goetz case, *see* Fordham Law School, *Revisiting The Trial of Bernard Goetz*, YouTube (Feb. 13, 2014), https://www.youtube.com/watch?v=K7-iunXZtC4 (Presentation of the Forum on Law, Culture and Society).

which leads to discussions about whether the jury should take into account the defendant's racist beliefs when deciding the subjective and objective reasonableness of his decision to use force. The recent case of a white police officer, Amber Guyger, who killed Bothan Jean, a Black man sitting in his own home, provides another example, as she relied on the Castle Doctrine, a version of defense of the home.[7] The use of either of these cases can introduce students to the layers of inquiry involved in a self-defense claim and provide an avenue to discuss the way the defense has been used historically to justify the killing of Black men.[8]

Before starting the trial, we take some time to talk about the role of the jury. This is an opportunity to discuss what we expect from juries, what their purpose is in the criminal system, and how we hope jurors behave when deciding a person's fate. The textbook I use includes some readings on juries, including the role of jury nullification.[9] But there are many terrific articles you can assign to the class regarding the role and purpose of the jury.[10] At some point in this conversation, the students should reflect on the dual nature of a jury as one body made up of twelve different people. Each of those jurors must each make their own determination about the defendant's guilt or innocence, while also committing to meaningful deliberation with their fellow jurors. In this sense, the students should understand that the jury functions only when each juror's voice is given weight.

The trial itself can take many forms. I give the students a number of real exhibits from the case with descriptions of each, along with a series of articles from the local newspaper about the case.[11] They have to review these materials thoroughly before class. In class I present closing arguments in the case, with a local criminal attorney arguing the other side. We both strongly advocate for our view of the evidence. We also explain self-defense to the students in a way that "wins" our case. I have my teaching assistant act as the judge. At the end of closing arguments, the judge reads to the students all

---

7. For more on the Guyger case, *see Amber Guyger: A curated collection of links*, MARSHALL PROJECT (Oct. 8, 2019, 03:25 PM), https://www.themarshallproject.org/records/6376-amber-guyger.

8. There are many sources that discuss the use of the self-defense defense as an excuse for violence against people of color. One source I would recommend is CYNTHIA LEE, MURDER AND THE REASONABLE MAN: PASSION AND FEAR IN THE CRIMINAL COURTROOM (NYU Press, 2003).

9. JOSHUA DRESSLER & STEPHEN P. GARVEY, CRIMINAL LAW: CASES AND MATERIALS (8th ed., 2019).

10. *See, e.g.*, PAUL BUTLER, LET'S GET FREE: A HIP-HOP THEORY OF JUSTICE (2009); Paul Andrew Guthrie Ferguson, *The Jury As Constitutional Identity*, 47 U.C. DAVIS L. REV. 1105 (2014); Julie A. Seaman, *Black Boxes*, 58 EMORY L.J. 427 (2008); Rachel E. Barkow, *Recharging the Jury: The Criminal Jury's Constitutional Role in an Era of Mandatory Sentencing*, 152 U. PA. L. REV. 33 (2003).

11. Many news sources will also post exhibits that were used at trials. If you pick a local case, you may also ask local defense attorneys and prosecutors if they would be willing to share exhibits that were in the public record, but not made otherwise available through the media. Finally, I would recommend the website, Famous Trials, which is produced and maintained by Professor Douglas O. Linder at the University of Missouri-Kansas City Law School, and provides a wealth of information on various famous trials, including the trial of George Zimmerman for the murder of Trayvon Martin. DOUGLAS O. LINDER, FAMOUS TRIALS, https://www.famous-trials.com.

the relevant jury instructions on murder, manslaughter, and self-defense, as well as the instructions on reasonable doubt and the meaning of deliberation.

Students then break out into groups of twelve, which have been randomly assigned beforehand. Ideally, each jury should be in its own room, uninfluenced by the other juries around them. The students are told to treat the exercise as if they were jurors and to make a decision based only on the evidence provided to them and the law as the judge has explained it. They have the remainder of the class period to deliberate. I give the students a copy of the jury instructions and, if I am asked a question, I refer them to the instructions. (Another variation is to have students only hear the jury instructions without receiving any written copy, which is the way many courts conduct this phase of a trial. This strategy would take more time and coordination but can lead to great conversation in the debrief about how jurors understand information.) At the end of class, they must return a verdict sheet (guilty on murder or manslaughter, not guilty on murder or manslaughter, or deadlocked). We spend the following class debriefing the exercise.

The debrief focuses on three major issues: First, what is the rule for self-defense? Second, now that the students have served as mock jurors, how should we understand the role of the jury in the criminal system? Finally, how did they and others take up space in their particular jury?

As to the first question—what is the rule for self-defense?—the students will likely see that even with access to the jury instructions and after hearing closing arguments, they still have a lot of questions about what constitutes self-defense. For instance, did they understand that the use of force must be reasonable? And did they understand the definition of reasonableness? Did they understand that if the defendant genuinely believed he was at risk of deadly force, even if that belief was not reasonable, he could mitigate the charge from murder to manslaughter? Or that the defendant may seemingly meet all the criteria for self-defense, but still fail to successfully invoke the defense because he could have retreated? What are the requirements for such retreat? This is just a small sampling of questions that you can raise about the doctrine. If there was confusion about the law (and I've found there almost always is *some* confusion), then what did they think self-defense was? Would they be able to explain self-defense to others?

This conversation sets up the elements we will cover in our study of self-defense in the next few classes, but also leads nicely into the second area of debrief. If there was confusion about self-defense, then why do we allow the jury to make the decision? What expectations do we have of the jury? Why do we have a jury? If the jury instructions are confusing, how might members of the jury be excluded from full participation because of issues with comprehension? This last question is especially useful to discuss the way lawyers and legislatures use language to exclude non-lawyers from understanding the law. Especially if you've decided to only read the jury instructions to the students, it can also be a good point to talk about how people take in and understand information and why it matters for the purposes not only of jury deliberation, but for how they, as lawyers, will communicate with clients. (To drive the point home, I like to note here that during the trial of John Hinkley Jr., who was charged with attempting to assassinate President Reagan, the jury asked for a dictionary to look up the words "fiction" and "poetry".)[12]

In this conversation you can return to the consensus that each juror's voice should be heard in making a decision on guilt or innocence, regardless of the juror's background; that each juror should be taking up space in the jury room.[13] With this in mind, students can then discuss whether each juror's voice *was* heard in their own jury exercise. How did their jury make a decision? Who spoke first? Who spoke most? Did anyone not contribute? Why was that? Unlike a classroom discussion, where students may perceive that whoever is the "smartest" person in the group should lead the discussion, there shouldn't be a sense that any one person is more deserving than another of voicing an opinion on the outcome. This is especially true since the students will have likely acknowledged that while the jurors' formal role is to apply the law to the facts, their actual position in the courtroom is much more expansive—as a check on government power.

This focus on the role of the jury can also help lead to discussions about the intersection between taking up space and race and gender. It allows students to speak about their own experiences of being a member of the mock jury, but also think about how racial and gender dynamics play out in actual juries. Students reflect on the space they took up and comment—in a respectful way—on the space that others in the group took up. In this way, students have an avenue to discuss the dynamics at play in the class more broadly.

Additionally, the exercise reminds students that the core of our criminal law class—learning the law and then applying it to facts—is something we entrust to non-lawyers every day. As such, it affirms that they are all capable and qualified to do the work of the class, and those who have, up until this point, not taken up much space in the classroom should feel some new sense of power and ownership over the materials. Students are often worried about getting the answer wrong, and this can discourage many students from venturing an answer in class. The exercise highlights that criminal law, like so many other areas of law, is simply the application of a set of laws to a body of facts with no clear right answer. The advocacy of the parties, the identity of the fact-finder and the cultural milieu in which the inquiry occurs all contribute to *an* answer, not some mythical right answer. (Indeed, I have never had each jury return the same verdict down the line, which drives home the point that in a single classroom of law students the "right" answer to the self-defense question may vary widely.)

---

12. Lincoln Caplan, *Annals of Law: The Insanity Defense*, NEW YORKER (June 25, 1984), at 45, https://www.newyorker.com/magazine/1984/07/02/the-insanity-defense. This article also provides a rich discussion of the history and debate over the insanity defense in modern American law.

13. This is also an opportunity to telegraph some of the issues that come up in a criminal procedure (adjudications) class about jury selection, namely the need for a fair cross-section in the venire and a petit jury that represents the defendant's peers. I've found that while class doesn't allow for the full conversation about race and jury selection that you can have in a criminal procedure class, you can still introduce some of these topics here.

In my experience students feel both challenged and excited by stepping into the role of jurors. I've found that students are particularly shocked by how difficult it was for them to understand the jury instructions and agree on the meaning of the law. (One additional exercise here, which demonstrates the importance and difficulty of writing the law in an accessible way, is to have them attempt to re-write the jury instructions for clarity.) This feeling is often underscored when we dig into the law of self-defense in earnest in the next several classes. In addition, students are often surprised by how heated the discussions in the jury room can get, but those heightened feelings can lead to meaningful conversations about the role of the jury, as well as the way they speak to and communicate with each other. I've gotten positive feedback on the exercise from students, but this exercise should be approached with care because of the conflicts that can arise between students and the vulnerabilities of those who discuss feeling marginalized in the exercise and in class more generally. But I find that by using the language of space, the students and I have the opportunity to probe those class dynamics that hinder an inclusive learning environment. It also gives us a concrete idea to return to when space issues arise in the future.

Conclusion

This exercise is, of course, just one of many terrific possibilities when teaching substantive criminal law. The class presents lots of opportunities to dig into meaningful conversations about social, racial and class justice. In fact a ton of useful resources exists on teaching the subject. For instance, I recommend the Guerilla Guides to Law Teaching, which have several excellent guides on how to integrate these themes into class.[14] Professor Cynthia Lee has written about how to incorporate race into the criminal law and criminal procedure curriculum,[15] a topic that was also recently tackled in a symposium at Boston University Law School.[16] In addition, the criminal law professor now has the benefit of many podcasts,[17] documentaries,[18]

---

14. GUERILLA GUIDES TO LAW TEACHING, No. 2: CRIMINAL LAW, https://guerrillaguides.wordpress.com/2016/08/29/crimlaw/.

15. Cynthia Lee, *Race and the Criminal Law Curriculum*, THE OXFORD HANDBOOK OF RACE AND THE LAW IN THE UNITED STATES (forthcoming), available at https://papers.ssrn.com/sol3/papers.cfm?abstract_id=3572334; Cynthia Lee, *Making Black and Brown Lives Matter: Incorporating Race into the Criminal Procedure Curriculum*, 60 ST. LOUIS U. L. J. 481 (2016).

16. Racial Bias, Disparities and Oppression in the 1L Curriculum: A Critical Approach to the Canonical First-Year Law School Subjects, Boston University School of Law (Feb. 28–29, 2020).

17. There are so many amazing podcasts available on criminal law topics. Here's just one example: In my criminal law class, I assign the students to listen to the *Life of the Law* podcast, episode *Ten Hours to Twenty Years*, to discuss how prosecutors prove "causation" in criminal law. But the podcast also allows the students to explore the vagaries of prosecutorial discretion and the way in which prosecutors can stack serious charges to pressure defendants into pleading guilty. In this way, the podcast allows the students to grapple with the granular legal issue of "what is causation?" and also explore how prosecutors make these decisions in the real world. Marylee Williams, *Ten Hours to Twenty Years*, LIFE OF THE LAW (Aug. 8, 2017), https://www.lifeofthelaw.org/2017/08/prosecutorial-discretion-2/.

18. See, e.g., *I Love You, Now Die* (HBO 2019), *13th* (Netflix 2016), *Thought Crimes: The Case of the Cannibal Cop* (HBO 2015).

mini-series,[19] and primetime legal procedurals[20] that can help students engage with the real-world issues that come up in the study of criminal law. There are, then, many ways to weave important conversations about diversity and inclusion into the criminal law classroom. This exercise is meant to encourage each student to contribute to that conversation in a meaningful way and to think about how they take up space in our shared world.

---

19. *See, e.g., When They See Us* (Netflix 2019).

20. *See, e.g., For Life* (ABC 2020), *For the People* (ABC 2018–19). In addition, The HBO show, *The Wire* (2002–2008), is taught as a stand-alone course at many law schools and has even inspired its own textbook, Adam M. Gershowitz, The Wire: Crime, Law, and Policy (2013).

Re-Tipping (Re-Balancing?) the Scale of Justice: A Selected Annotated Bibliography of Sources for Incorporating Issues of Diversity and Inclusion in the First Year Criminal Law Course

Ana Isabel Delgado Valentín[*]

The following is a selected bibliography on practical resources for law faculty who wish to integrate issues of diversity and inclusion into their criminal law course. This bibliography is by no means a complete list of resources, but a sample of materials available for consultation. Although the list of available resources is not lengthy, it is worth highlighting the quality of the examples available. After each entry, I have added a brief description of its most appealing features.

Books

Cole, David. *No Equal Justice: Race and Class in the American Criminal Justice System.* New York: New Press. 1999.

Professor Cole, who is both a law professor and National Legal Director for the American Civil Liberties Union, argues in this work that "while our criminal justice system is explicitly based on the premise and promise of equality before the law, the administration of criminal law ... is in fact predicated on the exploitation of inequality." (5) This relatively short and highly readable work provides an introduction suitable for a new law student to contemplate the extent to which racial discrimination is tied to disparities in policing, prosecution, and sentencing.

---

[*] Legal Research Librarian, Suffolk University Law School.

Karakatsanis, Alec. *Usual Cruelty*. New York: New Press. 2019.

Karakatsanis, a former public defender and civil rights attorney, published this short book of essays to argue that lawyers working within the criminal justice system risk becoming desensitized to daily injustices, causing them to reach a point when they may unconsciously uphold systems they would otherwise hope to change. The central section, titled "The Human Lawyer," presents a series of vignettes, many involving law students and the challenges they face in confronting injustice and brutality in the criminal justice system.

Kennedy, Randall. *Race, Crime, and the Law*. New York: Vintage. 1997.

This expansive work, which won the Robert F. Kennedy Book Award in 1998, addresses the issue of race in the criminal justice system. Professor Kennedy's work provides a historical survey of bias and discrimination in policing, jury selection, and imposition of capital punishment. Over two decades after it was first published, many of the racial disparities described remain disturbingly pervasive. Kennedy's framing of the work, which emphasizes finding common ground and advocates a "politics of respectability" (21), may be instructive for teachers who seek to illustrate how responses to unequal treatment under American law have shifted in the 21st century.

Schlanger, Margo, Sheila Bedi, David M. Shapiro, and Lynn S. Branham. *Incarceration and the Law, Cases and Materials*. St. Paul, M.N.: West Academic Publishing, 2020.

Now in its tenth edition, this casebook is a leading source for teaching the law of incarceration. The authors address criminal justice spanning from pre-trial to post-conviction. Chapter 10 part III, discusses prisoner populations and issues specific to different groups, including race and national origin discrimination, women prisoners, and LGBTQ prisoners. Chapter 19 covers the issue of accountability, by voting, standards, and external oversight.

Articles

Balos, Beverly. "Teaching Prostitution Seriously." *Buffalo Criminal Law Review* 4, no. 2 (2001): 709–753.

In this article, Professor Balos explores how the crime of prostitution is framed in leading criminal law casebooks and their accompanying teacher's manuals, with the goal of encouraging law teachers and authors to recognize the gendered implications of their treatment of sex work. In her review, the author found most texts used prostitution as a means to discuss other legal concepts, such as statutory interpretation, treating prostitution "as a moral issue or vice crime within the context of questions about what should or should not be criminalized and punished." (721) Despite years of critique from feminist scholars, these texts perpetuate stereotypes and give little attention to gendered disparities in punishment between prostitutes and their clients. Balos' work is a helpful framework for analyzing omissions and stereotypes while selecting a casebook.

Fradella, Henry F. "Integrating the Study of Sexuality into the Core Law School Curriculum: Suggestions for Substantive Criminal Law Courses." *Journal of Legal Education* 57, no. 1 (2007): 60–76.

Professor Fradella identifies a deficit of scholarship on the integration of matters of sexual identity into core law courses, finding even excellent existing work using Queer Theory to approach these issues may not sufficiently sensitize future lawyers to address GLBT issues. However, he insists that students should be told about the "centrality of incorporating diversity into the curriculum at the outset of a course" (65) and offers a wealth of cases, discussion topics, and readings beyond typical legal scholarship that may help faculty address issues of sexual identity, social class, gender, race, and ethnicity. The author also emphasizes the readings and examples that he integrates into specific areas of the criminal law curriculum are not meant to be all-encompassing. However, he covers examples in which materials on sexuality fit in quite naturally, including basic concepts of criminal law, philosophies of crime and punishment, theories of criminal liability, homicide, sex crimes, crimes against the person, and variations of self-defense. (This article was published before the landmark case *Obergefell v. Hodges.*[1])

Goodmark, Leigh. "Should Domestic Violence Be Decriminalized?" *Harvard Women's Law Journal* 40, no. 1 (2017): 53–114.

Professor Goodmark examines the intersection between the criminalization of domestic violence and the phenomenon of mass incarceration. The article begins by examining the perspectives of several feminist scholars on criminal interventions in intimate partner violence. Goodmark's work explores topics that arise in typical criminal law courses, including theoretical justifications for criminalization and punishment, and may be helpful to spark classroom discussion on the interplay of gendered and racialized harms in American criminal law.

Jones, Cynthia E. "I Am Ronald Cotton: Teaching Wrongful Convictions in a Criminal Law Class." *Ohio State Journal of Criminal Law* 10, no. 2 (Spring 2013): 609–612.

Professor Jones shares an in-class exercise for her criminal law course, in which students research the case of a person who was wrongly convicted and subsequently exonerated. Then they share the person's story as a first-person oral presentation reported in the character of the exonerated individual. Professor Jones describes how, in the years she has been using this exercise, the presentations have been filled with passion and outrage about the injustice committed. This exercise provides a chance to discuss a variety of issues, such as the fallibility of

---

1. 576 U.S. 644 (2015).

the criminal justice system. As the author explains, this exercise primes students to engage in a critical discussion and examination of criminal law doctrine.

Kuo, Susan S. "Culture Clash: Teaching Cultural Defenses in the Criminal Law Classroom." *Saint Louis University Law Journal* 48, no. 4 (Summer 2004): 1297–1312.

Professor Kuo outlines how to incorporate the concept of cultural defense into the criminal law course. Cultural defenses emerge from a criminal defendant's argument: because an admitted act is not a crime in the perpetrator's culture of origin, it should not be judged by the laws of the place where it was committed. The author believes that discussing the use of cultural defenses creates a space within the classroom for consideration of perspectives other than those inherent in traditional legal analysis. Kuo's teaching plan addresses cultural defenses at three points: 1) the relevance of culture to the criminal law, 2) the propriety of cultural defenses in the criminal law, and 3) the culture of the law school classroom. "Teaching cultural defenses opens our students' eyes to alternative and new arguments to be raised in the criminal law context. It also sheds light on the dominant culture that reigns over the creation, construction, and enforcement of our criminal laws. Finally, it offers the opportunity to provide students with a framework in which to contemplate their legal education and the legal process." (1311) This work also includes extensive references to other works on cultural defenses in criminal law.

Lawson, Tamara F. "Mainstreaming Civil Rights in Law School Curriculum: Criminal Law and Criminal Procedure." *Saint Louis University Law Journal* 54, no. 3 (Spring 2010): 837–856.

This article was part of the St. Louis University Law Journal's 2010 symposium issue "Teaching Civil Rights." Professor Lawson calls for careful and strategic planning in criminal law and criminal procedure courses to accomplish both adequate coverage of core concepts and the inclusion of civil rights issues. Lawson analogizes her role as a law professor to a prosecutor carrying the "burden of proof and persuasion" and provides several practical tips for managing that burden. First among these is selecting the right text; she recommends selecting a nontraditional text that incorporates civil rights or adding in supplemental readings. She also suggests several cases to focus on and advises incorporating video clips that illustrate pertinent civil rights issues;[2] providing vivid detail of the impact of discrimination can be more impactful than the cold record of a legal opinion. She concludes that using innovative and provocative course materials and presentations that incorporate civil rights issues enhances student interest in the course and challenges them to consider multiple perspectives, particularly race, in understanding criminal justice.

---

2. For example, in footnote 52, the author highlights *'Dateline' Gives a Shocking Look at Racial Profiling*, SEATTLE POST-INTELLIGENCER, Apr. 9, 2004, at E2, http://www.seattlepi.com/tv/168304_tv09.html.

Murray, Melissa. "Teaching Gender as a Core Value: The Softer Side of Criminal Law." *Oklahoma City University Law Review* 36, no. 2 (2011): 525–530.

This essay was part of the Oklahoma City University Law Review's 2011 symposium, "Sex in the Classroom: Teaching Gender as a Core Value." Professor Murray's essay acknowledges that in teaching criminal law, it may be more challenging to discuss gender issues than in other courses such as family law. While the family-law canon has many examples of how gender shapes the construction and application of law, criminal law narratives in the leading casebooks are populated largely by men. "As a professor in a law school where female students are the majority of the student body," she explains, "I believe it is important to challenge the criminal law's entrenched assumptions about men as offenders and enforcers and women as cowed and silent victims." (526) The author provides a list of assigned materials that help foster a robust discussion about the law of rape and public policy responses, with accompanying questions to ask the students to drive the in-class discussion and beyond.

Pinard, Michael. "Teaching Justice-Connectivity." *Louisiana Law Review* 80, no. 1 (2019): 95–108.

Professor Pinard provides a practical foundation for legal educators who are looking to impart in their students a holistic view of lawyering. The author provides an additional model that he calls justice-connectivity. With this model, Pinard aims for students to understand the connection between the different institutions, systems, and standards of laws that affect different individuals and communities.

Williams, Gregory Howard. "Teaching Criminal Law: 'Objectivity' in Black and White." *Harvard Blackletter Journal* 9 (1992): 27–42.

This article provides a foundational, and personal, critique of the concept of "neutrality" in law teaching, particularly in the criminal law context. Professor Williams argues that criminal law teaching must incorporate and speak to the diverse life experiences of faculty and students, describing how he uses his own background as a Black man and former deputy sheriff to un-settle student beliefs and pre-conceptions about criminality. He cautions, however, that "in order to be able to bring personal experiences such as these into the classroom, law schools must hire persons who have those diverse experiences," and support faculty with diverse backgrounds for leadership roles.

Podcast

In the Dark, season 2, hosted by Madeleine Baran and produced by American Public Media, https://features.apmreports.org/in-the-dark/season-two/.

This podcast follows the life of Curtis Flowers, a black man from Mississippi who was sentenced to death in 1996 and has been tried six times for the same crime. The podcast has an investigative tone and provides documents and interviews about the process and its aftermath.

Websites

Kupenda, Angela Mae. "As easy as "1, 2, buckle my shoe" 10 steps for addressing race intentionally in doctrinal classes," *Law Teaching Blog. Institute for Law Teaching and Learning,* May 16, 2019, http://lawteaching.org/2019/05/16/ addressing-race-intentionally-in-doctrinal-classes/.

In this short blog entry, Professor Kupenda offers ten steps to address race intentionally and facilitate unplanned racial discussions in doctrinal classes. The steps apply to doctrinal law courses, generally. However, she dedicates a few sentences to highlight specific issues with criminal law, among other doctrinal law courses, as a way of providing examples of how race is already present in your courses, and you need to address it. The blog entry also offers tools on how to address the topic of race, in class, before class, or after class.

"No.2 Criminal Law," *Guerrilla Guides to Law Teaching,* created August 29, 2016, https://guerrillaguides.wordpress.com/2016/08/29/crimlaw/.

The Guerrilla Guides to Law Teaching are a combined effort of a group of legal educators from around the United States. This evolving project highlights a variety of current events affecting the everyday life of people with a critical eye towards the legal system. Particularly relevant to this chapter is the post on August 29, 2016. Here the authors present a guide to deepen the discussion of core issues central to the teaching of the first year criminal law course. As a first step, the authors present a section titled "Methods" as a way to incorporate topics like mass incarceration, the relationship of crime and poverty, and other related topics alongside the theories of punishment traditionally taught in the criminal law class. The authors provide examples to make the criminal law course more relatable and closer to the current student experience with discussion for topical areas such as misdemeanors and drug laws, police violence, study prosecutorial power and discretion, among many other examples.

Chapter 5

Constitutional Law

"Why are you making us read such hateful cases?"

*Ruthann Robson**

The challenge in constitutional law courses, especially those that concentrate on or include "rights," is not integrating diversity or including minoritized persons or perspectives. The cases themselves do the work. Almost every case explicitly raises an issue of race, gender, disability, immigration, sexuality, poverty, class-exploitation, colonialism, or even enslavement.[1] Instead, the problem is how to negotiate the difficulties, disagreements, and misunderstandings inherent in diversity and inclusion. To further aggravate the problem, this negotiation occurs in the challenging context of mastering doctrine, confronting theoretical perspectives, and acquiring the necessary skills of analysis and argument. How should professors "manage" all this?

For nearly 30 years, I have been teaching a course entitled Liberty, Equality, and Due Process to students at CUNY School of Law. Unsurprisingly, throughout this time, much has changed: the doctrine covered, the cases assigned, the composition of the United States Supreme Court, the students, me, and perhaps most importantly the legal and political environment. By scheduling the required course for the students' first semester, it is intended to serve not only as a standard constitutional law course (even if a bit unusually putting "rights" before "structures"), but also as an embodiment of the twin missions of the law school: increasing access to the legal profession and educating lawyers to practice in the "public interest." At its core, this constitutional law course is intended as an introduction to the possibilities of lawyers working toward diversity and inclusion.

As is typical in constitutional law courses, our readings are almost entirely United States Supreme Court cases. Even as the case method for teaching law has been roundly critiqued, it persists. It seems to have special tenacity in American constitutional law. Certainly, cases exist alongside theoretical texts, histories, critiques, and narratives.

---

* Professor of Law & University Distinguished Professor, City University of New York (CUNY) School of Law.

1. Cases involving religious identities might not be included in a first year Constitutional Law course but treated separately in a First Amendment course. For a discussion of integrating various religious identities, see Ruthann Robson, *"Losing My Religion": Extended Role Play and the First Amendment Religion Clauses*, 21 Law Tchr. 49 (2014).

But students are struggling to move away from their undergraduate or graduate education and learning to "think like lawyers." Non-case materials are supplemental and appear in the notes in some casebooks (often too lengthy and complicated), as optional readings, or in professors' teaching that contextualizes and expands. The centerpiece, however, remains the case.

The case—as text—is heavily freighted. As students read, they labor with unfamiliar terms, syntax, and style. They grapple with the new categories necessary to complete their case briefs for class such as "facts," "procedural history," "reasoning," and "holding." All of this is what legal education anticipates and even celebrates. But students also treat the case as "text," a tendency I certainly shared as a law student. It is a phenomenon that professors can too easily disregard, even as we paradoxically stress "close reading." The difficulties intrinsic to language itself can overlap with the difficulties of diversity.

"Why do I have to read such hateful words?" student after student has asked me. So many of the cases we read in constitutional law can accurately be described as antithetical to a pluralistic and diverse democracy. There is *Dred Scott*, in which the Court denied citizenship and the right to sue for freedom to Dred Scott, and also found the Missouri Compromise unconstitutional, hastening the Civil War.[2] There is *The Civil Rights Cases* in which the Court found that despite the Reconstruction Amendments, Congress did not have the power to pass a statute prohibiting racial discrimination in public accommodations.[3] There is *Plessy v. Ferguson* in which Congress upheld a Louisiana statute mandating racial segregation in public accommodations, establishing the "separate and equal" doctrine which would last for decades.[4]

It is easy to explain that these cases are "foundational" and that we must understand the past in order to understand doctrinal development and constitutional argument.

Yet.

For some students in some years, such explanations do not satisfy. Instead, the words in the cases themselves are assaultive, disrespectful, hostile. Some semesters, the cases seem to mirror and magnify the contentious politics outside the classroom. The words seem inappropriate for a law school with a student body that is among the most diverse in the United States and that prides itself on its progressive pedagogy.

Several students tell me they object to the word "Negro" which appears in these cases.

Yet.

It cannot simply be that word, can it? Although it is a word we do not use now, it was the preferred term at the time used by such Black luminaries as Frederick Douglass.[5] I want to answer that what is wrong with the Court's opinions in *Dred Scott*

---

2. Scott v. Sandford, 60 U.S. (19 How.) 393 (1857).

3. The Civil Rights Cases, 109 U.S. 3 (1883).

4. Plessy v. Ferguson, 163 U.S. 537 (1896).

5. *See, e.g.*, Frederick Douglass, *The Present Condition and Future Prospects of the Negro People*, 2 THE LIFE AND WRITINGS OF FREDERICK DOUGLASS: PRE-CIVIL WAR DECADE, 1850–1860 244 (Philip S. Foner ed., 1950).

and *The Civil Rights Cases* and *Plessy v. Ferguson* is not the use of the word "negro," but the decisions themselves; the recitation of the facts, the reasoning, and especially the holdings.

Yet.

I understand, or think I do, that for more than a few students, the term becomes a metonymy for all the injustice manifest in the opinions. And for other students, who are not as focused on the term, it nevertheless becomes a flashpoint, so that quotations and references to the text of the case during class are fraught. The opposing viewpoints amongst the students do not fall neatly along racial identity lines: it is not only or primarily Black students who object or do not object to the word. It could be that experience before law school might make a difference: American history majors, whatever their race or ethnicity, seem most likely to defend the language of the case as part of historical context.

Yet.

I do not utter that word in class. Maintaining a distance between the "text" and what we say as professors in class seems not only acceptable, but critical. And in short: that was then, and this is now.

Yet.

A student says to me, "I notice you don't say it, but you make us read it." The classroom is different, I try to explain.

And yet.

When a student says it during class, reading from the case in response to a cold-called question, and shaping their fingers into "air quotes," another student comes for office hours to complain. I should have "shut down" and "called out" the student reading from the case. It does not escape me that the complaining student is white and is asking me, their white professor, to censure the Black student who answered the question in class. I decide that this is an illustration of the contours of academic diversity that the Court upheld in *Grutter v. Bollinger*: no one should be a "spokesperson" for their race and stereotypes bear reexamination.[6] It is also an example of the "educational benefits that flow from a diverse student body," as the Court will emphasize (and yes, narrow) *Grutter* a few years later in *Fisher II*.[7] I also decide that I will not use this example when we study these affirmative action cases a few weeks later in the semester.

The hateful language is not confined to the nineteenth century. Even in the cases that do not seem "hateful" in holding or even reasoning, there are repugnant arguments and aspects.

---

6. Grutter v. Bollinger, 539 U.S. 306, 333 (2003).

7. Fisher v. Univ. of Texas at Austin, 136 S. Ct. 2198, 2203 (2016) ("[A]sserting an interest in the educational benefits of diversity writ large is insufficient. A university's goals cannot be elusory or amorphous—they must be sufficiently measurable to permit judicial scrutiny of the policies adopted to reach them.").

Consider *Loving v. Virginia*.[8] In *Loving*, the state advanced racial purity as one of its government interests to support its criminalization of interracial marriages, specifically including the prevention of "a mongrel breed of citizens."[9] Mongrel. The desire to prevent the children who would be born from interracial marriages is especially painful to contemplate in a racially diverse classroom.

Yet.

Is it misguided to also experience a sense of triumphalism? The very "biracial" and "multi-racial" people that Virginia had sought to forbid were now adults sitting in a classroom preparing to become lawyers. Moreover, the Court's use of the term "white supremacy" in the opinion — one of the few times the Court uses the phrase[10] — seems like a great success: the naming of it and the explicit rejection of it.

Yet.

For some students it is the term "mongrel" that reverberates. "Maybe you could cross that out in the next edition of the casebook," one student suggests.[11]

In *Cleburne*, the term is "mentally retarded."[12] To even attempt to delete such a term from the majority and dissenting opinions in the case would render it indecipherable. In 1985, the Court was considering the constitutionality of an ordinance in the city of Cleburne, Texas which required special permits for homes for the "feeble-minded" including the Cleburne Living Center. The advocates in their oral arguments and briefs, as well as the Justices in their questions and opinions, employ variants of the term "mental retardation," eschewing the seemingly offensive and antiquated term "feeble-minded." But fifteen years after the decision, it is the term "mental retardation" that vibrates with offense.

In *Lawrence v. Texas*, the word is "homosexual."[13] In overruling *Bowers v. Hardwick* which upheld the constitutionality of criminalizing "sodomy,"[14] the majority opinion in *Lawrence v Texas* still employed the term "homosexual." Kennedy's opinion for the Court in *Lawrence* does this even when not describing the opinion in *Hardwick* and

---

8. 388 U.S. 1 (1967).

9. *Id.* at 7 (These purposes were "to preserve the racial integrity of its citizens," and to prevent "the corruption of blood," "a mongrel breed of citizens," and "the obliteration of racial pride.").

10. The Court uses the term "white supremacy" in various opinions in fifteen cases including *Loving*. A few of the cases are discussions of *Loving*; the majority of the cases include "white supremacy" in a discussion of the facts rather than as part of the legal analysis. *See, e.g.*, Virginia v. Black, 538 U.S. 343, 354 (2003) (quoting a Ku Klux Klan publication).

11. See Ruthann Robson, Liberty, Equality, and Due Process: Cases, Controversies, and Contexts in Constitutional Law (2nd ed. 2019). This book is available from CALI's E-Langdell Bookstore, at https://www.cali.org/books/liberty-equality-and-due-process-cases-controversies-and-contexts-constitutional-law.

12. City of Cleburne, Tex. v. Cleburne Living Ctr., 473 U.S. 432 (1985).

13. Lawrence v. Texas, 539 U.S. 558, 567 (2003).

14. Bowers v. Hardwick, 478 U.S. 186, 187 (1986), *overruled by* Lawrence v. Texas, 539 U.S. 558 (2003).

even when reaching an opposite result: "the liberty protected by the Constitution allows homosexual persons the right to make this choice."[15]

In *Plyler v. Doe*, the word is "aliens."[16] Justice Brennan, writing for the Court in 1982, concluded that not only are the "illegal aliens who are plaintiffs in these cases" able to claim the benefit of the Fourteenth Amendment's guarantee of equal protection, but that the Texas statute withholding state school funding for any student who was not a "citizen of the United States or a legally admitted alien" violated the Equal Protection Clause. Brennan's opinion does use the term "undocumented," although at times this is coupled with "alien" (as in "undocumented aliens"). The holding of the case, however, rejects the interests Texas advanced.[17] And the opinion ends:

> If the State is to deny a discrete group of innocent children the free public education that it offers to other children residing within its borders, that denial must be justified by a showing that it furthers some substantial state interest. No such showing was made here.[18]

Yet.

For some students, this favorable outcome does not erase the insult of the word "alien," especially when coupled with "illegal." During office hours, two students tell me how disturbed they are and wonder if they can ever become attorneys. A few years earlier, the law school had been at the forefront of arguing for admission to practice law of an undocumented graduate.[19] But these students, who discussed their own immigration statuses, were just as concerned by the words that they would have to write or say in judicial proceedings. "Can't you just tell the judge you object to that word and are just not going to use it? We noticed you did not say it in class." I tell them most of the time you can avoid it, but sometimes it will be the name of a statute, for example, the Alien Tort Claim Act.[20] And now I have said the word.

This office meeting occurred during the heightened tensions caused by President Trump's anti-immigration pronouncements. By the time a challenge reached the United States Supreme Court, at least one Justice would validate the approach I had tried to express during those office hours. Dissenting in *Trump v. Hawai'i*, in which the Court upheld the third iteration of the so-called Muslim travel ban, rejecting the Establishment Clause challenge, in a footnote Sotomayor wrote:

---

15. *Lawrence*, 539 U.S. at 567.

16. Plyler v. Doe, 457 U.S. 202 (1982).

17. *Id.* at 228–30 (These were "protecting" from "an influx of "illegal immigrants""; relieving schools from the "special burdens" imposed by "undocumented children"; and not spending money on those who because of "their unlawful presence within the United States renders them less likely than other children to remain within the boundaries of the State, and to put their education to productive social or political use within the State.").

18. *Id.* at 230.

19. *See* In re Vargas, 10 N.Y.S.3d 579 (N.Y. App. Div. 2015); Janet M. Calvo, *Professional Licensing and Teacher Certification for Non-Citizens: Federalism, Equal Protection and A State's Socio-Economic Interests*, 8 COLUM. J. RACE & L. 33 (2017).

20. Alien Tort Claims Act, 28 U.S.C. § 1350.

It is important to note, particularly given the nature of this case, that many consider "using the term 'alien' to refer to other human beings" to be "offensive and demeaning." I use the term here only where necessary "to be consistent with the statutory language" that Congress has chosen and "to avoid any confusion in replacing a legal term of art with a more appropriate term."[21]

Justice Sotomayor has also inspired one of my favorite strategies to combat some of the hateful words that we encounter throughout the semester and to try to enact a classroom that supports diversity and inclusion.[22]

Sotomayor dissented in *Schuette* v. *Coalition to Defend Affirmative Action, Integration & Immigrant Rights & Fight for Equality By Any Means Necessary (BAMN)*.[23] In *Schuette*, the Court upheld the constitutionality of a Michigan state constitutional provision banning "discrimination" or "preferential treatment" on the basis of "race, sex, color, ethnicity, or national origin."[24] The amendment was the result of a voter referendum, passed as a consequence of the Court's decision in *Grutter* upholding "diversity in higher education" as a compelling state interest.[25]

Sotomayor's lengthy dissent, joined by Justice Ginsburg, includes a subsection addressing the view of her colleagues on the Court who argued "that we should leave race out of the picture entirely and let the voters sort it out."[26] She begins "race matters."

I tell the class we will treat our discussion of this section as a "choral reading" and for students to volunteer to read aloud a phrase or a sentence or two at most from the opinion, trying not to repeat. I tell them I will not call on them. I stand back, moving away from the lectern and away from the front of the class. There follow moments of confusion. But invariably, one student will start and read aloud a sentence, and then other students, one by one, will follow.

Here are some of the things they read:

- Race matters in part because of the long history of racial minorities' being denied access to the political process.

---

21. Trump v. Hawaii, 138 S. Ct. 2392, 2444 n.7 (2018) (Sotomayor, J., dissenting) (quoting Flores v. United States Citizenship & Immigration Servs., 718 F.3d 548, 551–52, n. 1 (6th Cir. 2013)).

22. Another strategy is also inspired by Justice Sotomayor, as well as the Feminist Judgments projects, *see e.g.*, FEMINIST JUDGMENTS: REWRITTEN OPINIONS OF THE UNITED STATES SUPREME COURT (Kathryn Stanchi, Linda Berger & Bridget Crawford, eds., 2016). This assignment asks students to briefly rewrite any opinion we have studied from the perspective of their favorite Justice (including any future Justice they might envision including themselves). I've received some excellent revisions of *Dred Scott, Plessy, Cleburne,* and *Lawrence,* as authored by Sonia Sotomayor.

23. Schuette v. Coal. to Defend Affirmative Action, Integration & Immigrant Rights & Fight for Equality By Any Means Necessary (BAMN), 572 U.S. 291, 337 (2014) (Sotomayor, J. dissenting).

24. *Schuette,* 572 U.S. at 299 (quoting MICH. CONST. ART. I § 26).

25. Grutter v. Bollinger, 539 U.S. 306 (2003). In the companion case of *Gratz v. Bollinger,* 539 U.S. 244 (2003), the Court found that the undergraduate admissions program was not sufficiently narrowly tailored and thus unconstitutional.

26. *Grutter,* 539 U.S. at 380 (Part IV B of Sotomayor's dissent).

- Race also matters because of persistent racial inequality in society—inequality that cannot be ignored and that has produced stark socioeconomic disparities.
- [T]he many ways in which "the effects of centuries of law-sanctioned inequality remain painfully evident in our communities and schools," in areas like employment, poverty, access to health care, housing, consumer transactions, and education.
- [R]ecognizing that the "lingering effects" of discrimination, "reflective of a system of racial caste only recently ended, are evident in our workplaces, markets, and neighborhoods."
- And race matters for reasons that really are only skin deep, that cannot be discussed any other way, and that cannot be wished away.
- Race matters to a young man's view of society when he spends his teenage years watching others tense up as he passes, no matter the neighborhood where he grew up.
- Race matters to a young woman's sense of self when she states her hometown, and then is pressed, "No, where are you *really* from?", regardless of how many generations her family has been in the country.
- Race matters to a young person addressed by a stranger in a foreign language, which he does not understand because only English was spoken at home.
- Race matters because of the slights, the snickers, the silent judgments that reinforce that most crippling of thoughts: "I do not belong here."
- The way to stop discrimination on the basis of race is to speak openly and candidly on the subject of race, and to apply the Constitution with eyes open to the unfortunate effects of centuries of racial discrimination.
- [W]e ought not sit back and wish away, rather than confront, the racial inequality that exists in our society. It is this view that works harm, by perpetuating the facile notion that what makes race matter is acknowledging the simple truth that race *does* matter.[27]

There are some repetitions and some faltering and some silences. But it is incredibly moving and gives voice to the diversity within the room—or at least some of the diversity—in a way we rarely experience.

Yet.

There are complaints. For every student who will tells me they found it "powerful" or "affirming" or "cool," there is another student who will have a "suggestion": I should have announced the assignment in the syllabus; I should have only allowed students of color to talk; I should have cold-called; I should have stepped-in when a student spoke twice or when another student repeated a phrase that had already been spoken. And I definitely should have said something when *that* classmate read aloud the case name *and* citation.

---

27. *Id.*

They seem to want—or at least some students seem to want—the diversity managed. At least sometimes.

I am sympathetic to the impulse to supervise. As professors, we engage in classroom "management," especially in large doctrinal classes, for how could we accomplish our numerous teaching goals otherwise? And I have orchestrated this "choral reading" of Sotomayor's words for five years, usually with two different classes (full time and part time), for more than 500 students. I have certainly developed ideas for what would make the best performance, which would admittedly include some of the student suggestions.

Yet.

Performance is not the point. We must resist the impulses to merely perform diversity, to make it smoother and shinier, to render it less messy and riddled with imperfections, misunderstandings, and even disagreements. We cannot protect our students from the past. Or even the present.

And yet.

We continue to struggle with them towards a more just future with fewer hateful cases.

Naming Them

Nancy Leong[*]

Each semester, I begin my first year constitutional law class with an "introductory survey." Some of the questions are serious ("What do you want your life to look like in ten years?") while others are just for fun ("What television show should I be watching right now?" and "Which are better, cats or dogs?").

I get a lot of information from these serious and silly questions before I ever meet the students face to face, probably more than they intend to tell me. I learn what they value; what makes them laugh, even their pets' names; how they present themselves. The questions change from semester to semester as the world changes around us ("Who should sit on the Iron Throne?" and "Are you experiencing any obstacles to your learning as a result of the COVID-19 pandemic?").

But I also ask two questions that never change. They are: "What name would you like to be called in class? Please include a phonetic pronunciation"; and "What pronouns do you use to refer to yourself?"

These two questions—asked in the first email students ever receive from me— set the tone for the semester. They both establish the classroom environment and, more subtly, lay the groundwork for our study of the Equal Protection Clause. These questions are also critical to nurturing diversity and fostering inclusion for two reasons. The first relates to race, ethnicity, and dialect. Many people—but disproportionately people of color—routinely experience mangling of their names. This experience is often remarkably "othering." Put yourself in the shoes of a student watching an old white professor, standing at the front of the classroom, entirely in charge of their upcoming semester to say nothing of their grade, looking at their name on the class roster with befuddlement. It is a painful and cringeworthy scene that suggests the person attached to the confounding name simply does not belong in the classroom in the same way as classmates with more familiar anglophone names.

When a person charged with your education struggles with your name, it is an intensely alienating experience. It is also a deeply racialized event. As an undergraduate majoring in music and English, I watched professors who flawlessly pronounced

---

[*] Professor of Law, University of Denver Sturm College of Law.

names like "Tchaikovsky" throw up their hands at the sight of my last name, which is five letters long, pronounced Lee-ONG, and rhymes with other common English words like "song." The first day of each class was a cringeworthy event; I always knew my name was next on the list by the pregnant pause with which the professor preceded it.

I resolved early in my law teaching career I would not do the same to my students. As a native speaker of English, I will readily admit that I find some names harder than others, but this is *my* problem, not my students' problem. I drill pronunciation of every name until every single one is easy by the first day of class. Thus, every student begins class on equal footing.

Names are important. The referent for each student—their name—is presented as valuable and worthy of correct pronunciation *on the first day of class*. I got this idea from Barack Obama, who, I have read, routinely practiced pronouncing names of foreign leaders and less-familiar names of regular individuals with whom he was scheduled to meet.[1]

The other question, about pronouns, serves two purposes. Most obviously, it informs me about students' pronouns so that I can memorize them accurately for the first day of class. More subtly, it again places the class on a level playing field. *Everyone* has to take two seconds and let me know their preferred pronouns. The answer isn't assumed for anyone. This shifts the dynamic even before day one of class. Plenty of professors say that people are welcome to let them know if they have "different pronouns from what I might expect." But that solution still places a disparate burden on trans or gender non-conforming students. Moreover, it requires students to attempt to read their professors' minds: how do they know what their professors are going to expect? As with the pronunciation of names, everyone deserves to have others use their preferred pronouns without going to any more effort than anyone else.

These two questions lay a foundation for productive discussion of the important legal issues we will face throughout the semester—including, a few months in, the Equal Protection Clause. What does equality mean? What does justice mean? While students may have widely divergent views on these topics, creating a baseline of equal treatment on the basis of race and gender identification creates an environment in which students know they will be heard and respected.

In classes where professors do not bother to learn how to say their students' names or pronouns, approaching the Equal Protection Clause yields an irony both painful and obvious. Why should students of color and gender non-conforming students believe that the Equal Protection Clause will protect their rights alongside those of their white cisgender classmates when the person tasked with teaching them about that provision cannot be bothered to treat them equally in the most basic way?

---

1. Carol E. Lee, *Obama, a stickler for pronunciation*, Politico (July 3, 2009), https://www.politico.com/story/2009/07/obama-a-stickler-for-pronunciation-024466.

For a cisgender student named Jessica Smith, the correct pronunciation of her name and the use of she/her/hers pronouns may be a given. For other students these expectations are a small miracle. "You are the only professor who has ever bothered to say my name correctly," a student with a Vietnamese first and last name once told me. I thought of this student—an immigrant child of a single mother, for whom simply attending college was a miracle—and felt angry and sad that they spent four years of college listening to mostly white, highly privileged professors fumble through their name.

Doubtless some of my colleagues will be resistant to the idea that it is a core responsibility of our job—rather than a nice but non-essential task—to get their students' names and genders correct. I disagree. To disregard the basic features of your students' identities is to say you don't mind if you treat students of color differently and worse, in the aggregate, or that you don't really care if you treat gender nonconforming students differently and worse.

While schools probably cannot *require* professors to treat their students equally in this basic way, deans and other members of the administration can lead from the front. First, they can tell faculty that getting names right really is part of the job. Second, they can include a question on evaluations inquiring as to whether the professor pronounced their names and used their pronouns correctly. Finally, they can model the practice in their own spheres by ensuring that they pronounce faculty members' names correctly and use the correct pronouns.

Names and other identifiers alone will not make the constitutional law classroom a welcoming environment—one that embraces the spirit of the Equal Protection Clause. But professors can make a good start toward these goals by taking steps to include all their students—by naming them.

Integrating Diversity into the Constitutional Law Classroom: *Roe*, Abortion, and Reproductive Justice

*Tiffany C. Graham**

Introduction

The project of incorporating diversity into the constitutional law classroom can sometimes feel like a self-evident task. Teaching equal protection, for instance, forces students to consider questions about race,[1] gender,[2] sexual orientation,[3] and more. In addition, some casebook authors are beginning to evaluate the way under-explored historical events like Chinese exclusion and Japanese internment played a critical role in understanding executive and legislative power.[4] Comprehensive survey courses that cover the Free Exercise and Establishment Clauses will necessarily expose students

---

* Associate Professor of Law, Touro College, Jacob D. Fuchsberg Law Center.

1. Brown v. Bd. of Educ., 347 U.S. 483 (1954) (finding that racial segregation in public schools violated the Fourteenth Amendment to the U.S. Constitution).

2. United States v. Virginia, 518 U.S. 515 (1996) (finding that the state of Virginia failed to articulate a sufficiently persuasive justification for excluding women from admission into the Virginia Military Institute).

3. Obergefell v. Hodges, 576 U.S. 644 (2015) (finding that the Fourteenth Amendment required states to provide marriage licenses to two individuals of the same sex and further, that it required states to recognize same-sex marriages validly performed in another state).

4. Professors Randy Barnett and Josh Blackman have published a constitutional law casebook that considers the power of the executive to detain American citizens without a trial by exploring the three major cases that legalized different facets of the regime that defined the detention and internment of Japanese-Americans during World War II. *See* RANDY E. BARNETT & JOSH BLACKMAN, CONSTITUTIONAL LAW: CASES IN CONTEXT 572–597 (3d ed. 2017) (citing Hirabayashi v. United States, 320 U.S. 81 (1943); Korematsu v. United States, 323 U.S. 214 (1944); and Ex parte Endo, 323 U.S. 283 (1944)). *See also* STEVEN GOW CALABRESI & GARY LAWSON, THE U.S. CONSTITUTION: CREATION, RECONSTRUCTION, THE PROGRESSIVES, AND THE MODERN ERA 744–754 (2020) (incorporating Ping v. United States, 130 U.S. 581 (1889) and Fong Yue Ting v. United States, 149 U.S. 698 (1893), cases that arose from Chinese exclusion and which articulated Congress' plenary power to regulate immigration).

to claims advanced by practitioners of minority faiths. Even though the traditional Constitutional Law I course, primarily focusing on the structure of the federal government and the powers of each branch, is less likely to examine the role that marginalized groups played in the development of doctrine, Constitutional Law II—with its emphasis on individual rights—is replete with examples of constitutional engagement with the lives of minorities, women, and other groups who have lived on the sidelines.

To a significant degree, then, one might successfully incorporate diversity into constitutional law simply through inertia: as one progresses through the standard casebook, the class will eventually consider cases like *Brown v. Board of Education*,[5] *U.S. v. Virginia*,[6] *Obergefell v. Hodges*,[7] *Korematsu v. United States*,[8] *Church of Lukumi Babalu Aye v. City of Hialeah*,[9] and more. On balance, then, is this a course that is sufficiently inclusive, or would it still benefit from giving more attention to the role that diverse groups of people played in shaping the doctrine? The answer, of course, to the latter question is yes.

There are certainly many areas that are ripe for greater inclusion, especially within the structure and powers section of the course. Instructors, however, should not shy away from opportunities to incorporate more diverse considerations into the rights section, as well, even though this part of the class organically lends itself to such consideration. As an initial matter, it is always valuable to facilitate deeper student knowledge about a subject, but beyond that, there are various avenues that instructors can explore which will expose students to the intersectional factors that complicate constitutional jurisprudence. An excellent example arises when instructors cover substantive due process and the unit on abortion.

Low-Income Women of Color & Abortion Jurisprudence

It is fairly unremarkable to teach abortion by breaking the topic into three rough time periods. First, there is the early period that begins with *Roe v. Wade's*[10] articulation of the right and the subsequent impact of *Roe* on American politics, in particular, the growth and development of the Religious Right. Next, there is the period of doctrinal refinement and limitation, as represented by cases like *Casey v. Planned Parenthood of Pennsylvania*[11] and *Gonzales v. Carhart*.[12] Finally, there is the most recent

---

5. 347 U.S. 483 (1954).
6. 518 U.S. 515 (1996).
7. 576 U.S. 644 (2015).
8. 323 U.S. 214 (1944).
9. 508 U.S. 520 (1993).
10. 410 U.S. 113 (1973).
11. 505 U.S. 833 (1992).
12. 550 U.S. 124 (2007).

period characterized by the Supreme Court's response to state-level TRAP laws, or Targeted Regulation of Abortion Providers laws, where the Court has continued to address efforts by the states to limit abortion access and establish test case opportunities that might lead to the reversal of *Roe* and *Casey*. Less common, however, might be a sustained focus on the intersections among sex, race, and class that the lived reality of abortion reveals. Engaging with the actual experience of abortion could offer valuable insight for students as they consider the impact of doctrine on one of the most private, personal decisions that a woman might face in her life.

Constitutional law professors who wish to highlight the experiences of low-income women of color who encounter multiple anti-abortion regulatory barriers that are increasingly difficult to navigate might consider doing so after covering the Supreme Court decisions in *Harris v. McCrae*[13] and *Casey*. As described by Rhonda Copelon and Sylvia Law, the decision in *McRae* to uphold the Hyde Amendment's exclusion of most medically necessary abortions from Medicaid coverage "gutted the right to abortion for poor women"[14] and "set the stage for restrictive approaches to constitutional protection of fundamental rights affecting the poor, reproductive rights, and previously assumed rights more broadly."[15] *Casey* affirmed that trend toward restriction when it adopted the undue burden standard for evaluating abortion regulations, abandoning the strict scrutiny test articulated in *Roe*. Consequently, and due to the growing influence of the anti-abortion movement, state legislatures began to pass an ever-expanding array of laws that made abortions much harder to obtain for poor women.

The Reproductive Justice Movement

Engaging students here regarding the intersection of race, class, and abortion is valuable for another reason: the period after *Casey* coincides with the beginning of the movement for reproductive justice. The movement began at a pro-choice conference in 1994, when a group of African-American women decided that the rights-based approach to abortion insufficiently served the needs of Black women, who not only needed that protection, but also needed support in addressing access-based concerns.[16] Unlike the reproductive rights movement, the reproductive justice movement does not situate itself within a space that is primarily concerned with limiting the scope of government power to regulate personal liberty; instead, it is a human rights movement,

---

13. 448 U.S. 297 (1980).

14. Rhonda Copelon & Sylvia A. Law, *"Nearly Allied to Her Right to Be"—Medicaid Funding for Abortion: The Story of Harris v. McRae*, in WOMEN AND THE LAW STORIES 208 (Elizabeth M. Schneider & Stephanie M. Wildman, eds., 2011).

15. *Id.*

16. *See* Abigail Abrams, '*We Are Grabbing Our Own Microphones': How the Advocates of Reproductive Justice Stepped Into the Spotlight*, TIME (Nov. 21, 2019), https://time.com/5735432/reproductive-justice-groups/.

largely comprised of and organized by grassroots activists of color.[17] Reproductive justice locates the conversation about abortion within a fuller context that looks at access to healthcare overall, and further interrogates other structural barriers that contribute to poverty, inequality, and a distributional lack of power, especially to the degree that this last concern undermines the ability of poor women of color to exercise control over their lives.[18] A full accounting of the reproductive justice movement is beyond the scope of this essay, but instructors could use the concerns of this movement to highlight the importance of the right to many women, as well as the strategic limitations that come with a narrow focus on little more than securing it.

Using Abortion Access and Reproductive Justice as Lenses for Exploring Movement Organizing

Introducing students to the reproductive justice movement has another benefit— it provides an opportunity to expose students to the different modes of organizing that one often sees in social movements to secure legal rights and related policy goals. For example, students could explore the idea of "cause lawyering" and identify the attorneys who work within the reproductive rights movement as fitting within that framework. Moreover, they would have the opportunity to think about what it means to be a cause lawyer. For instance, how do cause lawyers attend to their ethical obligations when they are both serving clients who are the faces of each test case while also advancing the overarching goals of the cause? In addition, lawyers can occupy the position of privileged elites; how, then, do cause lawyers account for this potential barrier when serving vulnerable clients who, quite often, will not possess the same advantages?

By contrast, the organizers who serve as leaders within the reproductive justice movement—often women of color—offer a model of grassroots advocacy in pursuit of a particular set of goals. The tools of grassroots organizing and advocacy are distinct from the tools of litigation, but when deployed effectively, they can be as powerful. As young attorneys in training, students can use the example of this movement to consider how lawyers might partner with grassroots activists in ways that serve their complementary goals.[19]

---

17. This contrasts with the reproductive rights movement, which is largely shaped by lawyers and litigation. *See, e.g.*, Sarah London, *Reproductive Justice: Developing a Lawyering Model*, 13 Berkeley J. of African-Am. L. & Pol'y 71, 83–88 (discussing the impact of lawyers on building, driving, and sustaining the rights movement, often to the detriment of poor women of color).

18. *Id.*

19. It is also worth noting that a class discussion along these lines could have the future benefit of informing the way students think about the precedents that undergirded *Brown v. Board of Education*, as well as the legal backdrop for the Civil Rights Movement. Specifically, students would be prepared to think about the roles of and interaction between the NAACP Legal Defense Fund and the activists in groups like the Student Nonviolent Coordinating Committee (SNCC), as both were working to dismantle centuries of racial injustice.

One concrete example of a grassroots activist organization that instructors could use as an entry point into this conversation is the Mississippi Reproductive Freedom Fund (MRFF). MRFF describes itself in the following way:

> We're a dedicated group of Mississippians who believe in access to full reproductive health care that includes abortion as a human right and an essential part of reproductive justice. We recognize and affirm that the right to parent, not to parent, have access to full reproductive health care and education and to raise children in safe environments with full support and your needs met are ALL basic human rights.

> We do our part by offering financial assistance and practical support to persons seeking abortion as well as free emergency contraception, community based comprehensive sex education and fighting for reproductive justice in Mississippi. We strive for a world where every person experiences full reproductive justice.[20]

This organization is a lifeline for women in the state who need access to reproductive care—in particular, abortion services—but who are stymied by state law regulatory barriers that are increasingly difficult to surmount. The organization functions as a way station for women who need financial and other forms of assistance as they navigate the rules that govern abortion, both in Mississippi and across the South. But for the intervention of MRFF, many of the most vulnerable women in Mississippi and the surrounding region would effectively lose their right to terminate an unwanted pregnancy.

Groups like MRFF have become invaluable sources of support for women around the country who would otherwise not be able to terminate their pregnancies because of the obstacles they face.[21] They are part of a national network of grassroots abortion activists who fill a critical gap that public policymakers have, in many cases, chosen not to fill. The role of these organizations is particularly vital in states whose laws have made obtaining an abortion increasingly difficult, especially for poor women.[22]

---

20. Mississippi Reproductive Freedom Fund, *Who We Are*, https://www.msreprofreedomfund. org/about (last visited Oct. 9, 2020).

21. *See, e.g.*, Lornet Turnbull, *How Grassroots Funds are Ensuring Abortion Access Despite Bans*, Yes Mag. (May 16, 2019), https://www.yesmagazine.org/social-justice/2019/05/16/abortion-ban-grassroots-funds-access-healthcare/ ("Across conservative states and cities such as Jackson, home of [Mississippi's] only abortion clinic, or in Tuscaloosa, Alabama, grassroots organizations like [Laurie Bertram] Roberts' [Mississippi Reproductive Freedom Fund] are working nonstop to support reproductive justice. Funding cuts and increasingly restrictive legislation have transformed large swaths of the Southeast into abortion deserts, where low-income women increasingly have come to depend on these groups to access abortion."); *see also* Susan Dunlap, *An abortion fund for Native people is more than just a fund*, The NM Political Report (March 6, 2020), https://nmpoliticalreport.com/2020/ 03/06/an-abortion-fund-for-native-people-is-more-than-just-a-fund/ (discussing the activities of grassroots organization Indigenous Women Rising, which is the only group dedicated specifically to providing abortion funding for Indigenous women).

22. This is particularly true in the Southeast. Organizations like the New Orleans Abortion Fund, https://www.neworleansabortionfund.org/, the Yellowhammer Fund in Alabama, https://yellowhammer fund.org/, Access Reproductive Care—Southeast in Georgia, https://www.arc-southeast.org/, and Carolina Abortion Fund in North Carolina, https://www.carolinaabortionfund.org/, are examples of

The groups are nonprofit funding organizations and they are highly focused on practical concerns: they provide transportation or gas money for the drive to clinics, find free overnight lodging that is near the clinic locations, provide food during the trip, and otherwise support women who lack the resources to do many of these things on their own.[23]

As MRFF can attest, Mississippi is an excellent example for students of a state whose harsh legal landscape places the need for these grassroots efforts into stark relief. The Mississippi state legislature consistently attempts to restrict abortion as much as the Constitution will permit. By way of example, state law requires that women seeking an abortion receive in-person counseling, after which they must wait twenty-four hours before receiving an abortion.[24] As a result, women must make two trips to the clinic. This is a burden on working class and poor women, many of whom must drive a substantial distance to get to the clinic and who may struggle to take more than one day off work. Mississippi also limits the availability of abortion after eighteen weeks, a point in time which is well within the viability standard established by *Roe* and *Casey*.[25] In addition, Mississippi recently passed a series of laws governing the operation of abortion clinics that purports to protect maternal health, but has little to no connection to that specific goal. Instead, the laws simply impose so many restrictions on the functioning of an abortion clinic that remaining open has become increasingly burdensome.[26]

Working class and poor women, a disproportionate number of whom are Black, feel the impact of these laws most acutely. In fact, data shows that, as recently as 2016, Black women accounted for eighty percent of the individuals who had an abortion in the state, while White women only accounted for nineteen percent of the total.[27] There are multiple explanations for the difference in the rates at which White and Black Mississippians choose to terminate their pregnancies, ranging from disparate access to health care (including access to high-quality contraception), to differences

---

groups within the national network of funders who work to ensure that poor women have full access to their reproductive rights.

23. Zoë Beery, *What Abortion Looks Like in Mississippi: One Person at a Time*, N.Y. Times (June 13, 2019), https://www.nytimes.com/2019/06/13/magazine/abortion-mississippi.html (discussing the challenges that women in Mississippi face when they seek to terminate a pregnancy).

24. See *Mississippi—Abortion-Care Policies*, NARAL, https://www.prochoiceamerica.org/state-law/mississippi/ (last visited Oct. 9, 2020) (describing the kinds of TRAP laws that Mississippi has passed, including, for example, a requirement that all physicians who are associated with an abortion provider be board certified in obstetrics and gynecology).

25. *Id.*

26. *Id.*

27. See *Reported Legal Abortions by Race of Women Who Obtained Abortion by the State of Occurrence*, Kaiser Family Found., https://www.kff.org/womens-health-policy/state-indicator/abortions-by-race/?currentTimeframe=0&sortModel=%7B%22colId%22:%22Location%22,%22sort%22:%22asc%22%7D (identifying by race the percentage of women receiving abortions in each state in 2016). While the percentage of Black women in Mississippi who terminate their pregnancies is higher than the percentage of White women who do the same, the percentage of White women who receive an abortion is higher than the percentage of Black women on a national basis. *See id.*

in income and socioeconomic status, to other factors reflecting the harms perpetuated by structural inequality.[28] Regardless of the reason, Black women in Mississippi, who are disproportionately poor or working class, shoulder the brunt of the access burdens that have been legislatively imposed. Ultimately, the attacks on abortion, and the material consequences that flow from these attacks, highlight the manner in which race, gender, and class intersect in a set of policy choices that result in Black women shouldering most of the burden of disadvantage.

Conclusion

Based on my own teaching experiences, students generally respond well to the inclusion of a reproductive justice focused sub-unit when studying abortion. They rarely have the opportunity to think about abortion within the contexts of race, poverty, and healthcare more broadly, and the intersections that link these issues. In addition, they often do not realize the degree to which access burdens are disproportionately borne by women of color. These materials can be eye-opening for students and help them internalize information about the ways in which the abortion debate is grounded in concerns about structural inequality as well as a focus on individual rights. To be clear, I have also had students with strong moral objections to abortion and who resist anything that they interpret as an attempt to persuade them to alter their views. I have found that anchoring the discussion within the context of movement organizing—and in particular, the way social movement actors attempt to impact the law—helps to keep them on board because they can more readily understand the connection between the in-depth exploration of the topic and its connection to their legal training.

As one can see, Constitutional Law instructors who wish to diversify the standard syllabus have multiple avenues for achieving this goal. The story of abortion—especially as it relates to the women who are most acutely affected by the limits that lawmakers have steadily placed on the exercise of the right—is one that provides a rich opportunity for directing students' attention to the impact of marginalization on the operation of the law.

---

28. In 2018, a study by the Kaiser Family Foundation showed disparities in health insurance coverage between White and Black residents of Mississippi. Data showed that 16% of nonelderly Black residents were uninsured, compared to 13% of nonelderly White residents; 41% of Black residents had employer-based insurance while 59% of White residents had the same; and finally, 36% of nonelderly Black residents received insurance through Medicaid while 16% of White residents received the same. *See Mississippi: Health Coverage and Uninsured*, Kaiser Family Found., https://www.kff.org/state-category/health-coverage-uninsured/?state=ms. The last figure is particularly relevant in light of the fact that the Hyde Amendment prevents the use of Medicaid funds to pay for abortions except in the cases of rape, incest, or when the life of the mother is at stake. *See State Funding of Abortion Under Medicaid*, Guttmacher Inst. (Oct. 1, 2020), https://www.guttmacher.org/state-policy/explore/state-funding-abortion-under-medicaid ("First implemented in 1977, the Hyde Amendment, which currently forbids the use of federal funds for abortions except in cases of life endangerment, rape or incest, has guided public funding for abortions under the joint federal-state Medicaid programs for low-income women.").

Annotated Bibliography on Diversity and Inclusion Practice in the Constitutional Law Classroom

Jingwei Zhang[*]

Introduction

Constitutional law is a subject that innately touches on issue of diversity and inclusion. In this bibliography, several articles discuss how to create an open-minded, safe learning environment for students in constitutional law classes when dealing with sensitive issues such as those involving race or gender that might cause conflicts among students, or between students and instructors. Other articles provide practical teaching ideas for innovative ways of teaching this subject and examples of non-traditional teaching resources. There are also research guides that offer lists of suggested reading or other learning materials for faculty and students to be more mindful of the issue of diversity and inclusion while learning/teaching constitutional law.

Books

Carrasco, Gilbert Paul. "The Pedagogics of Poverty in Constitutional Law." In *Vulnerable Populations and Transformative Law Teaching: A Critical Reader*, edited by the Society of American Law Teachers and Golden Gate University, 73–87. Durham, N.C.: Carolina Academic Press, 2011.

This chapter discusses the idea that the Constitution protects poverty-based rights and how those rights have changed over time. Carrasco points out that recent litigation indicates an increasing lack of protection for the underprivileged. To remedy this issue, the author discusses some innovative approaches for delivering

* Reference Librarian, Rutgers Law School Library, Camden, New Jersey. The author would like to thank all the editors for their collective work, especially for Genevieve B. Tung who offered great advice and encouragement throughout the process.

constitutional law instruction. In addition to the traditional focus on the litigation and policy aspects in this area, Carrasco suggests positing change in the context of federalism by thinking beyond the Supreme Court and examining possible changes in state constitutions. Carrasco also discusses protections for the poor outside the courtroom with legislative and executive branch authorities.

Harkins, Anne Marie, and Robin Clark, "Planning for the Worst-off in the Worst Case Scenarios: Emergency Planning for the Economically Disadvantaged." In *Vulnerable Populations and Transformative Law Teaching: A Critical Reader,* edited by the Society of American Law Teachers and Golden Gate University School of Law, 201–225. Durham, N.C.: Carolina Academic Press, 2011.

In this chapter, Harkins and Clark offer teaching methods for encouraging emergency liability planning by incorporating emergency scenarios into doctrinal courses. The authors list examples of topical legal materials concerning the economically disadvantaged populations in emergencies. For a constitutional law class, Harkins and Clark suggest using the Commerce Clause and the Spending Clause to address services during emergencies for those in need. The authors also suggest using film and media, cross-disciplinary journals, and field trip exercises to pair with cases and statutes as more traditional legal instruction resources.

Articles

Ansley, Frances Lee. "Race and the Core Curriculum in Legal Education." *California Law Review* 79, no. 6 (1991): 1511–1597.

In this article, Ansley argues that race should be incorporated into the law school curriculum. While not specifically discussing a constitutional law class, this article is discussing a case study which could be used in a constitutional law class. Ashley states law schools are in a better position to achieve consensus on the centrality of race to the legal discipline and its core texts. In her discrimination class, Ansley examined the drafting of the Constitution with respect to slavery. She shares her questions used in class to facilitate student discussion and how students reacted to those questions. Ansley acknowledges that instructors can feel discomfort when attempting to teach issues of racial differences, regardless of the consensus that such issues should be addressed in law school curriculum. However, she argues that the reward outweighs the difficulties and that it should be an indispensable part of legal education.

Boles, Anastasia M. "The Culturally Proficient Law Professor: Beginning the Journey." *New Mexico Law Review* 48, no. 1 (2018): 145–172.

This article starts with a real-life situation; a race-related discussion between faculty and students in a constitutional law classroom that leads to a student-faculty forum, addressing issues of discussing race in culturally sensitive ways. The author draws upon her observation of this event and suggests that law instructors need to become culturally proficient when addressing diversity issues in class. Boles discusses the benefit of providing culturally proficient instruction in legal education. She also suggests that law instructors need to focus first on the "inside out" endeavor of cultural transformation before taking outward steps to change the classroom environment.

Instructors should start with identifying their own cultural values and associated biases. Boles then elaborates on the cultural proficiency continuum and essential elements and barriers that one might encounter. Finally, the author offers threshold steps law professors can take to become culturally proficient, including 1) seeking training on this matter, 2) mitigating unconscious racism from implicit bias to racial anxiety or stereotype threat, and 3) recognizing and reducing macroaggressions.

Deo, Meera E. "The Promise of Grutter: Diverse Interactions at the University of Michigan Law School." *Michigan Journal of Race and Law* 17, no. 1 (2011): 63–118.

Deo starts this article with an analysis of the diversity rationale in *Grutter v. Bollinger*.[1] After examining previous literature on diversity and interaction, Deo points out that despite the expected benefits of diversity through affirmative action, there is a difference between diversity in numbers (structural diversity) and actual diverse interactions in class (interactional diversity and classroom diversity). The author shares the results of her empirical research on this matter that prove her earlier observation. Specifically, for diversity discussions, data shows that greater diversity leads to greater learning, open minds, more comfort participating with less tokenism. It is also noteworthy that Deo shares some data on missed opportunities that instructors could have utilized to promote diverse interactions. The cause and subsequent effect of such missed opportunities are discussed.

Hanna, Cheryl. "Gender As A Core Value in Teaching Constitutional Law." *Oklahoma City University Law Review* 36, no. 2 (2011): 513–524.

In this article, Hanna offers practical advice for incorporating gender as a core value into constitutional law cases when the case decisions have obscured their central gender implications. Hanna points out the rising need for teaching cases that traditionally do not directly impose equal-protection analysis with a stronger focus on gender issues. She then offers teaching ideas in several areas of constitutional law. The author suggests teaching topics such as: affirmative state duties to end gender discrimination, due process, gender in the First Amendment, and sexual-orientation discrimination as sex discrimination. Hanna also lists various teaching methods and class activities that facilitate these discussions, including drafting statutes that touch on relevant issues, using documentaries and films for historical context, and using a class poll before and after the showing of those documentaries/films. She also offers possible class activities, like a single-gender law school (to have the same lecture delivered to students in the same manner with women or men in each session of the lecture). Hanna also stresses the im-

---

1. 539 U.S. 306 (2003).

portance of approaching gender issues free of gender stereotype. As the author states, gender is an issue that is relevant to all the students in constitutional law classes. She observes that, with the help of the above in-class activities, students could engage more in conducting complex legal analysis in a relatively safe and welcoming environment.

Kupenda, Angela Mae. "On Teaching Constitutional Law When My Race Is in Their Face." *Law and Inequality: A Journal of Theory and Practice* 21, no. 1 (2003): 215–218.

Kupenda shares an encouraging story of teaching constitutional law right after the September 11, 2001 attacks as a minority law professor. Her initial approach was to be direct and challenging when hearing and debating different perspectives, which she describes as "hitting a brick wall." After getting pushback and having more constructive conversation with her students, she decided not to be controlled by fear: fear of being challenged or rejected by her students and fear of bad student evaluations. She emphasizes the importance of a welcoming environment of diverse viewpoints in class and encourages students to embrace different opinions. Despite fear and uncertainty, the author argues that it is inevitable to face those moments as it entails the core value of constitutional law.

Kupenda, Angela Mae. "Collaborative Learning in the Constitutional Law Classroom: Adapting the Concept of Inevitable Disagreement in Seven Steps." *Journal of Legal Education* 68, no. 2 (2019): 284–302.

In this article, Kupenda provides insight on how to utilize collaborative learning in courses where inevitable disagreement is common in classroom discussions. Constitutional law being one of those courses, it can be used as a great opportunity for students to work collaboratively and strengthen advocacy skills. Kupenda offers a seven-step approach for pedagogical success in promoting collaborative learning. The first two steps advise instructors to reflect on their own experiences to understand the value of inevitable disagreement and work collaboratively as legal professionals. The next two steps focus on building relationships with students and remembering that student success is the ultimate goal. Steps five and six suggest some group activities and a final project that helps students work with disagreement through a positive learning experience. The final step goes back to building relationships with students and encourages instructors to be a model of collaboration and empathy during inevitable disagreement.

Merritt, Deborah Jones. "Who Teaches Constitutional Law." *Constitutional Commentary* 11, no. 1 (1994): 145–162.

This article introduces an empirical study done in the early '90s on the various factors that play a role when scholars apply for constitutional law teaching positions. Both positive and negative factors are examined and analyzed. The author used data from five successive editions of the AALS Directory of Law Professors (1986–1991). The results indicated that among all the factors, male scholars who had served as editors of law review, graduated from a prestigious law school or had clerked for appellate court judges are all positive factors when applying for constitutional law teaching positions while being a female scholar and having private law firm experience imposed a significant negative impact. Although this study was done in the early 1990s, it still reveals phenomena that currently exists in many law schools. Would professors who have none or very limited private law firm experience think and teach differently in constitutional law class? The author also points out that the lack of female constitutional law scholars may affect both the substance of scholarship in this field, as well as the rendering of court decisions. Their own education and work histories inform the way professors incorporate diversity and inclusion issues into their classroom teaching. Greater diversity of backgrounds for constitutional law teachers would naturally create a more inclusive, diversified learning environment.

Perea, Juan F. "Race and Constitutional Law Casebooks: Recognizing the Proslavery Constitution." *Michigan Law Review* 110, no. 6 (2012): 1123–1152.

In this review, Perea introduces George Van Cleve's work[2] on the proslavery origins of the Constitution. After using this as a starting point to establish a baseline, Perea carefully examines and compares several leading constitutional law casebooks on how they incorporate the proslavery nature of the Constitution in the text. He finds that even though most casebooks acknowledge the interpretation of the Constitution as proslavery, none of them present this interpretation as a core understanding of the original Constitution. Perea suggests sources that constitutional law casebooks can strengthen their discussion on the proslavery origin of the Constitution, such as using excerpts from Madison's notes from the Constitutional Convention, excerpts from the Federalist and Anti-Federalist papers, or excerpts from state ratification debates. Perea concludes with an examination of the racial implication of the Constitution along with an analysis of the importance to incorporate the proslavery interpretation into the constitutional law curriculum.

Rand, Kathryn R. L., and Steven Andrew Light. "Teaching Race without a Critical Mass: Reflections on Affirmative Action and the Diversity Rationale." *Journal of Legal Education* 54, no. 3 (2004): 316–335.

Rand and Light discuss their observation of teaching affirmative action in university admissions in their constitutional law classes at University of North Dakota (UND). The authors suggest that because UND is a homogeneous campus, the practicalities of demonstrating the diversity rationale endorsed by *Grutter* have some significant limitations. In their classes, they used an integrated approach of individual and group activities and the showing of a relevant documentary (*Secrets of the SAT*)[3] as supplements to casebook readings. In the group activities,

---

2. George William Van Cleve, A Slaveholders' Union: Slavery, Politics, and the Constitution in the Early American Republic 391 (2010).

3. *Frontline: Secrets of the SAT*, (PBS television broadcast Oct. 5, 1999), https://www.pbs.org/wgbh/pages/frontline/shows/sats/.

students were asked to role-play as a college admissions committee member. Rand and Light observe that the group exercise and the documentary set the stage for students to assess more critically the relevant case law and they provide a successful module of teaching affirmative action. From that class experience, the authors also discuss some barriers for teaching and learning diversity in a homogeneous classroom. Without a critical mass of diverse students within the student body, instructors need to employ creative pedagogical strategies to promote cross-racial understanding.

Ross, Thomas. "Teaching Constitutional Law Stories." *Journal of Legal Education* 55, no. 1 (2005): 126–137.

In this article, Ross reviews *Constitutional Law Stories*[4] as a supplement course material for teaching constitutional law classes. The author emphasizes the importance of teaching constitutional law to students beyond simple case analysis. He emphasizes the notion of doing justice for actual people who are "before the court." Ross criticizes chapters of *Constitutional Law Stories* that have failed in serving this purpose. Ross points out chapters that lack detail; some touch on irrelevant stories with masked ideologies as well as shifting or elusive meaning. Ross also alerts that some stories in the book can be biased and need caution while being used in class. However, Ross acknowledges that with the appropriate mindset, this book can be a useful tool for including discussion of diversity and inclusion in a constitutional law class. Overall, the author recommends using this book to explore with students the role lawyers play in the construction of constitutional law.

Websites

University of Washington School of Law Gallagher Law Library. "Diversity Readings in Constitutional Law." https://guides.lib.uw.edu/law/diversity1L/conlaw.

A research guide created by the Gallagher Law Library of University of Washington School of Law with a focus on topics typically covered in the first year constitutional class, including topics of the Census, Commerce Clause, Dormant Commerce Clause, Federalism, Same-Sex Marriage, Fugitive Slave Clause, Immigration and Citizenship, and Indian Sovereignty.

Harvard Law School, "Diversity and Legal History: A Harvard Law School Lecture Series," YouTube. https://www.youtube.com/playlist?list=PL2q2U2nTrWq0Kix VOa11hBv8wOssEtgLu.

This series of lectures was delivered by several Harvard Law School professors, a Divinity School professor, along with three guests professors from other law schools. The purpose of this lecture series was to respond to a growing interest on how diverse groups of people were treated in the U.S. legal system over the

---

4. CONSTITUTIONAL LAW STORIES (Michael C. Dorf ed., 2004).

time. The lectures approach several constitutional law issues with more diversified lenses, such as the discussion of a "liminal figure" of Latinos in racial division issues.[5]

---

5. This lecture series is a companion to the Diversity and U.S. Legal History Reading Group led by Professor Mark Tushnet. *See* Mark Tushnet, *Presenting Issues of Diversity and Social Justice in the 1L Curriculum: A Report on a Lecture Series and Seminar*, in Chapter 1 of this book.

Chapter 6

Legal Writing

Integrating Diversity through Design of Legal Writing Assignments

Bonny L. Tavares[*]

Introduction

All students should be able to see themselves and their communities reflected in the curriculum at various times throughout their legal education. Designing legal research and writing assignments with diverse characters broadens students' perspectives about their potential place within the profession, and helps them to prepare for a diverse client base and increasingly global legal marketplace. Students are reminded that some of the people that they will encounter in the practice of law (whether they are clients, colleagues, judges, or jurors) will undoubtedly be from different cultural backgrounds than themselves. Therefore, infusing their legal writing assignments with issues of equity and inclusion helps to influence our students' developing professional identities as they discuss and revisit these issues throughout the academic year.

Furthermore, infusing writing assignments with issues of equity will give our students opportunities throughout the semester to engage in deeper analysis of legal issues, beyond the Black Letter law. Analyzing issues of equity will allow students to discuss underlying policies which may not be overtly presented in the decisional law or in the plain language of a statute, and to consider decision maker bias and how it may manifest in an "objective" legal opinion. In addition, classroom discussions about equity viewed through the lens of their legal writing assignments will allow students to practice cross-cultural conversations in a professional setting and give them opportunities to participate in educating each other about diversity and inclusion.

[*] Associate Professor of Law, Temple University James E. Beasley School of Law. Thank you to my LRW colleagues at Temple—Lee Carpenter, Susan DeJarnatt, Mary Levy, Ellie Margolis, Kristen Murray, and Robin Nilon. Also, thank you to Professor Raquel Gabriel and the editors of *Integrating Doctrine and Diversity* for inviting me to contribute to this publication. And finally, a special "thank you" to my daughter, Haley Simone Tavares. Your interest in diversity and social justice makes me proud!

Integrating Diversity and
Inclusion through Problem Design

One challenge facing professors when creating writing assignments is keeping our students engaged while meeting the course's pedagogical goals, including the goal of promoting diversity and inclusion. If assignments do not capture our students' attention, they will have a more difficult time mastering the challenging array of skills that are presented in a legal research and writing course. Therefore, problem design is critical! To keep our students engaged, assignments should be based on facts that are interesting enough to sustain several weeks or even an entire academic year of instruction. The discussion that follows includes suggestions for: 1) building writing assignments around issues in which equity is integral to the legal analysis; 2) promoting inclusion by creating diverse characters; and 3) adding realism to problem design through authentic and effective facts.

Issue Selection

In the law school classroom, discussions of equity and inclusion are most effective when directly related to the legal issues underpinning the course. An important goal of a legal writing course is to teach our students how to communicate legal analysis, rather than simply sharing their personal opinions. Differentiating between objective analysis and opinion can be a difficult transition from the type of essay writing that many students were accustomed to as undergraduates or even as graduate students. Therefore, to provide context for legal analysis of equity, diversity, and inclusion, issue selection is vital. When designing the course, consider basing at least one assignment on a cause of action that involves constitutional or statutory civil rights or civil liberties. For example, my past assignments have included a Title VII hostile work environment sexual harassment issue ("Title VII assignment"), and a discriminatory discharge based on sexual orientation issue under the New Jersey Law Against Discrimination ("NJLAD assignment").[1] These causes of action naturally require legal analysis of case law discussing gender and sexual orientation. Furthermore, relevant case law involving other protected classes opens the door to discussion and analysis of race, age, and disability discrimination.

Family law is another subject that provides context for discussions about diversity and inclusion, because the legal analysis requires students to evaluate the litigants' personal traits. For example, I have assigned a memorandum in which students must discuss who is likely to be named the legal parents of a child whose birth was the result of an in vitro fertilization error ("IVF assignment").[2] Due to the diverse characters in the IVF assignment (for more on creating diverse characters, see below),

---

1. The NJLAD assignment was the idea of Professor Leonore F. Carpenter, Temple University Beasley School of Law.

2. The IVF assignment was created by Professor Susan DeJarnatt, Temple University Beasley School of Law.

the relevant legal analysis included discussion of ethnicity, religion, socio-economic status, and gender roles, to name only a few.

In choosing an issue, take care to consider the complexity of the analysis. Early in my teaching career, I chose a Fourteenth Amendment due process issue as the basis of a writing assignment for first semester 1Ls. Rookie mistake! The students struggled to grasp the concepts, and their confusion was only magnified by the fact they were not due to take constitutional law until their 2L year. To prevent the difficulty of the issue from interfering with your pedagogical goals, professors should base writing assignments on a straightforward cause of action. Legal tests with a limited number of elements or factors work best. A professor may also choose to further simplify the analysis by assigning only a few elements at a time. For example, when teaching the Title VII assignment, I initially assigned only the first two elements of the cause of action. The remaining elements were assigned a few weeks later.

Character Diversity

Almost any legal issue can elicit discussion of equity and inclusion when the facts involve diverse characters. However, to ensure context for classroom discussions, place at least one diverse character at the center of the controversy, not just on the periphery of the facts. Beyond the central character, professors might consider additional ways to add diversity, for example, including an equal number of male and female characters, or adding an individual with a disability, or a non-Christian character, or an LGBTQIA character. Furthermore, consider "intersectionality,"[3] or multiple dimensions of diversity. For example, the central character in the aforementioned NJLAD assignment is a lesbian, and a Latina, and has recently married her fiancée. Adding these layers of diversity also adds depth to classroom discussions of equity and inclusion.

Diverse characters can be introduced overtly (for example, "Sue Brown is a Black transgendered woman") or subtly. One subtle way to add diversity to a writing assignment is to choose character names from a well-known[4] TV show with a diverse cast. Students will inadvertently imagine the characters in your assignment as the actors who starred in the show. You can also subtly add diversity by incorporating names from different ethnicities, nationalities, or religions. This will give students practice in correctly spelling and pronouncing unfamiliar names, which will matter to clients, colleagues, judges, or anyone else that an attorney is expected to address formally.

---

3. Professor Kimberlé Crenshaw defines "intersectionality" as "denot[ing] the various ways in which race and gender interact to shape the multiple dimensions of Black women's employment experiences." Kimberlé Crenshaw, *Mapping the Margins: Intersectionality, Identity Politics, and Violence Against Women of Color*, 43 STAN. L. REV. 1241, 1244 (1991). Here, I use the term more broadly to mean a character with multiple cultural identities.

4. By "well-known" I mean known to the average twenty-five-year-old. I have used characters from *The Wire, Arrested Development*, and *The Good Wife*. Shows like *Walking Dead, This is Us*, and *Grey's Anatomy*, are also possibilities.

Professors do not necessarily have to reinvent the wheel to create a writing assignment with diverse characters. An old writing assignment can be given new life by revising the assignment's central characters. For example, the IVF assignment described above involved a Puerto Rican/Catholic family and a white/Jewish family. Both of the couples in the IVF assignment were heterosexual and both were United States citizens. However, two other colleagues taught the same basic set of facts, but changed the central characters. One colleague taught the IVF assignment with one heterosexual couple and one same-sex couple; the other taught the assignment with heterosexual couples from two different countries. Altering the central characters resulted in changes to the applicable law (California law versus international law) and brought a different dimension to classroom discussions about what a court was likely to consider in the best interests of the child. You may also be able to integrate diversity into one or more of your existing writing assignments by making a few thoughtful changes to the facts.

Factual Development

To keep your students engaged, base assignments on facts that are interesting enough to sustain several weeks or even an entire academic year of analysis and discussion. However, balancing the degree of difficulty with the amount of detail necessary to make the facts come alive for your students can be a challenge. One solution to overloading your students with too many facts at once is the portfolio method. With the portfolio method, all assignments are interrelated and build toward a final assignment that incorporates all of the students' work in the course. This method has three advantages: 1) professors are able to gradually increase the difficulty of the assignments, 2) professors have multiple opportunities to introduce diverse characters and facts, and 3) students are able to reengage with the material and practice their analytical and writing skills throughout the course. When using the portfolio method, the first research and writing assignment typically involves limited facts applied to a straightforward cause of action. As the semester progresses, however, additional facts and new issues are revealed with each subsequent assignment. By the final assignment, the facts have grown in complexity to span an entire case file or court record. By gradually introducing new facts, professors are more likely to maintain students' interest and increase their engagement with the course.

Another way to add realistic factual details to writing assignments is to draw inspiration from media reports, or cases that are "ripped from the headlines." For example, the IVF assignment was modeled on a real-life scandal that came to light in the spring of 2000. Doctors at a New York fertility clinic were discovered to have accidentally implanted a Black couple's genetic embryos into a white patient without the knowledge or consent of either of the families involved.[5] Relocating the families to a different state and altering other details of the real-life case provided the basis for an excellent writing assignment. In general, borrowing factual details from several

---

5. *See* Perry-Rogers v. Fasano, 715 N.Y.S.2d 19 (N.Y. App. Div. 2000).

related cases, rather than basing your entire set of facts on a single judicial opinion or news story, is the best option for creating a unique set of facts.

Regardless of the inspiration for the assignment, the facts you choose to include must not be graphic, disturbing, or otherwise likely to offend, trigger,[6] or embarrass students. For example, do not offend students by including any stereotypes based on identity, such as, race, gender, religion, disability, etc. Students are distracted from learning when they become offended. Finally, confer with colleagues or community members from various cultural backgrounds to build in authenticity and to ensure that the fact pattern has the intended effect.

Integrating Diversity and Inclusion through Classroom Discussion

Now that you have created your writing assignments, how do you create a classroom environment that supports discussions of equity and inclusion? Writing assignments that incorporate a variety of scenarios outside the common experience of the predominant culture can invite discussions that raise the students' awareness of other cultures. Furthermore, discussing issues related to diversity and inclusion is "a way to increase engagement in the law school classroom and to help the law come alive for students."[7] To encourage meaningful and effective discussions, I suggest that professors adapt the role of neutral moderator and work toward creating an inclusive, safe and respectful learning environment. The goal is a classroom environment in which students feel comfortable speaking and asking questions; a classroom environment in which no student feels isolated or alienated. To communicate the professor's expectations concerning the tone of classroom discussions, professors may want to consider including a diversity policy in the course syllabus, along with a set of ground rules for positive and productive class discussions.[8]

Classroom discussions are most likely to be effective when professors plan ahead to incorporate diverse perspectives that are relevant to the central legal issues and consistent with the pedagogical objectives of the course. This is an essential component of "teaching through the problem."[9] All components of classroom instruction, including discussions of diversity and inclusion, should be relevant to the legal analysis and not tangential. However, finding relevant background materials will require a bit of research. This section includes suggestions for: 1) finding and incorporating "diversity stories" to serve as background for class discussions, and 2) transitioning from objective writing to persuasion and oral argument.

---

6. When students are triggered, they are in effect re-traumatized and learning may stop altogether.

7. Bonny L. Tavares, *Changing the Construct: Promoting Cross-Cultural Conversations in the Law School Classroom*, 67 J. LEGAL EDUC. 211, 214 (2017).

8. *Id.* at 226.

9. *See generally* Ellie Margolis & Susan L. DeJarnatt, *Moving Beyond Product to Process: Building a Better LRW Program*, 46 SANTA CLARA L. REV. 93, 116–23 (2005).

Finding and Incorporating "Diversity Stories"

To add depth to classroom discussions of equity and inclusion, find out the background stories of the case law and the legislative history of the statutes that will be discussed in class. You may discover behind-the-scenes information that will be helpful in demonstrating to students when cultural identity is a legally significant fact. Look behind the cases to gain insight into the people involved. Search to see if any of the relevant cases have been covered by the media (photos from media reports may also be interesting to show on slides as you discuss the relevant authorities). You might find details about the litigants and the underlying facts that will add depth to your discussion of the law. This may involve research in nonlegal sources, such as books, blogs, podcasts, documentaries, etc. Note that professors may sometimes need to provide an overview of relevant historical facts to provide context for students who are unfamiliar with events that occurred "before their time." This can be achieved through classroom discussion or by assigning supplemental readings or multimedia, such as a documentary. Furthermore, throughout the course, keep an eye towards the media and integrate additional news stories and recent developments that are related to your assignments.

Before discussing any background materials that I have discovered, I prefer to initially cover the legal principles established in all of the relevant authorities. I want the students to absorb those legal principles and understand their relevance to the facts before introducing another layer of analysis. However, any background information that is discussed in class should be relevant to the question presented. For example, in the IVF assignment, where the genetic embryo of a Puerto Rican couple was mistakenly implanted in a white woman, students needed to determine whether cultural identity was a legally significant fact. In other words, in deciding the child's legal parents, would a court consider the race of the potential parents?

One landmark California case that indirectly addressed this question was *Johnson v. Calvert*.[10] In *Johnson*, the California Supreme Court applied an intent test to determine the legal parents of a child in a surrogacy case. Both the genetic parents and the gestational surrogate wanted to raise the child. However, under the California Family Code, a child could only have one legal mother, "despite advances in reproductive technology rendering a different outcome biologically possible."[11] The court determined that the genetic parents were the legal parents of the child because they had always intended to raise the child, evidenced by the contract providing for payment to the surrogate for her services and relinquishment of the resulting baby to the genetic parents.

---

10. Johnson v. Calvert, 851 P.2d 776 (Cal. 1993).

11. *Johnson*, 851 P.2d at 781; *but see* K.M. v. E.G., 117 P.3d 673 (Cal. 2005) (holding that a child may have two legal mothers when a lesbian couple intend to raise the child jointly in their own home). The California Family Code has since been amended to allow more than two legal parents.

However, the California Supreme Court did not mention the cultural identities of the parties in *Johnson*.[12] In fact, Anna Johnson, the surrogate, was Black; Mark Calvert was white, and his wife, Crispina Calvert, was Asian. Examining the background of a case may elicit discussions of point-of-view and decisionmaker bias. I informed the students about the ethnic backgrounds of the parties in *Johnson* and asked them to consider what the court left unsaid. Was the decisionmaker really objective? What cultural assumptions possibly influenced the analysis? Although race was an unspoken factor, did the court nevertheless consider the cultural identities of the parties when deciding legal parentage?[13] And if so, should the students include discussion of the parties' race in their legal analysis? If they decided to include ethnicity as a factor in the parentage analysis, what was the best way to incorporate such analysis into their writing?

The policies underlying the California Family Code and the case law interpreting that statute provided a rich array of underlying issues to discuss in class. In addition to the *Johnson* case, a trio of landmark lesbian parentage cases[14] provided opportunities to discuss sexual orientation, same-sex parents, gender discrimination, and reproductive rights. Similarly, the NJLAD assignment directly related to a discussion of sexual orientation discrimination. However, case law interpreting the statute opened the door to discussion of age, disability, and race discrimination. In each instance the authorities assigned and the topics of classroom discussion all related to the central legal issue that the students would ultimately analyze in their memoranda or briefs. Viewing these issues of equity and inclusion through the lens of their legal writing assignments provided opportunities for the students to practice cross-cultural conversations in a professional setting and to participate in educating each other about diversity and inclusion.

Transitioning to Persuasion

Discussions of diversity and inclusion continue to be relevant as the focus of a writing course shifts from objective analysis to persuasive writing. As students develop

---

12. The intermediate appellate court did not mention the parties' race either. Instead, media reports revealed the parties' ethnicities. Perry-Rogers v. Fasano, 715 N.Y.S.2d 19 (N.Y. App. Div. 2000), the case that inspired the IVF assignment, also involved parents of different ethnic groups. The genetic parents (the Rogers family) were Black, and the woman who was mistakenly implanted with the Rogerses' embryo was white. Both families wanted to keep the child. The *Perry-Rogers* court did not mention race either, but since it applied the *Johnson* intent test in reaching its decision, I was able to assign both cases and incorporate them into the classroom discussion.

13. The same question could also be asked about socio-economic class, since the Calverts were obviously more affluent than Anna Johnson. In the IVF assignment, the Jewish family had a nanny, while the Puerto Rican family's daughter (the genetic sister of the child in question) was in day care, which implied a possible difference in socio-economic class.

14. *See* K.M. v. E.G., 117 P.3d 673; *Elisa B. v. Superior Court*, 117 P.3d 660 (Cal. 2005); *Kristine H. v. Lisa R.*, 117 P.3d 690 (Cal. 2005).

arguments, they should be reminded that effective advocacy involves writing for different and diverse audiences: clients, colleagues, opposing counsel, and judges. The opportunity to serve as an advocate for someone of a different culture is a valuable tool for broadening awareness and building empathy. Stepping into the shoes of someone from a different background allows students to gain perspective on the issues from their client's point-of-view; However, attempts at zealous advocacy sometimes lead students to articulate insensitive arguments. Driven by the desire to win, a student will occasionally form an argument without considering how it may be received by the decisionmaker.

Furthermore, as the course transitions to oral advocacy, students may discover that articulating arguments that reference their client's personal traits may be more challenging at oral argument than on paper. Students often struggle, for example, with how to effectively make arguments that specifically reference their client's ethnicity or religion. The professor's role when teaching oral argument is to serve as a sounding board and to help students consider whether certain arguments are likely to persuade or offend. I ask my students to imagine the people in the room who are watching and listening to every word of their argument. What if the judge, opposing counsel, or someone else in the room belongs to the same religion or ethnic group, or has the same sexual orientation, or has the same disability? How would that affect your argument?

For example, in the IVF assignment, the Jewish family had a nanny, while the Puerto Rican family's daughter (the genetic sister of the child in question) was in day care. During practice oral arguments, students representing the Jewish family would sometimes argue that it would be in the best interests of the child for their clients to be named the legal parents because child care provided by a nanny was superior to child care provided at a day care facility. When giving feedback, I asked the students to consider whether that argument would be effective if the judge assigned to the case had her children in day care. Would they feel comfortable articulating the pro-nanny argument to that judge? However, once the question was raised, I left it up to each student to decide whether to revise the argument. Most students decided to omit the argument, concluding that the argument was not strong enough to risk offending the judge. This ability to view legal issues from multiple perspectives is invaluable as students prepare for practice in an increasingly diverse legal marketplace.

Conclusion

After you have incorporated some of these ideas into new legal writing assignments, review your course evaluations to assess whether your efforts have been well-received and where improvement is needed. Have fun with this! The storytelling involved in creating a balanced, realistic, engaging and diverse writing assignment is one of my favorite aspects of teaching legal research and writing. I hope that you will take on this challenge and enjoy the process of adding diversity to your writing assignments.

Small Tweaks, Big Effect: Fitting Diversity and Inclusion into the "Puzzle" of Any Legal Writing Problem, Involving Any Legal Issue

*Christine Tamer**

Introduction

First year legal writing provides a unique opportunity to incorporate diversity and inclusion in the classroom and particularly to address the importance of empathy and the role of implicit bias in the legal profession. This is because, in comparison to other first year doctrinal courses, legal writing is distinctly "real world" focused; students learn to write like lawyers through the use of an original, hypothetical client problem drafted by the legal writing professor.[1] This essay shows how an original, hypothetical client problem (and the assignments and class discussions that stem from it) can and should be used to foster diversity, inclusion, and empathy in legal writing each semester—*regardless of the topic of the problem*. While plenty of articles advocate that first year legal writing courses use problems with "social justice" issues (such as discrimination, harassment, immigration, etc.) to foster diversity and inclusion,[2] the use of such a narrow set of issues every semester is not always viable.

---

* Director of Legal Writing and Assistant Professor at UNT Dallas College of Law; J.D. with highest honors from University of Texas School of Law 2011.

1. Charles R. Calleros, *Training A Diverse Student Body for A Multicultural Society*, 8 La Raza L.J. 140, 155 (1995) (explaining how "legal writing courses are particularly salient vehicles for confronting issues of diversity, both because they permit students to immerse themselves in a sophisticated problem with fully developed characters, and because the instructor has unusual freedom to select the topics and issues that will serve as the vehicle for developing skills of critical analysis and expression").

2. *See, e.g.*, Sha-Shana Crichton, *Incorporating Social Justice into the 1L Legal Writing Course: A Tool for Empowering Students of Color and of Historically Marginalized Groups and Improving Learning*, 24 Mich. J. Race & L. 251, 257 (2019) (advocating for the incorporation of "social justice as a mandatory component of the first year law school curriculum, starting with the first year legal writing course").

Thus, while this essay recognizes the value of social justice problems (and also encourages the use of such), it will show how any problem, involving any topic, and any area of law can be used to incorporate diversity and inclusion, as well as the importance of empathy and the role of implicit bias, into a legal writing course.[3] That is, this essay recognizes the enormous and unique workload of a legal writing professor, the competing and sometimes conflicting needs an original legal writing problem must address, and shows how diversity and inclusion can be fostered by even small tweaks to an existing legal writing curriculum — as opposed to a major overhaul or the use of a specific social justice problem. Indeed, according to a survey of legal writing programs, "incorporating social justice into the legal writing classroom or curriculum, even on a small scale, helps spark student interest and motivation."[4]

Any legal writing professor who has created an original problem to be used in a first year legal writing course knows that the cliché "easier said than done" rings painfully true. Putting together an original problem is "like putting together a jigsaw puzzle."[5] First, legal writing professors need to find a topic (i) with a clear overarching rule that is accessible to first year law students and has a logical organizational structure (often factor- or element-based), (ii) that is set in a jurisdiction that has sufficient precedent case law analyzing the applicable rules and reaching fact-based outcomes that go both ways, and (iii) does not involve "rabbit trail" side-issues or other complications that would overwhelm and distract students. Second, legal writing professors need to write problem facts that fit into the topic, are realistic but not overly complex, are engaging and interesting to students, are analogous to and "fall between the cracks of the precedent cases,"[6] and are sufficiently balanced so that arguments on both sides of the issues can be made.

Putting together this "puzzle" is both challenging and time-consuming. And, if legal writing professors want to reduce the risk of cheating, the puzzle cannot be reused and instead must be created anew each semester. How then can legal writing professors consistently create problems that meet the needs listed above but also address diversity and inclusion? While the most straightforward way is to make the problem's topic and legal issue one involving social justice, it is not the only way.

Below are some ideas of how to incorporate principles of diversity and inclusion when drafting an original legal writing problem, regardless of topic or legal issue.

---

3. Calleros, *supra* note 1, at 154 ("Whether the issues of diversity are the central point of a problem or are raised only indirectly, they tend to excite, or at least provoke, students and thus can be effective vehicles for developing skills of expression and critical analysis.").

4. Kirsten Clement & Stephanie Roberts Hartung, *Social Justice and Legal Writing Collaborations: Promoting Student Engagement and Faculty Fulfillment*, 10 DePaul J. for Soc. Just. 1, 16 (2017).

5. Judith Rosenbaum, *Putting the Puzzle Together: Choices When Creating a Closed-Universe Memorandum Assignment*, 17 Persp.: Teaching Legal Res. & Writing 11, 12 (2008).

6. *Id.* at 23.

Consider making the client in the problem "controversial" to teach students empathy:

The traditional law school curriculum has been criticized for "devot[ing] little emphasis to teaching students about clients or about the role of empathy and compassion in law practice."[7] This is problematic because overcoming stereotypes requires students to have a "motivation to empathize."[8] Put another way, stereotypes can be seen as "empathy deficits"[9] created by dissimilarity with a person of a different race, gender, ethnicity, or social background.[10] One way to teach empathy is by having a student "stand in the shoes" of a client — that is represent a client — who is "controversial" because of beliefs shaped by stereotype. Professor Camille Campbell gives the example of students being tasked with representing a female client opposing her ex-husband's petition to relocate their child to another state.[11] The client — a big law associate, who works 90 hours/week and aims to become the firm's first female managing partner — relinquished custody of her child to the father in exchange for weekend and holiday visits. Professor Campbell described how students initially did not want to represent the "bad mother" and how using the controversial client forced students not only to confront their own implicit bias (automatically assuming the client was a bad mother because she was ambitious in her career)[12] but also to discuss "how empathy deficits such as stereotypes and implicit biases can influence who a lawyer chooses to represent and creates serious access to justice issues for controversial clients."[13]

---

7. Kristin B. Gerdy, *Clients, Empathy, and Compassion: Introducing First-Year Students to the "Heart" of Lawyering*, 87 Neb. L. Rev. 1, 4, 31 (2008) ("Perhaps the most stinging critique of modern legal education is that it teaches students to disregard, if not ignore, the client whom the lawyer is called to serve."); Ian Gallacher, *Thinking Like Nonlawyers: Why Empathy Is A Core Lawyering Skill and Why Legal Education Should Change to Reflect Its Importance*, 8 Legal Comm. & Rhetoric: JALWD 109 (2011) (noting that law schools "likely have given little thought to the important role empathy plays in real-life lawyering").

8. *See, e.g.*, Andrew E. Taslitz, *Why Did Tinkerbell Get Off So Easy?: The Roles of Imagination and Social Norms in Excusing Human Weakness*, 42 Tex. Tech L. Rev. 419, 432–33 (2009); Nicole E. Negowetti, *Judicial Decisionmaking, Empathy, and the Limits of Perception*, 47 Akron L. Rev. 693, 750 (2014).

9. Camille Lamar Campbell, *Who's Gonna Take the Weight: Using Legal Storytelling to Ignite A New Generation of Social Engineers*, 50 J. Marshall L. Rev. 231, 232 (2017).

10. Andrew E. Taslitz, *Police Are People Too: Cognitive Obstacles to, and Opportunities for, Police Getting the Individualized Suspicion Judgment Right*, 8 Ohio St. J. Crim. L. 7, 22 (2010) (noting that "different social backgrounds make empathy harder" and that "[w]hen empathy fails, observers judge others based more on stereotypes than a true understanding of the others' nature or situation.").

11. Campbell, *supra* note 9, at 234.

12. *Id.* at 242–43.

13. *Id.* at 232.

Make students confront implicit bias and discuss the dangers of such in the context of the law:

Regardless of the problem used, first year legal writing is a natural course to teach students about implicit bias—and the role it plays in both their own decision making and that of others. Implicit bias can be defined as "the unintentional or unaware act of grouping persons or things into categories that can lead to discriminatory behaviors."[14] Put another way, implicit bias can act "as a lens through which we view the world" that "automatically filters how we take in and act on information."[15] Because the first step to fighting implicit bias is awareness, it is important that law students be first taught about implicit bias and then, specifically how it affects the legal system.[16] Indeed, research shows that most people have a "bias blind spot," meaning they believe they are bias-free or they "over-estimate their ability to control their judgments and feelings."[17]

One way of making students aware of their own implicit bias is by assigning them as homework a Project Implicit computer-administered test ("IAT") relevant to the original problem facts. IAT tests, which are available for free at https://implicit.harvard.edu/implicit/ and have been taken by millions of people, measure one's "strength of associations between concepts (e.g., Black people, gay people) and evaluations (e.g., good, bad) or stereotypes (e.g., athletic, clumsy)."[18] These tests "have revealed widespread bias on the basis of race, gender, and disability, and have shown that these biases take hold even for test-takers who are members of the group against whom the bias is exhibited."[19] For example, if the problem involves a witness who was Black, the professor could assign as homework the "Race IAT,"[20] coupled with a self-reflection assignment.[21]

The homework could then be used as a springboard for a class discussion about how "[a]wareness of implicit bias is critical to developing effective

---

14. Samia E. McCall, *Thinking Outside of the Race Boxes: A Two-Pronged Approach to Further Diversity and Decrease Bias*, 2018 B.Y.U. EDUC. & L.J. 23, 60.

15. Nicole E. Negowetti, *Navigating the Pitfalls of Implicit Bias: A Cognitive Science Primer for Civil Litigators*, 4 ST. MARY'S J. LEGAL MAL. & ETHICS 278, 284 (2014) (citing Shawn C. Marsh, *The Lens of Implicit Bias*, JUV. & FAM. JUST. TODAY, Summer 2009, at 16, 17, available at https://www.ncjfcj.org/wp-content/uploads/2012/09/The-Lens-of-Implicit-Bias_0.pdf).

16. Campbell, *supra* note 9, at 244.

17. Andrea A. Curcio, *Addressing Barriers to Cultural Sensibility Learning: Lessons from Social Cognition Theory*, 15 NEV. L.J. 537, 554 (2015).

18. PROJECT IMPLICIT, ABOUT THE IAT, https://implicit.harvard.edu/implicit/iatdetails.html (last visited Aug. 7, 2020).

19. Debra Chopp, *Addressing Cultural Bias in the Legal Profession*, 41 NYU REV. L. & SOC. CHANGE 367, 378 (2017).

20. *See* PROJECT IMPLICIT, TAKE A TEST, https://implicit.harvard.edu/implicit/selectatest.html (last visited Aug. 7, 2020).

21. Curcio, *supra* note 17, at 555 (2015) (discussing self-reflection "as a methodology that helps students develop their cultural sensibility skill").

lawyering skills,"[22] the effects of implicit bias on the legal system;[23] and then, more narrowly, what it means for them as a legal writer in the context of the problem in front of them. For example, in persuasive writing, students are tasked with telling their client's side of the "story" to the court. Because "each element of the story is the product of conscious and unconscious choices made by the storyteller" (here, the student), the student must understand that her "own experiences, biases, and values can affect her ability to convey the client's story."[24] Moreover, students are reminded implicit bias can affect the audience of the story—in persuasive writing, the judge—and are introduced to methods of combatting potential implicit bias, at least temporarily. For example, one way to combat potential implicit bias is to "convey[] the multidimensional complexity of human beings who may otherwise be understood by reference to one label or group."[25] Thus, for instance, "to preclude a judge from activating racial or gender stereotypes, an attorney should highlight the individual and complex characteristics of the client."[26]

Replace the generic with a realistic, diverse world:

When creating an original problem for first year legal writing, one of the goals is for the problem to mirror a real-life legal issue that a real-life client could face. Yet, sometimes we create problems composed of generic parties (i.e., Plaintiff Paula and Defendant Dan), generic characters (i.e., John Smith), generic settings (i.e., Greenacre), and generic things (i.e., a border collie named Lassie). While these generic problems can adequately set a student up to analyze a legal issue, they are a missed opportunity to introduce students to the "messy" worlds in which their clients will reside, they will practice, and their case will be decided.[27] "[I]f we want our students to seriously address

---

22. McCall, *supra* note 14, at 60.

23. Chris Chambers Goodman, *Shadowing the Bar: Attorneys' Own Implicit Bias*, 28 Berkeley La Raza L.J. 18, 19 (2018) (summarizing studies on implicit bias with respect to jurors, judges, and attorneys); Judge Mark W. Bennett, *Unraveling the Gordian Knot of Implicit Bias in Jury Selection: The Problems of Judge-Dominated Voir Dire, the Failed Promise of Batson, and Proposed Solutions*, 4 Harv. L. & Pol'y Rev. 149, 158 (2010) (noting that research shows "implicit bias likely permeates our civil and criminal justice system"); Jeffrey J. Rachlinski et al., *Does Unconscious Racial Bias Affect Trial Judges?*, 84 Notre Dame L. Rev. 1195, 1232 (2009) (discussing study of trial judges and implicit bias and concluding that "judges, like the rest of us, possess implicit biases").

24. Negowetti, *supra* note 15, at 299.

25. Gary Blasi, *Advocacy Against the Stereotype: Lessons from Cognitive Social Psychology*, 49 UCLA L. Rev. 1241, 1279 (2002).

26. Negowetti, *supra* note 15, at 310. As more than one schema applies to people, "causing people to focus principally on one of those categories … 'inhibits the activation of stereotypes associated with another category.'" Pamela A. Wilkins, *Confronting the Invisible Witness: The Use of Narrative to Neutralize Capital Jurors' Implicit Racial Biases*, 115 W. Va. L. Rev. 305, 331 (2012). Professor Wilkins gives the example of someone who is three different schemas—Asian, female, and mechanic—and how focusing on the role schema (mechanic), can "trump racial and gender schemas." *Id.*

27. Brook K. Baker, *Incorporating Diversity and Social Justice Issues in Legal Writing Programs*, 9 Persp.: Teaching Legal Research & Writing 51, 51 (2001) ("[W]hen we create paper clients with whom students do not have to interact, students learn incorrectly that legal writing is an

issues of diversity in the legal problems we assign, even at the margins, we must create a diverse world."[28] Any issue can be set in diverse world composed of multiethnic experiences and, as such, can "promote cross-cultural discussions."[29] For example, what if "Plaintiff Paula" was replaced with "Plaintiff Maria Vasquez," who is a medical student at University of Texas and was born in Mexico but is a U.S. citizen? The plaintiff's ethnicity and job may not have any real bearing on the specific legal issue, but by nevertheless including them "students develop an appreciation of the pluralism of American society."[30] To the contrary, failing to make the problems detailed and reflective of a diverse world will cause students to fill in the blanks themselves with pictures that "may reflect the dominant white culture or the students' own experiences and prejudices."[31]

Make the original problem free of stereotypes; and consider including counter-stereotypes:

When drafting an original problem, we also must be mindful to avoid stereotypes. "Stereotypes are categorizations of people based on favorable or unfavorable traits" and "are formed as a result of the brain's need to develop cognitive schemas to sort and process incoming information efficiently."[32] One's automatic or unconscious use of stereotypes often occurs in circumstances where one is short on time, overwhelmed, lacks time to reflect, and is tired.[33] Thus, it is easy for legal writing professors—who are sometimes all of these things—to unintentionally include stereotypes in the original problem they are drafting. For example, as I was writing this chapter, I thought back to a problem I used in a prior semester, involving a dram shop statute. Two of the actors (witnesses) in the problem were a bartender and a server. The bartender was male, and the server was female. Because I do not recall being thoughtful of combatting stereotypes at the time and because the genders of those witnesses had no bearing on any issue in the problem, I assume the genders aligned with my unconscious stereotype of these roles. While the stereotype may not have been particularly harmful, it is important

---

instrumentalist, self-directed skill instead of a representation skill, one that is responsive to the needs, goals, and perspectives of a real, but 'messy' client.").

28. *Id.*

29. Bonny L. Tavares, *Changing the Construct: Promoting Cross-Cultural Conversations in the Law School Classroom*, 67 J. Legal Educ. 211, 233 (2017) ("Coursework will also be more relevant to students who 'view themselves as outside the mainstream culture' when professors deliberately include some cases and problems with diverse cultural contexts.").

30. Linda Karen Clemons, *Alternative Pedagogies for Minority Students*, 16 T. Marshall L. Rev. 635, 636 (1991).

31. Miki Felsenburg & Luellen Curry, *Incorporating Social Justice Issues into the Classroom*, 11 Persp.: Teaching Legal Research & Writing 75, 75 (2003).

32. Renee Nicole Allen & Deshun Harris, *#socialjustice: Combatting Implicit Bias in an Age of Millennials, Colorblindness & Microaggressions*, 18 U. Md. L.J. Race, Religion, Gender & Class 1, 14 (2018).

33. *Id.*

that legal writing professors creating problems be aware that "[e]ven the 'subtle activation of stereotypes' can negatively affect learning and performance."[34] Moreover, in addition to avoiding stereotyping, it can be helpful to use the problem to expose students to counter-stereotypes as a means to help decrease bias.[35] "Counter-stereotypes attack the validity of a stereotype by presenting concrete evidence that it does not apply for all individuals in a group."[36] For example, if one of the witnesses in the problem was a pilot, even if the problem does not directly involve the issue of gender, you could make the pilot female.[37] This counter-stereotype can help reduce implicit gender bias.[38]

Make students grapple with how to label or describe people in the problem:

"[T]o be culturally competent lawyers, law students need to be aware of the bias embedded in word choices."[39] Another way to incorporate diversity and inclusion in any legal writing problem is make students confront their word choice with respect to a racial, ethnic, cultural, or other group. This can be built into any problem. For example, if a party in your problem is identified as being a member of the Cherokee Nation, first you could ask students if the party's race is legally relevant and should be included in a statement of facts, thereby creating an important conversation about diversity and inclusion in and of itself.[40] Second, if the answer was yes, you could ask students if that party's race should be referred to in the statement of facts as, for example,

---

34. Tavares, *supra* note 29, at 233.

35. Jerry Kang & Mahzarin R. Banaji, *Fair Measures: A Behavioral Realist Revision of "Affirmative Action,"* 94 Cal. L. Rev. 1063, 1105 (2006) (summarizing how bias can be decreased by exposure to counterstereotypic exemplars).

36. Allen & Harris, *supra* note 32, at 25.

37. Only seven percent of pilots are female. *See* Ian J. Twombly, *The 7 Percent*, APOA Pilot (April 1, 2019), https://www.aopa.org/news-and-media/all-news/2019/april/pilot/the-seven-percent.

38. Kathleen Nalty, *Strategies for Confronting Unconscious Bias*, Colo. Law. 45, 48 (2016); Irene V. Blair et al., *Imagining Stereotypes Away: The Moderation of Implicit Stereotypes Through Mental Imagery*, 81 J. Personality & Soc. Psychol. 828, 829–30, 837 (2001) (research suggests that people can reduce stereotyping by "through the activation and strengthening of [counter-stereotype associations"); Kang & Banaji, *supra* note 35, at 1109 ("A debiasing agent is an individual with characteristics that run counter to the attitudes and/or the stereotypes associated with the category to which the agent belongs. Examples include women construction workers, male nurses, Black intellectuals, White janitors, Asian CEOs, gay boxers, and elderly marathon runners."). *But see* Blasi, *supra* note 25, at 1279 (noting that while "[i]ntroducing counterstereotypical exemplars of the stereotyped category is another way of affecting, through information, the stereotypes of advocacy targets," the "strategy is limited by the fact that people tend to respond by creating subtypes for the exemplars rather than modifying their preexisting stereotypes").

39. Lorraine Bannai & Anne Enquist, *(Un)examined Assumptions and (Un)intended Messages: Teaching Students to Recognize Bias in Legal Analysis and Language*, 27 Seattle U.L. Rev. 1, 12–13 (2003); Natalie Bucciarelli Pedersen, *A Legal Framework for Uncovering Implicit Bias*, 79 U. Cin. L. Rev. 97, 144 (2010) ("[T]he promotion of counter-stereotypes may also ameliorate the effect of automatic stereotypes.").

40. Bannai & Enquist, *supra* note 39, at 13–14 ("While some scholars argue that to include race when it is not legally significant works to perpetuate racial tension, others argue that race is always

American Indian, Indian, Native American, or something else. You can teach students that not only does legal writing require that lawyers be specific in making sure the words they choose convey their intended meaning, they also must know whether any term they are using is "controversial, potentially offensive, or preferred by the members of a given group or the individual being named."[41] Legal writing professors should encourage students to do research when confronted with such an issue — putting the responsibility on students for "updating [their] own cultural knowledge."[42] If students were to do the research with respect to the example above, they would find that, while "[a]ll of these terms are acceptable," the "consensus … is that whenever possible, Native people prefer to be called by their specific tribal name" and that many prefer the "terms American Indian or indigenous American," as opposed to the term "Native American."[43] Additionally, legal writing professors can explain to students that relying on their own assumptions about terminology — and neglecting to update their cultural knowledge — can negatively affect not only their writing, but it can also affect their legal research. Namely, if students only rely on their own assumptions about terminology, then their search terms and, correspondingly, search results risk being incomplete. And, this incomplete legal research would ultimately affect their larger legal analysis of an issue.

Conclusion

Incorporating diversity and inclusion into a legal writing program is important not only to prepare students for the diverse world in which they will practice law, but also — more specifically — it is important because it will make students more precise, more empathetic, and more effective legal writers. While adding another objective to an already demanding and crowded legal writing course seems initially overwhelming, as set forth in this essay, small, mindful tweaks to an existing curriculum can make a big difference in fostering a more diverse and inclusive learning environment.

---

relevant in a racially charged culture like the United States. In any case, students should think through why they are or are not including such a fact rather than unthinkingly including or omitting it.").

41. *Id.* at 12.

42. Tavares, *supra* note 29, at 234 (noting that "the onus is on the person using the language, not on someone from that particular culture to bear the burden of teaching everyone else in the classroom the 'right thing' to say").

43. NATIONAL MUSEUM OF THE AMERICAN INDIAN, NATIVE KNOWLEDGE 360°, https://american indian.si.edu/nk360/didyouknow.

Teaching with Feminist Judgments

Kathryn Stanchi,* Bridget Crawford,** &
Linda Berger***

Introduction:
The Feminist Judgment Projects

Beginning in Canada, spreading to the United Kingdom, the United States, and around the globe, feminist judgments projects emerged from an informal, international collaboration of feminist scholars and lawyers who decided to rewrite significant judicial opinions using feminist methods and reasoning. One of the primary goals of these projects is to demonstrate that the law has a vast, but often unrealized potential for social justice.

The feminist judgment methodology requires the authors of rewritten opinions to act as judges in following the rules of precedent and custom—and to be bound by the same facts and law as in the original opinion—while demonstrating that cases can still be decided in ways that address social justice concerns. The academics, activists, and lawyers who collaborate on these volumes provide rewritten opinions accompanied by commentaries that help law students and other readers understand the social and historical context of the original judgment, as well as the ways in which feminist theories and approaches influenced the feminist judgment's reasoning or outcome or both.

While the most obvious use of feminist judgments in the classroom is in feminist or critical theory seminars, feminist judgments can also be a rich source of alternative analysis and arguments in first year legal writing, as well as first year or upper level doctrinal courses. In this article, we give several examples of how exposing students

---

   * E.L. Cord Professor of Law, University of Nevada, Las Vegas, William S. Boyd School of Law. Many thanks to the editors of this project for the opportunity to write about this important issue. Also thank you to Sue Liemer, Teri McMurtry-Chubb, Melynda Barnhart, Ellie Margolis, Dan Barnett, Laura Graham, George Mader, Charles Calleros and Lori Johnson, who generously shared their wisdom and experience with legal writing problems using Title VII.

   ** Professor of Law, Elisabeth Haub School of Law at Pace University.

   *** Professor of Law Emerita, University of Nevada, Las Vegas, William S. Boyd School of Law.

to the alternative judgments of the feminist judgments project in a variety of courses can help students develop a more realistic and nuanced view of law that is simultaneously aspirational and based in the real world. These alternative judgments are excellent tools to incorporate diverse perspectives in the law classroom because they counter the narrative that law is objective while other perspectives are political or biased. The first book in the Feminist Judgments series focuses on the Supreme Court of the United States.[1] Other books typically have a specific subject-matter focus, including taxation;[2] reproductive justice;[3] family law;[4] trusts and estates;[5] employment discrimination;[6] and torts.[7] Future volumes are expected in other areas as well.

Using Feminist Judgments in First Year Legal Writing

Generating Creative Arguments and Problem Solutions

Because legal writing is often thought of as a wholly practical "skills" course, it may be difficult for some to see how feminist judgments might be useful in teaching it. But the sheer breadth of skills taught in legal writing courses provides an array of opportunities to use feminist judgments to incorporate diverse viewpoints. Moreover, it is the pigeon-holing of legal writing that makes it such an important context for teaching that understanding diversity and different perspectives is, in fact, a critical lawyering skill.

In the first semester, when students learn the basics of legal research and legal analysis, including analogical reasoning and problem solving, feminist judgments can give students a fresh perspective on the law's application to a client's problem and help students think of creative ways to further the client's goals. In the second semester, when students are introduced to persuasive writing, feminist judgments can stimulate students to generate "outside the box" legal arguments. In both semesters, reading alternative judgments can help students think creatively when re-

---

1. FEMINIST JUDGMENTS: REWRITTEN OPINIONS OF THE UNITED STATES SUPREME COURT (Kathryn M. Stanchi, Linda L. Berger & Bridget J. Crawford eds., 2016).

2. FEMINIST JUDGMENTS: REWRITTEN TAX OPINIONS (Bridget J. Crawford & Anthony C. Infanti eds., 2017).

3. FEMINIST JUDGMENTS: REPRODUCTIVE JUSTICE REWRITTEN (Kimberly Mutcherson ed., 2020).

4. FEMINIST JUDGMENTS: FAMILY LAW OPINIONS REWRITTEN (Rachel Rebouché ed., 2020).

5. FEMINIST JUDGMENTS: REWRITTEN TRUSTS & ESTATES OPINIONS (Deborah S. Gordon, Browne C. Lewis & Carla Spivack eds., 2020).

6. FEMINIST JUDGMENTS: REWRITTEN EMPLOYMENT DISCRIMINATION OPINIONS (Ann C. McGinley & Nicole Buonocore Porter eds., 2020).

7. FEMINIST JUDGMENTS: REWRITTEN TORT OPINIONS (Martha Chamallas & Lucinda M. Finley eds., 2020).

searching, show students how to do deep factual research, and help with cultural competence.

As an example, consider a typical first year legal writing problem involving sex discrimination or sexual harassment. This area of law is a fertile source of legal writing assignments, as it teaches statutory analysis in a fact sensitive context. A quick survey of the participants on the Legal Writing Institute Listserv along with a perusal of the Legal Writing Institute Idea Bank show numerous Title VII based problems used in first year writing. These assignments cover a diverse array of topics, from pregnancy discrimination, gender stereotyping (including some involving transgender discrimination), hostile work environment sexual harassment, discrimination in appearance or dress, and the defense of bona fide occupational qualification. These assignments also serve as excellent vehicles to raise diversity issues.

The rewritten judgments can be assigned at varying points in the semester. They could be assigned during the research phase, when students are likely to encounter the original opinion. They can be assigned for the same class during which the original opinion will be discussed, or during a class when the analysis or arguments for the assignment are being discussed. For class discussion, the professor can put students in groups and assign them to discover and point out the differences in factual context and reasoning in the original and the alternative and brainstorm about how the new factual context in the alternative judgments might help them see the facts of their own problem, or their client, in a new way. The professor could also charge students with creating arguments out of the different reasoning in the alternative judgments. The rewritten judgments have a wide utility in showing students how to shift perspective in developing reasoning and arguments in their assignments.

Teaching Intersectionality and Cultural Competency

The rewritten judgments can be excellent tools to introduce the concept of intersectionality as a source of creative analysis and argumentation. They can also serve as a way of teaching students that learning about people with different life experiences is a critical lawyering skill. For example, in the sex discrimination assignments reviewed for this article, few identified the race of the plaintiff, unless the assignment involved a race or ethnicity claim, and almost none identified the race of the defendant. This fact alone provides an excellent springboard for class discussion, as the absence of any identification raises a number of questions. Are students supposed to assume that the parties are white unless otherwise identified? Are the assignments subtly teaching students that the law is, or should be, "race neutral" or "color blind" in sex discrimination claims? What difference might race make in the analysis of a sex discrimination claim? How might race be introduced, in the assignment or in the resulting documents, in a way that acknowledges its significance without being discriminatory? All these questions can lead to an important discussion of intersectionality and to glimpses of how cases that allege only sex (and not race or ethnicity) discrimination might raise issues of gender-race dynamics.

In this situation, a legal writing professor could assign Angela Onwuachi-Willig's rewritten opinion in *Meritor Savings Bank v. Vinson*, a case involving workplace sexual harassment.[8] Onwuachi-Willig's feminist rewrite could be assigned at multiple points in the semester: if the assignment will lead students to research and read the original *Meritor*,[9] Onwuachi-Willig's rewrite could be assigned around the time that *Meritor* is likely to be discussed in class. But even if *Meritor* is not directly applicable to the assignment, Onwuachi-Willig's rewrite could be assigned prior to classes in which the professor expects to challenge students to discuss and explore the legal arguments or reasoning related to the assignment.

The rewritten opinion provides a rich education in racial gender politics and shows students intersectional analysis articulated in judicial language. If the legal writing assignment does not identify the race of the parties, Onwuachi-Willig's opinion can serve as a tool to push students to ask questions related to race and intersectionality and can encourage them to become more aware of the different experiences and challenges confronting people of color. If the assignment does specify race or ethnicity, the professor can use Onwuachi-Willig's opinion to explore how race or ethnicity might impact the analysis or use it to encourage students to broaden their research to include secondary sources that explain intersectional issues in sex discrimination or harassment cases.

Teaching Students to Reach beyond Traditional Reasoning

The rewritten judgments can also help students see deeper issues of diversity and inclusion and catch embedded or unconscious bias they may have missed in the original opinions. In one of the assignments I reviewed, for example, a woman employee sues her employer for hostile work environment sexual harassment. In one version of the assignment, a male co-worker shows the employee pornography on his computer and she objects to this, causing her other co-workers, including female co-workers, to ostracize her and call her a "prude." In another version of the same assignment, a junior female law firm associate is accosted by her supervisor's husband at a work party, and another lawyer sees what looks like an embrace between the two. The female associate is then ostracized by the female supervisor, and both male and female coworkers, as a "cheater" and a "homewrecker." These assignments raise difficult

---

8. Angela Onwuachi-Willig, *Rewritten Opinion in* Meritor Savings Bank v. Vinson, *in* Feminist Judgments: Rewritten Opinions of the United States Supreme Court, *supra* note 1, at 303–321.
    9. 477 U.S. 57 (1986).

issues of gender stereotyping, particularly because in both cases female employees either contribute to the harassment or are not bothered by it.[10]

In analyzing these assignments, students might research and read, among other cases, *Price Waterhouse v. Hopkins,* the leading case on sex stereotyping, *Meritor Savings Bank v. Vinson,* or *Oncale v. Sundowner Offshore Services,* the case holding that same-sex sexual harassment is actionable under Title VII.[11] These cases contain valuable information the students need to conceptualize the legal issues. But the reasoning of the original opinions does not address the more complicated gender dynamics raised by the facts; the original opinions contain reasoning that seem to reflect gender or race bias.

Assigning one of the rewritten versions of these cases would allow students to read analysis that helps them see a deeper picture of the complicated dynamics of stereotyping. Again, the teacher could assign the rewritten case around the time that the students are likely to encounter the original case in their research, or may assign the rewritten case to coincide with the day the original case would be discussed in class. Because the analysis of the rewritten judgments is written in a judicial style, they give the students a model for "translating" critical theory into law practice prose.

For example, a professor could assign Martha Chamallas's rewritten *Price Waterhouse v. Hopkins,* which uses the trial testimony of Dr. Susan Fiske to elaborate on what stereotyping is and how it can infect a workplace.[12] Seeing a concrete example of how a decision maker might use social science in decision-making can help students be more expansive and creative in their research and argument crafting. In a persuasive writing class, the professor could ask students to outline how Chamallas's rewritten opinion helped them understand more deeply what stereotyping and implicit bias are. They can then challenge students to think about how this new knowledge might enrich their understanding of their own client's case. The professor can challenge students to come up with ways that social science research might help them better understand the issues in their assignment and how social science research might influence or enhance their own research or reasoning process. Chamallas's use of Dr. Fiske's testimony can help students resolve the tougher factual issues, such as the seeming indifference of the other female employees to the pornography and the participation of women in the "homewrecker" harassment.

---

10. The pornography Title VII assignment was originally created by Professor Ellie Margolis at Temple University Beasley School of Law. Several assignments (including the 'homewrecker' assignment) were created using Professor Margolis's original assignment as a foundation. Both of these assignments are based, in part, on *Spain v. Gallegos,* 26 F.3d 439 (3d Cir. 1994) (holding that a female employee ostracized because of rumors of an affair with her boss stated prima facie case of hostile work environment).

11. Price Waterhouse v. Hopkins, 490 U.S. 228 (1989); Meritor Sav. Bank, FSB v. Vinson, 477 U.S. 57 (1986); Oncale v. Sundowner Offshore Servs., Inc., 523 U.S. 75 (1998).

12. Martha Chamallas, *Rewritten Opinion in* Price Waterhouse v. Hopkins, 490 U.S. 228 (1989) *in* Feminist Judgments: Rewritten Opinions of the United States Supreme Court, *supra* note 1, at 345–360.

Teaching Students to Recognize Hidden Bias in the Law

In addition to helping students understand complex issues of human behavior and to show how social science research can enhance their arguments, the alternative judgments can also help students see hidden bias in the law. Because the alternative judgments often confront the thornier points of discrimination explicitly, they can often help students manage those issues more easily than the originals, which tend to avoid explicit acknowledgement of racism or gender bias.

For example, Ann McGinley's rewritten majority in *Oncale v. Sundowner Offshore Serv., Inc.*[13] gives concrete help to students wrestling with how women can sexually harass other women, and how to articulate or explain possible underlying motives. Although the original *Oncale* decision clearly stands for the proposition that same sex harassment can create a hostile work environment, it misses the opportunity to address why same sex harassment might occur, and the original indicates Title VII might tolerate "ordinary socializing in the workplace" such as "male on male horseplay" and "intersexual flirting." Students confronting a hostile work environment problem involving a complex workplace dynamic may be puzzled by what these terms mean—what is the difference between "horseplay" and abuse? What is the difference between ordinary social dynamics and ostracizing someone based on sex? Does Title VII really force you to socialize with someone you just do not like?

McGinley's opinion can help with those questions. She gives a number of helpful additional examples, exploring the varying and complicated motivations for harassing behavior. For example, she notes that "some women engage in discriminatory behavior against other women in order to assure their own position among men" and that people may go along with discriminatory behavior to enhance their self-worth.[14] McGinley's opinion gives students thought-provoking examples that can help them reconcile and articulate why some women might participate in the harassment of another woman or tolerate pornography or other inappropriate workplace behavior.

Teaching First Year Doctrinal Courses with Feminist Judgments

Strengthening Doctrinal Understanding while Studying Persuasion and Decision Making

Large-enrollment courses with heavy doctrinal coverage provide natural—if surprising—opportunities to work with feminist judgments. By integrating feminist judgments into doctrinal courses, instructors can deepen students' engagement with

---

13. Ann McGinley, *Rewritten Opinion in* Oncale v. Sundowner Offshore Svcs., *in* Feminist Judgments: Rewritten Opinions of the United States Supreme Court *supra* note 1, at 414–425.
14. *Id.* at 420.

doctrinal material while also inviting more explicit consideration of how judicial reasoning works and how it may be affected by an advocate's argument choices. For example, when read in comparison with the original opinions, the feminist judgments may prompt students to think more carefully about how their construction of legal arguments and incorporation of critical perspectives could affect the judge's approach to a problem. Reading the original opinion to compare and contrast it with the feminist judgment helps students gain a deeper understanding of not only the particular substantive law under consideration, but also how an advocate's choices influence a case's presentation, and how a judge's world view informs judicial reasoning or outcomes. Feminist judgments have the added benefit of revealing the false divides between and among skills-oriented courses (including legal writing and reasoning), theory-oriented courses (like jurisprudence), and doctrinal classes.

Feminist judgments volumes are being published in a range of doctrinal subject matter areas taught in law schools. First year torts is an excellent course for introducing the lessons of feminist judgments.

Comparing the Original and the Feminist Judgment in a Torts Classic

Years after they graduate from law school, lawyers remember *Tarasoff v. Regents of University of California*[15] as the case that imposed an affirmative duty to warn on psychotherapists. *Tarasoff* is in the canon: excerpts can be found in every leading torts casebook, and the California Supreme Court opinion is said to have helped courts "reconceptualiz[e] the nature and source of duty and of tort liability."[16]

But the excerpts that made their way into the casebooks—like the majority opinion itself—omit facts, context, and theory that support a broader societal duty to protect individuals from the violent acts of others. The original opinion recounted the murder of a female college student at the University of California at Berkeley by a male student. It mentioned that the male student had sought mental health counseling and that his University therapist informed campus police about threats made during the counseling. After interviewing him and determining that he was "rational," campus police released the male student. The California Supreme Court held that psychotherapists had a duty to warn identifiable third parties of threatened harm from their patients, but exempted campus police from the same duty.

When torts professors assign their first-year law students to read the re-envisioned *Tarasoff* opinion from *Feminist Judgments: Rewritten Tort Opinions*[17] alongside the original majority California Supreme Court opinion, students encounter a recurring theme against a complex cultural backdrop: society's reluctance to impose respon-

---

15. Tarasoff v. Regents of Univ. of California, 551 P.2d 334 (Cal. 1976).

16. Peter F. Lake, *Revisiting Tarasoff*, 58 ALB. L. REV. 97, 98 (1994).

17. Sharmila Lodhia & Stephanie Wildman, *Rewritten Opinion in* Tarasoff v. Regents of Univ. of California, *in* FEMINIST JUDGMENTS: REWRITTEN TORT OPINIONS, *supra* note 7, at 102–118.

sibility on its members to protect individuals from harm caused by third parties. In the feminist judgment, a concurrence and partial dissent, Justices Sharmila Lodhia and Stephanie Wildman agree that the therapist had a duty to warn, but they would also impose a duty on campus police.[18]

One way of introducing the legal and policy issues underlying *Tarasoff* is to have students first read the full majority opinion (a necessary first step because the casebook excerpts do not address the court's reasoning on the responsibility of the campus police) and then the feminist judgment. The professor could also ask students to draft and bring to class an argument on the issue of the duty owed by the campus police — arguing either on behalf of Tatiana Tarasoff's parents or the campus police. The professor could structure the class discussion around the arguments the students have drafted, using guided questions such as:

1. The feminist authors believe that their more detailed factual background "provides significant insight into the cross-cultural and gender realities that bear on understanding why a duty by defendants to warn Tarasoff of her physical peril existed in this case." Do the additional facts provided about Prosenjit Poddar (the male student), Tatiana Tarasoff (the female student), and the actions taken by the psychotherapist and the campus police significantly change your understanding of the motivations and actions of the parties? How did this affect the arguments you made on behalf of one or more of the parties?

2. For example, the feminist judgment states that "[m]ore careful scrutiny of the behavior of individuals involved in this case by the therapist and/or police might have revealed the volatility of this particular intimate relationship.... Dr. Moore asserted in his letter to the campus police that one of the causes of Poddar's severe emotional distress was his perception that Tarasoff had violated 'his honor.'" Should this fact (as just one example) have been included in the original judgment? How did the absence of such facts affect the reasoning and the outcome, if at all?

3. The feminist judgment points to race- and gender-linked patterns of violence. If you included such patterns in your argument, how did you provide evidence of them? How would you? Should judges take these patterns into account in determining the question of the duty of the University and its agents to warn an individual who has been threatened by a patient of the University? How are the patterns relevant? Are they prejudicial?

4. The feminist judgment begins by referring to the "Good Samaritan conundrum" in tort law and points out that traditionally there has been no duty to rescue except when a special relationship exists. But it goes on to find justification for a duty to warn in democratic principles and in "the cultural and gender context in which the question of duty to protect arises on

---

18. *Id.*

the basis of these facts." Are these two new rationales equally persuasive? Did you present either or both of them in your argument? Would you present either or both of them to a court?

5. The California Supreme Court majority held that the campus police owed no duty to Tarasoff because unlike the defendant therapists, they had no "special relationship to either Tatiana or to Poddar sufficient to impose upon such defendants a duty to warn respecting Poddar's violent intentions." The feminist judgment's third rationale for imposing a duty is the majority's failure to delineate any actual distinction between the two sets of university employees. Is the feminist judgment more or less persuasive when it relies on this disagreement with the majority opinion?

6. The feminist judgment explicitly adopts feminist argumentation methods. For example, the authors more extensively use (1) narrative facts to illuminate what happened and to explain the motivations and actions of the parties; the authors provide more information about the (2) broader cultural and social context within which the murder took place; and the authors cite (3) a law review article rather than a case or statute for one of their main legal theories. Are any similar argumentation methods used in the majority opinion? Comparing the two opinions, which seems the most persuasive? Why?

7. If you were writing an alternative judgment rather than an argument on behalf of one of the parties, what would be the basis of your reasoning on the issue of the duty of the campus police? Your outcome?

This assignment deepens law students' understanding of *Tarasoff* while introducing alternative sources and methods of argument that they are unlikely to encounter in their first year torts course. As a result, it helps students become more sophisticated readers of judicial opinions and more knowledgeable and resourceful authors of legal arguments.

Teaching Upper Level Doctrinal Courses with Feminist Judgments

Uncovering the Lack of Neutrality in Seemingly Neutral Law

"Money law"[19] courses like federal income taxation might at first seem unlikely candidates for introducing feminist judgments. But, in fact, these courses are especially hospitable to working with feminist judgments because students who are intimidated

---

19. The phrase is Alice Abreu's. *See* Alice G. Abreu, *Tax Counts: Bringing Money-Law to LatCrit*, 78 Denv. U.L. Rev. 575, 575 n.1 (2001) ("By 'money-law,' I mean the areas traditionally viewed as comprising the business curriculum: tax, corporations, securities, commercial law (UCC), securities, banking, antitrust and the like").

by the subject are glad to encounter more accessible material. Students who think they already know something about the subject are challenged in their assumption that the tax law is neutral and unbiased. Students who fall somewhere in the middle of that spectrum bring to the material an openness to any pedagogical methods that illuminate a complex topic.

Doing a "Blind" Comparison of the Original Opinion and Feminist Rewrite

A particularly provocative way of integrating feminist judgments into a large federal income tax class—or indeed any large doctrinal course—is to ask students to read a feminist judgment and a published case without revealing which is which. In the part of the federal income tax course devoted to medical expense deductions, for example, students typically read the relevant section of the Internal Revenue Code that permits a deduction for "expenses paid during the taxable year, not compensated for by insurance or otherwise, for medical care...."[20] Students also read the related treasury regulations, one or more cases that explore the meaning of "medical care," and rulings by the Internal Revenue Service about what can and cannot be deducted as medical expenses.[21] Cult deprogramming? Not deductible.[22] That pilgrimage to a religious shrine? Not deductible.[23] But clarinet lessons, when recommended by an orthodontist as a treatment for crooked teeth? Deductible.[24]

A professor can integrate into this typical set of reading assignments one of the opinions from *Feminist Judgments: Rewritten Tax Opinions*,[25] along with the original case. For this exercise, the instructor should take care that the differences in format do not give away, by typeface or otherwise, that one is a real court opinion and one is an alternative judgment. As one example, when teaching deductions, the instructor could assign the United States Tax Court's decision in *O'Donnabhain v. Commissioner*,[26] which held that many (but not all) of the taxpayer's expenses for what the court called "sex reassignment surgery" did constitute medical care for tax purposes along with the feminist judgment in that case, written by Professor David B. Cruz. Professor Cruz's reimagined majority opinion allows a deduction for all of the taxpayer's expenses and evinces a degree of humanity and understanding that is lacking in the original opinion.[27]

---

20. 26 U.S.C. § 213(a) (allowing for medical expense deduction).

21. *See, e.g.,* JOEL E. NEWMAN, DOROTHY A. BROWN & BRIDGET J. CRAWFORD, FEDERAL INCOME TAXATION: CASES, PROBLEMS & MATERIALS (7th ed. 2019).

22. I.R.S. Priv. Ltr. Rul. 80-21-004 (Feb. 26, 1980).

23. Ring v. Commissioner, 23 T.C. 950 (1955) (denying deduction for taxpayer's pilgrimage to Our Lady of Lourdes Shrine in France).

24. Rev. Rul. 62-210, 1962-2 C.B. 89.

25. FEMINIST JUDGMENTS: REWRITTEN TAX OPINIONS, *supra* note 2.

26. O'Donnabhain v. Commissioner, 134 T.C. 34, *action on dec.,* 2011-47 (Nov. 21, 2011).

27. David B. Cruz, *Rewritten Opinion in* O'Donnabhain v. Commissioner, *in* FEMINIST JUDGMENTS: REWRITTEN TAX OPINIONS, *supra* note 2, at 274–96.

Without any introductory framing, the professor can guide students through a series of questions. The initial focus should be on how the two opinions vary in terms of the language the judges use to describe the taxpayer and what facts the judges highlight in their opinions. Students quickly identify that one opinion (which later is revealed as the actual, original opinion) focuses on the fact that the taxpayer was born as a male, served in the military as a man, married a woman, was the biological father of three children, and received extensive psychological counseling and a medical diagnosis of "severe" gender identity disorder.[28] The other opinion (which is later revealed as the feminist judgment) begins with the simple sentence, "Rhiannan O'Donnabhain is a taxpayer," and then takes brief note of her life experience as a man and her medical diagnosis before turning to the core of the opinion: a discussion of the taxpayer's medical expenditures.[29]

Students then explore whether the facts and contextual background that come to the forefront in one opinion but not the other, and how that emphasis (or deemphasis) impacts their views of the taxpayer. The instructor might ask whether the students sensed any shift in their own personal view of the taxpayer—as sympathetic or unsympathetic, for example—after reading one opinion versus both opinions. Depending which opinion the student reads first, the subjective impression of the taxpayer might vary considerably.

Students easily identify the differences in the holding of each opinion. One (later revealed as the original opinion) disallows a deduction for the taxpayer's breast augmentation surgery "because the petitioner already had normal breasts before surgery."[30] The other (later revealed as the feminist judgment) permits a deduction for all of the taxpayer's transition care, including the breast augmentation, reasoning that "[d]ue regard for the well-being of transgender persons counsels more tolerance for conclusions regarding the necessity of their attempts to bring their bodies into alignment with the gender identity disorder...."[31] Although both the original opinion and the feminist judgment are "pro taxpayer" in that they allow deductions, what is the significance of permitting a deduction for breast augmentation of "normal breasts"? Who decides what breasts are "normal"? Some instructors might be understandably reluctant to discuss such a seemingly non-tax subject as human anatomy (and corresponding socially constructed views of the "normal" woman or man), but it serves the larger pedagogical point that taxation is, indeed, implicated in all aspects of life, and that lawyers must be able to talk about difficult, uncomfortable, or "private" topics with professionalism and in a manner that recognizes humanity and dignity of all people.

Students then can turn to the language of the Internal Revenue Code and treasury regulations to ground their views of which of the opinions is correct as a matter of

28. 134 T.C. at 35, 39.
29. Cruz, *supra* note 27, at 274–75.
30. 134 T.C. at 72.
31. Cruz, *supra* note 27, at 296.

law. To do so, they must grapple with the meaning of "medical care," and how the tax law result in this case (i.e., deductibility) depends on the labeling of the trans-taxpayer as having a "disease." That is because medical care, for purposes of Internal Revenue Code § 213, is defined as amounts paid "for the diagnosis, cure, mitigation, treatment or prevention of disease, or for the purpose of affecting any structure of function of the body."[32] In one of the opinions (later revealed as the feminist judgment) the judge (Professor David B. Cruz writing as Judge Cruz) embraces the disease model "advisedly and not without hesitation, not wanting to reinforce a notion that the tax-payer was defective in any way or that she needed to be 'cured.' "[33] At the same time, the feminist judgment recognizes that the taxpayer's "disease" diagnosis is crucial to the finding that her expenditures are deductible. This is an opportunity in the class-room discussion to talk about judicial decision making and tone—the two opinions have radically different ways of talking about the taxpayer and her medical treatment. If the class discussion appears to be replicating some of the biases embedded in the original opinion, the instructor can ask students to take a short one-minute writing break, to take quick notes for themselves about the words they find themselves using when talking about or reflecting on the taxpayer, and comparing—as a matter of self-reflection only—how their vocabulary and tone is closer to one opinion or the other. The instructor might choose at that point to move the discussion in another direction.

At any point during the discussion, or at the end, the professor can reveal which opinion is the original and which is the shadow judgment. Students generally un-derstand the larger feminist judgments project once they learn of its goals to show by doing that the law could be different if a feminist perspective applies. In a course in federal income taxation, students typically are not expecting to hear the word "feminist." Therefore, in describing the larger feminist judgments project, the in-structor has an opportunity to explain how feminist legal theory, just like other critical perspectives, can serve as a lens for evaluating both substantive law and its interpre-tation. For students who resist the term "feminist" as applied to the rewritten opinion in *O'Donnabhain* (or any opinion), they might be asked to identify a term that seems more accurate to them. Students might suggest "humanist," or "rights-based," among other labels. The "feminist" identifier may not sit easily for some students; others will be open to it. For those of us for whom feminism and justice are synonymous, securing student acceptance of the label is not an especially important pedagogical goal. If the students recognize the differences in the opinion, the goal has been met: they can see in the side-by-side opinions what a difference perspective makes.

If students can conclude their reflections with consideration of what impact the feminist judgments might have had on the subsequent development of the law, they are themselves doing the same work that the contributors to the feminist judgments projects are doing. By asking how the feminist judgment squares with or challenges

---

32. 26 U.S.C. § 213(d)(a) (defining "medical care").
33. Cruz, *supra* note 27, at 282.

traditional measurements of tax law—efficiency, neutrality, and horizontal equity—students acquire a new perspective on a subject they either thought they knew, or did not, but now appreciate more deeply. This ability to reflect critically is a skill that transports across the curriculum and throughout a lawyer's career. Honing that skill through "money law" courses is an unexpected but memorable learning experience.

Conclusion

These are just a few of the possible ways that feminist judgments can be incorporated into law teaching. Because the rewritten opinions use the same law and precedent in effect at the time of the original decision, any differences in reasoning or result invite consideration. The fact that the opinion rewriter reached a different (or the same) holding with language that departs from (or comports with) the original opinion forces students to confront the malleability of law. How one interprets and applies the law is the product of historical context, (typically unmentioned) intellectual commitments, and what the judge determines "counts" as important in decision making—which might relate to how much of the parties' individual stories factor into the judicial opinion and what sources are treated as the basis for that opinion. By heightening students' awareness of the importance of perspective, feminist judgments are invaluable and flexible teaching tools.

Teaching Diversity, Inclusion, and Social Justice in Legal Writing: A Selected Annotated Bibliography

*Alyssa Thurston**

Due to their skills-based components and orientation around real-world client issues, as well as the relative liberty of instructors to customize class content, legal writing classes offer "especially rich"[1] opportunities to incorporate diversity, inclusion, and social justice in "pedagogically progressive"[2] ways.[3] This bibliography summarizes selected materials that set out practical suggestions, assignment examples, or considerations for legal writing professors seeking to adopt teaching methods that, for instance, consciously acknowledge law students' varied life experiences, perspectives, and backgrounds. The listed resources also provide guidance in training law students to recognize and address bias in legal language and inequities in legal procedure, or to represent clients from vulnerable or historically underrepresented populations.

---

* Senior Research Law Librarian, UC Davis Mabie Law Library.

1. Charles R. Calleros, *Training a Diverse Student Body for a Multicultural Society*, 8 La Raza L.J. 140, 149 (1995) [hereinafter Calleros, *Training a Diverse Student Body*].

2. Cynthia D. Bond, *The Legal Writing Classroom in the World: Teaching Skills in a Social Context*, *in* Vulnerable Populations and Transformative Law Teaching 163, 164 (Soc'y of Am. Law Teachers & Golden Gate Univ. Sch. of Law eds., 2011).

3. *See, e.g.*, Calleros, *Training a Diverse Student Body*, *supra* note 1, at 149, 155 ("[In] legal writing courses ... [students] work intensively on realistic problems with fully developed characters. Moreover, first year legal writing is typically part of the required curriculum and thus, will reach more students than clinical offerings or other elective courses.... [In addition,] the instructor has unusual freedom to select the topics and issues that will serve as the vehicle for developing skills of critical analysis and expression."]; Johanna K.P. Dennis, *Ensuring a Multicultural Educational Experience in Legal Education: Start with the Legal Writing Classroom*, 16 Tex. Wesleyan L. Rev. 613, 614 (2010) ("The legal writing classroom, with its small size and skill-based instruction format, particularly lends itself to the introduction of multiple issues in law and culture.").

Books

Bond, Cynthia D. "The Legal Writing Classroom in the World: Teaching Skills in a Social Context." In *Vulnerable Populations and Transformative Law Teaching: A Critical Reader*, edited by the Society of American Law Teachers and Golden Gate University School of Law, 163–182. Durham, N.C.: Carolina Academic Press, 2011.

Bond details strategies for legal writing faculty to "integrate social and political context into first-year skills training" for "'post-politically correct' student[s]." (165) These students are defined as "superficially acquainted with the discourses of multiculturalism, minority rights, and diversity but convinced that [they have] already absorbed them...." Id. (165–166) Her suggested methods, constructed around the teaching of predictive writing skills, include: "foregrounding the legal struggles of low income clients; reversing typical gender roles in hypothetical materials; choosing case law to diminish racial stereotyping ... structuring problems to highlight the economic and social ramifications of law ... [and] dealing with the hegemonic implications of the legal writing style...." (166) She attaches an example ungraded closed memo assignment.

Oates, Laurel Currie, Anne Enquist, and Jeremy Francis. "Effective Words." In *The Legal Writing Handbook: Analysis, Research, and Writing*, 7th ed., 595–640. New York: Wolters Kluwer, 2018.

In this legal writing textbook chapter on making more precise, up-to-date word selections, sections 29.4 and 29.5 provide detailed guidance on how to incorporate bias-free and more inclusive language. The authors directly address reasons why many traditional word choices, such as a default use of masculine pronouns or certain racial/ethnic descriptors, are now considered outdated or problematic. They provide copious examples of alternative language options that are gender-neutral or more appropriate for referring to members of minority groups, maintain sensitivity to self-identification preferences, or avoid prejudicial, "patronizing[,] overly euphemistic or ... victim[izing]" (639) descriptors.

Runge, Robin R. "Increasing Awareness and Understanding of Representing Vulnerable Populations and Their Economic Realities by Integrating Domestic Violence into Law School Curricula." In *Vulnerable Populations and Transformative Law Teaching: A Critical Reader*, edited by the Society of American Law Teachers and Golden Gate University School of Law, 183–200. Durham, N.C.: Carolina Academic Press, 2011.

Domestic violence law is increasingly taught in law school clinics and courses, and Runge situates domestic violence victims within the categories of vulnerable clients that law students should learn to represent and advocate for. She provides two in-class group assignments developed for her courses that are centered on domestic violence victims and emphasize the development of lawyering skills. For both assignments, she details her teaching process and how her students engaged with the materials and questions raised.

Simpson, Doug. "The Unseen, Unheard, Unknowledgeable, and Underrepresented—How Can Law Schools Develop Student Interest in Helping Disadvantaged People?" In *Vulnerable Populations and Transformative Law Teaching: A Critical Reader*, edited by the Society of American Law Teachers and Golden Gate University School of Law, 227–248. Durham, N.C.: Carolina Academic Press, 2011.

Emphasizing the importance of integrating values-based teaching in law school, Simpson advocates for a "cross-curricular" (228) approach incorporating "professor-created multidisciplinary fact patterns [that] can be used to promote positive social change by sensitizing law students to issues facing the disadvantaged." (Id.) In this approach, professors teaching across several subjects would coordinate the design of fact patterns, and legal writing assignments would be structured to unify fact patterns and associated legal topics. Simpson provides a detailed example fact pattern and describes how it ties into various law school subjects. He also suggests potential related writing assignments.

Articles

Atkins, Tiffany D. "Amplifying Diverse Voices: Strategies for Promoting Inclusion in the Law School Classroom." *Second Draft* 31, no. 2 (Fall 2018): 10–14.

Atkins promotes strategies she has used to "amplify" or "elevate diverse voices" (11) in her legal writing class. Strategies include: "direct amplification," (Id.) where faculty members and fellow students praise or properly credit the contributions of minority students in class; creating legal writing hypotheticals centered on minority characters and life experiences; and using educational technology, such as polling software, that encourages greater in-class participation by more introverted students.

Bannai, Lorraine, and Anne Enquist. "(Un)Examined Assumptions and (Un)Intended Messages: Teaching Students to Recognize Bias in Legal Analysis and Language." *Seattle University Law Review* 27, no. 1 (Summer 2003): 1–40.

The authors examine the impact of cultural bias on legal analysis and language; they discuss how to address that bias in the teaching of legal writing. Suggested methods include teaching students to recognize bias inherent to common language; to read cases with an understanding of how they can reflect different types of bias; and to recognize one's own tendencies to apply cultural bias into their legal analysis or argument. They also discuss challenges that may arise for faculty in attempting to incorporate bias issues in the legal writing classroom and propose ways to respond to these challenges.

Bishop, Emily A. "Avoiding 'Ally Theater' in Legal Writing Assignments." *Perspectives: Teaching Legal Research and Writing* 26, no. 1 (Spring 2018): 3–13.

In "ally theater," a member of a majority group, in "'call[ing] out' oppressive behavior," actually "magnifies the problems faced by … marginalized groups." (4)

It can be a particular risk in the "overwhelmingly white" (3) legal writing profession, and Bishop breaks down specific burdens faced by law students of color in the legal writing classroom. For example, it tends to be a "white space [where] human actions and events are evaluated mainly by reference to white perspectives and experiences" (5), and where students' emotional reactions to issues of race and oppression, or their past experiences of or perspectives on racism or representation, are often discouraged or discounted. She proposes strategies and communication techniques for white legal writing professors to "deconstruct the white space" (9) in their classroom and directly address these burdens, without also exacerbating them.

Blumenfeld, Barbara P. "Integrating Indian Law into a First Year Legal Writing Course." *Tulsa Law Review* 37, no. 2 (Winter 2001): 503–520.

Blumenfeld addresses reasons to include American Indian and Alaska Native law in the law school curriculum and in legal writing classes in particular. She discusses her processes for designing related persuasive legal writing assignments, introducing the problems to students, and addressing their reactions to the American Indian and Alaska Native law component (which can vary based on their prior exposure to the subject and their individual backgrounds and biases).

Calleros, Charles R. "In the Spirit of Regina Austin's Contextual Analysis: Exploring Racial Context in Legal Method, Writing Assignments and Scholarship." *John Marshall Law Review* 34, no. 1 (Fall 2000): 281–320.

An author of several works emphasizing and providing examples of teaching diversity in legal writing and in law school generally,[4] Calleros writes from the premise that law school instructors should teach in ways that "acknowledge[] and confront[], rather than ignore[] ... race or other facets of 'otherness.... '" (282) He shares over fifty examples of legal writing assignments "requir[ing] students to confront issues of diversity" (282) on topics including "race, economic class, ethnic culture, gender, sexual orientation, HIV status, medical condition, [and] mental or physical disability." (Id.) This list of assignments was originally compiled by Nancy Wright for the Society of American Law Teachers in 1994.

Campbell, Camile Lamar. "Who's Gonna Take the Weight: Using Legal Storytelling to Ignite a New Generation of Social Engineers." *John Marshall Law Review* 50, no. 2 (2017): 231–248.

Campbell concentrates on a "curricular deficiency" (232) in modern-day law schools that "treats clients as abstractions" (Id.), which results in law students'

---

4. *See, e.g.,* Charles R. Calleros, Legal Method and Writing (7th ed. 2014) (interspersing ethnic names and the alteration of male and female pronouns throughout the text and assignment examples, and providing several examples of writing problems integrating diverse settings or characters); Charles R. Calleros, *Diversity in the Legal Writing Curriculum, Fostered by Faculty* with *Color,* Second Draft, Fall 2011, at 4; Charles R. Calleros, *Training a Diverse Student Body, supra* note 1.

implicit biases and stereotypical beliefs going unaddressed. This has negative implications for how lawyers might select clients in practice, especially in ways that may adversely affect traditionally marginalized and underrepresented groups. To counteract this deficiency, she proposes implementing "legal storytelling" into the 1L legal writing curriculum. Legal storytelling "stimulates empathy which empowers students to build plausible counter-narratives that ease the psychological discomfort of representing controversial clients." (242) For instance, 1L professors might incorporate classroom exercises that facilitate open discussion about stereotypes of particular groups, or "visualization exercises" (247) (for example, asking students questions that place them in the shoes of a hypothetical client).

Castello, Rosa. "Incorporating Social Justice into the Law School Curriculum with a Hybrid Doctrinal/Writing Course." *John Marshall Law Review* 50, no. 2 (2017): 221–230.

Castello describes the structure of a hybrid writing/doctrinal course, "Perspectives on Justice,"[5] that is required for students working on the St. John's University School of Law's *Journal of Civil Rights and Economic Development.* The course emphasizes the use of narrative to "help students understand the ways in which laws and society work injustices against certain groups." (224) For instance, students are asked to read and discuss excerpts from court opinions dealing with discrimination, which may prompt students to share their own stories, and to review media such as videos, news clips, and interviews relevant to cases and statutes being discussed. An assignment to write a scholarly paper on a social justice topic of their choice helps students develop critical thinking and problem-solving skills as they work toward a resolution of the examined social justice problem.

Clement, Kirsten, and Stephanie Roberts Hartung. "Social Justice and Legal Writing Collaborations: Promoting Student Engagement and Faculty Fulfillment." *DePaul Journal for Social Justice* 10, no. 1 (Winter 2017): 1–18.

This article is based on the idea that "a collaboration [in legal writing classes] premised on a partnership with legal aid or other public interest organization can directly address the social justice gap," (1) while still advancing the learning and professional goals of law students and faculty. The authors discuss the results of several surveys from the past two decades by the Legal Writing Institute's Pro Bono Cooperation Committee. These surveys revealed an increase in the number of legal writing courses incorporating some social justice components; including collaborations between legal writing, pro bono, and clinical faculty; or including collaborations with outside public interest or social justice programs. They detail several models used in first year and upper-division legal writing courses at different law schools: a "'public interest partnership'" (11) model for the 1L cur-

---

5. *See also Perspectives on Justice*, ST. JOHN'S UNIV. SCH. OF LAW, https://www.stjohns.edu/law/academics/course-descriptions (select "P") (last visited Aug. 10, 2020).

riculum;[6] a "clinical collaboration" (12) model";[7] an upper-level course involving a partnership with a wrongful conviction legal nonprofit;[8] and models of collaborations outside of the traditional classroom. Finally, they address the pros and cons of integrating social justice-oriented content or collaborations into the legal writing curriculum.

Crichton, Sha-Shana. "Incorporating Social Justice into the 1L Legal Writing Course: A Tool for Empowering Students of Color and of Historically Marginalized Groups and Improving Learning." *Michigan Journal of Race & Law* 24, no. 2 (Spring 2019): 251–298.

Crichton addresses the serious impacts of "elevated and sustained" (254) stress, fear, and anxiety experienced by many law students of color or who belong to historically marginalized groups, often brought on by "constant and ubiquitous reminders of psychosocial stressors associated with belonging to a marginalized group, including discrimination in all of its iterations—stereotype threats, microaggressions, and racial biases." (255) She reviews research addressing the diverging impacts of positive and negative emotions on the brain and the learning process. Crichton writes that including social justice issues in the first year curriculum can help provide a more positive, empowering, and motivating learning environment for impacted students, and explains further that the legal writing classroom is a particularly appropriate place to incorporate these topics. She describes various relevant assignments used throughout her 1L legal writing course at Howard University School of Law.

Dennis, Johanna K.P. "Ensuring A Multicultural Educational Experience in Legal Education: Start with the Legal Writing Classroom." *Texas Wesleyan Law Review* 16, no. 4 (2010): 613–644.

Dennis defines "multicultural education" as both "educating on multicultural topics and educating multicultural students." (614) Having studied multicultural education efforts in eight law schools throughout the United States, in Part IV. B. she highlights

---

6. For additional details of the public interest partnership model, see Nantiya Ruan, *Experiential Learning in the First-Year Curriculum: The Public Interest Partnership*, 8 Legal Comm. & Rhetoric: JALWD 191 (2011); *see also* Mary Nicol Bowman, *Engaging First-Year Law Students Through Pro Bono Collaborations in Legal Writing*, 62 J. Legal Ed. 586 (2013) (describing Seattle University School of Law's Legal Writing Collaborative, partnering with university and community programs to construct social justice-oriented assignments for 1L legal research and writing students. This program today appears to be called "Real Clients in the First Year." *See Real Clients in the First Year*, Seattle Univ. Sch. of Law, https://law.seattleu.edu/academics/programs/legal-writing-program/our-curriculum/real-clients-in-the-first-year (last visited Aug. 10, 2020)).

7. For additional details of the clinical collaboration model, see Sara K. Rankin, Lisa Brodoff & Mary Nicol Bowman, *We Have a Dream: Integrating Skills Courses and Public Interest Work in the First Year of Law School (and Beyond)*, 17 Chap. L. Rev. 89 (2014).

8. For additional details of this upper-level model, see Stephanie Roberts Hartung, *Legal Education in the Age of Innocence: Integrating Wrongful Conviction Advocacy into the Legal Writing Curriculum*, 22 B.U. Pub. Int. L.J. 129 (2013).

Northeastern University School of Law's integration of social justice-oriented projects in the 1L legal writing course[9] as a successful example of multicultural education. In this course, students work in small sections designated as "law offices" and participate in real-world legal research projects for local community or nonprofit organizations on a wide range of social justice topics. Recognizing that institutional resources to implement similar programs will vary among law schools, Dennis outlines several goals for multicultural education and lists ways that instructors can begin to work towards these goals in their own courses.

Evers, Christopher G. "Other Useful Statutes for Challenging Your Students to Analyze Issues of Diversity." *Second Draft* 25, no. 2 (Fall 2011): 19–21.

Evers suggests several federal statutes that raise issues of diversity and provide accessible case law universes on which to base 1L writing assignments. He provides several sample brief and memo assignments. This article is part of an issue focusing on "the connection between social change and effective legal research, writing, and advocacy."[10]

Johnson, Greg. "Controversial Issues in the Legal Writing Classroom: Risks and Rewards." *Perspectives: Teaching Legal Research and Writing* 16, no. 1 (Fall 2007): 12–18.

Johnson contrasts the term "controversial" with that of "social justice," (12) defining the former as "any issue that can evoke a student's passion, interest, and emotion" (Id.) and the latter as more limited to specific topics such as race, class, gender, sexual orientation, and religious concerns. He recommends expanding the universe of legal writing subjects beyond social justice-related concerns to "cover the entire spectrum of political and personal views." (13) Johnson suggests ways to effectively design writing problems around topics that reflect this spectrum, which he believes better incorporates " 'outsider' voices of every persuasion." (Id.)

McMurtry-Chubb, Teri A. "The Practical Implication of Unexamined Assumptions: Disrupting Flawed Legal Arguments to Advance the Cause of Justice." *Washburn Law Journal* 58, no. 3 (Summer 2019): 531–576.

A scholar on diversity and issues of race in legal education and the law,[11] McMurtry-Chubb presents a study of students' motions and briefs on affirmative action topics "to reveal how legal education both prepares and fails to prepare

---

9. *See Legal Skills in Social Context*, NORTHEASTERN UNIV. SCH. LAW, https://www.northeastern.edu/law/experience/lssc/index.html (last visited Aug. 10, 2020).

10. Mary Ann Becker et al., *Letter from the Editors: Legal Writing as a Civil Rights Imperative*, 25 SECOND DRAFT 2, 2 (2011); *see generally Diversity*, SECOND DRAFT, Fall 2011, at 2 (including brief articles on teaching about LGBT law, tribal law, and different legal systems, as well as incorporating pro bono clinical work into legal writing classes and effectively teaching legal writing to students with diverse dialects and speech patterns).

11. *See, e.g.*, Bridget J. Crawford et al., *Teaching with Feminist Judgments: A Global Conversation*, 38 LAW & INEQUALITY 1 (2020); Teri A. McMurtry-Chubb, *The Rhetoric of Race, Redemption, and Will Contests: Inheritance as Reparations in John Grisham's Sycamore Row*, 48 MEMPHIS L. REV. 889 (2018); Teri A. McMurtry-Chubb, *On Writing Wrongs: Legal Writing Professors of Color and the Curious Case of 405(c)*, 66 J. LEGAL EDUC. 575 (2017); Teri A. McMurtry-Chubb, *Writing at the Master's Table:*

students to represent diverse client groups in a manner that helps rather than harms." (532–533) The legal writing classroom can "operate[] as a place of liberation." (535) To illustrate her point, the author lists six social justice-oriented "litigation universe[s]" (536) used in her legal writing classes and details several pedagogies she has employed to "disrupt students' normalization of the legal academy as a White space [and] a Western-colonized space...." (567) The litigation universes, designed to simulate legal practice, each "require[d] students to grapple with their own implicit and explicit biases to make effective legal arguments." (567) She includes a case file on legacy admissions as affirmative action to illustrate her method.

McMurtry-Chubb, Teri A. "Still Writing at the Master's Table: Decolonizing Rhetoric in Legal Writing for a 'Woke' Legal Academy." *The Scholar: St. Mary's Law Review on Race and Social Justice* 21, no. 2 (2019): 255–292.

McMurtry-Chubb's aim in this article is to present ways to "decolonize Western rhetorical practices ... [and] canon ... throughout the law school curriculum" (288–89), starting with legal writing instruction. She summarizes the characteristics of, and suggests exercises based on "oppositional [Indigenous, African Diasporic, Asian Diasporic, and Latinx] rhetorics." (274)

Moppett, Samantha A. "Acknowledging America's First Sovereign: Incorporating Tribal Justice Systems into the Legal Research and Writing Curriculum." *Oklahoma City University Law Review* 35, no. 2 (Summer 2010): 267–338.

Moppett points out that the first year law school curriculum emphasizes coverage of U.S. federal and state law and legal systems at the exclusion of American Indian and Alaska Native tribal governments and justice systems. She covers thorough foundational information about tribal justice systems for law professors, then outlines ways for legal writing faculty to teach this information. Methods include conceptually introducing tribal systems alongside federal and state systems in class, incorporating tribal justice systems into writing assignments, and using tribal cases and codes in discussion of statutory or case analysis.

Rose, Leslie M. "Teaching Gender as a Core Value in the Legal-Writing Classroom." *Oklahoma City University Law Review* 36, no. 2 (Summer 2011): 531–536.

Rose succinctly describes her efforts to normalize a more balanced use of gender in her appellate advocacy class, a required part of the legal writing program at her law school. She deliberately incorporates female-majority characters in her hypotheticals in order to "consciously avoid[] gender stereotypes" (531) and to make "the predominance of women appear *normal* rather than special." (532) In addition, she promotes the use of gender-neutral language in her course materials and in feedback on student assignments, with the goal of counteracting

---

Reflections on Theft, Criminality, and Otherness in the Legal Writing Profession, 2 Drexel L. Rev. 41 (2009).

the typical default use of "male-gendered generics" (533) in casebooks and legal writing textbooks.

Stanchi, Kathryn M. "Resistance Is Futile: How Legal Writing Pedagogy Contributes to the Law's Marginalization of Outsider Voices." *Dickinson Law Review* 103, no. 1 (Fall 1998): 7–58.

In this highly cited work, Stanchi critiques "the two prevailing methods of teaching legal writing: the process view and the social view ... [which both] emphasize that ... the writer or speaker must become a member of the culture and community of legal practice." (8) While effective, both methods "reflect[] the biases in legal language" (9) and can result in further suppression in the legal academy of the voices of already marginalized groups. To address this problem, she explores ways to incorporate critical theory and methodology throughout all levels of the law school curriculum, starting with first year legal writing classes.

Stephenson, Gail S., and Linda C. Fowler. "Keeping It Real: Developing a Culturally and Personally Relevant Legal Writing Curriculum." *Journal of Gender, Race & Justice* 10, no. 1 (Fall 2006): 67–92.

The authors discuss the creation of a legal writing curriculum at Southern University Law Center, a diverse and historically black institution, that accounted for differences in students' cultural and personal backgrounds, as well as disparate learning styles and problem-solving skill sets. Strategies included: having faculty become more familiar with regional and local culture; selecting cases and other learning materials with a focus on civil rights; developing in-class discussions and assignments that relate to students' personal interests or experiences; and diversifying teaching strategies, such as the inclusion of visual or audio aids into the classroom. They offer suggestions for developing similar curricula at other law schools.

Websites

"Diversity and Inclusion Committee," Legal Writing Institute, accessed Aug. 10, 2020, https://www.lwionline.org/diversity-committee.

This committee "foster[s] and support[s] diversity and inclusion in legal writing education" and has posted about proposed projects on diversity and equity, inviting input from legal writing faculty.[12]

---

12. As an example, the Committee has publicly posted about a "Common Case Project" inviting legal writing faculty to submit ideas for civil cases that "touch[] on diversity, equity, and inclusion concerns ... [with the goal of] 3–4 [1L] classes across both semesters using the case.... The purpose of the project is to encourage more professors to include cases that address diversity issues and, through repetition, increase the likelihood that students would remember the case and the lessons taught." Letter from Betsy Brand Six, University of Kansas School of Law, to Legal Writing Colleagues (Apr. 23, 2019), https://www.lwionline.org/sites/default/files/Common%20Case%20Project.docx.

Chapter 7

Legal Research

Integrating Diversity into Legal Research: Building an Essential Skill for Law Students

*by Raquel J. Gabriel**

Introduction

As of this book's publication, legal education will still be dealing with the repercussions of two seismic disruptions that occurred in the first half of 2020: 1) the COVID-19 global pandemic that forced a substantial number of schools into remote learning with different levels of success, and 2) the murder of George Floyd that galvanized nationwide protests and brought into mainstream awareness the systemic racism and oppression of Black people in the United States and around the world. Both of these events will undoubtedly change how current and future law students will learn and engage with the profession, and it is foolish for legal educators to believe or act otherwise. Any argument that professors should teach students to "think like a lawyer" without acknowledging the impact of the outside world on a student's ability to learn is doing a disservice to their students, as well as to the future clients of those students.

Legal research presents the perfect opportunity to introduce students to concepts of diversity contextualized within the framework of learning how to be a lawyer. The ability to conduct legal research professionally and efficiently is an ABA requirement[1]

* Professor of Law and Director of the Law Library, City University of New York (CUNY) School of Law. This piece was originally workshopped in a vastly different format at the Seventh Annual Boulder Conference on Legal Information: Teaching & Scholarship held at the University of Pennsylvania Law School, Philadelphia, Pennsylvania. Heartfelt thanks to the CUNY School of Law Library faculty and staff, as well as the community at CUNY Law as a whole for their support. Special thanks to Sue Bryant for reading those earlier versions and for her comments and encouragement.

1. Legal research is specifically listed as a Learning Outcome by the ABA. Am. Bar Ass'n, Standards and Rules of Procedure for Approval of Law Schools 2020–2021, Standard 302(b), https://www.americanbar.org/content/dam/aba/administrative/legal_education_and_admissions_to_the_bar/standards/2019-2020/2019-2020-aba-standards-chapter3.pdf.

that the profession holds in high regard as a necessary skill to for practice, even if as a whole, law schools do not.[2] While offering a stand-alone legal research course is the most obvious way a law school accomplish these goals, even in situations where legal research is part of the legal writing course or taught in a few separate sessions, the opportunity to integrate diversity[3] issues exists.

Instructors can adapt the examples articulated in this essay to their particular situation, whether it be a full semester course or a singular session. Many students see the ability to perform legal research as a beneficial, practical skill; leveraging that assumption is key to helping students become receptive to integrating diversity into their development as attorneys. Doing so helps them realize they do not need to think about such issues as siloed off from learning about the law, but gives them a basis to anchor the diversity of their life experiences into how they relate to learning the law and its real-life impacts.

This essay echoes a growing number of voices declaring that students should be introduced to ideas of diversity and cross-cultural competence in their legal education.[4] It draws upon the ideas laid down in Sue Bryant's seminal piece on the Five Habits[5] in clinical settings, Bryant and Jean Koh Peters' *Five Habit for Cross-Cultural Lawyering*,[6] as well as subsequent literature in clinical legal education[7] to illustrate that con-

---

2. Very few law schools hold Legal Research as a required, stand-alone course in the first-year curriculum, even though it is a learning outcome required by Standard 302. A legal research course is a perfect opportunity for an experiential law course under ABA Standard 304, which directly references Standard 302 as a guide to how to implement experiential law courses. In most law schools, the topic of legal research is folded into the Legal Writing course. The amount of course time dedicated to legal research across U.S. law schools appears to vary widely depending on the school's particular history with its legal writing program, and very often, the library. While some law schools have librarians teach the legal research sections of the legal writing course, that is not always the case. From the beginning of its existence, CUNY School of Law has a required legal research course taught by the library faculty (who each hold a J.D. and M.L.S.), in the first year of the 1L full and part-time programs. My colleague Sarah Valentine outlined some of the reasons why legal research should be a priority in law schools and offers recommendations on how and why legal research could be folded into the larger law school curriculum. Sarah Valentine, *Legal Research as a Fundamental Skill: A Lifeboat for Students and Law Schools*, 39 U. Balt. L. Rev. 173 (2010).

3. I define diversity very broadly; it not only encompasses race, gender, and sexual orientation, but also mental and physical abilities. I also believe an individual can hold multiple diverse identities within them at once, reflecting an integrated experience that shifts and changes depending on their circumstances and surroundings. For further explanation of what I mean, see Raquel J. Gabriel, *Diversity Dialogues: Diversity in the Profession*, 102 Law Lib. J. 147 (2010).

4. However, to the best of the editorial team's knowledge (of which I am a member), this volume is the first one specifically addressing integrating these ideas into the first-year curriculum.

5. Susan Bryant, *The Five Habits: Building Cross-Cultural Competence in Lawyers*, 8 Clinical L. Rev. 33 (2001).

6. Susan Bryant & Jean Koh Peters, *Five Habits for Cross-Cultural Lawyering* in Race, Culture, Psychology & Law (Kimberly Barrett & William George, eds., 2005).

7. There are numerous articles that cite Bryant and Koh Peters as an example of how the literature has developed around cross-cultural competency and issues concerning diversity specifically in clinical settings. Some examples are: Muneer I. Ahmad, *Interpreting Communities: Lawyering Across Language Difference*, 54 UCLA L. Rev. 999 (2007); Jeffrey Blumberg, *Sitting by the Well: The Case for Intercultural Competency Training in International Experiential Learning*, 43 U. Balt. L. Rev. 395 (2014); Ascanio

sciously incorporating ideas about diversity into the law school curriculum and legal educational pedagogy assists students in their development as attorneys. By consciously integrating techniques that recognize the diversity of the classroom in the first year curriculum, students have a foundation to build upon to prepare them for law school clinics or related experiences, as well as their future careers.

The techniques explored in this essay draw upon my teaching experiences, from readings over the years on instructional design and teaching pedagogy, but most importantly, from the discussions I have been fortunate to have with colleagues within my law school and the law library profession. Through the years, many of these conversations have reflected observations I have had about teaching at different points in my career—first as an untenured faculty member of color, then as a more experienced teacher reaching out for feedback from colleagues on how to handle issues in the classroom. As technology, legal research methods, students, and I have changed over time, such discussions have been invaluable in my ongoing examination of what I teach and more importantly, *how* I teach to optimize reaching students in the classroom.

Laying the Groundwork

For any new class, whether it be the beginning of a course or guest lecture, teachers usually spend significant amounts of time preparing their teaching materials. There are several ways to approach thinking about diversity and acknowledge how integrating ideas about diversity can better help you prepare for classroom instruction.

Introduce yourself and your expectations before class begins and take the opportunity to learn a bit about students.

I used to have each student introduce themselves in our first class, and give a sentence or two about their interests; in my acknowledgment, I would tie their interest to a faculty member, clinic, or course within the curriculum. The goal was to immediately let a student know that they were a part of our community and that someone in the building had something in common with them from day one.

As some students were always clearly uncomfortable, these days I prefer sending out a *Student Information Sheet* with an introductory email before our first class session. I ask students to fill it out and return it to me a few days before class starts. On the sheet, I have them provide me with the name they prefer in class, as well as their favored pronouns. I ask for undergraduate/graduate majors, legal areas of interest, and if they would categorize themselves as a specific type of learner. Finally, I ask if

---

Piomelli, *Cross-Cultural Lawyering By the Book: The Latest Clinical Texts and a Sketch of a Future Agenda*, 4 HASTINGS RACE & POVERTY L. J. 131 (2006). It is hoped that this book leads to the same robust development in moving forward the discussions of diversity not only across legal research pedagogy but the entire law school curriculum.

there is anything I should know that might impact their ability to learn in the class-room. I also let them know that any information they disclose to me is voluntary.[8]

Every semester, I gain a wealth of information from students that assists me in preparing or revising how to handle particular classes or exercises. Some students disclose issues that explain why it would be difficult for them to answer me if I cold-called on them in class, or why they might seem distracted. Others will admit they hope they do not have to work in small groups, while others will say they would prefer learning that way exclusively. Some might need accommodations during class or for out of class assignments. I see which students already have strong interests or experience in certain subjects, as well as those who haven't yet formed a path. Surprisingly, almost every student can identify what type of learner they believe themselves to be and what they believe helps them learn best in the classroom. Many already know their strengths in auditory, visual, or hands-on learning, as well as their weaknesses. Often, several students can give me a detailed explanation of their learning style, and will often mention in what ways they may be limited in what would be considered immediate participation in class (e.g., raising their hands, handing in a completed exercise at the end of class) due to a specific learning disability or other issue.

Who was an immigration paralegal? Who switched careers from social work to the law? Who came straight from college? Is there anyone who needs to know about alternative methods of completing a timed in-class exercise? Has anyone highlighted topics that will be uncomfortable for them if we discuss them? Does a student explain a situation at home that will make it difficult to complete classwork if we are doing it during a scheduled class session versus doing something asynchronously?

Knowing all of this information does not mean I necessarily change the subjects I use as demonstrations in my course, or that I limit the kinds of exercises I do in the class. But it does mean I will go back and take another look at each exercise once I have reviewed their student information sheets to see if I could potentially modify it slightly to make it more accessible to students. Sometimes that means breaking down the directions into more steps so that I am clearer about what type of answer I am looking for, or I give them a specific example of the citation format. It may mean giving them strict guidelines on how long to spend on a particular portion of an exercise before seeking me out for further assistance, or if we are all in the same room, asking them to let me know what their group has gotten for a specific answer before moving on to the next question. It may mean stopping the entire class from time to time to be sure we are all heading in the same direction. In some classes, I may need to incorporate all of those techniques in order to ensure that students have

---

8. I currently use Slack as my learning management system, and have students upload their Student Information Sheet via Dropbox. The syllabus is also available, outlining course requirements, which informs them of the levels of professionalism expected in the classroom. I have students volunteer any information they may want to share with me, but I also let them know in my introduction to the course that they should feel free to contact our Director of Student Disability Services for additional information or guidance.

the opportunity to ask questions in a way that they believe best helps them navigate the material and the work I am asking them to do in class.

Being conscious of their diversity and the ways in which they define their own challenges to learning before I even meet them is a relatively easy way to respond to students' diversity and think about how my coursework might need to be adjusted in ways that will optimize their learning. I tend to review these sheets before the first few classes to remind myself there is no one way to assess student progress that will be reflective of *all* students within a particular class session or topic, so I should be ready with different types of assessment throughout the course to help maximize the opportunity for them to learn. With the reality of a remote learning environment in the fall of 2020, I am likely to be more reliant upon the student information sheets, since any information I have that can help me better refine my materials is useful in adapting the course to remote learning.

Be transparent when designing your learning outcomes.

Recall your years as a law student. Other than perhaps cringing at all the things you potentially did wrong in your pursuit of the study of law, do you remember the intensity of it? How it made you insecure or nervous? On the other side, many faculty members might say the same thing about how they felt when they first started teaching. Imagine how your students' fears may be amplified learning remotely in their first semester of law school.

Think how it might have alleviated your fears if your professor told you, "We are doing A because I want you to learn B, and the reason I'm choosing to teach it this way is because of C, which ties in our course/lesson/session as a whole as D." Applied to legal research, one could state, "We are learning about legal encyclopedias because we've learned a secondary source is a good place to start when you don't know a lot about an area of law. We are using Westlaw because they own the state encyclopedia for our jurisdiction. We can look at how a Table of Contents and Index works on that research system giving you a baseline for how materials are organized within the system. Finally, remember how it ties into the legal research process that we've talked about and how secondary sources are critical to making sure you find the appropriate legal authority."

While perhaps not necessary for every lesson, or for you to speak it aloud, I find it helps me rescan my entire course each semester. What kinds of tasks am I assigning, and does it match my pedagogical goals? If I need to create material that will be done asynchronously, does it reflect an actual learning goal? Am I transparent in either my directions or in the exercise itself what those goals are? Is there information from the student information sheets that can help me improve the learning environment for more students? Does someone have an advantage if they've worked in that subject area, or conversely, has expressed anxiety about it? When we move to classroom exercises, I often tell students why we're doing it a particular way within the context of the specific learning outcome, and this hopefully forestalls any feeling that an activity is classroom filler.[9]

The sudden shift to remote learning in spring of 2020 made me go back and rescan my material again, conscious of the stress levels both the students and I were experiencing. I revised my final assignment and told them why I was doing so. Frankly, I spent most of my time with them in our remaining lectures trying to assess their overall mental and physical health and trying to reassure them that it was fine if they didn't retain everything. I reminded them that I would be available during the rest of their law school careers to help them relearn any and all of it, and for me, in that moment of time, that was a perfectly acceptable learning outcome. Teaching in the part-time program, where almost half of the students are from diverse backgrounds already balancing the stress of work with law school study, I felt it was critical to alleviate the sudden anxieties several of them expressed to me.

Acknowledge limitations of your knowledge and comfort levels, and seek assistance, guidance, and support from colleagues.

In addition to reaching out to the usual avenues such as Academic Affairs or Student Affairs offices when dealing with student issues, I find it tremendously helpful to consult with colleagues. Our legal research faculty makes it a practice to meet once a week during the semester and discuss how the week's classes went, and share what worked and what didn't in terms of the flow of each class. We bounce ideas off of each other for new ways to do things, and if one of us tries something, the others can modify it for their use. While we work from a standard curriculum and provide teachers with the sample exercises to work from, many of us have tweaked the samples over the years to match what we think works best for our teaching style and the particular group of students that semester. While we all teach the same material, there is no requirement that we teach it the same way, given our personalities and teaching styles. Forcing one of us to do something they were uncomfortable with as a teacher would likely be readily apparent to students. Our regular meetings are a way to make sure we have the opportunity to discuss things that might be of concern, including those around diversity, and we can talk to one another how best to address those

---

9. For example, I've taught seminars where several students wanted to make sure they knew how to use materials in print, so revised an exercise where they could choose to use print or not based on their preference but needed to report their findings back to the whole class. For another seminar that seemed to divide between wanting to work alone or work in groups, I often have the same exercise do both — they first work alone for a few minutes, then in small groups, and report out to the whole class. What I have found tremendously helpful is letting students know that I am assigning these different ways of engaging the material specifically because they do have different learning styles, as they've told me in their Student Information Sheets. I then explain I am trying to accommodate those styles as much as possible, but always open to working with them outside of class if they need assistance or review.

concerns and try to alleviate them,[10] with a final advantage being that we have found it an excellent way to help transfer the knowledge of more experienced teachers to newer ones.

Techniques and Examples

The methods described above can help consciously prepare for diversity issues in the classroom. The following are examples of how to integrate those ideas into classroom exercises in legal research, and how to do so all within an overriding framework: acknowledge and integrate diversity issues within the context of the development of professional skills that will help them in assisting a future client.

Use diverse names or settings consciously to help students determine implicit bias, OR deliberately neutralize names for legal research issues before introducing diversity issues.

Shamika Dalton and Clanitra Stewart Nejdl have written about how to incorporate race and cultural competency into a legal research class[11] and offer excellent examples on how to incorporate diverse names into legal instruction. Their work also highlights some of the issues one should think about before doing so and it offers practical tips on navigating the sometimes contentious issues that may arise from the discussion of diversity in the classroom.[12]

---

10. During the summer of 2020, we met regularly to re-examine our curriculum, revise some exercises, and overall, just to discuss how those of us who were forced to suddenly teach remotely in the spring had handled the course. The discussions we had about how we each approached the course and the different ways we worked towards achieving the same benchmark goals was enlightening and helpful towards re-energizing us in preparation for the fall. At the same time, the larger CUNY faculty had weekly discussions during the first half of the summer, talking about remote teaching, lessons learned from the spring semester, and how we might pedagogically move forward teaching remotely in the fall.

I have also found connecting with colleagues through AALL (American Association of Law Libraries) Annual Meetings, webinars, and discussion forums helpful as well. If you do not have a colleague within your institution to turn to, reach out to someone else! I have found it rare that a librarian will not reply with some sort of answer from another librarian who seeks assistance.

11. Shamika Dalton, *Incorporating Race into Your Legal Research Class*, 109 Law Libr. J. 703 (2017); Shamika Dalton & Clanitra Stewart Nejdl, *Developing a Culturally Competent Legal Research Curriculum*, AALL Spectrum, March/April 2019, at 18–21. I have had the pleasure with co-presenting with Shamika and Clanitra, along with Michelle Rigual, at the 2018 American Association of law Libraries (AALL) Annual Meeting (Baltimore) and the inaugural Teaching the Teachers Conference (Atlanta, 2019) where we presented the program *Diverse Interactions: Addressing Race & Implicit Bias in Legal Research Instruction*. Shamika Dalton provides additional insight on teaching Legal Research in a separate essay within this chapter.

12. In the summer of 2020, I moderated the program *Fear and Loathing in Legal Research Instruction: Addressing Cultural Competence and Managing Implicit Bias*, at the 2020 American Association of Law Libraries (AALL) Annual Meeting with panelists Mike Martinez, Jr., Sherri Thomas, and Ronald E.

I agree with the advice they give in their work, and for those who might still hesitate, offer an alternative method. Deliberately strip the names from any hint of diversity, as simplistic as John and Jane Doe, or even X and Y, as well as other significant identifying factors such as location, time of day, or the age of individuals.[13] When students report out their findings, acknowledge their research methods, and instruct them as you normally would on their efforts. However, when done, step back, tell them not to answer aloud and ask them to simply think on the following question: "What assumptions did you make about the client?"

Some will look confused, but I explain that each of them made assumptions they were likely not even consciously aware of in executing their search: assumptions about what words were important in the fact pattern I gave them, about what the legal issue was, and where to go first to do their research. Then I ask them to think about how their research methods might have changed if I added or altered some facts. I might tell them the client was Asian, a member of the LGBTQIA community, in a wheelchair, or was 89 years old. That the location featured was on the Upper West Side, Flushing, Queens, or the Hamptons. I stop for a few moments after each iteration and then ask them to be honest with themselves: Did their assumptions change how they might have done the research based on who/what/where their client was? That recognition is key to understanding they hold implicit biases[14] that affect their ability to understand their future clients. Holding such bias is not inherently wrong, but legal research in the real world does not exist in a vacuum. Many students instinctively realize that research must be contextualized within the needs of their clients, yet may not recognize that ideas about identity and diversity can limit the ability to serve their clients' best interests if they are not aware they hold them. This type of self-reflection does not require students to share something they may be uncomfortable with about the assumptions they may have made. Still, I hope it helps them recognize, from the start

---

Wheeler, Jr., where we were able to discuss some of these ideas. *See* Victoria Hudgins, *Why Acknowledging Implicit Bias is Key for Better Legal Research,* Law.com (July 14, 2020), https://www.law.com/legaltech news/2020/07/17/why-acknowledging-implicit-bias-is-key-for-better-legal-research/.

13. For the past few years, I have used a landlord/tenant issue that focuses on water damage to the apartment when introducing secondary sources. I do not give a name nor gender to the client but ask them to research the issue. If a student asks me aloud while researching for more information about who the client is, I ask them to go on and research based on what they think they know. Inevitably, this helps me circle the conversation back to that same question when I discuss the problem with the entire class.

14. Many students are already familiar with the concept of implicit bias. If not, I give a brief definition and stress that we all carry them, whether we are aware of them or not. There are also numerous sources discussing implicit bias in the legal profession. *See generally* Debra Chopp, *Addressing Cultural Bias in the Legal Profession,* 41 NYU Rev. L. & Soc. Change 364 (2017); Nicole E. Negowetti, *Implicit Bias and the Legal Profession's "Diversity Crisis": A Call for Self-Reflection,* 15 Nev. L. J. 930 (2015); Joan C. Williams et al., *You Can't Change What You Can't See: Interrupting Racial & Gender Bias in the Legal Profession, Executive Summary,* Am. Bar Ass'n, Commission on Women in the Profession & Minority Corp Counsel Association (2018), https://www.americanbar.org/content/dam/aba/administrative/women/you-cant-change-what-you-cant-see-print.pdf; Am. Bar Ass'n, Section of Litigation, *Implicit Bias Initiative,* https://www.americanbar.org/groups/litigation/initiatives/task-force-implicit-bias/ (last visited Sept. 9, 2020).

of building their practical skills, that there is a distinct identity to each client that influences the research into their legal issue.

Use current news stories to frame an issue.[15]

Another way to integrate diversity in ways that may engage students is by using current news stories as a starting point for research. For example, a current news article about stopping American citizens at the border to question their "loyalty" to the United States may form the backbone of delving into secondary sources that discuss lawsuits that challenge such stops. Assigning the individuals in a story as their clients help ground them in something that feels more urgent and practical in terms of developing their skills. I may assign them a news story where their natural inclination is to disagree with one of the parties, and assign them to support that particular party. I do so to reinforce that they may need to set aside their biases to help a client, and to remind them there will be times they do not always agree with all of a client's decisions. For example, at a law school that trains students to work in the public interest, I often find students bristling a bit when I inform them the day's fact pattern deals with someone's Second Amendment rights, or with defending a large corporation. Exposing students to ideas of diversity they are comfortable with—and those they are not—is critical to reinforcing the concept that ideas about diversity are integrated inextricably within their professional work as attorneys.

Create exercises that will have them practice working with diverse clients and colleagues by having them work with one another.

My class requirements indicate that I expect a certain level of professionalism from my students, which includes appropriate, respectful, and professional conduct with each other and in all class communications. It also requires that they sometimes have to work individually or in small groups. While dependent on the dynamics of a particular semester, at times, I will have students work with partners in class whom I sense they do not regularly interact with or have them count off to work in groups away from their friends. I circulate through the classroom to see how they are interacting with one another, encouraging the different approaches they may take within a group. I always try to communicate the reality of what happens in legal research— there are usually several paths to the right answer—and I remind them that someone else's approach isn't necessarily wrong, it may just be different from theirs. I point out that it is very rare for lawyers to work completely alone, as it's a very collaborative

---

15. While I have used current events to help develop classroom exercises, I have started to use recent news stories more consciously in the classroom based on discussions with the library faculty at CUNY as well other law librarians, including Shamika Dalton, Mike Martinez, Jr., Clanitra Stewart Nejdl, MIchelle Rigual, Sherri Thomas, and Ronald E. Wheeler, Jr.

profession. Respecting and recognizing the diversity among their colleagues is also key to becoming an effective lawyer.

Students have generally been positive about such exercises, even when they are working with others with whom they previously have had limited interactions. There are usually at least a few minutes of awkwardness, especially in the beginning of the semester. But as time goes on, (either in that initial session or in subsequent ones) I am usually pleased to see that if I pair them up with different students, they are more likely to complain I don't give them enough time to talk with each other about the varying ways they got to the same answer! Finally, I try to remember to reinforce the idea that most lawyers work in teams to get things done, and the way I am asking them to interact in the classroom is a way to get them used to the idea of doing so when they move into real world practice.

Incorporate diversity into teaching legal research based on the organizational culture of your institution.

There may be those who would argue that there is not enough time to integrate diversity issues into legal research teaching, especially if there are limitations on the time allotted to teaching the material or there is personal discomfort in how to structure classroom lessons. I strongly disagree and believe acknowledging and integrating diversity into teaching legal research is a requirement for all legal research teachers.

Integrating diversity into your teaching helps you examine your pre-conceptions of who is sitting in front of you in the classroom, or on the other side of the computer. It makes you think more broadly about how to get your goals across to your students, and in the end, creates more paths of accessibility to the material. It helps you to start laying the groundwork for your students' understanding that they need to think of legal research as a process that ultimately helps them advocate for their client, and to do so, they must be conscious of the diversity of the clients they may have in the future.

I understand that this may seem radical or intimidating to those who are afraid to get it wrong standing in a classroom. I have felt the apprehension and panic that a teacher may feel about risking classroom conflict if students clash with each other—or with you—if something goes wrong. But it is unwise to think that current or future law students will not be much more aware of issues involving race and diversity, and will question why their legal education does not address inequalities in the law.

Conclusion

Legal research is an essential skill that I believe should be taught by professional law librarians invested in training our future attorneys. Law librarians are the experts in conducting the process of legal research, and best equipped to train law students in how it should be done, in much the same way that clinical faculty are commonly understood to be the experts in teaching clinical offerings. Understanding the current reality of the limitations of legal education in many institutions, I know that many librarians are not as fortunate as I am to be allowed to teach. But I would encourage librarians, who are interested in integrating diversity and may have fewer opportunities, to think about how to adapt some of the observations into their interactions with students. Even in a single bibliographic session, one could consider using a news story as a basis or taking a few minutes after the session to remind students of the different types of clients they may have in the future. Thus, legal research can be used to bridge the experiences and identities of students before law school and tie them directly to their legal education and the development of a legal skill that will assist their future clients.

Teaching legal research has been the most enjoyable part of my career as a librarian. I firmly believe that when given the opportunity, librarians are perhaps the most naturally inclined among a law school's community to teach, as many of us gravitated towards the profession with a simultaneous love for learning, providing access to information, and educating others on how to find it. Adapting those skills to teach in a classroom is a transition that can rarely be done in a single session or year. Along with trial and error, and a willingness to keep improving, instructors should realize they have the tools to become effective teachers over time with effort. The same applies when thinking of adopting ways to integrate diversity concepts into teaching legal research. Integrating diversity into the legal research curriculum is required if we are to prepare students for their careers as practicing attorneys engaged with an increasingly diverse world. And thinking about how to do that within the context of teaching legal research—a required, valuable skill that is necessary to becoming an effective attorney—is an exciting process well worth the engagement.

Teaching Cultural Competency through Legal Research Instruction

Shamika D. Dalton*

Introduction

The racial demographics of the United States have undergone significant changes over the past forty years. In 1980, racial minorities made up approximately 20% of the U.S. population.[1] According to the 2019 U.S. Census population estimates, the percentage of racial minorities in the U.S. has doubled to nearly 40%.[2] By 2060, it is projected that the U.S. will be a "majority-minority" nation with the non-Hispanic white population only making up 44% of the general population.[3] As the U.S. becomes more and more racially diverse, lawyers will inevitably have to represent clients from different racial backgrounds.[4] Cultural competency is a critical set of skills that lawyers need to be effective advocates for their clients in a multicultural society.[5] To be a culturally competent lawyer, law students need to understand that "we all have multi-

---

* Associate Director and Associate Professor, University of Tennessee College of Law Joel A. Katz Law Library.

1. Nat'l Ass'n Soc. Workers, Standards and Indicators for Cultural Competence in Social Work Practice 8 (2015), https://www.socialworkers.org/LinkClick.aspx?fileticket=PonPTDE Brn4%3d&portalid=0; Soc. Sci. Data Analysis Network, *Population By Race*, CensusScope (2001), http://www.censusscope.org/us/chart_race.html (last visited Sept. 9, 2020).

2. U.S. Census Bureau, Population estimates, July 1, 2019, https://www.census.gov/quickfacts/fact/table/US/PST045219 (last visited Sept. 9, 2020).

3. Sandra L. Colby & Jennifer M. Ortman, *Projections of the Size and Composition of the U.S. Population: 2014 to 2060: Population Estimates and Projections*, U.S. Census Bureau (Mar. 3, 2015), https://www.census.gov/library/publications/2015/demo/p25-1143.html.

4. Serena Patel, *Cultural Competency Training: Preparing Law Students for Practice in Our Multicultural World*, 62 UCLA L. Rev. Discourse 139, 143 (2014).

5. *Id.* at 142.

faceted cultural backgrounds, experiences, and biases that affect how we perceive and analyze legal problems and how we interact with clients and colleagues."[6]

The need for cultural competency in the legal profession is evident in the American Bar Association's professionalism and accreditation standards.[7] As legal educators, we need to develop an inclusive law school curriculum that educates students about different cultures and challenges personal and structural cultural biases and stereotypes. "[B]ecause the law is an expression of social values[;] students need to be aware that those values may be culturally biased."[8] An explicit consideration for cultural issues, coupled with legal analysis, "will strengthen and expand a student's intellectual capacity, as well as his or her capacity for passion and compassion."[9] Cultural awareness and sensitivity to cultural issues will also help students understand "the limits of legal doctrines and, in some cases, how the doctrine itself undermines the overriding purpose or goals of the law."[10]

The responsibility to teach law students about cultural competency should not be limited to doctrinal, clinical, and legal writing faculty. Legal research instructors should also incorporate cultural competency into their courses. Understanding legal issues begins with legal research, and students need to be able to identify potential diversity issues and bias at the onset of analyzing a legal problem. We can create legal research exercises that "give students practice thinking about legal issues from a variety of cultural perspectives" and help them understand how bias in the criminal justice system can adversely affect marginalized groups.[11] Without this keen awareness, students can miss key legal arguments that could help their client's case.

Cultural competency encompasses an awareness of differences based on one's race/ethnicity, religion, sexual orientation, socioeconomic class, etc.[12] In this essay, I will focus on racial competency. Racism and racial biases are deeply rooted in American culture and have significant implications in the legal system. However, many educators avoid the topic of race due to its emotionally-charged nature and the potential to cause acute levels of discomfort in confronting racial biases. But I firmly believe that avoiding the topic does a disservice to our students. When we avoid the topic of race, we minimize and dismiss the unequal treatment that racial minorities have been subjected to for hundreds of years in the U.S.; push a false narrative that we live in a

---

6. Andrea A. Curcio, *Addressing Barriers to Cultural Sensibility Learning: Lessons from Social Cognition Theory*, 15 Nev. L.J. 537, 538 (2015).

7. Shamika Dalton & Clanitra Stewart Nejdl, *Developing a Culturally Competent Legal Research Curriculum*, AALL Spectrum, Mar./Apr. 2019, at 18, 19–20.

8. Bonny L. Tavares, *Changing the Construct: Promoting Cross-Cultural Conversations in the Law School Classroom*, 67 J. Legal Educ. 211, 215 (2017).

9. Okianer Christian Dark, *Incorporating Issues of Race, Gender, Class, Sexual Orientation, and Disability into Law School Teaching*, 32 Willamette L. Rev. 541, 544 (1996).

10. *Id.*

11. Tavares, *supra* note 9, at 213.

12. Ellen Yaroshefsky, *Waiting for the Elevator: Talking about Race*, 27 Geo. J. Legal Ethics 1203, 1206 (2014).

post-racial or colorblind society;[13] and miss an opportunity to train the next generation of lawyers and policymakers to be advocates against racial injustices.

Getting Started

A diversity statement in your syllabus is a great way to communicate your commitment to an inclusive, supportive learning environment. It is important to let students know that you value and respect their thoughts, opinions, and experiences. There are diversity statement examples online to help inspire you.[14] In your statement or first class, you should also let students know upfront that they will be researching and discussing sensitive topics, such as race, to build upon the cultural competencies they need to be effective lawyers in our diverse society.

If you are going to discuss sensitive topics in the classroom, you need to communicate a set of ground rules to "help clarify expectations, cultivate a sense of belonging among students, and facilitate students' ability to engage productively with one another across their differences."[15] As with diversity statements, you can find examples of ground rules online.[16] You should review your ground rules with students on the first day of class and before discussing sensitive topics. If you or a student violates any of these ground rules, it must be addressed promptly. Rules without enforcement are merely suggestions. You must be willing to follow through on your commitment to creating a positive, productive learning environment for ALL students.

When I am creating race-based hypotheticals, I scour news stories and agency websites for inspiration. Unfortunately, in our nation's current climate, it is easy to find news articles covering racial discrimination in the workplace, voter suppression, the inhumane treatment of immigrants, or the senseless killing of Blacks by police and racist vigilantes. Basing your legal research exercises on current events "can increase law students' interest in legal research by leveraging their potential excitement at dealing with a 'real' legal issue in class."[17] It can also further solidify "the practical value of legal research courses and reinforce the importance of legal research as a necessary skill."[18] Due to time constraints, it is common for legal research instructors

---

13. *Id.*

14. Yale Univ., Poorvu Center for Teaching and Learning, *Diversity Statements*, https://poorvu center.yale.edu/DiversityStatements (last visited Sept. 9, 2020); Carnegie Mellon Univ. Eberly Center Teaching Excellence & Educ. Innovation, *Diversity Statement on a Syllabus*, https://www.cmu.edu/ teaching/designteach/syllabus/checklist/diversitystatement.html (last visited Sept. 9, 2020).

15. Univ. of Michigan Center for Research on Learning and Teaching, *Guidelines for Classroom Interactions*, https://crlt.umich.edu/examples-discussion-guidelines (last visited Sept. 9, 2020).

16. *Id.*; *see also* Vanderbilt Univ. Center for Teaching, *Difficult Dialogues*, https://cft.vanderbilt.edu/ guides-sub-pages/difficult-dialogues/ (last visited Sept. 9, 2020); Washington Univ. in St. Louis, Center for Teaching and Learning, *Establishing Classroom Ground Rules*, https://teachingcenter.wustl. edu/resources/inclusive-teaching-learning/establishing-ground-rules/ (last visited Sept. 9, 2020).

17. Clanitra Stewart Nejdl, *This Really Happened: Incorporating Legal News Items and Current Events into Legal Research Courses*, Second Draft, Fall 2017, at 45, 45.

18. *Id.*

to recycle the same hypotheticals year after year. Using recent news articles can stimulate legal research instructors intellectually and encourage us to update our assignments and exercises regularly.[19] Agency websites are another great place to find ideas for legal research exercises. The U.S. Equal Employment Opportunity Commission (EEOC) website, for example, lists significant race/color discrimination cases adjudicated by the EEOC since 1964.[20] I have used some of the facts in those cases to create new hypotheticals.

First Class

To effectively engage students in research and discussions about race, you need to get to know your students beyond learning their names and foster rapport amongst your students.[21] Before student introductions, I pass out index cards with questions aimed at learning more about who my students are: their culture, values, and norms.[22] Here are some of the questions/prompts I use:

- Tell me about one or two traditions, celebrations, or rituals your family participates in.
- Tell me about where you grew up.
- Why do you want to become a lawyer? Was there a situation or incident that sparked your interest in being a lawyer?
- What is success to you? Where do you get your drive/work ethic?
- What organization are you most excited to join while in law school?

With this activity, I can get to know my students on a deeper level and build a sense of community in the classroom. I also use the information I learn during the student introductions to create diverse research groups with students of different races, genders, generations, and hometown geographic locations.

Formulating a Research Plan

Generating search terms is a critical component of formulating a research plan. I encourage students to think about synonyms when brainstorming search terms to ensure they receive the most comprehensive search results (e.g., car OR automobile OR vehicle OR conveyance). I also talk about the importance of synonyms when dealing with issues of race. Terms used to identify underrepresented groups have

---

19. *Id.* at 46.

20. U.S. Equal Employment Opportunity Comm'n, *Significant EEOC Race/Color Cases*, https://www.eeoc.gov/eeoc/initiatives/e-race/caselist.cfm#types (last visited Sept. 9, 2020).

21. Harvard Univ., Derek Bok Center for Teaching and Learning, *Inclusive Moves*, https://bokcenter.harvard.edu/inclusive-moves#navigating-difficult-moments (last visited Sept. 9, 2020).

22. Due to COVID-19, I taught my legal research classes online for the 2020–2021 academic year. I utilized the Discussion feature on the Canvas platform for this exercise.

evolved. To capture cases from the 1920s and the 2000s, students will need to consider the evolution of such terms in their Boolean searches (e.g., Indian OR "American Indian" OR "Native American" OR "Indigenous"). Professors Lorraine Bannai and Anne Enquist wrote an article that "discusses how law school courses, specifically legal writing courses, can address cultural bias and its effects on legal analysis and language."[23] In the article, they provide a brief history of the evolution of terms used to identify racial minorities.[24] This article would be great supplemental reading for your students before the lecture.

Conducting Secondary Source and Interdisciplinary Research

Certain legal issues may require students to consult resources outside of the law. Rule 2.1 (Advisor) of the ABA's Model Rules of Professional Conduct states that "a lawyer may refer not only to law but to other considerations such as moral, economic, social, and political factors that may be relevant to the client's situation."[25] The legal profession relies on research in disciplines such as sociology, psychology, economics, and medicine to help lawyers and judges better understand the specific circumstances of a client's problem or dispute. For the past few years, I have used an employment discrimination hypothetical that involves Tyrone Bennett, a 32-year-old Black male, who works at a local restaurant. Due to a medical condition called pseudofolliculitis barbae (PFB), he is unable to shave off all his facial hair. Tyrone was denied a promotion to Head Chef because of the restaurant's "no beard" policy. I asked students to determine if Tyrone has a case against the restaurant.[26]

When students start formulating their research plan, most students do not identify Tyrone's race as a significant fact and focus their legal question on a violation of the Americans with Disabilities Act. It is not until they start reading legal secondary sources and medical journals that they learn Tyrone's illness is a condition that disproportionately affects men of color, and having a "no beard" employee policy may be discriminatory. This exercise illustrates the interdisciplinary nature of legal research and teaches students that they cannot overlook their client's race as a significant factor. If you wanted to change the facts, you could sub-out PFB for other medical conditions such as sickle cell anemia, which also predominantly affects Blacks. What if Tyrone was fired because he refused to cut this beard due to religious reasons? You could alter the facts to teach religious competency.

---

23. Lorraine Bannai & Anne Enquist, *(Un)Examined Assumptions and (Un)Intended Messages: Teaching Students to Recognize Bias in Legal Analysis and Language*, 27 SEATTLE U. L. REV. 1 (2003).

24. *Id.* at 14–19.

25. ANNOTATED MODEL RULES OF PRO. CONDUCT (Am. Bar Ass'n, E. J. Bennett & H. W. Gunnarsson eds., 2019).

26. Shamika Dalton, *Incorporating Race into Your Legal Research Class*, 109 LAW LIBR. J. 703, 707–708 (2017).

I have used the "no beard" policy assignment for several years, so for next year's class, I plan to use the following hypothetical:

> In 2013, Marc Sanchez was convicted of the armed robbery of a convenience store and sentenced to 10 years in prison. At the trial, Ms. Miller, the store cashier, identified Mr. Sanchez as the robber. In her statement to the police on the night of the incident, Ms. Miller, a white, middle-aged woman, said that a Latino man entered the store with a gun and demanded the money in the register. She also said the suspect wore a baseball cap, which made his eyes hard to see. A few days after the robbery, police received an anonymous tip that identified Mr. Sanchez as a suspect. The police showed Ms. Miller a photo lineup that included Mr. Sanchez. When she first saw the lineup, Ms. Miller said, "Oh, my! All of these men look alike." After looking at the lineup for a few minutes, she identified Mr. Sanchez. Ms. Miller said she was 85% sure that Mr. Sanchez was the robber. Based on Ms. Miller's identification, the police arrested Mr. Sanchez. During interrogation and at the trial, Mr. Sanchez was adamant that he was attending his niece's Quinceañera ten miles away from the convenience store on the night of the robbery. Mr. Sanchez's mother corroborated Mr. Sanchez's whereabouts testifying that he was at the celebration with her. While she could not say with 100% certainty that he was at the party the whole time, Mrs. Sanchez testified that Mr. Sanchez does not own a vehicle, so he did not have transportation to leave the party.
>
> You work as an intern for Mr. Sanchez's new appeals attorney, Mr. Peters. Mr. Peters plans to challenge Ms. Miller's photo lineup identification. Mr. Peters wants you to research the reliability of cross-racial identification.

This hypothetical requires students to examine the reliability of cross-racial identification by researching law review articles and articles in psychology and social science disciplines. In their research, students may also learn about the significance of a Quinceañera in Latin American culture.

Finding Primary Authority (Statutes)

For a statutes class, you could create a hypothetical that involves a person of color suing her employer for making highly offensive and derogatory racist comments. However, I think it is far more impactful to educate students about the subtle forms of racial discrimination. Recently, states like California and New York have passed the CROWN Act to address hair discrimination.[27] Recent studies have assessed the

---

27. CAL. GOV'T CODE § 12926 (West 2020) (defining "race" to include traits including hair texture and protective hairstyles); CAL. GOV'T CODE § 212.1 (West 2020) (same); *see also* N.Y. EXEC. LAW § 292 (McKinney 2020); N.Y. EDUC. LAW § 11 (McKinney 2020).

impact of bias, either implicit or explicit, towards natural or textured hair.[28] It is well-documented that hair discrimination has harmful effects on Black women—in healthcare, policing, education, and other workplaces.[29] In one study, twenty-five percent of Black women felt social pressure to straighten their hair for work, which is double the percentage of white women.[30] In another study, 83% of Black women reported being judged harshly on their looks, and they were 1.5 times more likely to be sent home from work because of their hair.[31] To avoid scrutiny, 80% of Black women reported straightening their natural curls to conform to the office setting.[32] These biases also exist for Black men who chose to wear afros, braids, or dreadlocks.

Next year, I am excited to use the following hypothetical regarding hair discrimination.

> North Carolina Senator Dalton attended a local summit hosted by the Black Women Coalition last night. During the event, a Black woman shared that she was denied an executive job because she refused to cut her dreadlocks. Other Black women at the event shared stories about bosses and colleagues telling them that their afros and braids were "unprofessional" in the workplace. The Coalition has asked Senator Dalton to introduce a bill that prohibits hair discrimination. Senator Dalton knows that Virginia, our neighboring state, recently passed similar legislation. Senator Dalton has asked you to 1) find any research studies regarding hair discrimination; and 2) locate Virginia's CROWN Act. Senator Dalton wants to know about the history of the statute (the bill and session law number, who introduced the bill, and when the bill was passed).

In addition to finding the statute and interpreting the history table, students will learn about the social and economic effects of hair discrimination for people of color.

Locating Dockets

Since the killing of Eric Garner, media outlets and organizations such as Black Lives Matter have shed light on the violent murders of Black men and women at the hands of police officers. This hypothetical brings awareness to this historical racial injustice and explores legal remedies for the victims' families, especially since many police officers avoid criminal prosecution.

---

28. A.M. Johnson, Rachel D. Godsil, Jessica MacFarlane, Linda Tropp & Phillip Atiba Goff, *The "Good Hair" Study: Explicit and Implicit Attitudes Toward Black Women's Hair*, Perception Inst. (2017), https://perception.org/wp-content/uploads/2017/01/TheGood-HairStudyFindingsReport.pdf.

29. *Id.* at 1.

30. *Id.* at 12.

31. Dove, The CROWN Research Study (2019), https://static1.squarespace.com/static/5edc69fd622c36173f56651f/t/5edeaa2fe5ddef345e087361/1591650865168/Dove_research_brochure 2020_FINAL3.pdf.

32. *Id.* at 4.

Mr. and Mrs. Walker's son, Cameron Walker, was shot and killed by a police officer during a routine traffic stop. At the time of the shooting, Cameron, a Black man, was unarmed. Officer Shelia Johnson, a white female, insisted that Cameron was acting "aggressively" and was attempting to reach into his glove compartment to retrieve what she believed to be a gun. After an internal investigation, the shooting was ruled as justified, so Officer Johnson was not criminally charged. The Walker family wants to file a wrongful death lawsuit against the police department and Officer Johnson. Mr. Williams is a civil rights attorney in St. Louis, Missouri, and has agreed to represent the Walker family.

This case is eerily similar to the Michael Brown Jr. case in nearby Ferguson, Missouri.[33] Mr. Williams gives you a *New York Times* article detailing the wrongful death suit filed by Mr. Brown's family.[34] Since this will be Mr. Williams's first wrongful death case, he wants to review the docket from the Brown's lawsuit. He has asked you to find the docket and the contact information for the attorney(s) representing the Brown family. If available, he would also like for you to locate a copy of the initial (or amended) complaint and the final judgment.

This assignment alerts students to an injustice that has plagued our country for decades while engaging them in the prickly process of pulling case dockets through such limited information as can be found in a news article. It further provides a vehicle for discussing the types of case files that build the docket.

Conclusion

I hope this essay will inspire you to incorporate the topic of race into your legal research course. In addition to the hypotheticals in this essay, I provided three race-related hypotheticals in an earlier article, and I encourage you to use any of my examples in your curriculum.[35]

---

33. U.S. Dept. of Justice, Department of Justice Report Regarding the Criminal Investigation Into the Shooting Death of Michael Brown by Ferguson Missouri Police Officer Darren Wilson, (Mar. 4, 2015), https://www.justice.gov/sites/default/files/opa/press-releases/attachments/2015/03/04/doj_report_on_shooting_of_michael_brown_1.pdf.

34. John Eligon, *Family of Michael Brown Settles Lawsuit Against City of Ferguson*, N.Y. Times, June 20, 2017, at A17, https://www.nytimes.com/2017/06/20/us/family-of-michael-brown-settles-lawsuit-against-city-of-ferguson.html.

35. *See* Dalton, *supra* note 30.

Service-Learning in the First Year Research and Writing Classroom[*]

Alyson Drake[**] & Brie Sherwin[***]

Introduction

At some point in their career, most legal research and writing professors are looking for a way to incorporate a real legal issue into research and memo-writing that will resonate with their students. In the current social and political climate, it is more important than ever to introduce discussions of inclusion and the law into our classrooms. The goal of this chapter is to illustrate how valuable it is to pair with community partners to bring local legal issues into the classroom. The benefits for law students are vast; connecting them to social justice issues and people impacted by the law's inequity make them more invested in improving their legal research and writing skills. We have found that the benefits for the community are tremendous, as well, for it receives acknowledgement, support, and hopefully, a long-term interest from our law students in working to serve the community.

Service-Learning, Diversity, and Training Lawyers

There is a tremendous amount of literature on the benefits of service-learning, especially regarding benefits students gain in the areas of understanding diversity and inclusion.[1] In working with diverse communities including those communities students may not otherwise encounter in their lives, students gain an appreciation of other

---

[*] The authors want to recognize the contributions of attorneys Adam Pirtle, Advocacy Co-Director of Texas Housers, and Michael Bates, attorney at the Legal Aid of Northwest Texas's Community Revitalization Project, in helping inspire and develop these programs.

[**] Instructional Services Librarian & Adjunct Professor of Law, Fordham University School of Law.

[***] Professor of Law, Texas Tech University School of Law.

1. *See infra* Part I text and notes.

cultures and are less likely to accept stereotypes.[2] Additionally, outside the often contentious classroom atmosphere, students use their skills to solve real-life problems in a way that breaks down any defensiveness and allows for a more informal, relaxed dialogue about topics that can be controversial.[3]

Defined as "a teaching and learning strategy that integrates meaningful community service with instruction and reflection to enrich the learning experience, teach civic responsibility, and strengthen communities,"[4] service-learning balances service to the community with academic learning to give students an opportunity to go beyond the intellectual component of a course.[5] In *Where's the Learning in Service Learning*, Janet Eyler and Dwight E. Giles describe the impact service-learning has had on their students:

> [I]t engaged our students' hearts as well as their heads and helped them understand the complexity of what they were studying. It also provided opportunities to apply what they learned and think critically about assumptions they had never questioned before. We have been impressed by the ability of students to bring the information and skills learned in the classroom to bear on a project and help a community group achieve an important goal. We have been impressed by the power of service to motivate students to want to know more. We have been impressed by the ways in which service-learning creates connections — between feelings and though, between studies and life, between self and others, and between college and community.[6]

With service-learning, students realize they can have an impact in their communities as they help solve local problems.[7] Additionally, service-learning boosts student learning as they apply their skills to solving community problems through service-learning.[8]

In a study conducted by Eyler and Giles, not only did students indicate a greater appreciation of other cultures and increased tolerance of others, but large percentages of students reported an increased awareness and tolerance as one of the most important learning outcomes from the course.[9] Another study by Patricia Gross and Virginia Anne Maloney found students gained "a greater appreciation for the privileged

---

2. Janet Eyler & Dwight E. Giles, Jr., Where's the Learning in Service-Learning? 26 (1999).

3. *Id.* at 28.

4. Maureen Barry, *Librarians as Partners in Service-Learning Courses (Part I)*, LOEX Q., Spring 2011, at 8.

5. Eyler & Giles, *supra* note 2, at 2.

6. *Id.* at xiv.

7. Maureen Barry, *Research for the Greater Good: Incorporating Service Learning in an Information Literacy Course at Wright State University*, 6 Coll. & Rsch. Libr. News 72 (2011).

8. *See* Maureen Barry, *Librarians as Partners in Service-Learning Courses (Part II)*, LOEX Q., Summer 2011, at 8; Jadig Garcia & Debra Harkins, *Brief Report on Service Learning and Diversity Acceptance*, 4(1) Pedagogy & Hum. Sci. 1, 1 (2014) (describing two studies showing "incorporating diversity into the curriculum ... increases the complexity of student thinking as well as their willingness to participate in civic engagement").

9. Eyler & Giles, *supra* note 2, at 31–32.

lives they have lead" while interacting with local community members; students also had a greater understanding of the diversity in and the need for more outreach within their local communities.[10] Finally, a 2012 study by Matthew Holsapple, reviewing 55 studies on service-learning's impact, found six outcomes relating to diversity: (1) tolerance of differences, (2) stereotype confrontation, (3) recognition of universality, (4) interactions across differences, (5) knowledge about the served population, and (6) belief in the value of diversity.[11]

Studies[12] showing service-learning's positive impact on students' awareness and appreciation of issues of diversity and inclusion is likely due to service-learning's tendency to place students in contexts that challenge their world view.[13] Service-learning forces students to see the world in new ways and provides them with the opportunity to seek out information and experiences to better foster new understanding.[14] Service-learning courses provide students with spaces to grapple with their own identities and how identity affects their place within the systems that create inequality.[15]

Service-learning also helps students develop skills in civic engagement.[16] Notably, service-learning can "positively influence the quality of students' interactions with diverse peers,"[17] a skill helpful both during and after law school. The ability to empathize and communicate with diverse communities is an important community lawyering skill. Service-learning gives students an opportunity to exercise their empathy skills with diverse communities and cultivate a true interest in the client and not just

---

10. Patricia A. Gross & Virginia Anne Maloney, *Embracing Diversity Through Service Learning*, 85 CLEARING HOUSE 192, 194–95 (2012); *see also* Rachel A. Willis, *Socks, Trains, and Wheelchairs: Service Learning as the Vehicle for Teaching Diversity*, ASS'N AM. COLL. & UNIV., https://www.aacu.org/diversitydemocracy/2008/spring/willis ("By listening to perspectives different from their own, they came to appreciate the impact of 'stochastic variation' (i.e., luck) and gender-based circumstances that they had seen play out in the disaggregated economic data.").

11. Garcia & Harkins, *supra* note 8, at 3 (citing Matthew A. Holsapple, *Service-Learning and Student Diversity Outcomes: Existing Evidence and Directions for Future Research*, 18(2) MICH. J. CMTY SERV. LEARNING 5–18 (2012)).

12. *See* Barry, *supra* note 8, at 9 ("Service-learning students must think critically to discover how the information they might find might solve a community problem. This task often becomes more complicated by the fact that the students may have been largely unaware that such a problem existed prior to the service-learning experience."); David D. Blouin & Evelyn M. Perry, *Whom Does Service Learning Really Serve? Community-Based Organizations' Perspectives on Service Learning*, 37 TEACHING SOCIO. 121 (2009) ("[A] great deal of research reports numerous pedagogical and personal benefits for students ... [including] improved grades and learning, increased civic engagement, enhanced job skills, and greater appreciation for diversity."); Marcia Hernandez & Lorrie A. Knight, *Reinventing the Box: Faculty-Librarian Collaborative Efforts to Foster Service Learning for Political Engagement*, 16(1) J. CIVIC ENGAGEMENT 1–2 (2010) ("SL activities result in students' increased tolerance for diversity, compassion for others, commitment to engaged citizenship, and increased cognitive skills.").

13. EYLER & GILES, *supra* note 2 at 17.

14. *Id.*

15. Garcia & Harkins, *supra* note 8, at 2.

16. Maria J. Agostino, *Fostering a Civically Engaged Society: The University and Service Learning*, 14(2) J. PUBLIC AFFAIRS EDUC. 192 (2008).

17. Garcia & Harkins, *supra* note 8, at 1.

the exercise.[18] Teaching these skills allows students to see beyond the facts on a page and begin to understand the history and context behind clients' unique stories, which may involve inequality created by economic, political, and social realities.[19]

Service-Learning: A Case Study

Background

In the spring of 2019, a group of Texas Tech law professors led by Dr. Brie Sherwin began a series of discussions with two attorneys, Adam Pirtle, Advocacy Co-Director for Texas Housers, a non-profit organization that assists Texans in achieving decent, high quality affordable housing, and Michael Bates of the Legal Aid of Northwest Texas, about ways Texas Tech law students could help with local legal issues in Lubbock, Texas. Of the potential initiatives discussed, forming a first year open memo problem around an issue relevant to the local community was one of the first two initiatives to take root.[20] Taking a team approach to teaching legal research and writing, we adapted our first year Legal Practice course for the fall 2019 semester to include a service-learning component.

During the first semester of Legal Practice, students are instructed in basic legal research methods and objective analysis and writing, similar to many Legal Research and Writing (LRW) course plans. We first assign a short, objective analysis assignment based on a "closed problem," and then later assign a second objective analysis assignment for which students must conduct independent legal research. Many first semester LRW classes utilize a pre-packaged office memorandum assignment based on a fictitious client and set of facts. While these assignments can be effective in teaching basic skills, they require students to "pretend" they are working for a client. Students often struggle to relate or empathize with this client because there is no real chance to connect with the client and allow students to practice their empathy skills.

The initial challenge was determining what problem we could do with first year students. The problem had to be straightforward enough for first year students to successfully research, analyze, and communicate their findings in writing. We worked together with Mr. Bates and Mr. Pirtle to develop legal research problems for both first year and upper-level law students that assisted both organizations with researching legal issues faced by the residents of East Lubbock. For the first year students, we landed on set of facts from which a private nuisance claim could arise. The problem

---

18. *See* Mary Juetten, *Attorney Well-Being: Start with Emotional Intelligence*, ABA: Law Prac. Today (Aug. 17, 2017), https://www.lawpracticetoday.org/article/attorney-well-being-emotional-intelligence/.

19. Monika Batra Kashyap, *Rebellious Reflection: Supporting Community Lawyering Practice*, 43 N.Y.U. Rev. L. & Soc. Change 403, 410–11 (2019).

20. The other took place in Professor Drake's upper-level Texas Legal Research course, in which students each engaged in a semester-long research projects on environmental quality and historical inequity in Lubbock.

had a good set of secondary and primary sources for the research component, as well as a set of factors that would allow good practice of the students' analytical skills. The facts were based on a situation drawn from current events in Lubbock.

As in other cities nationwide,[21] East Lubbock has been affected by the city's land use policies that segregated communities of color and subsequently concentrated industry in and around those communities. These land use policies began with a 1923 ordinance signed by the mayor forcing African-Americans to live in a designated section on the southeast side of the city.[22] In 1943 and later in 1959, Lubbock's land use plans purposefully sited industry near communities of color, despite planners' acknowledgment that ideal neighborhoods should be "free from the noxious odors, sounds, and sights of industry."[23]

Residents in these communities have struggled with the air quality in their neighborhoods for years due to their close proximity to several industrial sites, including cottonseed oil refining and concrete batch plant operations.[24] Residents report high rates of asthma and other respiratory illnesses, foul smells, and even an oily film which collects on windows and cars.[25] The first year students took on this air quality issue by analyzing certain elements of a private nuisance claim on behalf of a "representative resident" of the community.[26] The class focused on the particulate matter emitted from a concrete batch plant[27] and the conditions it created for our client.

Introducing the Problem

When we introduced the assignment, we felt it was important to orient the students to the community, as well as the history of racially discriminatory zoning in East Lubbock, instead of simply providing a typical handout outlining the details of the assignment. To do so, we arranged for the Legal Practice classes to have two guest lectures at the law school.

The first lecture, led by Adam Pirtle, introduced students to Lubbock's history and the racially discriminatory ordinance practice that required zoning for communities of color and industry to be placed on the east side of town. The day of Mr. Pirtle's presentation, Professor Drake opened class with a short discussion of the civic responsibilities lawyers have in their communities. Speaking on the values of the citizen-lawyer, she discussed the important role lawyers, as people of privilege, have in advocating on behalf of those whose voices are ignored in their communities. She

---

21. *See* Richard Rothstein, The Color of Law: A Forgotten History of How Our Government Segregated America (2017).

22. Audra Brigham, Katie Main, & Mary Onishi, *Why is East Lubbock Coughing? The Discriminatory Past and Present of Lubbock's Land Use* (Dec. 2018), https://spark.adobe.com/page/i1W4Fv1uEG4Pt/.

23. *Id.*

24. *Id.*

25. *Id.*

26. For the sake of anonymity, Professor Sherwin worked with Michael Bates to create a "client" based on the actual situation residents of several of the neighborhood cases currently face.

27. Again, a fictitious concrete batch plant was created based on the local industries.

explained this project was an educative opportunity to see how the law treats people differently in our own backyard.

Next, with Mr. Pirtle as their guide, students examined the texts of the Lubbock ordinances that led to an array of problems, including a disproportionate placement of communities of color near industrial sites and lack of access to public transportation and lending, among others. Students viewed a series of maps depicting the current racial and economic divisions within Lubbock, which tie back to those ordinances. The presentation included clips from residents of the East Lubbock neighborhoods immediately adjacent to industrial sites describing their experiences living near cotton processing facilities.[28] Mr. Pirtle concluded by talking about some of the important skills needed to be a community lawyer. He emphasized the importance of research and writing, as well as the importance of educating the community, creating helpful narratives, and listening.[29]

During a second lecture, students heard what community activists and non-profit attorneys were currently doing to bring awareness to these problems. Our students heard from Mr. Bates as well as A.J. McCloud, a local resident and community activist, who further addressed the environmental justice issues plaguing Lubbock's east side. Our students were noticeably shocked and emboldened by the information presented in each session, and many participated in the Q&As that followed, asking what they could do in addition to completing the legal research and memo assignment.

The Open Memo

After being introduced to the problem, students were ready to undertake the research for the project. Over a series of five workshops, Professor Drake introduced the students to the four-step research process we teach at Texas Tech. The workshops covered the following topics:

- Research Planning
- Secondary Sources
- Introduction to Statutory Research
- Introduction to Regulatory Research
- Introduction to Binding & Persuasive Cases

In each class, students were introduced to basic research skills and given an in-class exercise to practice their skills. Each exercise was tied to the open memo topic—private environmental nuisance—and gave students a head start on their open memo research. Basing the assignments on the open memo helped students invest deeply in their research.

---

28. Presentation slides on file with authors.

29. *Id.*

In the research planning class, students created a research plan based on the facts of the open memo and drafted strategies to begin their research. For the secondary sources class, students used Texas secondary sources, such as *O'Connor's*[30] and *Texas Jurisprud*ence,[31] to get an overview of private nuisance and to identify primary sources to further their research. In the last three classes, students used various strategies to locate primary authority on their issues. In addition to gaining familiarity with each type of source, students were able to see how efficient research can be when using the four-step process to lead them from source to source.

Client Counseling

During the first semester of Legal Practice, the professors at Texas Tech place a high emphasis on client counseling skills. Students are assigned supplemental readings and faculty discuss the process and ethical issues associated with client counseling. In practicing client-centered counseling, students must learn to discern client goals, while showing empathy and respect so clients can make good decisions for themselves.[32] The classroom materials and lectures focus on lawyering as a multidisciplinary profession and that a lawyer's job will be to acknowledge all of the client's concerns, including legal, economic, and emotional aspects, in developing the best strategy for the client.[33] Therefore, our classes talked about the issues in East Lubbock in a holistic sense: What was a reasonable solution for the residents? What is feasible? The class came to the conclusion that, although we performed research and wrote a memo on a legal cause of action, there were other alternatives that could be employed, such as advocating on behalf of the community during city council meetings, as well as providing educational materials to empower residents. After their lectures on client counseling, students were able to come watch Professor Drake's upper-level Texas Legal Research students present their semester-long research projects on related environmental justice issues to the affected Lubbock community members—modeling a different approach to client counseling.[34]

Finally, students worked in groups to author a client letter explaining their findings to the client in an easy-to-understand way that minimized the need for legalese. These groups also worked to create educational flyers for the community that provided residents with easy to follow steps for reporting an air quality complaint to the Texas Commission on Environmental Quality. The students also considered the facts that some residents did not have ready access to the internet and that some communities were primarily Spanish-speaking. The result was an array of excellent flyers, which

---

30. O'Connor's Texas Causes of Action (Thomson Reuters 2019).

31. Texas Jurisprudence 3d (Thomson Reuters 2020).

32. Jack W. Burtch, Jr., *The Lawyer As Counselor,* Apr. 2020, at 26, 27.

33. *Id.*

34. Students in Texas Legal Research also wrote research memos that we shared with Texas Housers and Legal Aid of Northwest Texas.

were submitted to our community partners for the possibility of distribution at future community meetings.

The Results and Lessons Learned

As instructors, we learned many helpful lessons along the way. First, it is critical to have excellent community partners. Mr. Pirtle and Mr. Bates not only helped us develop the problem, but shared their enthusiasm with our students; their infectious passion for their work inspired our students to engage deeply with their open memos.

Service-learning requires excellent project organization—and the earlier, the better. Bringing in speakers meant some re-arranging to our traditional schedule. We got started a little late on developing the problem and finalizing the schedule, so we would recommend starting coordination early to get the schedule and problem set in advance. Our late start meant we had trouble scheduling other activities we would have liked to include in the project, such as attending a local neighborhood association meeting and advocating at city council. Students actually reported they wished there had been more interaction with the community members, so fitting in those opportunities is a priority for future semesters.

One of the most challenging aspects of the project was finding a problem that would work for first-semester students. As novices not only to legal research and writing, but to substantive law, we knew the problem had to be kept purposely simple. Mr. Pirtle and Mr. Bates sent us a few ideas related to constitutional law, but when we tested those problems to see how the research would go and considered how the students would analyze the issues, we decided those issues might be too challenging for first year students. Ultimately, we decided we needed a problem with elements or factors the students could use to analyze their problem. This led us to settle on private nuisance as the issue.

One other helpful point is to prepare for any difficult discussions that may occur. With a diverse set of students in our classes, we were cognizant of the emotions students could rightfully feel at discussing issues of racial and socio-economic inequality, and we prepared ourselves for an open dialogue about those issues. We were floored by our students' professional, supportive response to engaging in these discussions, even as many learned about Lubbock's history of redlining for the first time.

Ultimately, what our students took away from this exercise went far beyond the assigned research and office memorandum. Not only did our students engage deeply in the law, but with their community as well. Our students established connections with community leaders and non-profit organizations, developed a passion and interest in pro bono work, and expressed interest in continuing to work with the community after the courses ended. The quality of their research and open memos also matched or exceeded the quality of other semesters and their flyers were excellent. Students overwhelmingly reported their appreciation for working on a real-world problem and how much they valued the experience because it allowed them to help local community members.

Selected Annotated Bibliography on Legal Research

*Malikah Hall**

Introduction

This annotated bibliography is designed to provide helpful resources on integrating issues of diversity and inclusion in the legal research classroom. I believe in the power of storytelling, so I prefer resources that include some kind of personal story, whether that be the story of the student, the teacher, or the administrator. The stories used by the authors in these resources helpfully frame why they have made the recommendations they do.

Books

Vulnerable Populations and Transformative Law Teaching: A Critical Reader. Edited by the Society of American Law Teachers and Golden Gate University School of Law. Durham, N.C.: Carolina Academic Press, 2011.

Includes essays written by faculty that address issues of diversity and inclusion including issues of race, gender, sexual identity, disability, etc. The essays also provide different methods for incorporating these issues into the law school curriculum. Chapter nine of the text, titled "Leveraging Legal Research" by Sarah Valentine encourages the restructuring of first year legal research to address issues of diversity and inclusion. Methods discussed include integrating the materials from doctrinal courses to build connections between legal research and the doctrinal classes and suggesting techniques for connecting administrative legal research with underserved and marginalized populations.

* Reference Librarian and Instructional Assistant Professor, Texas A&M University School of Law, Dee J. Kelly Law Library. I would like to thank my incredible team at the Texas A&M University School of Law, Dee J. Kelly Law Library. Thank you to Lisa Goodman, Cynthia Burress, and Kristen Rowlett, Joan Stringfellow, Wendy Law, Lillian Velez, Sharon Jefferson, Perren Reilly, and Aaron Retteen. Your teamwork truly makes the dream work.

Articles

Calleros, Charles R. "Training a Diverse Student Body for a Multicultural Society." *La Raza Law Journal* 8, no. 2 (1995): 140–65.

This is a great source of information for instructors who are looking for tools to integrate issues of diversity into legal research courses. The author provides strategies to effectively address issues of diversity and inclusion in law school classrooms. The article includes commentary from ten "ethnically diverse law students who met with the author to discuss their law school experience." (141) The themes of these personal stories still ring true. Additionally, Part III subsection B of the article provides techniques and strategies for addressing issues of diversity and inclusion in legal research and writing courses and Part IV discusses problems and challenges of addressing diversity and inclusion in the assignments. (149–64)

Dalton, Shamika. "Incorporating Race into Your Legal Research Class." *Law Library Journal* 109, no. 4 (2017): 703–10.

Shamika Dalton writes on the importance of incorporating issues of race and diversity inclusion into legal research courses. She advises that although this work can be difficult or uncomfortable, it is necessary to incorporate diversity and inclusion in your classroom in order to better prepare our students to address issues of race in their lives. Moreover, the students surveyed wanted to talk about these issues in the classroom. There are four hypotheticals and helpful tips for creating a more inclusive classroom.

Dalton, Shamika, and Clanitra Stewart Nejdl. "Developing a Culturally Competent Legal Research Curriculum." *AALL Spectrum*, 23 no. 4 (Mar./Apr. 2019): 18–21.

This brief article provides simple instructions on implementing cultural competency into legal research courses. The authors' "Pointers for Addressing Race and Diversity in Legal Research Instruction" includes simple suggestions for incorporating issues of diversity and inclusion into assignments, lectures, and classroom discussions. (20–21)

Dennis, Johanna K.P. "Ensuring A Multicultural Educational Experience in Legal Education: Start with the Legal Writing Classroom." *Texas Wesleyan Law Review* 16, no. 4 (2010): 613–44.

This article calls for legal educators "[to] begin the transformation towards multicultural education by training the Atticus Finches of tomorrow today." (632) Beginning in section IV. B., the author provides examples and suggestions for raising issues of diversity and inclusion in mandatory first year legal research and writing courses including problems she has used in her own courses. (636–39)

Jolly-Ryan, Jennifer. "Bridging the Law School Learning Gap through Universal Design Education Article." *Touro Law Review* 28, no. 4 (2012): 1393–1442.

Universal Design offers law professors an exciting opportunity to help a greater variety of law students achieve success in the classroom. In providing tips that adhere to the "Seven Principles of Universal Design to Law Teaching" (1419–1430), the author provides methods that help professors improve legal education accessibility for people with disabilities and diverse groups including English as a Second Language (ESL) Law Students. (1430–35).

Moppett, Samantha A. "Acknowledging America's First Sovereign: Incorporating Tribal Justice Systems into the Legal Research and Writing Curriculum." *Oklahoma City University Law Review* 35, no. 2 (2010): 267–338.

When the author moved to the Southwest, she was introduced to a new for her legal system: the tribal legal system. Moppet suggests instructors introduce students to tribal justice systems. "By failing to expose students to the tribal justice systems, law schools are not adequately preparing students to practice in today's legal arena." (269) This is true not only in the Southwest part of the U.S. but in other areas of the country where tribal justice systems apply (269–70, footnotes 5, 7–8). The author provides best practices for incorporating tribal justice into legal research assignments including how and where to locate historical information, tribal court systems resources and jurisdictional issues, sources of tribal law, and other helpful resources.

Tavares, Bonny L. "Changing the Construct: Promoting Cross-Cultural Conversations in the Law School Classroom." *Journal of Legal Education* 67, no. 1 (2017): 211–41.

The author suggests instructors prepare before introducing topics of diversity and inclusion. Article suggestions include: creating a group of research assignments in the first week of class to give students an opportunity to build relationships from the start, assigning historical legal research problems that include issues of diversity, and using nonlegal sources that "analyze ideas from diverse perspectives, such as books, magazine and newspaper articles, blogs, podcasts, documentaries, etc."(229) She also incorporates reproduction issues including in-vitro fertilization since the "relevant cases involved explicit and implicit cultural diversity issues, including race, gender, and sexual orientation." (231) The paper is divided into three sections: "priming the classroom environment," "techniques for promoting cross-cultural conversations," and how to "[deal] with resistance and classroom incivility." (217–41)

Other Materials

Presentations

Dalton, Shamika, Clanitra Stewart Nejdl, Michelle Rigual, and Raquel Gabriel. "Diverse Interactions: Addressing Race and Implicit Bias in Legal Research Instruction." Presentation, from Teaching the Teachers conference, Atlanta, GA, May 31, 2020. https://elibrary.law.psu.edu/cgi/viewcontent.cgi?article=1016&context=tttconference

Presented at the inaugural Teaching the Teachers conference, this presentation document includes "tips for incorporating cultural competence in the classroom," a definition of implicit bias, and a listing of "implicit biases in the law."

Martinez, Jr., Mike, Michelle Rigual, Sherri Thomas, Ronald E. Wheeler, Jr., and Amy Carr. "Addressing Diversity and Implicit Bias in Your Classroom and Your Law School." Webinar, from American Association of Law Libraries (AALL), November 14, 2019. https://elearning.aallnet.org/products/addressing-diversity-and-implicit-bias-in-your-classroom-and-your-law-school.

This hour-long AALL webinar begins by defining implicit bias and common fears about addressing implicit biases and issues of equity. The moderator then leads our speakers through discussion topics including why addressing implicit biases is important to law librarians, how our speakers have experiences explicit biases while teaching, and how to formally address issues in legal research instruction. The webinar ends by walking through two hypotheticals and a Q&A session.

Chapter 8

Civil Procedure

Diversifying Civil Procedure

*Frank Deale**

Introduction

Notwithstanding the many accomplishments of the civil rights revolution, there remains much to be done. This article focuses on a narrow subset of those remaining tasks: the diversification of the legal profession. As I write, a recent case is heading up to the appellate courts that could result in a major new decision by the Supreme Court of the United States on the future of affirmative action,[1] a chief means of providing this diversification. Yet, however that case is ultimately resolved, there will continue to be diversity students (those with ethnic ancestries, gender identities, and economic histories that have kept them out of the legal profession), attending law schools throughout the United States, and many diversity students will be doing so because they seek to bring some form of justice to their communities.[2] What can law school faculty do to help them in this endeavor?

I focus specifically on the course referred to as civil procedure, a class that most law schools require students to take in their first year that investigates the practical legal issues that arise in litigating a federal civil case. Numerous students,[3] if asked what the class was about, would probably say something like: "this class is about the court rules that have to be followed when litigating a case." Indeed, this is an accurate description of what the class is about; but who looks forward to taking a class that sounds, at best, like a predictable semester of memorization and drudgery? And, if this is a general reaction to taking a required civil procedure class, the reaction may be more anxiety provoking for diversity students. So, for starters, it will be

---

* Professor of Law, City University of New York (CUNY) School of Law.

1. Students for Fair Admissions, Inc. v. President and Fellows of Harvard University, 980 F.3d 157 (1st Cir. 2020).

2. This is admittedly a broad definition of "diversity students" that would only exclude privileged white males. However, law school presents problems to diversity students because so much of the law school culture has been structured for privileged white males.

3. It must be said at the outset of this discussion that we, as faculty, need to speak with the greatest circumspection in speaking about teaching students, in recognition of the reality that we are constantly being "fact checked" by them.

helpful to think of ways that the course can be described both accurately and with greater appeal to new law students. I tend to describe it as a course where we learn "how to sue people." Others might think of it as a search for the best procedures for effectuating justice after negotiation attempts have been exhausted. There are, of course, numerous other ways of describing civil procedure. The basic idea, however, is to articulate the class description so that diversity students can somehow connect it to their own experience.

What is that life "experience" the faculty member is trying to connect the course to? A professor who has not been a diversity student might be at a loss in coming up with an answer to this question. And although there are multiple ways to formulate a response, a formulation that is not acceptable is the suggestion that the pre-law school experiences of diversity students are no different from those of non-diversity students. A faculty member unable to contemplate the experiences that diversity students bring to law school would do well to take a look at the publication, *Critical Legal Studies: A Primer* and the numerous references contained within this resource.[4]

As a person who was a diversity student, I am thrown back to my own experience as a student of color entering the profession; a step I most certainly would not have taken but for the public law revolution that Abram Chayes described in his captivating article.[5] For sure, this revolution was in its waning stages when my class entered law school in 1976, but it still had some room to run. Others have described that revolution in a way that makes it unnecessary for me to do so here[6] but what has been less frequently described is the effect that now-seemingly aberrant period in U.S. Supreme Court history had on thousands of prospective law students throughout the United States, many of them students of color. Who would have thought that by pursuing the ancient arts of rhetoric: reading, writing, speaking—arts traditionally utilized to preserve the privileges of those in power—one could end forms of discrimination in housing,[7] health,[8] education,[9] and employment,[10] keep someone out of jail,[11] and even prevent the state from executing people?[12] Yet, this access to law

---

4. KHIARA M. BRIDGES, CRITICAL RACE THEORY: A PRIMER (2019). Although this book is promoted as a "primer" on Critical Race Theory, it is actually far more than that. While tracing positions on issues that Critical Race scholars have addressed, it summarizes views held by critically oriented observers on race in the United States wherever they may be situated in intellectual communities. By skillfully articulating arguments about key issues of concern to race scholars: mass incarceration, affirmative action, health disparities, disabilities, and other issues, it provides insights that allows any non-diversity person to get some sense of where diversity students are on these issues.

5. Abram Chayes, *The Role of the Judge in Public Law Litigation*, 89 HARV L. REV. 1281 (1976).

6. ARCHIBALD COX, THE WARREN COURT: CONSTITUTIONAL DECISION AS AN INSTRUMENT OF REFORM (1968); GEOFFREY R. STONE & DAVID A. STRAUSS, DEMOCRACY AND EQUALITY: THE ENDURING CONSTITUTIONAL VISION OF THE WARREN COURT (2020).

7. Jones v. Alfred H. Mayer Co., 392 U.S. 409 (1968).

8. Roe v. Wade, 410 U.S. 113 (1973).

9. Brown v. Board of Ed., 347 U.S. 483 (1954).

10. Griggs v. Duke Power Co., 401 U.S. 424 (1971).

11. Miranda v. Arizona, 384 U.S. 436 (1966).

12. Furman v. Georgia, 408 U.S. 238 (1972).

school was the door to justice cracked open by the Warren Court. I certainly do not want to overstate the progressiveness of the Court or deemphasize the not-so-progressive decisions of the Court from those years, nor do I want to shift attention away from the tremendous work of unsung activists and organizers, many of whom have yet to receive the historic recognition to which they are entitled for their momentous contributions to the social changes of that period. But having come to law school to try to help fulfill some of the promises of the Warren Court era, I remember well that when filling out the evaluation form for my first semester civil procedure class, my beef was why did we have to study so many cases about airplane crashes?[13] This was not what I had come to law school to learn about. This brings me to the thesis of this article—that students in general, but especially diversity students, are more likely to enjoy and therefore succeed in a first year civil procedure class if they can identify with the struggles and concerns of the parties in the cases they are reading so closely.

Law professors enter class armed with two tools: their personality and their ability to explain the materials (books, etc.) they will be utilizing. Although these are both essential, my focus here is on the materials that we use, especially the casebooks. The large number of law school casebooks available to professors for required courses is extraordinary, and the choice of books for civil procedure compares favorably with other required first year classes. Although few professors will deem a book that she has not personally compiled to be "perfect," most of us manage to make do with what is available.

Professors who want to do all they can to assure diversity students succeed should give serious thought to evaluating whether the structure and content of the book selected will alienate, neutralize, or empower those students based on the professor's sense of those students' experiences. Is the layout of the material confusing or coherent? Do the cases and the parties represent the rich diversity of contemporary American life, or reflect a tiny sliver of the world dominated by the rich and powerful who continue to exercise disproportionate influence over the rest of us? My guess is that most casebook editors are not thinking along these lines as they are compiling their materials and few professors are asking themselves these questions as they choose which casebook to utilize.

The legal principles that govern Federal Civil Procedure come from the U.S. Constitution, various federal statutes, and a host of rules promulgated by the Judicial Conference of the United States and approved by the U.S. Supreme Court and the U.S. Congress. The court cases construing these rules are so numerous that there exists a special West reporter that publishes them, the Federal Rules Decisions (FRD). There are thus volumes and volumes of cases that professors can draw upon to obtain judicial constructions of the rules and provide illustrative examples of how they operate in the world. Most professors rely on casebook editors to peruse these volumes

---

13. This was not my only criticism of that class but it is the one most relevant to my discussion in this paper.

for cases that students should be familiar with, although many of us, as we get more confident with the material, either add cases of our own or even substitute cases for any number of reasons.

I have learned from years of teaching civil procedure that the cases one uses to illustrate or establish a rule can have a tremendous effect on the extent students engage with the material. If we take central areas that are taught in a first year civil procedure class and select cases with fact patterns that target the interests, concerns, and the backgrounds of diversity students, this closer communication of the material may enhance the ability of those students to engage more fully with the cases and obtain greater success. For sure, civil procedure casebooks already have cases that diversity students can immediately relate to and some of those cases are leading cases in the field. I do not suggest that one should attempt to construct an entire course around cases chosen for their suspected ability to engage diversity students. Diversity students can handle cases that do not trigger something from their own experience and are aware that civil procedure cannot be taught entirely as "civil rights" or "race and the law" by another name. The goal, however, is to intersperse such material to make general points about civil procedure in a way that diversity students can better appreciate.

Diversifying Joinder

I begin my teaching suggestions with the concept of "joinder." Although this is a word that one never hears when speaking "normal" English, in civil procedure jargon it refers to the expansion of a litigation to include claims beyond the standard paradigm of one plaintiff suing one defendant over one cause of action. Joinder rules provide for the addition of plaintiffs and defendants and allows them to assert multiple claims — most commonly cross claims and counter-claims. The most recognized of these devices is the class action mechanism, which allows for thousands of plaintiffs suffering similar harms to join together in one litigation against any number of defendants allegedly responsible for those harms. Class actions are discussed in the media quite frequently, especially with the advent of the so called "coupon" class action, where victorious plaintiff classes suing about a defective product often win nothing but a "coupon" to buy a similar product. Students often are themselves members of a class action, sometimes without being aware of it.

Notwithstanding the familiarity of the class action in the popular imagination, it is nonetheless a complex mechanism to teach because of the multilayered nature of Rule 23 which provides for its authorization.[14] While the number of pages devoted to class actions in casebooks varies, it can be large because of the complexity of the rule. So, in an introductory first year course faculty need to be selective in choosing their cases. Of course, these choices are influenced by what aspect of the rule faculty

---

14. Fed. R. Civ. P. 23.

choose to illustrate with cases. But whatever aspect of the rule we wish to cover, we should all be teaching *Wal-Mart Stores v. Dukes.*[15]

This case was certified as one of the largest class action suits ever filed with over 1.5 million women joining together in a single litigation against a popular multinational corporation, alleging claims of sex discrimination in violation of Title VII of the Civil Rights Act of 1964. In asserting that the employer made decisions regarding pay and promotions based on indefinable subjective criteria, the case raised issues which all groups protected by Title VII could immediately identify. Racial and ethnic minorities protected by the statute know well the feeling of being passed over for a promotion or raise because they somehow do not conform to "corporate culture."[16]

In this case, Justice Scalia could have reversed the class certification with a unanimous opinion had he stopped with the conclusion that the lower court improperly certified a class under 23(b)(2) when the plaintiffs were seeking both injunctive relief and damages, which required inquiry into certification under 23(b)(3).[17] Instead, his analysis resulted in a fractured 5–4 majority, holding that women plaintiffs did not have "common" claims allowing them to proceed via the class action mechanism.[18] My point here is not to take issue with the Court's reasoning (although it is a striking example of the Court going out of its way to harm class action plaintiffs suing corporations) but to state that in teaching class actions, this is a case that will more likely engage diversity students than a case that makes the same point but deals with two corporate parties and/or corporate claims.

The *Wal-Mart* case is an easy illustration of my point because of its timeliness and the significance of its holding. A more complicated example, also in the area of joinder, involves Rule 19, dealing with necessary parties.[19] Sometimes litigators commence a case that does not name all of the parties necessary for the court to do justice to the claims before it. Rule 19 sets out the circumstances in which those persons who are not before the Court, but should be, can be brought into the litigation. More importantly, the Rule allows the defendant to dismiss the case if the plaintiff has not sued a necessary person and the court concludes that the case may not go forward without that person.

I have found that I can increase student engagement with this rule by using a case from federal Indian law, an area many students never come across in law school; an area that has been singled out for law faculty to bring more into the curriculum.[20] In *Confederated Tribes of Chehalis Indian Reservation v. Lujan,*[21] tribal governments

---

15. Wal-Mart Stores, Inc. v. Dukes, 564 U.S. 338 (2011).

16. *Id.* at 345.

17. *Id.* at 360–67. All the Justices joined in this part of the opinion.

18. *Id.* at 348–60. This section of Justice Scalia's opinion was only joined by Justices Roberts, Kennedy, Thomas and Alito.

19. Fed. R. Civ. P. 19.

20. Maggie Blackhawk, *Federal Indian Law as Paradigm Within Public Law*, 132 Harv. L. Rev. 1787 (2019)

21. 928 F.2d 1496 (9th Cir. 1991).

brought suit against the United States because of its continuing recognition of the Quinault nation as the sole governing authority over the reservation on which a number of plaintiff Tribes resided. The United States government created the reservation in the 19th century under highly disputed circumstances, forcing Tribes on to the reservation over their objection and placing sole governing authority in the hands the Quinault nation because it favored creation of the reservation.[22] The 9th Circuit Court of Appeals dismissed the plaintiffs' attempt to force the United States to change the governance on the reservation because the Quinault nation was a necessary party defendant that was not named, even though it could not be named because of tribal sovereign immunity.[23] The case provides an example of the force of Rule 19 as a weapon for defendants, but also encapsulates the difficult balance played out in United States history between U.S. colonialism and tribal sovereignty.

Joinder also covers the concept of Intervention governed by Rule 24.[24] Sometimes an important case is pending in the courts and, although the parties involved in the case as plaintiffs and defendants are sufficient to allow the court to reach a proper disposition, there are individuals or groups who are not parties to the litigation but have interests in the litigation that can be adversely affected by the ruling that the court will issue. The intervention rule allows these interested non-parties to participate in the litigation upon a showing of certain circumstances, namely that they have an interest that would be affected by the outcome of the case, and the interest is not being represented by any of the current parties.

A case that will surely engage diversity students regarding this rule is *Thurgood Marshall Legal Society v. Texas.*[25] This was the first major law school affirmative action case after the fragmented *Bakke* decision narrowly upheld race-based affirmative action in medical school admissions for the purpose of attaining a diverse student body.[26] The *Bakke* result turned upon the opinion of Justice Powell, who concluded that medical school affirmative action plans could constitutionally be utilized, provided their sole purpose was to diversify the student body.[27] The University of Texas designed a law school affirmative action plan based upon the plan the Supreme Court upheld in *Bakke*. A rejected white applicant challenged the University of Texas Law School law school affirmative action plan arguing that Justice Powell's opinion and reasoning was not binding on the lower federal courts.

The Thurgood Marshall Student Association, a predominantly student of color organization, sought to intervene in the litigation, arguing that it had a strong interest in the continuation of the affirmative action plan that could be negatively impacted if the plan was held unconstitutional. They claimed that this interest was not being

---

22. *Id.* at 1497–98.

23. *Id.* at 1498–50.

24. Fed. R. Civ. P. 24.

25. 21 F.3d 603 (5th Cir. 1999). The case in which the proposed intervenors sought intervention was *Hopwood v. Texas*.

26. Regents of the University of California v. Bakke, 438 U.S. 265 (1978).

27. The other eight members of the Court split 4–4 on the constitutionality of the plan.

represented by the state university defendant because of the university's history of discrimination against Black applicants. This history of discrimination was the strongest argument in support of the affirmative action plan, but it was not one that the university would raise because it would open itself up to past liability. The Fifth Circuit denied the students' application to intervene, concluding that their interests were being represented by the defendant.[28] The Fifth Circuit later went on to hold the law school affirmative action plan unconstitutional, a decision that the Supreme Court declined to review.[29] Again, what is important for this discussion here is that this is an ideal case to engage diversity students in understanding a difficult rule of civil procedure.[30]

Conclusion

I have focused on the area of joinder because it is complex and one that the professor may only get to deep into the semester, when students are beginning to feel overwhelmed and anxious about exams. But there are ways to engage diversity students in the class material taught earlier in the semester that involves the "canonical"[31] Supreme Court decisions. For example, *Ashcroft v. Iqbal*,[32] concerning the US government's extraordinary mistreatment of Muslim detainees after 9-11, can be the source of engaging class discussions so long as the case is not reduced to a multiple-choice hypothetical of whether a federal trial judge can dismiss a case if she feels the claims asserted by the plaintiff are "implausible." *Burger King v. Rudzewicz*,[33] a rare modern case where the Supreme Court upholds the exercise of personal jurisdiction, can also be used to discuss how facially neutral procedural rules operate to provide benefits to wealthy litigants. If defendant Rudzewicz, a bankrupt franchisee in that case who was sued by a multinational corporation in a court 1400 miles from his home and place of business, had the resources to take an interlocutory appeal (as all similarly situated corporate defendants do) he might have benefited from the Supreme Court's suggestion that he move for a pre-trial change of venue.[34] Even discussion of the venerable case of *Pennoyer v. Neff*[35] could be energized by an inquiry into how

---

28. *Thurgood Marshall Legal Soc'y*, 21 F.3d at 605–06.

29. Hopwood v. Texas, 236 F.3d 256 (5th Cir. 2000), *cert. denied*, 533 U.S. 929 (2001). The University of Texas Law School afterwards promulgated a different affirmative action plan that was upheld. *See* Fisher v. Univ. of Texas, 570 U.S. 297 (2013).

30. The exact same issue was presented in similar circumstances in the recent challenge to affirmative action at Harvard College. *See* Students for Fair Admissions, Inc. v. President and Fellows of Harvard Coll., 807 F.3d 472 (1st Cir. 2015).

31. I use this phrase to refer to the cases "so central to the [law] that competence in the discipline requires fluency [with] the texts." Paraphrasing from Jamal Greene, *The Anticanon*, 125 Harv. L. Rev. 379, 385 (2011).

32. 556 U.S. 662 (2009).

33. 471 U.S. 462 (1985).

34. *Id.* at 484.

35. 95 U.S. 714 (1877).

Marcus Neff became the beneficiary of U.S. governmental schemes to swindle Native Americans of their land[36]—in other words, who did the land *really* belong to?

Having made the investment in matching students' experience with their learning of doctrine, it is essential to follow through making the investment with class examinations. Ideally, the examination process should itself be a learning experience. In trying to come up with fact patterns that reflect diversity student experience it helps to draw upon historical and contemporary events that they are aware of, such as #BLACKLIVESMATTER, #OCCUPYWALLSTREET and the circumstances that gave those movements their impetus. But the method as well as the substance of the exam are important. Making students do lawyer-like exercises for examination purposes can work, even for 1L students. Although the law school examination experience may not connect to anything they have done before, they will appreciate it once they see that it is connected to tasks they will do in their future as social justice lawyers.

---

36. *See* Eric Kades, *The Dark Side of Efficiency: Johnson v. M'Intosh and the Expropriation of American Indian Lands*, 148 U. Pa. L. Rev. 1065, 1110–52 (2000).

Teaching Federal Pleading Standards by Way of the "Elusive" Claim of Discrimination

*Mikah K. Thompson**

Introduction

Each semester, civil procedure professors find themselves struggling to convey to their students the importance of the federal pleading standard described in Federal Rule of Civil Procedure 8(a)(2). The rule states that a claim for relief must contain "a short and plain statement of the claim showing that the pleader is entitled to relief." This short and plain statement must provide the defendant with "fair notice of what plaintiff's claim is and the grounds upon which it rests."[1] Despite the standard's apparent simplicity, the U.S. Supreme Court has explained that a complaint fails to meet Rule 8(a)(2)'s requirement unless it is plausible on its face—that is, the complaint includes factual allegations from which a court could reasonably infer that the defendant is liable for the alleged misconduct.[2]

Most civil procedure textbooks include excerpts of *Bell Atlantic Corp. v. Twombly*[3] and *Ashcroft v. Iqbal*.[4] In *Twombly*, the Supreme Court first articulated the facial plausibility requirement,[5] and in *Iqbal*, the Court held that the facial plausibility requirement applies to all federal civil actions.[6] *Twombly* and *Iqbal* provide the civil procedure professor with an opportunity to improve students' understanding of the facial plausibility requirement while also educating them on the difficulty of alleging (and proving) discrimination based on protected status.

---

* Associate Professor of Law, University of Missouri-Kansas City.
1. Conley v. Gibson, 355 U.S. 41, 47 (1957).
2. *See* Ashcroft v. Iqbal, 556 U.S. 662, 678 (2009).
3. 550 U.S. 544 (2007).
4. 556 U.S. 662.
5. 550 U.S. at 556.
6. 556 U.S. at 684.

This essay describes the techniques I use in my civil procedure classroom to both animate the federal pleading requirements and challenge my students to consider the elusive nature of bias and discrimination. To utilize these techniques, the civil procedure professor need not be an employment discrimination expert. Indeed, any professor who would like to bring some cultural competency into the civil procedure classroom can use these methods to engage students on the topic of bias when they least expect it.

Pleading Discrimination in the Pre-Facial Plausibility Era

The civil procedure professor's first task is deciding whether or not to assign students federal pleading standards cases that pre-date *Twombly* and *Iqbal*. In order to have a robust discussion about the nature of bias and discrimination, I recommend assigning the 2002 case *Swierkiewicz v. Sorema*.[7] Before explaining the value of including *Swierkiewicz*, it is important to consider the reasons I do not recommend assigning the 1957 case *Conley v. Gibson*.[8] *Conley* is obviously important because it describes the notice pleading standard that remains in effect today;[9] however, *Conley* was partially overturned by the Court in *Twombly*. In *Conley*, the Court held that a complaint should not be dismissed pursuant to Rule 12(b)(6) "unless it appears beyond doubt that the plaintiff can prove no set of facts in support of his claim which would entitle him to relief."[10] In light of the clear contradiction between the "no set of facts" standard and the facial plausibility standard, the *Twombly* Court found that *Conley*'s standard had "earned its retirement."[11]

For purposes of a classroom discussion about bias and discrimination, I recommend against assigning *Conley* because the plaintiffs' complaint in that case so clearly met the federal pleading requirements in place at the time and would likely meet the facial plausibility standard described in *Twombly* and *Iqbal*. In *Conley*, the plaintiffs, a purported class of Black railway employees, sued their union, alleging that it had failed to represent them fairly because of their race.[12] Specifically, the complaint alleged that despite a contract between the plaintiffs' employer and their union that provided union members protection from discharge and loss of seniority, the union did nothing to stop the employer from discharging or demoting 45 Black union members and replacing them with white workers.[13] The complaint alleged that the union had failed in general to represent Black union members in good faith and that the

---

7. 534 U.S. 506 (2002).

8. 355 U.S. 41 (1957).

9. *See Conley*, 355 U.S. at 47 (stating that the complaint need only provide "fair notice of what plaintiff's claim is and the grounds upon which it rests.").

10. *Id.* at 45–46.

11. Bell Atlantic Corp. v. Twombly, 550 U.S. 544, 563 (2007).

12. 355 U.S. at 42.

13. *Id.* at 43.

union's actions violated plaintiffs' right to fair representation under the Railway Labor Act.[14] The *Conley* Court found that the complaint alleged sufficient facts pursuant to the "no set of facts" standard articulated in the case,[15] and I would argue that these allegations also satisfy the facial plausibility standard. Although the *Twombly* Court disavowed *Conley*'s "no set of facts" standard, it explained that the standard must be understood in light of the Court's consideration of the *Conley* plaintiffs' complaint, which the *Twombly* Court described as containing "concrete" allegations that "amply stat[ed] a claim for relief."[16]

It is the strength of the plaintiffs' claims in *Conley* that make it a less than ideal case for a discussion of bias and discrimination. The plaintiffs alleged that their union refused to protect them from discharge or demotion despite the existence of a contract between the union and the employer that should have protected them and that the union protected similarly situated white union members. Most students would agree that a court or jury could reasonably infer from these allegations that the union had failed to provide fair representation to the plaintiffs because of their race, especially in light of the *Conley* Court's statement at the outset of the case that it had repeatedly addressed labor unions' refusal to fairly represent Black union members.[17] Rather than engaging the students in a discussion about a case where discrimination was very likely, the civil procedure professor should offer students a factual scenario wherein a court or jury would have to make a greater inferential leap to find unlawful discrimination — such a factual scenario can be found in *Swierkiewicz*.

In *Swierkiewicz*, the plaintiff alleged that his employer demoted and discharged him because of his age and national origin. A native of Hungary, the plaintiff was 53 years old at the time he filed suit.[18] He alleged that for six years he was employed as senior vice president and chief underwriting officer for Sorema, a reinsurance company headquartered in New York and principally owned and controlled by a French parent corporation.[19] Plaintiff alleged that the CEO of Sorema demoted and replaced him with a 32-year old French national after stating that he wanted to "energize" the underwriting department. Plaintiff alleged that his replacement had just one year of experience at the time he was promoted and therefore was less qualified than plaintiff, who had 26 years of experience.[20] Plaintiff also alleged that he was excluded from business decisions following his demotion, causing him to request a severance package. He alleged that the employer responded by informing him that he

---

14. *Id.*

15. *Id.* at 46 ("If these allegations are proven there has been a manifest breach of the Union's statutory duty to represent fairly and without hostile discrimination all of the employees in the bargaining unit.").

16. 550 U.S. at 563.

17. *See* 355 U.S. at 42 ("In a series of cases ... this Court has emphatically and repeatedly ruled that an exclusive bargaining agent under the Railway Labor Act is obligated to represent all employees in the bargaining unit fairly and without discrimination because of race").

18. *See* Swierkiewicz v. Sorema N.A., 534 U.S. 506, 508 (2002).

19. *Id.*

20. *Id.*

could resign without a severance package or be terminated. Plaintiff alleged that he refused to resign and was fired.[21]

The *Swierkiewicz* Court considered whether an employment discrimination plaintiff is required to assert facts supporting the prima facie elements of the *McDonnell Douglas* burden-shifting framework in order to survive a Rule 12(b)(6) motion. The Court of Appeals had ruled that a plaintiff alleging discrimination must allege: (1) membership in a protected class; (2) that plaintiff was qualified for the job at issue; (3) an adverse employment action; and (4) circumstances supporting an inference of discrimination.[22] The *Swierkiewicz* Court found that an employment discrimination plaintiff need not allege facts supporting these elements because: (1) The *McDonnell Douglas* framework is an evidentiary standard, not a pleading standard. Thus, a plaintiff must come forward with evidence supporting these elements to survive a summary judgment motion, not a 12(b)(6) motion;[23] (2) The *McDonnell Douglas* framework does not apply in every case. If a plaintiff can offer direct evidence of discrimination, then the framework is unnecessary. It makes no sense to force a plaintiff to plead the prima facie elements where they are inapplicable;[24] and (3) A rule requiring the pleading of the prima facie elements is at odds with the notice pleading requirement of Rule 8(a)(2) and would effectively impose a heightened pleading standard in employment discrimination cases.[25] Ultimately, the Court ruled that plaintiff's allegations met Rule 8(a)(2)'s pleading requirement.[26]

Swierkiewicz serves as a good introduction to Rule 8(a)(2)'s pleading requirement because it allows students to consider the meaning of the "short and plain statement" requirement without the difficulty of the facial plausibility requirement. Moreover, because the Court ruled that the *McDonnell Douglas* elements do not affect the pleading requirements in an employment discrimination case, the civil procedure professor does not have to be well-versed in the framework to employ the techniques described herein.

When teaching *Swierkiewicz*, I summarize the plaintiff's allegations on a presentation slide. I attempt to make the allegations as short and simple as possible to make clear the inferences a court will need to make to determine whether the allegations are sufficient under Rule 8(a)(2). The summary is as follows:

I. <u>National Origin Claim</u>

    a. Plaintiff is Hungarian.

    b. Plaintiff has 26 years of experience in the underwriting industry.

    c. The CEO of the employer is French.

    d. Plaintiff was demoted and terminated.

---

21. *Id.* at 509.
22. *Id.* at 510.
23. *Id.* at 511.
24. *Id.* at 512.
25. *Id.* at 512–13.
26. *Id.* at 514.

    e. The man who replaced Plaintiff is French.

    f. The man who replaced Plaintiff has one year of experience in the underwriting industry.

Conclusion: Plaintiff was demoted and terminated because he is Hungarian.

II. <u>Age Discrimination Claim</u>

    a. Plaintiff is 53 years old.

    b. Plaintiff has 26 years of experience in the underwriting industry.

    c. In 1995, the CEO stated that he wanted to energize the underwriting department.

    d. Plaintiff was demoted and terminated.

    e. The man who replaced Plaintiff is 32 years old.

    f. The man who replaced Plaintiff has one year of experience in the underwriting industry.

Conclusion: Plaintiff was demoted and terminated because of his age.

After showing the students the summary, I ask them whether the plaintiff's allegations satisfy Rule 8(a)(2)'s pleading requirement. Many will likely agree that the allegations are sufficient, especially if I pose the question after we have discussed the Court's rationale in *Swierkiewicz*. At this point, I push the students to make an argument that these facts show the employer discriminated against the plaintiff. Some students will note the experience gap between Swierkiewicz and his replacement and argue that such a large gap in experience suggests a discriminatory motive. Others will argue that the allegations meet the notice pleading requirement because they provide the employer with sufficient notice of the grounds for the plaintiff's complaint. Some students may argue that these allegations on their own are not sufficient and that it would be unfair to allow the case to move forward without more. If no students make this argument, then the professor should certainly do so. Undoubtedly, some students will seek to add facts that would justify the plaintiff's demotion and termination. For example, students in my class sometimes state that it would be unfair to allow the case to move forward if it turns out that Swierkiewicz was terminated for engaging in some sort of misconduct like theft. At this point, I remind students that the defendant who seeks a dismissal pursuant to Rule 12(b)(6) is not allowed to offer a defense on the merits that might include helpful facts. Instead, the failure to state a claim motion is a "so what" motion—that is, even if the court assumes all facts alleged by the plaintiff are true, the defendant is still entitled to a dismissal because the claims are legally insufficient. I also preview the summary judgment motion as an opportunity for the defendant to offer undisputed facts that would justify the plaintiff's termination. This discussion of the summary judgment motion allows me to return to the fairness argument. If it turns out that Swierkiewicz was actually terminated for misconduct and there is no way for the defendant to get this fact before the court prior to a summary judgment motion that would likely be filed after months of costly discovery, are the plaintiff's allegations sufficient? Regardless of the students' answers, the professor should return to this question and the allegations of *Swierkiewicz* after covering *Twombly* and *Iqbal*.

Twombly, Iqbal, and Facial Plausibility

I utilize *Twombly* to chat with the students about Ma Bell, the Baby Bells, and landline phone service — three topics that may be foreign to the 21st Century law student. For purposes of a discussion about the legal sufficiency of discrimination complaints, the facts of *Twombly* are less relevant than the facts of *Iqbal*, wherein a Pakistani Muslim man alleged that government officials had adopted an unconstitutional policy targeting individuals based on their race, religion, or national origin.

In *Twombly*, a purported class of plaintiffs consisting of all subscribers of local telephone and/or high speed internet service sued the Baby Bells, alleging that they violated the Sherman Act.[27] The plaintiffs alleged that the defendants had conspired to block lower-cost competitors from entering their respective regional markets by engaging in parallel conduct that would inhibit the growth of these competitors.[28] The plaintiffs also claimed that the defendants entered into an agreement or conspired to refrain from competing against each other.[29] The defendants moved to dismiss the complaint for failure to state a claim, and the Supreme Court agreed that plaintiffs' allegation of an agreement or conspiracy was not supported by the factual allegations of the complaint.[30] During its discussion of Rule 8(a)(2)'s requirement of a "short and plain statement showing that the pleader is entitled to relief," the *Twombly* Court held that the complaint must include factual allegations that raise the right to relief above the speculative level rather than "a formulaic recitation of the elements of a cause of action".[31] The Court stated that while the notice pleading standard described in *Conley* and *Swierkiewicz* would remain in place, that standard requires "enough facts to state a claim to relief that is plausible on its face."[32]

Iqbal provided the Court with an opportunity to expound upon the facial plausibility standard it set out in *Twombly*. Iqbal alleged that the government's post-9/11 policy of designating individuals as "high interest" based on their race, religion, or national origin and subjecting those individuals to harsh conditions of confinement violated plaintiff's constitutional rights.[33] While much of plaintiff's complaint survived the government's motion to dismiss for failure to state a claim, the Supreme Court held that his claims against Attorney General John Ashcroft and FBI Director Robert Mueller should be dismissed because they failed to meet the facial plausibility standard

---

27. *See* 550 U.S. 544, 549–50 (2007).
28. *Id.* at 550.
29. *Id.* at 550–51.
30. *Id.* at 564.
31. *Id.* at 555.
32. *Id.* at 570.
33. 556 U.S. 662, 669 (2009).

described in *Twombly*.[34] Looking first to the substantive law underlying plaintiff's claims, the Court determined that government officials are immune from liability that might otherwise flow from the theory of respondeat superior. Thus, even if Ashcroft's and Mueller's subordinates had violated Iqbal's constitutional rights, Ashcroft and Mueller would only be liable if their individual conduct violated his rights.[35]

To establish Ashcroft's and Mueller's active involvement, Iqbal's complaint alleged that Ashcroft was the "principal architect" of the unconstitutional policy while Mueller was "instrumental in its adoption, promulgation, and implementation."[36] The Court found that these allegations failed to meet the facial plausibility requirement, which it defined as follows: "A claim has facial plausibility when the plaintiff pleads factual content that allows the court to draw the reasonable inference that the defendant is liable for the misconduct alleged."[37] The Court held that Iqbal's allegations against Mueller and Ashcroft were "bare assertions," "conclusory," and "nothing more than a formulaic recitation of the elements of a constitutional discrimination claim."[38] The Court also found that plaintiff's allegations about the role of Ashcroft and Mueller in creating the conditions of confinement were implausible in that a more likely explanation for their decisions was that they sought to keep suspected terrorists in the most secure conditions available until they could be cleared of terrorist activity. The Court found that such a motive would not violate Iqbal's constitutional rights and that he would need more factual content to "nudge his claim of purposeful discrimination across the line from conceivable to plausible."[39]

Pleading Discrimination in the Post-Facial Plausibility Era

After covering *Twombly* and *Iqbal*, the professor should ask whether the pleading standards described in *Swierkiewicz* remain viable. After all, while the *Twombly* Court explained that the facial plausibility standard does not conflict with the holding of *Swierkiewicz*,[40] *Iqbal* did not mention *Swierkiewicz*[41] and at least one circuit court has determined that the pleading standard described in *Swierkiewicz* was explicitly overruled by *Twombly*.[42] Because *Swierkiewicz* was a pre-*Twombly* case, the Court employed

---

34. *Id.* at 683, 687.

35. *Id.* at 676.

36. *Id.* at 669.

37. *Id.* at 678.

38. *Id.* at 681 (internal quotations omitted).

39. *Id.* at 683.

40. 550 U.S. 544, 569 (2007).

41. *See generally* 556 U.S. 662.

42. *See, e.g.*, Woods v. City of Greensboro, 855 F.3d 639, 648 (4th Cir. 2017).

Conley's "no set of facts" standard to analyze the plaintiff's complaint, a standard explicitly disavowed in *Twombly*.[43]

At this point, the professor should provide the students with a brief summary of post-*Twombly*/*Iqbal* case law to explain how lower courts have applied the facial plausibility requirement in employment discrimination cases. The lower courts seem to agree that based on the language of Title VII, plaintiffs must allege that: (1) the employer took adverse action against the plaintiff; and (2) that plaintiff's race, color, religion, sex, or national origin was a motivating factor in the employment decision.[44] While a plaintiff will likely have very little difficulty alleging facts in support of the first element, such as a termination, demotion, or failure to hire, it may be nearly impossible for a plaintiff, prior to discovery, to plead facts allowing for an inference that the adverse action was motivated by plaintiff's protected status. Lower courts have held that a Title VII plaintiff can satisfy the facial plausibility requirement by alleging facts that directly show discrimination[45] or that "give plausible support to a minimal inference of discriminatory motivation."[46] The professor should ask students what facts might give rise to a minimal inference of discriminatory motive. This question is best answered by returning to the facts of *Swierkiewicz*.

I usually return to the presentation slide summarizing the allegations of *Swierkiewicz* and ask students to consider whether they satisfy the facial plausibility standard. Students may disagree, but it is likely that more students will determine that the allegations lack facial plausibility in light of *Twombly* and *Iqbal*. These students may argue that there are a number of equally compelling lawful explanations for the employer's decision to demote and discharge the plaintiff, similar to the compelling, lawful explanations that resulted in the dismissal of Iqbal's claims against Ashcroft and Mueller, and that the plaintiff has not alleged facts that would allow for an inference of misconduct. Here, the professor should ask students what more the plaintiff should have alleged to "nudge" the complaint across the line from conceivable to plausible. Some students will suggest that a direct allegation, like a "smoking gun" email from the CEO explaining that he wants to terminate plaintiff because of his national origin, would be sufficient.

At this point, the professor should discuss the difficulty of proving discrimination in the workplace or elsewhere. The professor should ask, "If the CEO were motivated to terminate plaintiff because of his national origin, is it likely that he would have described that motivation in an email?" The students will agree that such direct evidence is very unlikely. On this point, it may be helpful to quote some language from the Second Circuit where the court noted the "elusive" nature of intentional discrim-

---

43. 534 U.S. 506, 514 (2002). *See also* Vega v. Hempstead Union Free School Dist., 801 F.3d 72, 83 (2d Cir. 2015) (noting that courts have questioned the continued viability of *Swierkiewicz* because of the Court's reliance on the "no set of facts" standard).

44. *See, e.g., Vega*, 801 F.3d at 86; Wolfinger v. Consolidated Edison Co. of New York, Inc., No. 17-CV-1710, 2018 WL 3637964, *8 (E.D.N.Y. July 31, 2018).

45. *See Vega*, 801 F.3d at 87.

46. Littlejohn v. City of New York, 795 F.3d 297, 311 (2d Cir. 2015).

ination and recognized that "clever men may easily conceal their motivations."[47] The Second Circuit has stated that because plaintiffs have such difficulty finding evidence of the unstated intent of their employers, they are usually left to rely on "bits and pieces" of information that support an inference or form a "mosaic" of intentional discrimination.[48] The professor should ask whether Swierkiewicz's allegations create a "mosaic" of intentional discrimination formed by the bits and pieces of information to which he had access at the time he filed suit.

Moreover, the professor should raise the issue of implicit or unconscious bias and ask students if the possibility of intentional discrimination based on implicit bias might impact a plaintiff's ability to meet the facial plausibility requirement. First, the professor should provide a bit a background on implicit bias. Implicit biases can be defined as "the plethora of fears, feelings, perceptions, and stereotypes that lie deep within our subconscious, without our conscious permission or acknowledgement."[49] Because of the covert nature of implicit or unconscious biases, individuals are usually unaware of the effect their biases may have on their decision-making process.[50] Lower courts have begun to acknowledge the existence of implicit bias in various contexts, even stating that when judges make determinations concerning facial plausibility, they should be aware of the ways in which their own unconscious biases may affect their decisions.[51] Furthermore, the Fourth Circuit has found that unlawful discrimination is more likely to be based on implicit rather than explicit bias[52] and that discrimination complaints based on "more subtle theories of stereotyping or implicit bias" are vulnerable to premature dismissal because the judge may "substitute his or her view of the likely reason for a particular action in place of the controlling plausibility standard."[53]

After sharing this background information, the professor should ask the students two important questions. First, if the CEO terminated Swierkiewicz because of the CEO's unconscious bias against Hungarians, is Swierkiewicz entitled to relief under Title VII? The students will likely agree that the plaintiff is entitled to relief regardless of whether the CEO understood the motive behind his decision because the plaintiff suffered a compensable harm. Next, the professor should ask, if it is possible that the CEO terminated Swierkiewicz because of the CEO's unconscious bias against Hungarians, what if any allegations should plaintiff add to the complaint? The professor should remind students that while Rule 9(b) allows the plaintiff to plead conditions of the mind generally, the *Iqbal* Court held that allegations regarding a

---

47. *Vega*, 801 F.3d at 86.

48. *Id.*

49. Mark W. Bennett, *Unraveling tie Gordian Knot of Implicit Bias in Jury Selection: The Problems of Judge-Dominated Voir Dire, The Failed Promise of Batson, and Proposed Solutions,* 4 Harv. L. & Pol'y Rev. 149, 149 (2010).

50. *Id.* at 150.

51. *Vega*, 801 F.3d at 86.

52. Woods v. City of Greensboro, 855 F.3d 639, 651–52 (4th Cir. 2017).

53. *Id.* at 652.

defendant's state of mind must have some factual context.[54] Some students may respond that the plaintiff should allege the CEO's unconscious bias. The professor should push back on this suggestion, asking the student for a factual basis that would support such an allegation. After all, Rule 11 requires that the factual allegations of a pleading "have evidentiary support or, if specifically so identified, will likely have evidentiary support after a reasonable opportunity for further investigation or discovery." Short of the court ordering the CEO to take the Implicit Association Test[55] or another measure of unconscious bias, the plaintiff would have difficulty finding evidentiary support for this assertion. The professor should return to the question of what additions, if any, the plaintiff should make to the allegations if the CEO's decision was based on implicit bias. The students will have difficulty identifying additional allegations. The point of this exercise is to show the students the challenge of crafting allegations that go to the decision maker's state of mind, particularly when the decision maker is not fully aware of the factors influencing the decision.

Conclusion

At the conclusion of my discussion about the federal pleading standards, I do my best to reconcile the holdings of *Twombly*, *Iqbal*, and *Swierkiewicz* by sharing my thoughts on how they might co-exist. In both *Twombly* and *Iqbal*, the plaintiffs could have forced a settlement by engaging in abusive discovery practices. The purported class of plaintiffs in *Twombly* included nearly every person who subscribed to local telephone service and/or high-speed internet service between 1996 and the present and named as defendants several very large telecommunications companies. Discovery in that case would have been extensive, and the Court expressed its concern about potential abuse of the discovery devices.[56] Similarly, the plaintiff in *Iqbal* sued 34 government officials including the Attorney General of the United States and the FBI Director. The Court ruled that the claims against Ashcroft and Mueller should have been dismissed, but Iqbal's claims against the lower-level government officials were allowed to proceed.[57] Had the Court allowed Ashcroft and Mueller to remain in the case, they would have been subject to discovery that the Court labeled as "disruptive" and counterproductive to the duties of high-level government officials.[58] *Swierkiewicz*, on the other hand, was a single-plaintiff employment discrimination case involving one defendant. The Court liberally construed Rule 8(a)(2) to allow the plaintiff the opportunity to build his case during discovery. The Court noted that the plaintiff was not required to plead the *McDonnell Douglas* elements in part because he might

---

54. 556 U.S. 662, 687 (2009).

55. The Implicit Association Test can be found at https://implicit.harvard.edu/implicit/.

56. 550 U.S. 544, 558–59 (2007).

57. 556 U.S. at 684 ("[W]e express no opinion concerning the sufficiency of respondent's complaint against the defendants who are not before us…. Our decision is limited to the determination that respondent's complaint does not entitle him to relief from petitioners.").

58. *Id.* at 685.

find direct evidence of discrimination during the discovery process.[59] Because the Court has not reaffirmed the holding of *Swierkiewicz* since it decided *Twombly* and *Iqbal*, I am not certain that the issue of discovery abuse fully explains how the cases should be read together.

As I approach the discussion of federal pleading standards each semester, it is my hope that the conversation reveals the obscure nature of discrimination and the attending obstacles plaintiffs face post-*Twombly/Iqbal*. Additionally, the discussion should allow the professor to introduce the topic of implicit bias in a non-threatening manner that ties the phenomenon to the drafting skills any good trial lawyer should have. In addition to learning about civil procedure, students participating in the discussion may gain some insight that will help them relate to their future clients and better understand the world around them.

---

59. 534 U.S. 506, 511 (2002).

Selected Annotated Bibliography in Civil Procedure

Anne Rajotte[*]

Introduction

The works included in this bibliography were chosen to demonstrate the breadth of thinking on how to present concepts in civil procedure to students in a way that allows them to connect the sometimes abstract concepts to people's real lives. Authored by scholars with many years' experience teaching civil procedure, the works included demonstrate that a first year civil procedure class offers numerous opportunities to integrate discussions of race, gender, class, and national origin. Further, these works show that including these topics does not detract from teaching substantive concepts, but instead, offers an opportunity to provide students with additional context and perspective.

Books

Clark, Robin, and Anne Marie Harkins. "Planning for the Worst-Off in the Worst Case Scenarios: Emergency Planning for the Economically Disadvantages." In *Vulnerable Populations and Transformative Law Teaching: A Critical Reader*, edited by the Society of American Law Teachers and Golden Gate State University, 201–225. Durham, N.C.: Carolina Academic Press, 2011.

The authors suggest including the experiences of vulnerable populations during emergencies or disasters into standard law school courses. As emergencies and disasters tend to shed light on existing economic or societal weaknesses, examining how legal rules, systems, and norms operate during these times provides the opportunity for critical evaluation. To incorporate this topic in a civil procedure class, the authors note a commonly used book, *The Buffalo Creek Disaster*, pro-

---

[*] Anne Rajotte, Head of Reference Services, Thomas J. Meskill Law Library, University of Connecticut School of Law.

vides a backdrop of a disaster in combination with issues of inequality to introduce concepts of civil procedure.

Clermont, Kevin M., ed. *Civil Procedure Stories*. 2nd ed. New York: Foundation Press, 2008.

This book provides additional information and analysis about standard cases taught in civil procedure classes. For each case, the author, who has taught and written about civil procedure for over 40 years, provides the social and legal background, the factual background, information about the lower court decision, what happened after the case, and the case's continuing importance. For example, although *Hansberry v. Lee*[1] is usually included in civil procedure curricula to demonstrate the concept of joinder and due process in relation to class actions; the author sets the case against the larger struggle for equality in housing, education, and employment. The chapter concerning *Hansberry* includes information about the advocacy career of the lawyer who argued the case, the background of Black migration to Chicago, and the creation of racially restrictive covenants in response. Likewise in *Lassiter v. Department of Social Services of Durham County, N.C.*,[2] the author provides background about the attitudes related to neglected children and the preference of removing them from their parents at that time, the background, the plaintiff, and details about how she fared in court without a lawyer, which clearly illustrate the hurdles self-represented litigants encounter.

Articles

Carlson, Bob. "Why Slavery Reparations are Good for Civil Procedure Class." *St. Louis University Law Journal* 47 (2003): 139–148.

Carlson sets forth a method for teaching class action suits using slavery reparation lawsuits. The author encourages this method because it provides an opportunity to teach the procedural requirements while also considering how class action suits can give voice to a movement or advocate for social change. The author suggests beginning with looking at other class action suits brought as the result of injustices perpetrated on racial or ethnic groups, and then applying the formal requirements for a class action suit to slavery reparations. An instructor may also incorporate discussion of the lasting impact of slavery, the still-existing corporations that benefited from slavery, and possible actions that can be taken concurrently with a class action suit to further bring attention to the issue of slavery reparations into the class.

Ford, Cynthia. "Integrating Indian Law into a Traditional Civil Procedure Course." *Syracuse Law Review* 46 (1996): 1243–1286.

---

1. 311 U.S. 32 (1940).
2. 452 U.S. 18 (1981).

This article provides suggestions for incorporating aspects of Indian Law into the first year civil procedure curriculum. The author, who teaches civil procedure and has also served as a judge on two tribal courts, cites a lack of exposure to Indian Law classes during law school and a lack of education about Native Americans in general as reasons to incorporate Indian Law into the law school curriculum. She offers that civil procedure is an ideal course in which to advance this content because it is a required course, and because incorporating Indian Law topics will build respect for tribal courts and tribal judges. The author includes several civil procedure topics that lend themselves to the inclusion of Indian Law, such as comparative federal, state, and tribal rules of procedure, subject matter jurisdiction, and enforcement of judgments. The article includes specific cases that can be used to teach the suggested Indian Law topics.

Ford, Cynthia. "Including Indian Law in a Traditional Civil Procedure Course: A Reprise, Five Years Later." *Tulsa Law Review* 37 (2001): 485–502.

This article is a follow up to Ford's earlier article "Integrating Indian Law into a Traditional Civil Procedure Course" (see above). The author describes student feedback she had received over five years of teaching Indian Law subjects in a civil procedure course. The article explains changes made to the course in response to both the changing law and student feedback. Ultimately, the author concludes that including Indian Law in a doctrinal course such as civil procedure is an effective method to engender respect for Indian Law and tribal jurisdiction, and urges other law professors to consider how to broaden their classes in order to widen the perspective of their students.

Hershkoff, Helen. "Integrating Transnational Legal Perspectives into the First Year Civil Procedure Curriculum." *Journal of Legal Education* 56 (2006): 479–501.

Hershkoff suggests methods of including transnational themes throughout a first year civil procedure class using a standard civil procedure casebook, of which she is the co-author.[3] The article touches on the main subjects in a first year civil procedure class: personal jurisdiction, subject matter jurisdiction, venue, pleading, and discovery, class actions, and alternative dispute resolution. Using standard civil procedure cases, the author suggests exploring ideas like the continental derivation of territoriality as the basis for personal jurisdiction (*Pennoyer v. Neff*[4]) and treatment of foreign litigants (*Asahi Metal Industry Co. v. Superior Court*[5]).

Hershkoff, Helen. "Poverty Law and Civil Procedure: Rethinking the First-Year Course." *Fordham Urban Law Journal* 34 (2007): 1325–1354.

This article lays out a framework for integrating issues of poverty and inequality into a first year civil procedure course using a standard casebook.[6] In addition

---

3. Jack H. Friedenthal, Arthur R. Miller, John E. Sexton, and Helen Hershkoff, Civil Procedure: Cases and Materials (9th ed. 2005) (currently in the 12th edition).

4. 95 U.S. 714 (1877).

5. 480 U.S. 102 (1987).

6. Friedenthal, et al., *supra* note 4.

to teaching civil procedure, Hershkoff is the co-author of two books about the legal rights of the poor. Using this combined expertise, she includes suggestions for bringing topics of poverty into discussions of due process, equal protection in the procedural context, adversarialism and inequality between litigants, transubstantivity, and economic disparity. The article includes a section that connects traditionally taught doctrinal areas with poverty and inequality. For example, *Burger King v. Rudzewicz*[7] can highlight the disparity between major corporations and those with fewer resources. Additionally, these cases draw attention to how procedural requirements can affect litigants with few resources, such as the impact of homelessness on reasonable service of process.

Johnson, Kevin R. "Integrating Racial Justice into the Civil Procedure Survey Course." *Journal of Legal Education* 54 (2004): 242–263.

The author demonstrates how to integrate issues of race, class, and gender into a standard civil procedure course using a leading casebook.[8] The article includes suggestions for integration of subjects related to racial justice into major aspects of the course, such as subject-matter jurisdiction, due process, class actions, and impact litigation. On the subject of jurisdiction, the author compares justification for diversity jurisdiction (bias against out-of-staters in state courts) with more prevalent discrimination, such as discrimination on the basis of race, national origin, or gender to demonstrate how to foster a class discussion about historical origins of certain aspects of civil procedure and their modern relevance. *Fuentes vs. Shevin,*[9] a case commonly used to teach the development of due process in prejudgment remedies, also opens an opportunity for students to consider the perspective of Fuentes, a person with low-income who had a stereo and stove repossessed by a sheriff without notice or hearing. This case also provides a vehicle to discuss the legal strategies used by legal aid groups to develop test cases. Finally, the author includes a section examining fairness to racial minorities in civil litigation and how language in cases can reveal underlying racial bias. There are similar sections on language as it relates to gender and class.

Kennedy, Deseriee A. "Witnessing the Process: Reflections on Civil Procedure, Power, Pedagogy, and Praxis." *Loyola of Los Angeles Law Review* 32 (1999): 753–760.

Kennedy, who has taught civil procedure for twenty-five years, offers that civil procedure is an ideal course for students to explore how well the rules of dispute resolution promote an equitable process. One approach is through "action pedagogy," which aims to present theory and practice as an integrated whole to demonstrate the impact of dispute resolution processes on individuals. Providing a connection between legal processes and the individual participants acts as a ve-

---

7. 471 U.S. 462 (1985).

8. JOHN J. COUND, ET AL., CIVIL PROCEDURE: CASES AND MATERIALS (8th ed. 2001) (currently published as JACK H. FRIEDENTHAL, ARTHUR R. MILLER, JOHN E. SEXTON, AND HELEN HERSHKOFF, CIVIL PROCEDURE: CASES AND MATERIALS (12th ed. 2018).

9. 407 U.S. 67 (1972).

hicle for integrating discussions of the impact of race, gender, and class on the litigants, attorneys, and judges. The author suggests making connections between classroom materials and actual practice by asking students to visit a variety of courtrooms, compare them, and critically evaluate the judicial process as it plays out in real settings. For example, students can compare the formality, characteristics of the parties, attorneys, and decisionmakers, the time spent of matters, and the nature of the disputes. This exercise allows students to assess the ideals of procedure against the realities.

Koh, Harold Hongju. "Two Cheers for Feminist Procedure." *University of Cincinnati Law Review* 61 (1993): 1201–1208.

The author argues that looking at procedure from a feminist perspective "add[s] to our ability to see the world" and that modern procedure reinforces values which could be classed as male such as "individualism, neutrality, formality, separateness, and autonomy" and minimizes values that can be considered female, such as "connectedness, reciprocity, empathy, relationship formality, and context." In the classroom, feminist procedure is valuable for explaining why procedural rules were applied in a certain way and can reveal less apparent reasoning behind rule application. Additionally, the feminist perspective on procedure is successful as a critical approach which allows students to consider courts and procedure apart from the idea of neutrality and question the existence and reasoning behind rules.

MacKinnon, Catharine A. "Mainstreaming Feminism in Legal Education." *Journal of Legal Education* 53 (2003): 199–212.

MacKinnon is a well-known and influential feminist legal scholar who has authored dozens of books and articles on sex equality, sexual harassment, feminist theory, and gender-based crime. In this article, she explores the role of feminism in education and how law schools can prepare lawyers to recognize and remedy gender inequality. Part II considers how to integrate gender across the curriculum, including how subjects in civil procedure can be considered through the lens of gender inequality. For example, the author questions whether the norms about personal jurisdiction, which are structured to favor resolving disputes in forums "close to home," reflect a male dominant perspective.

Marder, Nancy S. "Teaching Civil Procedure Stories." *Journal of Legal Education* 55 (2005): 138–151.

This book review looks at what *Civil Procedure Stories* (described above) can offer professors and law students. Law professors can learn additional information and perspectives about the standard cases used to teach civil procedure. For first year students, the book provides details about the parties and the circumstances of the case and illustrates the role of lawyers and judges. For second and third year students, the book can remind them that the standard civil procedure cases do not tell the whole story, that information in included and excluded from court opinions for particular reasons, that a judge must work within a system that has limitations on remedies, and the legislature's role in changing laws when the courts cannot.

Rand, Spencer. "Social Justice as a Professional Duty: Effectively Meeting Law Student Demand for Social Justice by Teaching Social Justice as a Professional Competency." University of Cincinnati Law Review 87 (2018): 77–137.

Rand proposes that law schools implement a school-wide learning objective of social justice and integrate instruction across the curriculum that promotes practice through a lens of social justice. The author includes suggestions for including discussions about inequality and social justice in several courses, including civil procedure. For example, a civil procedure course could examine how court rules can favor litigants with greater power and resources.

Resnik, Judith. "Revising the Canon: Feminist Help in Teaching Procedure." *University of Cincinnati Law Review* 61 (1993): 1181–1200.

Resnik takes a feminist theory perspective on civil procedure, specifically jurisdiction of the federal courts, the institutional identity of courts, and federal rule-making. In considering jurisdiction, the author links jurisdiction and gender through the Violence Against Women Act, jurisdictional disabilities of women, and the idea of a natural division between federal and state courts on matters in domestic relations law. The author also looks at the structure of the courts themselves; how non-litigant women, such as judges, attorneys, clerks, staff, and jurors, operate within the court system. Finally, the author examines the Federal Rules of Civil Procedure, looking at how the Rules are created and whether they should be amended in response to findings about gender bias.

Chapter 9

Torts

Issues of Diversity and Inclusion in Torts Cases

*Carol M. Suzuki**

Student Learning Goals in Traditional Doctrinal Courses

This essay discusses methods of advancing equity and inclusion through tort law while pointing out societal discrimination and bias reflected in some torts cases. A specific approach for teaching tort law is explained using a diversity and inclusion tort law project followed by in-depth use of this approach for two well-known tort cases.

Torts professors have a lot of material to cover, whether over one or two semesters, at three or five credits per semester. Incorporating diversity and inclusion into class discussions can pose a challenge. Some first-year casebooks have developed to include cases that raise issues of diversity and inclusion,[1] which would by themselves support relevant class discussion. Even if a law school has adopted a cultural competence student learning outcome,[2] a professor who wants to present diversity and inclusion matters in class may feel the pressure brought on by the need to teach first-year students how to read and analyze substantive law while ensuring subject material coverage over the semester.

The planning and facilitation of diversity and inclusion discussions in a torts course must not be too burdensome on the professor, or the cultural competence learning

* Dickason Professor of Law, University of New Mexico School of Law. Co-author of DOMINICK VETRI, LAWRENCE C. LEVINE, JOAN E. VOGEL, IBRAHIM J. GASSAMA & CAROL M. SUZUKI, TORT LAW AND PRACTICE (6th ed. 2020). The author thanks her casebook co-authors and acknowledges the Don L. and Mabel F. Dickason Professorship for its generous support of this endeavor.

1. *See, e.g.,* DOMINICK VETRI ET AL., TORT LAW AND PRACTICE (6th ed. 2020) (Carolina Academic Press). The sixth edition includes an Index of Diversity and Inclusion Materials.

2. *See* HOLLORAN CENTER FOR ETHICAL LEADERSHIP IN THE PROFESSIONS, UNIVERSITY OF ST. THOMAS SCHOOL OF LAW, LEARNING OUTCOMES 302(C) AND (D), https://www.stthomas.edu/holloran center/learningoutcomesandprofessionaldevelopment/learningoutcomesdatabase/learningoutcomes 302c/ (last visited September 4, 2020). This student learning outcome database indicates that at least 51 U.S. law schools have adopted a learning outcome focused on cultural competence.

goal will not be achieved. Also, a professor must consider that as first-year law students learn to find their voices in a new environment among new peers, their abilities and comfort levels to discuss issues of discrimination and bias in the law will be varied. Additionally, torts professors must be careful to control the increase in work when they assign students research into and class presentations of historical and current bias issues in the law beyond the casebook reading.

Diversity, Inclusion, Discrimination, and Bias in Torts

Any torts casebook is certain to include cases that lend themselves to consideration of diversity and inclusion. While teaching Black Letter law, torts professors can guide students to engage in meaningful and thoughtful discussion of these issues.

Looking at intentional torts, issues of diversity, inclusion, discrimination, and bias may surface claims for assault,[3] battery,[4] intentional infliction of emotional distress,[5] defamation,[6] or privacy.[7]

The elements of negligence offer opportunities to research and engage in discussion of diversity and inclusion. Cases covering the general duty of reasonable care may surface some issues of unequal treatment.[8] The reasonable care standard allows for discussion of who is the reasonably prudent person and whether that person has a gender.[9]

The element of causation, depending on the casebook, may cover the issue of proving future harm, perhaps with DES cases, where the daughters of women who took

---

3. *See, e.g.*, Vetter v. Morgan, 913 P.2d 1200 (Kan. Ct. App. 1995) (two men in vehicle threaten woman driving van in next lane late at night).

4. *See, e.g.*, Villa v. Derouen, 614 So. 2d 714 (La. Ct. App. 1993) (plaintiff burned by co-worker, perhaps as a form of racial harassment).

5. *See, e.g.*, Brandon v. County of Richardson, 624 N.W.2d 604 (Neb. 2001) (transgender man emotionally abused by law enforcement when reporting rape).

6. The #MeToo movement has led to a number of lawsuits by alleged victims and alleged perpetrators. *See, e.g.*, Complaint, Carroll v. Trump, No. 160694 (N.Y. Sup. Ct. Nov. 4, 2019) (journalist sues man she claims raped her, for making false, insulting statements about her).

7. *See* Scott Skinner-Thompson, *Privacy's Double Standards*, 93 Wash. L. Rev. 2051 (2018) (privacy rights are not equally granted to members of marginalized communities).

8. *See, e.g.*, Boyles v. Kerr, 855 S.W.2d 593 (Tex. 1993) (on appeal, woman loses lawsuit for emotional distress after man with whom she has consensual sex shares with his friends surreptitiously made tape of encounter) (dissenting opinion sets forth the disproportionate effect of the decision on women).

9. *See, e.g.*, Edwards v. Johnson, 152 S.E.2d 122 (N.C. 1967) (plaintiff successfully appeals dismissal after woman neighbor unintentionally shoots him); *see also* Lucinda M. Finley, *A Break in the Silence: Including Women's Issues in a Torts Course*, 1 Yale J.L. & Feminism 41 (1989). Depending on how a casebook discusses the elements of negligence, duty or breach may support more discussion of the reasonably prudent person. As to issues of diversity, beyond gender, one can consider physically different characteristics, mentally disabled persons, the child standard, and the status of children in regard to tort liability.

diethylstilbestrol to prevent miscarriage while pregnant suffered signature cancers.[10] Or perhaps the casebook will include lead paint cases,[11] which may surface the continuing problem of lead paint in public housing and poor communities nationwide.

The element of scope of liability (proximate cause) is often learned through discussion of unforeseeable plaintiff Mrs. Helen Palsgraf, set forth below. Beyond the unforeseeable plaintiff and unforeseeable consequences cases, one may look toward the cases that teach the exceptions to the foresight rule.[12] How is it that a plaintiff has an eggshell skull or is thin-skulled?[13] What is that plaintiff's susceptibility?

Damages are an element of negligence that are sure to support abundant discussion of diversity issues. With respect to earnings losses, how do race and gender affect past and future damages?[14] Do race- and gender-based worklife tables reflect historical and current bias in terms of who has had opportunities for employment and advancement?[15] How does one determine the worklife expectancy of a transgender person? Does the attorney of a transgender woman use a female table to align with the client's identity, or does the attorney strategically use the higher-wage male table?

The terrorist attacks of 9/11, a devastating event for the United States, resulted in significant developments in tort damages and will be noted in many torts casebooks. Students may have the opportunity to discuss the September 11th Victim Compensation Fund, where Special Master Kenneth Feinberg, the fund administrator, used an all-male earning capacity table instead of race- and gender-based tables in determining damages awards, thereby attempting to eliminate historical race- and gender-based earnings discrimination.[16]

Looking to loss of consortium, these damages for the loss of a spouse's services were originally only available for the husband for loss of services of his wife. Damages have historically been available to married spouses, and thus unavailable for same-gender couples who were not able to marry. Consortium losses are available to gay

---

10. *See, e.g.*, Hymowitz v. Eli Lilly & Co., 539 N.E.2d 1069 (N.Y. 1989).

11. *See, e.g.*, Thomas v. Mallett, 701 N.W.2d 523 (Wis. 2005).

12. Suicide as an exception to the foresight rule may serve as an opportunity to speak with first year students about the stress of law school and counseling services available at the law school.

13. *See, e.g.*, Pace v. Ohio Dep't of Transp., 594 N.E.2d 187 (Ohio Ct. Cl. 1991) (defendant operator of snowplow that injured plaintiff claimed plaintiff was current drug user).

14. *See* Ronen Avraham & Kimberly Yuracko, *Torts and Discrimination*, 78 Ohio St. L.J. 661 (2017) (challenging race- and gender-based wage, life expectancy, and worklife expectancy tables); *see also* Elizabeth Adjin-Tettey, *Replicating and Perpetuating Inequalities in Personal Injury Claims Through Female-Specific Contingencies*, 49 McGill L.J. 309 (2004) (suggesting gender-neutral method for calculating lost future wages).

15. *See, e.g.*, Reilly v. United States, 863 F.2d 149 (1st Cir. 1988); *see also* Martha Chamallas, *Civil Rights in Ordinary Tort Cases: Race, Gender, and the Calculation of Economic Loss*, 38 Loy. L.A. L. Rev. 1435, 1439 (2005); Adjin-Tettey, *supra* note 14; Sherri R. Lamb, *Toward Gender-Neutral Data for Adjudicating Lost Future Earning Damages: An Evidentiary Perspective*, 72 Chi.-Kent L. Rev. 299 (1996).

16. *See generally* Kenneth R. Feinberg, What Is Life Worth? The Unprecedented Effort to Compensate the Victims of 9/11 (2005). Life expectancy tables also may reflect gender and racial bias. *See, e.g.*, McMillan v. City of New York, 253 F.R.D. 247 (E.D.N.Y. 2008) (rejecting race-based life expectancy tables).

and lesbian married couples after the U.S. Supreme Court's decision in *Obergefell v. Hodges*.[17] Should consortium losses be available in other relationships, including to cohabiting unmarried couples?

The Diversity Research Project

The following is one approach to support diversity, inclusion, discrimination, and bias discussions in class that would require some advance planning and assignments while leaving most of the research to the students. A torts professor may assign students in advance throughout the semester to research cases in the torts casebook used in the course to consider how case opinions were or were not shaped by diversity issues, including gender, race, ethnicity, sexual orientation, gender identity, and class. This project suggests one method that can be adjusted to the professor's teaching style.

Below is a general assignment:

Torts: Diversity Research Project

This torts course provides an opportunity for you to research and discuss the context in which these lawsuits and judicial opinions were developed in order to better understand and appreciate diverse backgrounds and perspectives.

Throughout this semester, I will assign students to conduct research into specific cases in the book to identify historical and/or current unequal treatment of the parties.

For each case to which you are assigned [individually, in pairs, in groups], please read the full case opinion, along with prior and subsequent opinions, if reasonably available; also research secondary sources including news articles and law review articles. Please prepare a presentation up to [X] minutes, with two or three open-ended questions for your colleagues to discuss relevance to diversity, inclusion, equity, difference, discrimination, or bias. [As part of your preparation, please meet with me during my office hours to discuss your ideas, research results, challenges, etc.]

Please consider the following questions as you research your case:

• What is the relevant historical context at the time of the alleged negligent event, verdict, and/or appellate opinion?

• What do you remark about the parties and other people or entities involved?

• What does the case opinion raise with respect to issues of diversity, inclusion, discrimination, or bias?

• What is the opinion silent on with respect to issues of diversity, inclusion, discrimination, or bias?

---

17. 576 U.S. 644 (2015).

- Reflecting on this case, do you have concerns regarding fairness and justice with respect to issues including gender, race, ethnicity, sexual orientation, gender identity, and class?
- What do you remark as to the perspective of the court in its opinion?
- What are the values reflected in the opinion?

A professor could assign cases to students individually, or in panels, or to the class as a whole arranged into small groups, depending on the professor's teaching style. Whether a professor teaches by use of the Socratic method, or assigned panels, perhaps a group of three students would encourage student collaboration and support students who may be reticent about discussing diversity issues in class.

The project could be expansive and cover all cases in the casebook or, with some research and review, a professor could select cases where the casebook authors or the judges in their opinions identify issues of diversity, inclusion, discrimination, or bias. Students may not yet have started to study constitutional rights, but they do not need this background in order to begin a dialogue on discrimination in torts. An introduction to challenges to historical normative values in tort law may aid in student learning about civil rights and awareness that torts is an area of law that is developing in response to society's demands for equality, fairness, and justice.

Two Cases for Potentially Rich Discussions

In some case opinions, diversity and inclusion issues may be apparent or obvious, as the lesson objective and the reason that the case is contained in the casebook. In other cases, the diversity issue may only be found in the breach, or what is unwritten but discoverable with investigation.

Palsgraf v. Long Island Railroad Co.

Let's explore briefly a case that is routinely included in torts casebooks. Many, if not all, torts casebooks cover negligence, and more specifically scope of liability[18] (proximate cause), the element of negligence where we test whether the plaintiff was, or the consequences were, sufficiently unforeseeable such that we should limit liability despite the defendant's careless conduct. Enter Mrs. Helen Palsgraf, forever the unforeseeable plaintiff and victim of an accident involving exploded fireworks at a train station. Is there any first year torts casebook that does not include among its cases *Palsgraf v. Long Island Railroad Co.*?[19] The comparison of Chief Judge Benjamin Cardozo's opinion and Judge William S. Andrews' dissent makes for great analytical

---

18. *See* Restatement (Third) of Torts: Liability for Physical and Emotional Harm § 29 cmts. b, g (Am. L. Inst. 2010) (the term "proximate cause" may lead to confusion with causation).

19. Palsgraf v. Long Island R.R. Co., 162 N.E. 99 (N.Y. 1928).

class discussion and plentiful scholarship.[20] Among tort law professors and even be-yond, in class discussions, the *Palsgraf* majority and dissenting opinions are known for the actual facts not comporting with either judge's recitation of them. Judge Cardozo's majority opinion is noted for its lack of facts. Professor William H. Manz wrote a law review article[21] and then a book,[22] acknowledging how the actual facts may not align with the opinions.

After it occurred, the event was reported in many newspapers, including on the front page of the *New York Times*.[23] Delving further into the facts, the *New York Times* indicates that the boarding passenger who held and then dropped the package of fire-works that exploded, and his fellow passenger, were Italian. Perhaps to the credit of the court, this "fact" does not figure into the *Palsgraf* opinions, as it is not relevant. However, it is noted in *Palsgraf* scholarship[24] and a law student would have no difficulty finding this "fact" through searching on the internet.

The report of the nationality/ethnicity of the fireworks-carrying passenger has been discredited as having no basis. This description insinuates discrimination against Italians in the 1920s based on race. Columbus Day, a commemoration of the Italian explorer and his landing in the Americas in 1492, was approved as a legal public hol-iday in 1968.[25] These days, a number of jurisdictions no longer commemorate Colum-bus Day because it is seen as having racist origins for denying the existence of native peoples prior to the creation of the United States, and some have renamed the holiday as Indigenous Peoples' Day.[26] The progression of Italians as subjects of race discrim-ination to being considered endorsers of cultural bias provides challenges and allows an opportunity for students to engage in respectful and thoughtful dialogue.

Wassell v. Adams

Now let's look at a second case as an example for this project. The plaintiff in *Wassell v. Adams*[27] appealed the denial of her motion for judgment notwithstanding

---

20. *See, e.g.*, William L. Prosser, Palsgraf *Revisited*, 52 Mich. L. Rev. 1 (1953).

21. William H. Manz, Palsgraf: *Cardozo's Urban Legend?*, 107 Dick. L. Rev. 785 (2003).

22. William H. Manz, The *Palsgraf* Case: Courts, Law and Society in 1920s New York (2005).

23. *Bomb Blast Injures 13 in Station Crowd*, N.Y. Times, Aug. 25, 1924, at 1.

24. *See* Manz, *supra* note 21, at 791.

25. Pub. L. No. 90-363, 82 Stat. 250 (1968).

26. *See, e.g.*, Heather Murphy & Aimee Ortiz, *Columbus Day or Indigenous Peoples' Day? Depends Where You Are*, N.Y. Times (updated Oct. 14, 2019) (noting the controversy of Columbus Day), https://www.nytimes.com/2019/10/13/us/indigenous-peoples-day-columbus-day.html?searchResult Position=1; Brent Staples, *How Italians Became 'White'*, N.Y. Times (Oct. 12, 2019) (opinion) (noting President Harrison's 1892 Columbus Day proclamation following the lynching of eleven Italians in New Orleans, and 1920s laws restricting Italian immigration based on race, despite the declaration that Italians are white), https://www.nytimes.com/interactive/2019/10/12/opinion/columbus-day-italian-american-racism.html?searchResultPosition=1. New Mexico adopted Indigenous Peoples' Day and removed Columbus Day in 2019, and Columbus Day as a racist holiday has been a long-term subject of discussion at the author's law school.

27. 865 F.2d 849 (7th Cir. 1989).

the verdict or for a new trial after the jury found her ninety-seven percent at fault for rape committed upon her in a fourteen-room Chicago motel. Circuit Judge Richard Posner begins the majority opinion by describing the plaintiff, Susan Marisconish, as a woman who "grew up on Macaroni Street in a small town in a poor coal-mining region of Pennsylvania—a town so small and obscure that it has no name. She was the ninth of ten children, and as a child was sexually abused by her stepfather. After graduating from high school she worked briefly as a nurse's aide, then became engaged to Michael Wassell, also from Pennsylvania."[28]

The plaintiff lodged at the motel in order to attend her fiancé's graduation from the Navy. Judge Posner includes a description of the locality: "Four blocks to the west of the Ron-Ric motel is a high-crime area: murder, prostitution, robbery, drugs— the works."[29] Staying alone at the motel after graduation in order to look for a marital apartment, the plaintiff opened the motel door one night to "a respectably dressed black man whom Susan had never seen before."[30] The plaintiff was raped by the visitor, who was never identified. The jury, in assigning the plaintiff most of the blame for her rape, left her with an award sufficient to cover her therapy for her post-traumatic stress.

The opinion sets forth Judge Posner's risk-utility standard that has been criticized by Professor Ellen M. Bublick[31] and others for monetizing the right to be free from rape, itself a subject appropriate for this project. We could also talk about damages for assault and infliction of emotional distress as gendered issues. Additionally, the opinion is disturbing for its one reference to race. The rapist's race is mentioned; the opinion does not mention the race of the plaintiff, the fiancé, or the defendant motel owners. Why is that? What is the importance of the rapist's race to the affirmation of the denial of plaintiff's motion?

Diversity Project Challenges

Diversity and inclusion are relevant areas for discussion in a torts course. Each torts professor who includes diversity and inclusion discussion will need to determine how much professor and student time and energy to devote to this project. A professor could select only the cases where diversity, inclusion, discrimination, and bias are apparent, perhaps by focusing on issues of standing to sue or types of damages.

The *Palsgraf* case has been researched and analyzed beyond diversity and inclusion issues, but a first-year law student should be able to conduct reasonable research to find relevant material even if the student has not yet had training on legal database

---

28. *Id.* at 850.

29. *Id.* at 851.

30. *Id.* at 851.

31. *See* Ellen M. Bublick, *Citizen No-Duty Rules: Rape Victims and Comparative Fault*, 99 Colum. L. Rev. 1413, 1436 (1999); *see also* Lawrence A. Cunningham, *Traditional Versus Economic Analysis: Evidence from Cardozo and Posner Torts Opinions*, 62 Fla. L. Rev. 667 (2010).

searching. The *Wassell* case may be more challenging, and more uncomfortable for students and perhaps professors to discuss, because it involves rape[32] and race.[33]

This diversity project protocol has as a goal to not tax the professor to find additional cases beyond the selected course casebook. Realistically, some cases will not lend themselves to diversity discussion, and students should not be penalized if research does not reveal a fruitful case. Depending on casebook selection, case coverage during a semester, and student assignment protocols, each student should have the opportunity to research and analyze at least one case for diversity and inclusion issues.

Torts is an ideal class to introduce students to the importance of intentional focus on diversity and inclusion issues. With proper guidance, law students can learn to identify and analyze these issues, and to engage in thoughtful and respectful discussion of them.

---

32. *See, e.g.*, James J. Tomkovicz, *On Teaching Rape: Reasons, Risks, and Rewards*, 102 Yale L.J. 481 (1992) (discussion of teaching rape law in first year criminal law course).

33. *See, e.g.*, Alexi Nunn Freeman & Lindsey Webb, *Positive Disruption: Addressing Race in a Time of Social Change Through a Team-Taught, Reflection-Based, Outward-Looking Law School Seminar*, 21 U. Pa. J.L. & Soc. Change 121 (2018).

Reasonableness and Realism

*Pat K. Chew**

"Reasonableness" as Ambiguous Concept in Tort Law

Tort law is packed with legal principles that include undefined and ambiguous concepts subject to various interpretations. These concepts may heavily influence legal conclusions and therefore influence who wins and who loses (outcome-determinative effects). A few illustrative examples:

- The concept of "foreseeability" of the risk of harm is used in determining the defendant's duty and proximate cause in negligence and in determining strict products liability under the 3rd Restatement of Torts.[1]

- A "cost/benefit" analysis is used in determining if the defendant breached her duty of care, or in determining whether the risk-utility test in a strict liability design defects case is satisfied.

- The intentional tort of privacy or infliction of emotional distress requires a determination of "offensive," "highly offensive," or "outrageous" conduct based on social norms.

The concept of "reasonableness" may be the most ambiguous concept in tort law, yet it is also pervasive and recurrent. For example, whether or not a defendant is legally negligent and ultimately liable for the plaintiff's harm is dependent on the defendant acting "un-reasonably" under the circumstances. This inquiry is often stated as: Did the defendant act as "a reasonable person" would in this situation? If not, this is proof of the breach of the duty of care. It is often the most important element in a plaintiff's negligence case.

The reasonableness standard can also play an important role in intentional torts. For instance, was the defendant's use of force in a battery claim "reasonable and

---

* Judge J. Quint Salmon and Anne Salmon Chaired Professor, University of Pittsburgh School of Law.
    1. Restatement (Third) of Torts: Products Liability §2 (Am. Law Inst. 1998).

proportionate" under the circumstances? Or was the defendant's invasion of the plaintiff's privacy within the "reasonable" expectation of an individual in the plaintiff's situation?

Moreover, the "reasonableness standard" is particularly noteworthy for first year students because the concept is found in many non-torts subject areas as well — thus introducing and informing first year students about a concept they will encounter again and again in law school. To illustrate, a breach of a duty of care in corporate law requires an imagining of the *reasonably prudent* director or officer; also, the workplace sexual harassment requirements of "severe or pervasive" harassment and a "hostile work environment" in employment discrimination law is based on a *reasonable person's* assessment.

Consequences of this Ambiguity: Teaching Challenges and Opportunity

Because the concept of reasonableness is ambiguous, judges have to use their discretion in their decision making. Thus, they need to determine what the concept means for this particular legal issue and how to apply it to these specific facts. They have to decide whose vantage point is most relevant — the plaintiff's, the defendant's, or an "objective" third party? Among the myriad facts, which ones are relevant and what is the importance of that fact over another fact?

Furthermore, how and when judges exercise their discretion in their decision making is rarely transparent. They can rely on precedents and facts that best support their conclusions and ignore those precedents and facts that do not. Even in the absence of clear precedent, they can simply explain what seems reasonable under the circumstances, carefully articulating their logic and rationale.

Faculty can also link this discussion of judicial discretion to the "formalist" and "realist" models of legal decision making.[2] The formalist model, sometimes called legalistic model or professional-socialization model, assumes that judicial decision making is generally predictable and uniform, particularly when the legal principles and key precedents are clearly articulated (e.g., a defendant's duty of care is breached if he or she acts unreasonably). Thus, the formalist would argue that judicial decision making is essentially a deliberative and formula-driven process where, for instance, reasonable conduct is objectively ascertainable through a careful study of authoritative sources and precedents. This model argues that judges, through their legal and judicial training, are socialized to the profession's norms and that this socialization prevails over any personal attributes or experiences. Therefore, the demographics of an in-

---

2. Pat K. Chew, *Judges' Gender and Employment Discrimination Case: Emerging Evidence-Based Empirical Conclusions*, 14 J. OF GENDER, RACE & JUST. 359, 360–61 (2011).

dividual judge (e.g., their gender, race, religion, economic background) and their life experiences are unlikely to affect their decision making process.

In contrast, a realist model of judicial decision making makes different assumptions. It posits that the process—depending on the type of case, the applicable legal principles, and the particular facts—does involve some judicial discretion. "It argues that judges do not leave their humanness at the courtroom door. Judges' lives, including personal attributes and experiences, consciously or unconsciously influence how they interpret case facts and legal principles."[3] Therefore, the decision making process is more intuitive and the legal outcomes are sometimes less predictable than the formalist model suggests. In other words, judges can remain committed to their training and professional norms, while exercising some discretion.

My impression is that legal academics as a group are more likely to believe that judges are realists, but that judges as a group are more likely to believe they are formalists. And as is apparent, this essay supports a realist model of judicial decision making (as does the social science research described below). Torts textbooks typically do not directly discuss the formalist and realist models, but I think it is helpful if faculty do. It offers students one way to understand the seemingly incongruent and confusing judicial opinions and conclusions that are based on the same legal principles and very comparable facts.[4]

Discretionary Judicial Decision Making

Social Science Research

In what ways do judges use their discretion in assessing and reaching legal conclusions, for instance, in determining what constitutes "reasonable" conduct? Studies continue, but evolving social science research reveals many ways that humans unwittingly analyze information and make decisions using "cognitive heuristics."[5] These cognitive heuristics are intuitive rather than deliberate, in the sense that individuals are not necessarily aware they are using these heuristics. Nonetheless, these heuristics—such as generalizations based on social stereotyping, hindsight bias, anchoring bias, and motivated cultural cognition—are influential in how individuals identify and assess relevant facts, and then determine how to incorporate their assessments into their decision making.[6] So, in addition to using conscious logic and rationales,

---

3. *Id.*

4. The Nevada Supreme Court, in *PETA v. Bobby Berosini Ltd.*, 867 P.2d 1121 (Nev. 1994), for instance, illustrates in a tort case how a judge can cherry-pick facts to suit legal conclusions including various analyses of the "reasonableness" standard.

5. See e.g., Paul Brest and Linda Hamilton Kreiger, Problem Solving, Decision Making, and Professional Judgment: A Guide for Lawyers and Policymakers (2010).

6. Pat K. Chew, *A Case of Motivated Cultural Cognition: China's Normative Arbitration of International Business Disputes*, 51 Int'l Law. 469, 471–473 (2018).

judges like all humans are likely to incorporate into their discretionary decision-making, unconscious intuitive inclinations. Thus, a judge's determination of the reasonable person standard is not quite as objective and predictable as it might appear.

Research on Effects of Judges' Gender and Race

Given the homogeneity of the judiciary, namely that judges are mostly white and male,[7] researchers have considered whether a judge's race or gender makes any difference in how they exercise their discretionary judgement. Inferential empirical evidence indicates that a judge's gender or race can affect their legal conclusions in, for instance, discriminatory harassment cases.

How is this research related to our discussion of reasonableness? Reasonableness is also the standard for determining racial and sexual workplace harassment. In pre-trial motions, judges determine if a *reasonable person* would believe that harassment has occurred. In making this determination, judges often focus on two key inquiries: (i) Would a reasonable person believe the harassment was "sufficient or pervasive" enough to result in a "hostile work environment"? and (ii) Would a reasonable person believe that the harassment was "because of" the person's protected status (e.g., the employee's sex or race) or for other nondiscriminatory reason? Since these key inquiries are interpreted under the reasonable person standard, they open the door to the judge's interpretive discretion.

Race Effects:

In an empirical study of federal workplace racial harassment cases that span a twenty-year period, the researchers found that plaintiffs, who are mostly likely to be African American employees, have an uphill battle. They are successful in only 20% of the proceedings; losing in 80% of the cases. In addition, multiple analyses find that judges' race significantly affects outcomes in workplace racial harassment cases.[8]

Namely, African American judges rule differently than white judges even when one considers their political affiliation or characteristics of the case. Results suggest that judges of all races are attentive to the relevant facts of the cases but may reach different conclusions depending on their races.

While these results cannot predict how an individual judge might act, it suggests that African American judges as a group and white judges as a group perceive racial harassment differently.[9] African American judges are more likely than white judges to find for the plaintiffs. These findings counter the

---

7. Tracey E. George & Albert H. Yoon, *Measuring Justice in State Courts: The Demographics of the State Judiciary*, 70 VAND. L. REV. 1887 (2017); FEDERAL JUDICIAL CENTER, DEMOGRAPHY OF ARTICLE III JUDGES, 1789–2017, https://www.fjc.gov/history/exhibits/graphs-and-maps/race-and-ethnicity.

8. Pat K. Chew & Robert E. Kelley, *Myth of the Color-Blind Judge: An Empirical Analysis of Racial Harassment Cases*, 86 WASH. U. L. REV. 1117–18 (2009).

9. Pat K. Chew, *Seeing Subtle Racism*, 6 STAN. J. OF C. R. & C. L. 183 (2010).

traditional myth that the race of a judge would not make a difference—a myth premised on a presumption of a formalistic and objective decision making process.

Gender Effects:

In an empirical study of federal appellate cases, the researchers found significant differences in the way female and male judges rule in sex discrimination cases. Female judges were more likely to find for the plaintiffs (who are most likely to be female) than male judges.[10]

Furthermore, the researchers analyzed the effects of gender on the behavior of all-male appellate panels versus panels with at least one female judge (mixed-gender panels).[11] They found that a male judge was more likely to find in favor of the plaintiff in the mixed-gender panels. The difference between all-male versus mixed gender panels had measurable consequences for litigants. The probability of an all-male panel supporting the plaintiff never exceeded 20%, not even for the most liberal of male judges. In contrast, the probability never fell below 20% on mixed-gender panels, even for the most conservative male judges. For male judges who were "average" in their ideology, the likelihood of a pro-plaintiff vote increased by almost 85%.

What are possible explanations for the results in these studies? Consistent with a realist model of judicial decision making, judges may subconsciously tap into their experiences and knowledge—their humanness! In other words, female and male judges have different experiences, knowledge, and attitudes about sexual harassment. Given the ambiguity and subjectivity of the reasonableness standard, they draw on these experiences and attitudes in their understanding of the facts and their interpretation of the laws.

In racial harassment cases, judges must determine if a reasonable person in the plaintiff's position would consider the harassment "severe or pervasive" and motivated by the plaintiff's race. African American judges have different race-related experiences than white judges. Given these life experiences, African American judges may well acknowledge more subtle forms of racism than white judges and consider this subtle racism in their determination of what a reasonable plaintiff-employee (who happens to be African American) would consider severe or pervasive harassment. The judges' race becomes salient in these cases. Similarly, female judges may well recognize more subtle forms of sexism than male judges and consider this subtle sexism in their determination of what a reasonable employee (who happens to be a woman) would consider severe or pervasive harassment. Their gender becomes salient in these types of cases, while it may not be salient in other types of case. The analysis of mixed-gender versus all-male panels also suggests that judges of one gender may influence the decision making of the other gender through their sharing of particular insights and experiences.

---

10. Chew, *supra* note 2, at 366–69 (describing research by Christina Boyd and others).

11. *Id.*

In Summary

The reasonable person standard is critical in determining if a defendant is negligent in tort law. What a reasonable person would do, however, is often open to interpretation. Judges understandably draw on their own experiences and socialization in their interpretation — consistent with the realist model of judicial decision making.

In studying "reasonableness" in tort law, we can draw from empirical research in other areas of law where the reasonable person standard is also used. Empirical research in sexual harassment cases, for instance, indicates that female judges and male judges differ on what they think a "reasonable person" would consider sexual harassment; and in racial harassment cases, black judges and white judges differ on what they think a "reasonable person" would consider racial harassment.

Students tell me that studying "reasonableness" while also learning about judicial decision making models and the empirical research described above helps them realize two things:

a. Reasonableness is not as predictable as one might think.

b. Legal decisions about what reasonable persons would do or think depend in part on who judges are, their particular background (including gender and race), and their experiences.

Questions for Your Consideration

The federal judiciary is mostly male and mostly white.[12] Many state courts also reflect this same homogeneity in gender and race.

1. How does this lack of gender and racial diversity affect judges' determination of reasonableness and reasonable conduct in torts and other areas of the law? Are there tort issues and fact patterns where, for instance, a judge's gender or race might affect her or his determination of "the reasonable person"? What about other characteristics of a judge's profile (e.g., religion, social economic class, political party)?

2. Given a mostly male and mostly white judiciary, is the reasonableness standard and other ambiguous concepts in tort law, by default, based on the perspective of White male judges? What are the consequences of this?

3. What are the benefits of a more diverse judiciary?

4. What if the parties' perspectives on reasonableness vary considerably from those of judges, given their particular demographic profiles or other factors? Whose perspective should be considered or take priority?

---

12. *See* Chew & Kelley, *supra* note 8, at 1122–1129 (raw data available through Federal Judicial Center).

5. If judges' norms and values are homogeneous, legal results are more likely to be the same, and therefore, more predictable and more uniform. The legal system usually values this predictability, but it also values fairness and justice. Are fairness and justice better served with a more diverse judiciary?

6. Should answers to all these questions vary by the subject area of the law, where the history and policy goals may differ? For instance, corporate law has historically prioritized those laws encouraging capitalism and entrepreneurship, while the policy goal of employment discrimination law is to eliminate discrimination in the workplace. Torts is guided by the fairest distribution of liability for personal harms.

Tort Norms in Context: Fostering Discussions about Gender and Racial Bias in Tort

Alena Allen[*]

Introduction

Many professors begin the first class of torts by asking what a tort is. Hopefully, one student will define a tort as a civil wrong not arising out of a contract. The definition sounds straight forward enough but students should be challenged to view tort law as complex and interdependent on the historical norms of the time. The scope of wrongs for which the law provides a remedy is dictated by common law and state legislatures which have largely been populated by white men from wealthy backgrounds.[1] Simply acknowledging this truth is important. Thus, after we discuss what a tort is, I tell students:

> I am obviously a Black woman as such my life experiences inform how I view tort law. As a person of color and as a woman, I am particularly sensitive to how the evolution of tort law has largely evolved without input from women or minorities. I am also sensitive to ways in which tort law perpetuates inequality. I realize that some of you simply want to learn what the law is and that you might not be interested in the broader policy discussions. However, discussions about broader policy objectives are critical. As lawyers some of you will have an opportunity to argue for a change in the law or actually write legislation. The law is not static. It is constantly evolving, so it is my job to help you critically assess whether laws are achieving their purported goals. It is also my job to help you think about what the goals of tort law

* Director of Faculty Research and Associate Professor of Law at the Cecil C. Humphreys University of Memphis School of Law. A special thank you to my wonderful torts students who push me to continue growing as a teacher each year.

1. Catharine A. MacKinnon, *Reflections on Sex Equality Under Law*, 100 YALE L.J. 1281, 1281 (1991) (noting that "[n]o woman had a voice in the design of the legal institutions that rule the social order under which women, as well as men, live.").

should be. In order to do that effectively, we have to discuss how the law impacts all stakeholders and that necessarily involves a discussion of how the law impacts everyone including and especially marginalized and vulnerable groups. I will share my perspective, and I want you to feel comfortable sharing yours too. I learn a tremendous amount from my students each year, and I look forward to learning from you as well. So, now I am going to provide an overview of the broad theories related to the overarching goals of tort law. We will return to them time and time again throughout this semester and next semester."[2]

The twin questions: what a tort is and why does tort law exist, are foundational, but it is also important to create a classroom environment where students are comfortable engaging in tough and important conversations. I have found that it is easiest to create a safe space starting with the first class. I open with the speech I described earlier because I want students to understand that my race and gender have had a profound impact on my perspective, and I want them to know that I am open to and want to learn from them. At a recent town hall meeting with BLSA (Black Law Students Association) students, these students lamented how few of their professors talked about race in the classroom and how, in many classes, they did not feel comfortable talking about race. Providing a space where students from marginalized groups feel comfortable sharing is critical for achieving equity in the classroom. The most effective way to foster discussion is to genuinely and authentically want to hear from students.

Returning to the foundational question of why does tort law exist, tort law is typically summarized as (a) compensation, (b) deterrence, (c) corrective justice, and (d) fair process in the administration of justice. In addition, I discuss newer, less developed theories of therapeutic jurisprudence[3] and tort law as necessary for democracy or social change. I challenge students to think about ways in which tort law can drive social change. Here, the point is to highlight for students early that tort law on a macro level can be used to change perceptions even if the litigation is not ultimately successful.[4]

Tort cases do not exist in a vacuum. Often the litigants have histories that have been colored by discrimination; judges and juries are not immune from making decisions from a biased lens which has real consequences.[5] As such, the historical back-

---

2. A white male colleague asked me for assistance in helping to frame discussions about race in his class. Here is the script that I provided which he said has been very useful: "Everyone is not always treated equally under the law. At various points, I will try to highlight how the law has furthered inequality or has been used as a tool of oppression. Some of you have personal experiences which can enrich our understanding of how the law impacts people's lives. I encourage you to share those stories with me and the class and am eager to learn from you as we discuss how the law can be used to further the ideals of justice and equality for all."

3. *See, e.g.,* Daniel W. Shuman, *Therapeutic Jurisprudence and Tort Law: A Limited Subjective Standard of Care,* 46 SMU L. Rev. 409 (1993).

4. Melissa Mortazavi, *Tort as Democracy: Lessons from the Food Wars,* 57 Ariz. L. Rev. 929 (2015).

5. *See* Jonathan Cardi, Valerie P. Hans & Gregory Parks, *Do Black Injuries Matter? Implicit Bias and Jury Decision Making in Tort Cases,* 93 S. Cal. L. Rev. 507 (2020) (finding that participants who

drop of cases is often important. The facts of a case form a rich ground for discussing bias, discrimination, and structural racism. Sometimes reading the full case will provide ideas for developing a classroom discussion. Additionally, Tort Stories[6] provides a richer picture of classic tort cases. The forthcoming Feminist Judgements: Torts Opinions Rewritten[7] is another resource that can be used to spark classroom discussion. Finally, Tort Law and Practice (5th)[8] provides more coverage of how tort law has impacted marginalized groups than most casebooks.[9]

Deciding how to best incorporate discussions of equity and inclusion into a torts class is a matter of personal choice. What follows is a description of some the ways in which I foster those discussions.

Intentional Torts

Intentional torts are often the first subject covered in the first year class. The following cases are useful to assign to students:

Battery/Intentional Infliction of Emotional Distress

For a robust discussion about the impact of race and gender, I assign *Robinson v. Cutchin*.[10] In *Cutchin*, Mrs. Robinson, an African American woman, sued her doctor alleging battery, intentional infliction of emotional distress, and negligence. Her complaint alleged that during the caesarian delivery of her sixth child, Dr. Cutchin also performed an unconsented bilateral tubal ligation. The judge dismissed Mrs. Robinson's battery claim noting that the touching was not harmful because it did not cause additional pain or injury and was not offensive because "not [being] able to have a seventh child after previously giving birth to six children is hardly something which would offend her reasonable sense of personal dignity."[11]

This is a wonderful teaching case, and there are myriad ways to use the case. I typically reserve about 35 minutes at the end of class. After dividing the class into small groups, I hand out lightly edited versions of the case which include the facts and the battery and IIED claims. I ask the students to act as an appellate judge and decide

---

had IAT scores attributed significantly more legal responsibility to Black defendants than to white defendants and awarded less damages for injuries by Black defendants).

   6. TORTS STORIES (Robert L. Rabin & Stephen D. Sugarman eds., 2003).

   7. FEMINIST JUDGMENTS: REWRITTEN TORT OPINIONS (Martha Chamallas & Lucinda M. Finley eds., 2020).

   8. DOMINICK VETRI ET AL., TORT LAW AND PRACTICE (5th ed., 2016).

   9. Although it has not been updated recently, the casebook by Galligan and his coauthors provide critical insights related to race and gender in their notes. THOMAS C. GALLIGAN ET AL., TORT LAW: CASES, PERSPECTIVES, AND PROBLEMS (4th ed. 2007).

   10. 140 F. Supp. 2d 488 (D. Md. 2001).

   11. *Id.* at 493.

whether the trial court erred when granting the motion for summary judgment with respect to the battery and IIED claims. Unbeknownst to the students, the name of the plaintiff is different for certain groups. I typically use a name like La'Keisha Robinson or Maria Sanchez with a name like Joanna Schwarz or Ann Miller. Each group turns in a sheet explaining whether the trial court's ruling is affirmed or reversed along with their analysis.

In the three years that I have done this exercise, groups who have a plaintiff with a name that sounds Latino or African American are more likely to affirm the trial's court ruling. Groups who have a plaintiff with an Anglican or Jewish sounding name are more likely to reverse the trial court. The margin is typically 2 to 1. This leads to a robust discussion about gender and race. Although I enjoy free flowing discussions, the discussion can be guided in a number of ways. First, there is a robust literature on intersectionality. Drawing on the work of Kimberlé Crenshaw[12] and Angela Harris,[13] I try to demonstrate that Mrs. Robinson's suffering was trivialized in large part because she was an African American and a woman. I caution students about essentializing the case to only being about race or only being about gender. We talk specifically about the struggles that African American woman have faced including the stereotype of the promiscuous welfare queen. Secondly, I ask the students to think about whose perspective tends to dominate what we view as a reasonable sense of dignity. Third, I discuss the extent to which cross-cultural competency matters in medicine. I briefly highlight the work of Professor Kimani Paul-Emile on accommodating patient's racial preferences[14] and discuss the staggering differences in maternal fetal outcomes between African American and white women. Finally, foreshadowing a discussion that I return when covering damages, I ask them to think about the impact of race and gender on ascertaining damages.[15]

False Imprisonment

Peterson v. Sorlien[16] and *Eilers v. Coy*[17] provide an interesting backdrop for discussing the role of gender. These cases have similar but not identical facts. In *Peterson,* the plaintiff is a young woman who sues her parents and cult deprogrammers for false imprisonment. In *Eilers,* the plaintiff is a young man who sues cult deprogrammers hired by his parents for false imprisonment. The pair of cases forces students to think

---

12. *See, e.g.,* Kimberlé Crenshaw, *Demarginalizing the Intersection of Race and Sex: A Black Feminist Critique of Antidiscrimination Doctrine, Feminist Theory and Antiracist Politics,* 1989 U. Chi. Legal F. 139 (1989).

13. *See, e.g.,* Angela P. Harris, *Race and Essentialism in Feminist Legal Theory,* 42 Stan. L. Rev. 581, 585–86 (1990).

14. Kimani Paul-Emile, *Patients' Racial Preferences and the Medical Culture of Accommodation,* 60 UCLA L. Rev. 462 (2012).

15. *See, e.g.,* Martha Chamallas, *The Architecture of Bias: Deep Structures in Tort Law,* 146 U. Pa. L. Rev. 463 (1998).

16. 299 N.W.2d 123 (Minn. 1980).

17. 582 F. Supp. 1093 (D. Minn. 1984).

about whether the cases can be distinguished based on the facts and whether *Peterson* would have been decided differently if the plaintiff were male. I usually introduce Difference Feminism and the work of Carol Gilligan[18] to suggest that the plaintiff in *Peterson* was expressing lack of consent in a classically feminine way and ultimately that response was held against her.

Negligence

Robinson v. Cutchin can be revisited again. About half the states follow the "professional" malpractice standard of disclosure rule in negligent informed consent cases. The doctor's disclosure is based on what a reasonable physician would disclose. In other jurisdictions, the standard is based on the disclosure of information that a reasonable patient would consider material in making a decision. In revisiting *Robinson*, students have the opportunity to consider how a long history of experimentation on people of color might impact how they define material facts. It also creates a space to discuss whether professional standards of care are at least partially responsible for the continued health disparities in this country.[19]

Additionally, negligence cases present an opportunity to discuss how the conception of duty and the distinction between physical and emotional harm has been used in particular to deny women the right to recover for substantial harms.

In *Mitchell v. Rochester Ry. Co.*,[20] the defendant's car, pulled by a team of horses, turned toward the plaintiff in the street and did not stop until the horses' heads were on either side of her. The plaintiff collapsed from fright and suffered a miscarriage. The court denied the plaintiff's claim because she had not been touched. The court characterized the plaintiff's harm as fright and held that there could be no recovery for fright alone. The salient point here is that the law refused to provide a remedy for her emotional harm and her miscarriage. The failure of the law to provide a remedy in this case and others can be used to highlight for students that our legal norms were created to provide remedies largely for white men.[21] The common law was created by white European men who believed that they exclusively had the ability

---

18. The most influential source for the feminism of difference is Carol Gilligan's book, in which Gilligan argues that women speak "in a different voice." Gilligan argues for societal transformation based on the womanly values of responsibility, connection, selflessness, and caring rather than masculine values of separation, autonomy, and hierarchy. *See* CAROL GILLIGAN, IN A DIFFERENT VOICE (1982).

19. Steven W. Postal & Robyn Whipple Diaz, *A Remedy in Sight: International Clinical Research Regulation in the Wake of Guatemala and Nigeria*, 6 PITT. J. ENVTL. PUB. HEALTH L. 1 (2011). While most students know about the Tuskegee Study, most students are not aware of the Guatemala Study or the Pfizer Trovan Study.

20. 45 N.E. 354 (N.Y. 1896).

21. *See* Lucy Jewel, *Does the Reasonable Man Have Obsessive Compulsive Disorder?*, 54 WAKE FOREST L. REV. 1049, 1061–1070 (2019) (describing the men who created the reasonable man standard as white Anglo Saxon protestants who believed in the inferiority of people of color and the subordination of women).

to reason because women were emotional and people of color were believed to be intellectually inferior.[22]

This theme can be continued by discussing *Johnson v. Jamaica Hospital*.[23] In this case, the plaintiffs were parents of a girl, Kawana, who was born in the defendant's hospital in Queens. Kawana was abducted from the hospital's nursery by a stranger. She was recovered by the police four months later. The plaintiffs sued the hospital to recover for the emotional distress they suffered in the interim, alleging that the incident was the result of the hospital's negligence. The trial court held that the complaint stated a good cause of action and was reversed. The appellate court held that there was no basis for establishing a direct duty to the parents because the direct injury allegedly caused by defendant's negligence was abduction of the infant, and the plaintiffs' grief and mental torment which resulted from her disappearance were not actionable. The court went on to conclude that foreseeability, that such psychic injuries would result from the injury to Kawana, does not serve to establish a duty running from defendant to plaintiffs, and in the absence of such a duty, as a matter of law, there can be no liability.

Here, students should be challenged to think about whether duties should be expansive or limited. A more expansive view of duty is in keeping with goals that are often described as feminine. I describe Leslie Bender's work about how a feminine ethos of care could potentially change how we conceive of duty in tort.[24] Expanding our notion of duty furthers the basic tort goal of compensating injured plaintiffs and also uses the law to promote connection. In other words the law can be used to foster a sense of connection between unrelated parties. The current framing of duty has an individualistic nature where duties are based on individual actions and not based on the need to protect others or to think about the collective good. Emphasizing these points ensures that students understand that the law is value laden. What tort law prioritizes reflects who created tort law and their values.

Just like a limited view of duty, the choice to prioritize physical harm and preclude or limit emotional harm is intentional. Jurists have been skeptical of hysterical women and feared that emotional injuries could be faked. As such, courts routinely denied recovery for emotional injuries.[25]

A final case to illustrate how tort law fails to provide a remedy to women is *Kerr v. Boyles*.[26] In *Kerr*, the Texas Supreme Court held that negligent infliction of emotional

---

22. *See, e.g.*, CHARLES MILLS, THE RACIAL CONTRACT 59–60 (1999) (explaining that "David Hume's denial that any other race but whites had created worthwhile civilizations, Kant's thoughts on the rationality differentials between blacks and whites, Voltaire's polygenetic conclusion that blacks were a distinct and less able species, John Stuart Mill's judgment that those races 'in their nonage' were fit only for 'despotism'" influenced the creators of the reasonable person standard).

23. 467 N.E.2d 502 (N.Y. 1984).

24. Leslie Bender, *A Lawyer's Primer on Feminist Theory and Tort*, 38 J. LEGAL EDUC. 3, 33 (1988).

25. *See* Martha Chamallas & Linda K. Kerber, *Women, Mothers, and the Law of Fright: A History*, 88 MICH. L. REV. 814 (1990).

26. 855 S.W.2d 593 (Tex. 1993).

distress was not an independent cause of action noting that "tort law cannot and should not attempt to provide redress for every instance of rude, insensitive or distasteful behavior, even though it may result in hurt feelings, embarrassment, or even humiliation." The petitioner Dan Boyles, Jr., then seventeen years old, in concert with two friends videotaped nineteen-year-old Respondent Susan Leigh Kerr engaging in sexual intercourse with him. Boyles took possession of the tape shortly after it was made, and subsequently showed it on three occasions, each time at a private residence. Kerr was soon widely known by many to have starred in a porn tape. When Kerr became aware of the tape she was humiliated and distressed. Why is humiliation less worthy of compensation than a broken bone? Being humiliated can have lasting consequences and cause emotional harms that far exceed the recovery time for a broken bone. If tort law is about compensating plaintiffs for harms or deterring undesirable conduct, then it seems like Kerr should have been a case for liability. So, I challenge students to present arguments that make Kerr consistent with tort goals. Most students will conclude that this case is inconsistent with tort goals. So, the question then is why do we have the holding?

Damages

Most damage awards are comprised of lost wages, medical bills, and pain and suffering. There is a robust literature discussing how the harms suffered by women and people of color are undervalued in tort damage awards.[27] Many students are appalled to learn that many courts routinely rely on race-based mortality tables. I encourage discussion about why courts continue to rely on such tables and ask students how the tables impact tort judgments. One issue with the use of race-based life expectancy data is that the life expectancy for African Americans and Native Americans is lower than for white and Hispanic Americans. Average wages are lower for women and people of color as compared to white men. Thus, using wage data that is based on race and gender typically results in a lower damage award for women and people of color. Because lost earnings are typically lower for women and people of color tort reform, which most commonly imposes damage caps on non-economic damages, causes increased inequity.

---

27. *See, e.g.,* Kimberly A. Yuracko & Ronen Avraham, *Valuing Black Lives: A Constitutional Challenge to the Use of Race-Based Tables in Calculating Tort Damages,* 106 Calif. L. Rev. 325 (2018); Ronen Avraham & Kimberly Yuracko, *Torts and Discrimination,* 78 Ohio St. L.J. 661 (2017); Dariely Rodriguez & Hope Kwiatkowski, *How Race, Ethnicity, and Gender Impact Your Life's Worth: Discrimination in Civil Damage Awards,* Lawyers' Comm. for Civil Rights Under Law (July 2018), https://lawyers committee.org/wp-content/uploads/2018/07/LC_Life27s-Worth_FINAL.pdf; Martha Chamallas, *Questioning the Use of Race-Specific and Gender-Specific Economic Data in Tort Litigation: A Constitutional Argument,* 63 Fordham L. Rev. 73 (1994).

Selected Bibliography on Torts

*Margaret (Meg) Butler**

Introduction

The integration of diversity and inclusion into a doctrinal torts classroom may feel overwhelming to those whose lives have not given them significant lived experience as a member of a diverse group—based on categories including race, sex, gender, ability, sexual orientation, national origin, economic background, class, and so on. However, we live in a diverse world and our torts (and other) classrooms should reflect the ways in which the law interacts with and affects the lives of all types of people.

The selections included in this bibliography are made because they represent the experiences and analysis of those who teach torts inclusively, raising questions of equality and equity in the application of the law. Other selections, such as the movies included, are tools that illustrate tort issues in real life, useful for promoting thoughtful class discussion and possibly broadening students' understanding of others' lived realities. Constrained by length, it is not possible to include all scholarship in this area. Items selected are more likely to reflect recent analysis, though a few seminal pieces are mentioned. Neither are casebooks included (though there are excellent tools, such as the book *Tort Law and Practice* co-authored by Carol M. Suzuki who wrote a submission for the chapter accompanying this bibliography).

Books

Engel, David M., and Michael McCann, eds. *Fault Lines: Tort Law as Cultural Practice.* Stanford Univ. Press, 2009.

* Associate Director for Public Services, Georgia State University School of Law, I would like to thank Pam Brannon, Faculty Services Coordinator at the Georgia State University School of Law Library and graduate research Bethany Boatright for their assistance in gathering materials for consideration in this bibliography. Also, I would like to thank Merle Slyhoff, University of Pennsylvania Biddle Law Library, for generous interlibrary loan assistance.

Tort law serves a normalizing function, and the contributions to this anthology analyze the ways in which culture is reified, created, and modified by the action of tort law. An interdisciplinary collection, contributors include tort law scholars such as Professors Martha Chamallas and Jennifer Wriggins, each of whom has addressed issues of equality in her scholarship. In addition to discussion of damages, which Chamallas and Wriggins separately consider, Professor Ann Scales considers analysis of causation and the ways in which it disadvantages marginalized groups, including women.

Chamallas, Martha, and Lucinda M. Finley, eds. *Feminist Judgements: Rewritten Tort Opinions.* Cambridge Univ. Press, 2020.

An installment in the respected Feminist Judgments series, the book includes both canonical cases such as *Palsgraf v. Long Island Railroad*, 248 N.Y. 339 (1928), and lesser known cases. The opinions, accompanied by commentary, are rewritten by professors of law and other fields. The opinions may take the form of dissent, concurrences, or majority opinions based on the law available at the time and based on the facts of the underlying cases. The analysis considers core tort issues such as the existence of duty, what constitutes harm, and the role of social decency in decision making. The authors and editors use the rewritten cases to demonstrate the failures of past assumed gender-neutral principles and doctrines.

Richardson, Janice, and Erika Rackley eds. *Feminist Perspectives on Tort Law.* Abingdon: Routledge, 2012.

Largely reflecting the scholarly view of common law countries other than the United States, the collection addresses a variety of core tort concepts. The authors consider the duty of care and standard of care, negligence and reparation for harm, as well as the normalizing effect of tort law. Questions of equity and justice are raised in the context of particular torts, as well as in the context of remedies. The authors and editors focus primarily on doctrinal analysis and present little direct pedagogical discussion. However, the doctrinal concepts raised could easily be used to develop inclusive course materials for analysis and discussion. The calculation of damages in personal injury litigation provides a stark example of disparate impact of seemingly neutral principles that may be used to inform students' understanding of the law and its development.

Keren-Paz, Tsachi. *Torts, Egalitarianism and Distributive Justice.* Aldershot: Ashgate, 2007.

Tort law represents value judgments and has an extensive reach. Professor Keren-Paz analyzes the points of intersection for tort law, distributive justice, and the normative commitment of tort law, with the goal of demonstrating that tort law can be "used progressively, as one mechanism in the ongoing struggle to achieve a more just and egalitarian society" (4). After presenting a theoretical framework, Keren-Paz considers the application of the theory of distributive justice in terms of standard of care, duty of care, and negligence in the context of discrimination.

The analysis includes a table of cases and reflects the consideration and inclusion of materials from the United States, as well as Israel and the United Kingdom.

Articles

Banks, Taunya Lovell. "Teaching Laws with Flaws: Adopting a Pluralistic Approach to Torts." *Missouri Law Review* 57, no. 2 (Spring 1992): 443–45.

Professor Banks presents both an argument for teaching students the law in context, advocating for the recognition and consideration of cultural, political, class, and other characteristics in teaching students the law, using the battery case *O'Brien v. Cunard Steamship Co.*, 28 N.E. 266 (Mass. 1891), as an example. The comparison of the casebook version of the facts with the record from the case which is contextualized by a description of gender, class, and cultural influences, as well as a discussion of how legal analysis has (or may not have) changed form an example for law professors interested in embracing a more pluralistic approach in developing their courses.

Bender, Leslie. "Teaching Torts as if Gender Matters: Intentional Torts." *Virginia Journal of Social Policy & the Law* 2, no. 1 (Fall 1994): 115–164.

Professor Bender begins by noting that systematic oppressions are masked by apparent gender-neutrality and spends the balance of the article offering specific guidance about ways in which torts instruction can reflect consideration of gender bias in the law. In addition to the selection of teaching materials, Bender provides specific suggestions for teaching torts, such as adding new materials to the course, using cases written by female judges, sharing empirical studies regarding gender bias with students, and collaborating with others interested in bringing systematic oppression to light. Bender concludes with specific and detailed examples of her own experiences teaching intentional torts.

Bernabe, Alberto. "Do Black Lives Matter? Race as a Measure of Injury in Tort Law." *Scholar: St. Mary's Law Review on Race and Social Justice* 18, no. 1 (2015): 41–72.

Assisted reproduction provides the lens for the tort question arising when a sperm bank provided a purchaser with sperm from an African American donor, rather than the white donor that had been specified. Bernabe notes that the plaintiff fundamentally asserted that "giving birth to and raising a child of a mixed race is an injury" (54) and concludes that "recognizing the cause of action would support the view that life as an African American is worth so little that it is not worth living at all" (66).

Chamallas, Martha. "Discrimination and Outrage: The Migration from Civil Rights to Tort Law." *William and Mary Law Review* 48, no. 6 (May 2007): 2115–2188.

Outrageous conduct such as sexist or racist behavior can be used to support a claim of intentional infliction of emotional distress (IIED). Such claims, as arising in an employment and civil rights context, are the focus of Professor Chamallas's heavily cited analysis. Professor Chamallas describes the development of outrageous conduct or IIED claims, explicitly considering the dual roles of sexism and racism. Whether and how concepts such as hostile environment may be imported from employment discrimination into tort law are considered. Chamallas also discusses the severity requirement of a hostile environment workplace harassment claim, the recognition that sexual harassment serves a purpose of maintaining workplace hierarchy, and the role of perspective in identifying the reasonable person standard.

Dark, Okianer Christian. "Incorporating Issues of Race, Gender, Class, Sexual Orientation, and Disability into Law School Teaching." *Willamette Law Review* 32, no. 3 (Summer 1996): 541–576.

Professor Dark concisely explains the value of inclusion in the law school classroom, noting that the law is affected by "'diversity issues'" (542) and that attorneys need to be prepared to effectively address such issues in practice. In Part I, Dark notes that discussion of legal issues is enhanced and broadened by consideration of diversity issues, and she includes strong examples of how societal stereotypes inform the development of the law. Dark anticipates and addresses her readers' concerns about issues that might arise for the professor who raises diversity issues by providing both suggested teaching strategies in Part II. Dark shares in Part III student comments about what they learned in advanced torts (taken from anonymously reviewed exams). The article concludes with suggestions about both creating the classroom conditions to raise diversity issues and advice on how to begin and become more comfortable including diversity issues.

Finley, Lucinda M. "A Break in the Silence: Including Women's Issues in a Torts Course." *Yale Journal of Law and Feminism* 1 (1989): 41–74.

Professor Finely advocates thoughtfully for the consideration of women's issues in torts, including sexual harassment, valuation of 'women's work' which often takes the form of caretaking, and need for a reasonable woman, rather than a male-biased reasonable person, standard. Finely's call to action is based in part on the goal of "help[ing] women feel less like outsiders to the enterprise of the law ... which can only enrich class discussion and deepen the understanding of the material for everyone" (43).

Fox, Dov. "Reproductive Negligence." *Columbia Law Review* 117, no. 1 (January 2017): 149–242.

Professor Fox focuses his attention on the negligence of medical providers—ranging from pharmacists to embryologists—in their provision of medical services. With this perspective, he identifies misconduct including both the imposition and the denial of pregnancy or parenthood alone, as well as "procreation confounded," in which parents' seek, for example, to screen out genetic-linked disorders and their efforts are foiled by lab error. By focusing on professional misconduct by medical providers, Fox asserts the existence of "core reproductive interests" (161) and provides a schema in which attorneys and parents can discuss and ultimately recover for a claim of reproductive negligence. Included in the description of the claim is a discussion of the methods by which damages would be calculated.

Joslin, Courtney G., and Lawrence C. Levine, "The Restatement of Gay (?)." *Brooklyn Law Review* 79, no. 2 (Winter 2014): 621–662.

Part of a symposium regarding Restatements, the authors conclude that the American Law Institute (ALI) should update several Restatements to assure that lesbian, gay, bisexual, and transgender people are treated fairly under the law. In the context of torts, Professors Joslin and Levine offer specific examples of relational torts, intentional infliction of emotional distress (IIED), and defamation. The authors extrapolate from ALI's guidance regarding false imputations of race claims in their suggestions regarding the treatment of false imputation of homosexuality, for example, indicating that such a change would move "toward recognizing the dignity of the LGBT community" (661).

Weber, Mark C. "A Common Law of Disability Discrimination." *Utah Law Review* 2012, no. 1 (2012): 429–474.

Although statutory claims may exist for disability-based discrimination, as under the Americans with Disabilities Act (ADA), Professor Weber notes that individuals are not adequately protected by those claims and offers suggested protections under contract and tort law. In particular, Weber focuses on claims arising under the following theories: negligence based on duties of care such as that of a common carrier; retaliatory discharge as a public policy tort; tortious interference with contract; invasion of privacy or defamation; assault and battery; and intentional infliction of emotional distress (IIED). Though the discussion of each type of claim is brief, *in toto* Weber provides numerous opportunities for consideration of disability discrimination to be considered in a torts course. Further, Weber provides analysis of both the effectiveness of common law claims, as well as potential barriers to their success.

Weeks, Elizabeth. "Healthism in Tort Law." *Journal of Tort Law* no. 1 (2019): 81–126.

Weeks describes "healthism" as normative-based treatment of people due to their health status or habits, and the "article provides tort law examples of differential treatment" (82) and provides readers a starting point for the related analysis contained in Weeks's related book *Healthism: Health-Status Discrimination and the Law* (coauthored with Jessica L. Roberts). Following a brief description of the effects of race and gender discrimination in tort law and in tort reform, Weeks identifies ways in which health status is a factor in the application of tort law. Examples include the reasonably prudent person standard, the objective standard of care failing to adjust for mental health-related considerations, and tort law failure to award compensation for emotional distress alone. The discussion of unhealthy injured parties addresses contributory negligence and its interplay with the eggshell plaintiff doctrine through the lens of a diabetic New Jersey plaintiff who ultimately was not barred from recovery under contributory negligence, but had a duty to mitigate damages following injury. Assumption of the risk also offers the question whether "all risks are freely assumed" (115–116).

Wriggins, Jennifer B. "Toward a Feminist Revision of Torts." *American University Journal of Gender, Social Policy & the Law* 13, no. 1 (2005): 139–160.

Published as part of a Feminism and Legal Theory Project conference, Professor Wriggins applies the basic strategy of "'asking the woman question[s]'" to identify and examine ways in which existing legal doctrine overlooks women (140). The answers to the woman question make clear the importance of tort law and the ways in which feminist perspectives can be used to creatively change the development of tort law. Wriggins deconstructs two opinions to show the ways race and gender were historically used to reinforce those hierarchies. Through the analysis, Wriggins seeks to destabilize those hierarchies. Further, Wriggins asks the question why domestic violence, which may include the manifestation of a variety of traditional torts such as assault, battery, false imprisonment, has not been considered in tort law scholarship, an extension of her earlier scholarship "Domestic Violence in the First-Year Torts Curriculum," 54 J. Legal Educ. 511 (2004).

Yakren, Sofia. "Wrongful Birth Claims and the Paradox of Parenting a Child with a Disability." *Fordham Law Review* 87, no. 2 (November 2018): 583–628.

Professor Yakren focuses her attention on wrongful birth claims and calls for reform. These are claims based on the birth of a disabled child, following negligent medical care resulting in a completed pregnancy. Yakren notes that wrongful birth claims both stigmatize disabled people and tend to offer greater likelihood of recovery than 'wrongful conception' or 'wrongful pregnancy' claims. After relating the ways in which plaintiff-mothers are damaged by wrongful birth law, Yakren offers suggestions to allow for wrongful birth claims to continue while minimizing the negative effects on plaintiff-mothers and stigmatization of disabled people. The analysis of wrongful birth claims and their effects would be helpful in structuring class discussion in consideration of the perspectives of both women and disabled people.

Movies

Ava DuVernay, dir. *When They See Us* (2019; Netflix).

Ken Burns, dir. *The Central Park Five* (2012; Public Broadcasting Service).

The story of the five African American teens who were convicted of raping the Central Park jogger has been told repeatedly, drawing national media attention during the trial and subsequently when the young men were exonerated. Ken Burns produced a documentary reflecting the boys' experience, and Netflix produced a mini-series showing the perspectives of the young men. The two films provide a useful lens for instruction on the torts of malicious prosecution and intentional infliction of emotional distress. DuVernay's film also affords opportunity to consider prosecutor Linda Fairstein's claims that "When They See Us" is biased and defamatory.

Tom McCarthy, dir. *Spotlight* (2015; Participant).

The Boston Globe earned a Pulitzer prize for its investigative reporting on the accusations of sexual abuse and related cover up by priests and the Boston diocese of the Roman Catholic Church. "Spotlight" is the award-winning film presenting that series of events. Though a dramatization, underlying facts present opportunities to examine the roles of power, gender, and institutions as they affect lives. Further, connections may be made between the film and litigation against the Church.

Websites

Law and Political Economy, https://lpeblog.org/.

A website springing from a Yale Law School course and that is focused on the pursuit of equality and democracy, the scope of the site is inclusive of torts issues, as well as teaching suggestions. The site continues to be updated and is searchable by keyword, as well as by tags. Editors and contributors include a list of professors in endowed chairs, as well as some Ph.D. students. Contributions such as Conor Dwyer Reynolds's "Rules of Power & Wrongs: A Law & Political Economy Approach to Tort Law" shine light on the ways tort law simultaneously distributes and exercises power, and thus serve as a starting point for analysis of how tort law "reifies existing categories of power like class, race, and gender."

University of Washington Gallagher Law Library. *Diversity Readings in Torts*, https://guides.lib.uw.edu/law/diversity1L/torts.

Organized to include entries related to traditional torts topics such as negligence, intentional infliction of emotional distress, and damages, the value in this guide derives primarily from the variety of sources that are cited. For any torts professor interested in scholarship regarding diversity, equity, or justice in tort law from the early 1980s (e.g., Richard Delgado's *Words that Wound: A Tort Action for Racial Insults, Epithets, and Name-Calling*) to the time of this writing, a collection of canonical works is included and briefly either described or excerpted. The bibliography is part of a series and lists Research Services Librarian Mary Whisner as a contributor, as well as a number of interns.

Law Professor Blogs Network. *Torts Prof Blog*, https://lawprofessors.typepad.com/tortsprof/.

The blog, edited by Professor Christopher Robinette, fills a niche as a source of regularly posted notifications of recent torts scholarship, as well as shorter pieces addressing current torts issues, such as opioid litigation, damages verdicts, and data privacy. A sample entry of interest is the announcement of a California statute prohibiting the use of race, gender, and ethnicity when calculating earnings-related tort damages. The site includes a Google-powered search tool as well as a subscription service to assure that readers are notified of new posts.

Law Professor Blogs Network. *Race and the Law Prof Blog*, https://lawprofessors. typepad.com/racelawprof/.

With 10 editors, the Race and the Law Prof Blog includes a wide variety of information, ranging from legal analysis of current events and issues to posts highlighting books and articles of interest in the area of race law as well as pedagogy. An entry of particular interest is Jennifer B. Wriggins's post of Feburary 2020 in which she advises on ways in which a torts course can address issues of race and racism, noting cases for inclusion, addressing liability insurance issues, and the history of racism in tort law.

Jotwell: Torts, https://torts.jotwell.com/.

Jotwell: Equality, https://equality.jotwell.com/.

The purpose of Jotwell is to help readers identify great scholarship, particularly articles, in specific subject areas, including torts and equality. Many of the torts reviewers, such as Professors Martha Chamallas and Jennifer B. Wriggins, are known for their own scholarship in the area of diversity and inclusion in torts. The contributors to jotwell.com license their content to the cite under a Creative Commons license allowing others to use or modify the site's content—as for teaching—with acknowledgement and proper sourcing.

Acknowledgments

The editors would like to thank each of the contributors to this volume for their tremendous insight, thoughtfulness, and continuous collaboration throughout an unexpectedly difficult time. We would also like to thank Carol McGeehan, Ryland Bowman, and their colleagues at Carolina Academic Press for their guidance throughout the publication process.

We thank our respective institutions, Roger Williams University School of Law, University of Pennsylvania Carey Law School, City University of New York (CUNY) School of Law, and the Ninth Circuit Court of Appeals Library, for their support.

Finally, we would like to thank Dean Onwuachi – Willig for her leadership in antiracist lawyering and legal education, and for graciously sharing her thoughts with us in the Foreword to this volume.

Nicole P. Dyszlewski thanks her support system in Rhode Island and beyond, which includes family and friends and colleagues and law librarians in far-flung places. She wants to thank the law library staff at RWU Law. She also wants to thank Professor Nadiyah J. Humber and Professor Diana Hassel. Finally, she wishes to thank her co-editors for their tremendous patience, passion, and kindness. This project was just an idea until you four ladies came along, and then it was a book.

Raquel J. Gabriel thanks her fellow co-editors for their patience, enthusiasm, commitment, and sense of humor while we brought this project to fruition. She is grateful for the camaraderie of CUNY Law Library colleagues Karen Bean, Yolanda Clark, Douglas Cox, Ida Dulaney, Mary Godfrey-Rickards, Ricardo Pla, Jonathan Saxon, Sherry Scott, Yasmin Sokkar Harker and Kathy Williams. Finally, she would like to thank her family for their unwavering support.

Anna Russell thanks our amazing editorial team for its generosity of spirit and friendship. What project should we tackle next? Special thanks go to the creative imagination and unflagging spirit of Nicole Dyszlewski who lit the spark as well as kept this book project flame alive through the many requirements needed for completion. Finally, a heartfelt thank you to the author contributors who pushed aside or dropped tasks and otherwise made room for adding this project into work already made busier by the pandemic's shifting work requirements.

Genevieve B. Tung thanks Amanda Runyon, Associate Dean and Director of the Biddle Law Library, and all her Biddle colleagues as well as Nancy B. Talley, Charlotte D. Schneider, Heather Mitchell, and Jingwei Zhang, for their support and insight. Thanks also to Will and Juniper Tung for their patience.

Suzanne Harrington-Steppen thanks the creative, smart, and courageous RWU Law students, who deserve a law school curriculum and experience that reflects all of their experiences and histories. She thanks Nicole Dyszlewski for her vision and energy in driving this project, and her talented co-editors. She also thanks Laurie Barron, Eliza Vorenberg, and Lisa Quinn for their support and the space to work on this book.

Index